THE MAKING OF A
BLOCKBUSTER

THE MAKING OF A
BLOCKBUSTER

How
WAYNE HUIZENGA
Built a Sports and Entertainment Empire from Trash, Grit, and Videotape

GAIL DeGEORGE

JOHN WILEY & SONS, INC.
New York • Chichester • Brisbane
Toronto • Singapore

Publisher: Jim Childs
Editor: Ruth Mills
Managing Editor: Linda Indig
Composition: Publications Development Company of Texas

This text is printed on acid-free paper.

This publication is designed to provide accurate and authoritative
information in regard to the subject matter covered. It is sold
with the understanding that the publisher is not engaged in
rendering legal, accounting, or other professional services. If
legal advice or other expert assistance is required, the services
of a competent professional person should be sought.

Library of Congress Cataloging-in-Publication Data:

DeGeorge, Gail
    The Making of a Blockbuster: How Wayne Huizenga
    Built a Sports and Entertainment Empire from Trash, Grit, and
    Videotape / Gail DeGeorge.
    Includes bibliographic references and index.
ISBN 0-471-12269-6 (alk paper; cloth)

Printed in the United States of America

10 9 8 7 6 5 4 3 2 1

For Shawn and Kyle

Contents

Prologue

It was showtime. Stepping onstage into the spotlight, H. Wayne Huizenga took a deep breath. He looked out over the crowd of shareholders filling row upon row of the 2,700 deep-turquoise seats throughout the Broward Center for the Performing Arts in downtown Fort Lauderdale. This wasn't going to be easy. He hadn't been able to make it through practice runs all week without choking up. Seven years, seven months, and 18 days had culminated in this event at 11 A.M. on September 29, 1994.

In those incredible seven years, Huizenga and his team had taken a $7 million Dallas-based chain of 19 video stores and built it into a $4 billion video rental giant with more than 3,700 stores in 11 countries and 50 million card-carrying customers—more cardholders than American Express. Blockbuster was opening a new store every 24 hours and was larger than its next 375 competitors combined. Using the company's prodigious cash flow, Huizenga had already begun the transformation of Blockbuster into an entertainment giant, with stakes in television studios, music stores, children's play centers, and concert amphitheaters. Not bad for someone who had started in business in 1962 with a truck and a garbage route in Pompano Beach, Florida, had built two billion-dollar companies, and by now had amassed a fortune of more than $800 million and a sports menagerie with his Miami Dolphins, Florida Marlins, and Florida Panthers teams.

He hadn't been sure this day would come, and had alternately hoped it would and wished it wouldn't. After months of blistering blasts from Wall Street, shareholder suits to try and block the merger and his own wavering, now would come the vote on ceding control of Blockbuster to Viacom Inc. and its chairman, Sumner Redstone.

The tenacious Redstone had won the epic takeover battle of the 1990s by bidding $10 billion for Paramount Communications Inc., triumphing over rival Barry Diller and his home shopping channel QVC. Huizenga had allied Blockbuster with Viacom and helped line Redstone's war chest with much needed cash. What began as discussions about joint ventures and common interests had blossomed into a full-blown merger of Blockbuster into Viacom. Instead of fueling Blockbuster's continued diversification, the company would direct its cash flow into paying down part of the mammoth debt Viacom had taken on to win Paramount. Blockbuster would become part of one of the biggest entertainment companies in the world.

But there was a price. Unwilling to be second to anyone at this point in his storied career, Huizenga was stepping down as Blockbuster's chairman. This last shareholders' meeting was as much a farewell as a formality. Blockbuster insiders had already voted their 22% stake in favor of the merger, and Huizenga and others had spent weeks winning over reluctant institutional holders to support the deal. Now it was time to close it.

"There are very few events when the participants can know, at that instant, that something monumental is about to happen. Well, this is one of those events," he told shareholders. Standing at a podium, he read from a TelePrompTer, his image cast large on a huge video screen center stage. A woman at the foot of the stage translated into sign language for the hard of hearing. "As you know, the main purpose of our meeting today is to vote on the Viacom merger. It's been, a long nine months since all of this got started. And there have been many ups and downs along the way. When Viacom's stock dropped to the low twenties, I was down, too." Then he faltered from the prepared text, in which he was supposed to say, "But things have changed." Instead, he said, "But things haven't changed." He smiled grimly at the slip, which revealed his feelings, and went on to introduce Blockbuster's directors.

The night before, Huizenga had tried to keep the mood light at the last directors' meeting. He hosted it at one of his favorite haunts, Fort Lauderdale waterfront restaurant Burt & Jack's, owned by friend and actor Burt Reynolds and restaurateur Jack Jackson. In the private Oak Room, tucked away from the main restaurant, but still with spectacular views of ocean-going cruise ships, he presented the six directors with bronze statuettes of a bull and bear fighting—the classic stock market symbols—with the bull winning, of course. He also gave each of them a framed cover of a recent *Economist* magazine, which for a story about mergers, had featured a photograph of copulating camels. On the covers, he'd scribbled the inscription, "Thanks for the ride. Wayne."

They swapped Blockbuster stories, many of them focusing on Huizenga's initial doubts about the business. In the early days, when Huizenga was reluctantly thrust into managing Blockbuster, he'd often chew out his friend, fellow investor and company director John Melk. "He used to complain a lot," remembers Melk. "That I brought him into this crazy deal that has now consumed his life, which it did. The thing that always made it work out okay is that it was pretty profitable." Indeed, Blockbuster shares had risen over

4,000 percent, with a $25,000 investment in January 1987, worth $1 million seven years later.

Blockbuster vaulted Huizenga into a new stratosphere of corporate executive. It had erased some of the taint left by his years in the garbage business building the powerhouse Waste Management Inc. Now called WMX Technologies, the company had grown to be the largest waste disposal and treatment company in the world. But along the way, there had been antitrust charges, environmental violations, investigations by the Securities and Exchange Commission, and rumors—never proven and always staunchly denied—of mob connections. The rumors even plagued Huizenga for a time at Blockbuster. Early in the company's history, Huizenga suspected shortsellers, who profit when a stock price falls, of spreading stories of money-laundering and drug dealing to explain how the stores were doing so well. The ploys to discredit the company and its stock made Huizenga furious, but there was little he could do except spur the company on to even greater success. As Blockbuster's performance soared and its stock price rose, Huizenga took pleasure in burning the short sellers. Indeed, Blockbuster solidified Huizenga's place in the American business pantheon as a builder of businesses and a consummate dealmaker.

Now Huizenga had to explain to shareholders what they were getting with their new shares of Viacom stock. He gave highlights of the vastness of the new combined companies: a broadcast segment with a cable television system with more than one million subscribers, 12 television stations, and 11 radio stations. Cable television programming with some of the world's most popular shows, including MTV and Nickelodeon. Publishing, through Simon & Schuster and Macmillan. Films through Viacom Productions and Paramount Pictures, with current hits such as *Forrest Gump* and *Clear and Present Danger.* To that segment, Blockbuster had contributed its ownership of Republic Pictures, with its vast library of television and film classics, and Spelling Entertainment with its popular "Beverly Hills 90210" and "Melrose Place" television series. And "saving the best for last," Huizenga said, the retail segment with over 4,500 Blockbuster Video, Blockbuster Music, and Discovery Zone children's play center locations, generating over one billion customer visits annually. "We'll be able to make a movie, put it in our theaters, rent it in our video stores, sell it on our pay-per-view channels, show it on our cable networks, and play it on our television stations. And while we're doing that, we'll publish the book, release the soundtrack, and make the video game, and sell them in all of our stores."

So why sell? Huizenga had wrestled with that question for months. The 210-page proxy statement mailed to shareholders had all the legalese and rationale for the deal. But it boiled down to this: while Huizenga believed it would be years, maybe decades, before new technologies would take a toll on Blockbuster's mainstay video rental business, the threat would have created a constant cloud over the company and depressed the stock. It would be enormously expensive to build Blockbuster into a fully diversified entertainment empire since many prized properties were already owned by big entertainment companies or bid beyond reach. He worried about unfinished business, primarily the fate of Blockbuster Park, the 2,600-acre sports and entertainment complex he envisioned southwest of Fort Lauderdale with a baseball stadium and hockey arena to host his teams' games. But he had delivered value to shareholders, to employees, to executives, to himself. It was time to go, time to say good-bye.

"You know, we've come a long way together." His voice broke, "This is going to be tough." And then the man with the public image as the steely-eyed dealmaker, a tough-as-nails competitor, got tears in those famous laser-blue eyes. Accompanied by the strains of Louis Armstrong's "What a Wonderful World" rolled a short video of Blockbuster's history. Included were clips of Huizenga greeting employees in video stores, photos of Huizenga and his wife, Marti, and of his father, affectionately known around Blockbuster as Uncle Harry. The film even poked fun by incorporating highlights from franchisee meetings with their fabled themed costume parties, including a shot of Huizenga dressed as a hippie.

As the video rolled to an end and the song faded, Huizenga had one other point to make to assuage his honor, which had been assailed in media reports. There was widespread speculation about his reasons for doing the deal, a suspicion that there must be something more behind the public explanation. "Despite what some people have written, there is nothing extra in this deal for me," he said. No bonus, no severance pay, or golden parachute.

"Obviously, I'll miss all of you and all of this very much." His voice broke again. Struggling for composure, he thanked Blockbuster executives, employees, and franchisees. "And I thank you, our shareholders, for your years of loyalty and support." He left the podium in tears amid a thunderous standing ovation. Pausing sidestage, he took a few deep breaths, wondered whether to bother going out again, then decided he had to face whatever questions might still be left. The emotional high was burst when a few shareholders again questioned the terms of the deal. Huizenga countered calmly that Blockbuster shareholders were getting a fair price, that they could ride Viacom's upside as the newly combined companies paid down debt and became a greater force in the entertainment world. With that, Blockbuster's final shareholders' meeting was adjourned.

Huizenga came out of the dark auditorium into the brightly lit reception area, with its blue-and-rust patterned carpet, chandeliers, and sweeping staircases. His largesse and that of the companies he'd built had helped finance the center for his adopted hometown. One of the first people to greet him was a boy, about 10 years old, who held a proxy statement up to Huizenga. Like one of his ballplayers autographing a baseball, Huizenga the dealmaker signed it. Others crowded around, thrusting cocktail napkins and scraps of paper torn out of reporters notebooks for him to sign. Many weren't quite sure why they wanted his autograph, maybe they hoped his Midas touch might transfer. Huizenga was always sure it was his sports teams, not his business prowess, that had brought him celebrity status.

Waitresses served hors d'oeuvres of bacon-wrapped water chestnuts and crab-puff pastries with mimosas and glasses of Le Chandon champagne. Huizenga joined his wife Marti. "Don't you start," he told her as she blinked back tears. He shook hands with his son Ray and got a hug from his daughter Pamela. For more than an hour, he signed autographs, posed for photos, greeted old friends and strangers with warmth. Shareholders wished Huizenga well and pressed business cards into his hands, into his pockets, wanting to be part of his next deal, whatever it was.

Just outside the auditorium, three tables were laden with trophies of success: 82 plaques, inscriptions, statues, and momentos from the collection of his partner and chief lieutenant Steve Berrard. These were some of the momentos from the 110 deals and 8 financings since 1987, events like the listing of Blockbuster's stock on the New York Stock Exchange on April 27, 1989, to the four two-for-one stock splits, to key acquisitions like Cityvision, which gave Blockbuster needed clout in the United Kingdom, to high-profile events like the sponsorship of the former Beatles singer Paul McCartney's World Tour. "This is a combination of a wedding and a wake," said Chuck Lewis, a top executive with the Chicago office of Merrill Lynch, Pierce, Fenner & Smith Inc. A long-time advisor to Huizenga, Lewis had followed his business exploits since his days at Waste Management. "This part," Lewis said, nodding at the collection of memorabilia, "reminds me of the photos on the coffin."

As reporters got their interviews and left and shareholders downed the last sips of champagne, Huizenga lingered and chatted a few minutes longer with Barry Rosenblatt, founder of Video Library, the second company Huizenga had acquired in his race to build Blockbuster. "It was like he really didn't want to leave," Rosenblatt recalls. While cleaning crews whisked away the last of the hors d'oeuves and corked the champagne, Huizenga walked out into the gray, rainy afternoon. It was, after all, time to move on.

1

"One Man's Trash": Building a Garbage Kingdom

Wayne Huizenga waited patiently in front of Wilbur Porter's wood-frame house, the only one for miles around in the fields of palmetto scrub that stretched west of Fort Lauderdale. Porter chuckled to himself as he pulled up and saw the skinny, blond-haired kid with the strange name, pronounced HIGH-zeng-a, waiting for him again. This was a switch, a white man waiting for a black man in South Florida in 1962. For days now, the kid had come by, wanting to know if Porter was ready to sell him a garbage truck and part of his route. But Porter hadn't been willing to sell. Not yet. "No, Wayne, I'm just trying to hold onto my own and I just don't care to sell," Porter, now 88, remembers telling young Wayne Huizenga. "Well, if you do, if you change your mind, I'll be back," Huizenga replied.

Porter's Rubbish Service had been one of the best ventures Wilbur Porter had gotten into. Porter was a hustler, a hard-working Georgian who'd hopped a freight train to Florida in 1934 and whose sense of enterprise made up for his lack of education. He'd worked at a dairy, tried landscaping, fixed trucks. He owned 800 laying hens and when he delivered eggs, he'd started picking up garbage. He hired a white woman to solicit new customers for him and the rumble of growth shaking Broward County had brought him good fortune. His business had grown nicely, to some 1,300 customers with six men working for him. In the early days of the garbage business in Broward County, he says, you couldn't help but make money. "I never had $100 in my life until I got in the garbage business," he remembers. "Then I was making money head over heels. Gee whiz, we could take a trip to New York and spend $500 or $600 and not miss it."

But the business was changing. It was getting rough, with some New York-types with Italian surnames moving in. Already, he'd gone out to find his route picked up by an outfit with brand-new trucks, an intimidation tactic common in the garbage business. And here was this Huizenga kid, pestering him to sell. "He wasn't involved with the rest of the gang that had come down," Porter remembers. "He just wanted to get his foot in the door." After the Huizenga's fourth visit, Porter relented and sold him a beat-up truck and about 20 commercial accounts, a grocery store, a gas station, and some hotels on Fort Lauderdale beach. The whole route brought in about $500 a month.

For Huizenga, at age 25, it was the start he needed. He'd borrowed the $5,000 from his father-in-law to buy the truck and routes and on February 14, 1962, Southern Sanitation Service was incorporated. From that one truck, he would help create the largest waste handler in the world, Waste Management Inc. His father's construction business had gone bust and Wayne had spent the last few years managing a garbage business for a family friend. But working for someone else wasn't the Huizenga way. This was a chance to get into business for himself. Within a day, he signed up his first new customer, a Cadillac dealership. He was on his way.

* * *

The doctors attending Jean Huizenga during her labor at Little Company of Mary Hospital in Evergreen Park, Illinois, were worried. The baby, a boy, was breech and the labor had been long and difficult. The lives of both the mother and the child were at risk. There was no choice. One of the doctors deliberately broke the leg of the infant to speed the birth. With that rude welcome, Harry Wayne Huizenga arrived in the world on December 29, 1937. The doctors affixed a stiff cardboard brace to help the leg heal. Despite the break, he started walking early, at nine months.

Wayne, as he would be called, was the son of Gerrit Harry Huizenga, who was the fifth and youngest child of Harm Huizenga. His grandfather had died two years before his birth, but from him, Wayne inherited a strong sense of family, a propensity for hard work, and a knack for business.

Harm Huizenga at age 23 sailed the Holland American line from the Netherlands to the New World in 1893 and headed for Chicago to stay with a cousin. Trained as a blacksmith and a wheelwright, he loved horses, didn't speak English, and didn't mind hard work. He arrived in Chicago during the World's Fair. The bustling city spreading out from the shores of Lake Michigan was a magnet for immigrants. He landed a job for $5 a week and a year later, started his own business, hauling garbage for $1.25 a wagonload.

Harm saw it as honorable work. It appealed to the independent nature of his Dutch heritage. "My father always said working for somebody else never amounted to anything," says Harry Huizenga. "You have to be an entrepreneur." That saying would ring decades later in the years of Harm's grandson, Wayne. Trash hauling also attracted other Dutch in the ethnic enclave in west Chicago where Harm settled. They started businesses of their own, and the Dutch tended to hire other Dutch, giving rise to the saying among some of their countrymen, that they "had garbage in their blood."

Harm returned to Holland in 1897 to marry Altje Kremer. After their wedding in March of that year, they returned to Harm's basement flat in Chicago. Harm continued in the garbage hauling business. By 1907, he and Altje had two sons, Siert (Sam) and Tammes (Tom) and a daughter, Trientje, called Tena. A year later, a third son, Petro (Peter) was born. But tragedy struck the young family in 1913 when Altje died of pneumonia. The eldest child, Sam, was 15, the youngest, Peter, was just four. Harm hired a housekeeper to help care for the children, then wrote to his brother in Holland asking if he knew of a woman who would make a good wife. His brother replied that there was a middle-aged woman, 42, whose fiancé had died. Harm wrote to Aaltje Keizer, asking what she thought about marriage and moving to America. Her reply was curt, "I don't know who you are and I have no intention of going to America."

But Harm didn't take no for an answer, a characteristic his grandson Wayne would inherit. Harm sold his business for $6,000 and all the household goods and took his family to Holland in 1914, determined to woo this woman to be his wife. They wed in February 1915. Their only child from this union, Gerrit Harry, was born June 28, 1916. Harm at age 46, was retired, a state he detested, once proclaiming that "one ought to throw all retired men in the Boterdiep" (a canal in front of his home). Wayne would retire at the same age from Waste Management and feel equally ill-at-ease. His retirement, said his wife Marti, lasted "three weeks and 12 minutes." Harm hoped to get back into business, but found it impossible to buy into anything in Holland. Harm wanted to return to America, but Aaltje resisted. Finally, as the threat of war grew nearer, she reluctantly agreed to move. In October 1916, they sailed for America.

FAMILY BUSINESS

Upon returning to Chicago, Harm repurchased his garbage business and renamed it Huizenga and Son, as his second, son, Tom, began to work with him. Later, in the 1920s, Tom started his own company called Ace Scavenger Service and later entered into a partnership with other, mostly

Dutch, garbage men, called Chicago and Suburban Disposal (C&S) to provide service to suburbs of Cicero and Berwyn. Tom hired his older brother Sam, whose fortunes took a dive in the 1929 stock market crash, to manage C&S, while his younger brother, Pete, ran Ace Scavenger, which Tom still owned. During World War II, Tom sold Pete some of his northern routes, and for a while, both operated under the name "Ace" until Pete changed the name of his business, which was really just one truck at the time, to "Arrow." In a precursor to later run-ins with regulators, during World War II, Tom Huizenga raised prices without getting clearance from the Office of Price Administration. While the paperwork pended and the war lasted, Ace Scavenger racked up fines of $120,000. The war ended and the OPA disbanded before Ace had to fork over the money.

As the businesses and families grew, so did the involvement of the families in the businesses. Sons and sons-in-law were brought in to help run what would become a complicated tangle of companies and partnerships and associations. The businesses provided a steady and comfortable living for the Huizenga clan. "There was good money in garbage," says Betty Joanne (BJ) Buntrock, the eldest daughter of Pete Huizenga. "We lived simply but when they bought a car, they paid cash. When they bought a house, they paid cash." Her father would bring the truck home and park it in front of the house in Berwyn. "We were garbage men's children. We didn't try to impress people. We knew that no matter what we did, we were still garbage men."

Harm believed strongly in involvement in family, community, and his religion, serving as a deacon in the church. While the brothers were developing the garbage business, against her father Harm's wishes, sister Tena trained as a nurse and became a missionary, going to Nigeria in February 1937. She'd been a strong influence in Harry's life and in her later years, would be one in Wayne's as well.

Harry's brothers decided their youngest brother wasn't going to go into the garbage business. Instead, he became an apprentice to a carpenter and would later become a contractor. At age 20, he eloped with his high school sweetheart, Jean Riddering, on September 1, 1936. Theirs would be a tumultuous relationship. Harry was loving but demanding and quick tempered. Jean was blond and striking, but reclusive and at times emotionally fragile. They started their life together in a basement apartment in a building owned by Harry's brother, Tom. Harry was still working as an apprentice and money was tight. Jean swept the stairways and Harry did other custodial work in exchange for rent.

Harry became a contractor in the 1940s and his business followed the vagaries of the real estate market. He built ranch houses in the sprawl of Chicago's suburbs, mostly on speculation. Jean decorated the houses that Harry built, paying close attention to details, a trait she passed on to her son. To this day, Wayne Huizenga will straighten a picture in a room and takes great interest in design, such as the logos of his sports teams or the color and width of the stripes on his planes. In the building boom of the post-war years, business was good.

Harry and Jean lived in Evergreen Park, apart from the other brothers and cousins in Berwyn. Even so, son Wayne became steeped in the Dutch culture though he never learned the language. As was the custom, he attended private Dutch schools. Sundays were spent at church, the strict sect of Dutch Reformed, visiting relatives and having supper, then attending church services again Sunday evening. (The ethnic clannishness was passed on. Years into adulthood, Wayne would remark about a fellow Dutchman, "he's okay, he's a wooden shoe" as the Dutch referred to each other.) These visits, as Peter Huizenga recalls, were a time to smooth over differences that might have occurred during the course of business. "You might fight with each other business wise during the week, but this was a time for family." During the Sunday gatherings, Wayne, his sister, Bonnie, who was five years younger and the other children were allowed to listen in on the conversations of the adults as the Huizengas gathered to discuss business or family news, but as Harry Huizenga remarks, "they weren't allowed to repeat what they heard. What was said had to stay in the room."

But marital problems between Harry and Jean worsened. Even as a child, Wayne showed signs of the intensity that would be a hallmark characteristic later. When playing trucks or with toys, it was with a single-mindedness that his cousin, Peter, still remembers. The only indication that not all was well at home was that intensity. During a seventh-grade baseball game, Wayne argued with an umpire over a call, tears welling in his eyes as a clue that the emotional outburst wasn't just about the game.

That intensity was coupled with an innate inquisitiveness. On a family vacation to south Florida in 1947 when Wayne was nine years old, the family stayed at a hotel in Singer Island. Wayne struck up a conversation with a man in the hotel lobby who owned an auto dealership and quizzed him about the business. "The man was amazed at the questions Wayne was asking," Harry recalls. "Even at that young age he was never afraid to talk to strangers."

Jobs that were tedious or unpleasant held no interest for Wayne. While visiting his uncle Pete's cottage on Lake Michigan, he hid rather than help rake dead fish that had floated ashore, prompting his uncle to remark that "that boy won't amount to anything." But he could also be industrious. His first job was to help sweep floors in his father's millwork shop. When Harry was hospitalized when Wayne was 14, he started operating a bulldozer at a job site, though he couldn't legally drive a car. After Harry recovered, Wayne stayed involved in the business. He'd wake early before school to take the bulldozer to a job site, then pick it up after school, and move it

again. Harry says it was Wayne who suggested that equipment be moved to
the next job site the night before, so work could start promptly the next day.
Years later, in building Waste Management and Blockbuster, he'd fly at
night—and insist his executives do likewise—to be ready to do business
the next day.

Even as a teenager, Wayne didn't want to fail Harry. When he was about
16, Harry asked him to pick up a tool shed and bring it over to a job site.
Wayne called his cousin Peter and told him that he'd need some help. The
two sweated and shoved, but the shed wouldn't fit in the pickup and tilted
precariously. Peter advised Wayne to call his father and tell him he
couldn't do it. "No, I've got to pick it up, my job is to pick it up and bring it
back," Wayne answered. So they hoisted the tool shed on to the bed of the
pickup and Wayne backed the truck up gently against a telephone pole to
wedge the shed in and make sure it wouldn't bounce out. They'd figure out
how to get it out later, but he'd done the job his father had asked him to do.

It was through church that Wayne met Dick Molenhouse. They became
life-long friends and Molenhouse ended up marrying Wayne's grade-
school sweetheart, Pixie. In fifth grade, she remembers Wayne returned
from a family vacation to Florida and gave her a white ceramic slipper
filled with perfume. For Valentines Day, he sent her a card addressed,
"To My Sweetheart."

After the bus ride home from high school, Wayne would often stop in a
small village diner and order a cherry cola, and if other kids were there,
showing his streak of generosity, he'd buy them one, too. To Molenhouse,
he would confide on occasion about his parents' problems. "I think it made
him grow up in a hurry," Molenhouse says. "From the time his folks' problems started, he was basically on his own. He did his own thinking then as
he does today."

Tensions between his parents reached a breaking point during Wayne's
early teen years. There were constant arguments and fights that degener-
ated at times into physical violence. In the nasty divorce that followed,
Harry accused Jean of carrying on a long-standing affair with a Chicago
man. Jean would deny the affair, but was hospitalized in 1953 for a nervous
breakdown. After a reconciliation, Harry suggested moving to Florida to
remove her from the other man's influence and try to save their marriage.
They visited Florida in December, then Harry and 16-year-old Wayne
moved that winter and Jean and Bonnie followed in April.

FLORIDA BOUND

Fort Lauderdale, Florida in the 1950s: A golden place in a golden age.
By now, the settlement that had sprung up on the banks of the New River,

incorporated in 1911 and dubbed a city in 1917, had shed its rural beginnings as a site for packing plants for vegetables and catfish. It had survived the early boom-bust cycles of real estate speculators and its suburban sprawl was rapidly spreading into surrounding Broward County, named for Governor Napoleon Bonaparte Broward, who began the ditch-digging to drain the Everglades that would help create the city and make much of south Florida habitable, but become the bane of environmentalists decades later. Smudge pots gave way to planes spewing DDT to keep the voracious mosquitoes at bay. The gambling halls that had flourished in the 1930s and 1940s with their links to the mob and organized crime had been shut down, a prerequisite, civic leaders felt, to any solid, sustained growth.

The area boomed as a post-war nation on the move discovered the allure of south Florida's sun. Fort Lauderdale's beaches were already becoming a springtime mecca for students, with 10,000 collegians arriving in 1953 in response to invitations mailed by the Mayor's Hospitality Committee to 500 colleges and universities across the nation. In an object lesson about good intentions gone awry, the city would spend the next 30 years ridding itself of its "spring break" image. Shopping centers and subdivisions replaced palmetto scrub, pine trees, and live oak hammocks. By the end of the 1950s, 750 families a month were moving into the city, which numbered 83,648 by 1960. Within that same timespan, Broward County's population quadrupled to 329,431. Ten new cities were incorporated and roads, bridges, highways, and schools were built in an ever-losing battle to keep pace.

Into this flood of newcomers came the Huizenga family. The move to Florida seemed to help Harry and Jean's troubled marriage, at least initially. They rented a small, two-bedroom house on Andrews Avenue in the center of the city. Harry planned to build houses and would miss the building boom in condominiums and hotels that fueled fortunes in Fort Lauderdale in the fifties. Initially the business was successful, but then Harry gambled by building larger, custom homes. That would prove to be a mistake. "In people that had certain financial insecurity, a little personal insecurity in their lives, they become a little more business aggressive," says Wayne's first cousin, Peter Huizenga. "I think that probably formed a certain business aggression and purpose in Wayne's life."

Harry grew to depend on Wayne, more so as his own business ventures foundered and Wayne showed the focus and business knack he lacked. Whereas Harry was the youngest brother and was always being told what to do, "Wayne was the oldest one, he had to take responsibility and things were not always together," says Peter Huizenga. "His father tried to keep things glued together. He tried to be a success and he was adventurous. He did take risks, unfortunately, not always on the winning side. Since Wayne went into business, his father has always been his partner. Wayne has always had love and respect for his father." As he matured, Peter says, Wayne was constantly "trying to give his father the dignity that he always thought his father should have." Wayne made his father a partner in nearly every business venture, from one of his first garbage businesses to the baseball team, and included him in milestone events, like having him make the first trade of Blockbuster shares on the New York Stock Exchange in April 1989. One of Wayne's bitterest disappointments would be the bouts of depression his father grappled with when he was in his late 70s.

Wayne thrived in Florida. He learned to water ski and did so well, he ran a skiing school. He remembers one time putting his skis on and as he swung them over the side of the boat, a huge sea mammal called a manatee, a moniker quickly dismissed as a possible name for his professional baseball franchise years later, came up under the skis. "It was a great area to live," he says. His love of south Florida would be a trait friends and business colleagues would later indulge but never quite understand.

He enrolled in Pinecrest, a small private school then on Broward Boulevard that had gotten its start tutoring the children of seasonal tourists so they wouldn't fall behind in their studies. Whereas he'd made poor grades, near failing, in the two high schools he'd attended in Chicago, his grades improved to at least average or slightly above. With his wavy blond hair and striking blue eyes, he was popular and not particularly studious, remembers Bill McMillan, who taught American history at the time at the school his mother founded.

But after a few months, tensions between Wayne's parents escalated. After one particularly gruesome night in July in which Harry struck both Jean and Bonnie and punched Wayne when he tried to intervene, Jean had had enough. After 18 years of marriage and just five months of living in Florida, she filed for divorce on July 26, 1954. The court papers served Harry were left by the sheriff deputy with his teenage son.

Divorces in those days were not easily granted, and each side painted the worst picture of the other. In the divorce suit and countersuit, Harry and Jean traded charges of cruelty. Jean recounted Harry's physical threats and violent outbursts, Harry accused her of being mentally unstable and carrying on an affair. Both denied each others' charges.

Into the maelstrom were drawn Wayne and Bonnie, who both testified at the trial on behalf of their mother, collaborating accounts of Harry's outbursts. "He would push us down on the floor, hit mother, Bonnie, and myself," Wayne testified. Harry dropped his countersuit in the mistaken belief that Jean would withdraw the divorce case. Harry, for his part, didn't want the divorce to go through, and wrote an impassioned letter to the court pleading that Jean needed counseling and warning that he couldn't keep up with court-ordered support payments as creditors were hounding him for money. The court sided with Jean and granted the divorce on October 21, 1954. Harry was ordered to pay alimony of $500 a month plus legal costs, but he was already weeks behind on previous support payments. The divorce would be as tumultuous as their marriage, with repeated court filings dogging Harry for support payments. Wayne and Bonnie—as well as family friends—say despite this, the family remained close, still celebrating holidays together and spending many Sundays together. "I think we were always close," Wayne Huizenga says of his relationship with his father. With a pained expression, he adds, "you had to take sides in those days and sometimes you sided with one, sometimes you sided with the other." (Harry and Jean would remarry in 1978 at a ceremony attended by both Wayne and Bonnie.)

Money troubles would be constant as Harry's business hit the skids. As interest rates rose, the economy slowed and the houses didn't sell, Harry got squeezed. "He lost it all," Wayne says. "Some of the relatives and some friends came in and kept him out of bankruptcy, but he was an eighth of an inch away." From that experience, Wayne says, "I learned one thing. You don't want to go broke."

Wayne became heavily involved in school. He showed his interest in business early, serving as class treasurer and business manager for the school yearbook and student newspaper. Athletic, he joined the football team, where he played center. The 14-member team would play just three games, losing one, tying another, and winning the last. The rough sport could be even rougher in the hot Florida sun with sharp, pointy sandspurs and plenty of sweat. With such a small team, Wayne had to play both offense and defense. "He was a hard worker," says Bill Munsey, who coached the team. When it came time to choose the team name, Wayne lobbied heavily for his choice, the Panthers. He would use the same name for his National Hockey League franchise awarded in 1992. Though he won the contest, the experience etched one of his most mortifying moments of those years: Instead of saying he was going to pass out ballots, he slipped and said he would "piss out ballots," prompting howls of laughter among his fellow students.

Just weeks into the school year, Wayne befriended a classmate, Mike (Lowell) Clark, an Ohio native. The boys became inseparable. They drove Harry's 1953 Ford powder-blue convertible to school, dropping Bonnie off at her classes at Pinecrest and attending football practice together. Wayne took a job at a Texaco gas station after school. "He could understand people pretty quick, like the guy he worked for at the Texaco station," remembers Clark. "The guy was tough to work for, but Wayne'd make an assessment of what he wanted him to do and how to do it."

He loved fast cars. During summer breaks from high school, he'd head back to Chicago to work for a family friend, driving a dump truck. Along with Molenhouse and another friend, he fixed up a 1950 Buick to use in stock car races. "He could never go fast enough," Molenhouse says. Wednesday and Saturday nights were spent at the races and they'd sometimes sneak off after church on Sundays, too. He was also a bit of a daredevil. Back in Florida, in a rented white Cadillac convertible, he and Mike Clark spun around a traffic circle in nearby Hollywood at more than 70 miles an hour, the tire rims nearly scraping the pavement. Clark was scared but Wayne wasn't. Together, he and Clark bought a clunker, a 1939 black Pontiac, for $90 to use for cruising around. With fixing up the car, Wayne showed a particular persistence. "If it was something he liked to do or was interested in, he wouldn't give up," Clark says.

Schoolwork, on the other hand, was something for which Wayne never showed much patience. Girlfriends would correct his spelling on papers. Midway through the semester, Wayne was in danger of flunking a pre-law class. The night before midterms, Clark forced him to drink hot coffee and slapped him to keep him awake and study. Wayne passed the course. It was after this incident that Wayne dubbed him "Dad." (Years later, he'd bestow nicknames on favored executives at Waste Management and Blockbuster. And on memos, he would correct the spelling of executives, particularly one at Blockbuster who irked him by spelling "financial" with a "t" instead of a "c.")

Wayne was quite a charmer with women, classmates recall. They'd get fresh-squeezed orange juice at a local soda fountain (this being Florida), hang out at drive-in restaurants on Federal Highway, or cruise over to the beach for pizza. He organized beach parties in an undeveloped section north of Fort Lauderdale. His sunny disposition matched Florida's climate. "He didn't brood on anything, he'd just go on to what was next. Tomorrow's a new day for Wayne," says Clark.

Fellow football player John Leech, now a stockbroker in Fort Lauderdale, remembers even then how contagious were Wayne's powers of persuasion, enthusiasm, and sheer exuberance. Leech would eat lunch in his 1950 gray Ford convertible, usually with four or five other guys crammed in the car. One time, Wayne glanced at the odometer, which read 39,999 miles. "We've got to go around the block and see the numbers turn," he urged. Leech thought it rather silly but complied, starting up the car and dutifully driving. By the end of the short trip, "he had us so excited we were laughing and screaming like it was the last few seconds of a basketball game."

Not having something didn't get in the way of his goal, especially if it involved having fun. While visiting Wayne in Florida as a teenager, Molenhouse remembers, they wanted to go for a boat ride. Wayne looked in the classified ads under "boats for sale" and he and Molenhouse knocked on doors and asked if they could test drive the boats. They didn't buy a boat but they got their ride. "Just another way to negotiate," Molenhouse laughs.

Though he was friendly, that didn't mean everyone was a friend. "You had to blend into his temperament to get along with him," Clark recalls. "He was a funny guy because he either liked you or didn't like you—there was no inbetween with Wayne. He'd make the pretense, but he'd tell me different." With that quick assessment of people came a stubborn streak. "He was always a perfectionist, whatever he got into he would carry through on it."

Wayne had a quick temper. "Those blue eyes get a different color when he's mad. The powder blue gets a deep, deep blue." Wayne controlled his temper. "He wouldn't yell or scream, he would clam up," Clark remembers. "He'd control himself, but no doubt he was mad. You could read his face and tell how mad he was."

But like all good times, senior year at Pinecrest drew to a close in May 1954. Like other seniors, he expected a graduation gift. But Wayne's wish was a little different from the norm, remembers classmate William Rosse. "Everyone looks for presents on birthdays and Christmas. Wayne wanted a 10-wheel tandem truck to haul fill and he got the dump truck and was happy." Indeed, he got the truck, but had to borrow the down payment from his uncle because Harry didn't have the money. Wayne used it to haul fill for the endless road construction in Broward County, until the axle broke.

He moved to Chicago, happy to leave his parents' continuing spats. Wayne worked a bulldozer and drove a truck for a family friend's company. He considered hiring on to one of the family's garbage operations. Instead, his uncle Pete persuaded him to go to college with Peter and agreed to pay his tuition.

Wayne arrived on campus of Calvin College in Grand Rapids, Michigan, in a 1957 Chevy BelAir baby-blue convertible with a horn rigged to play "Mary had a Little Lamb." He was exotic for this strict, private college in the religious Dutch community of western Michigan with his convertible and pet alligator, Baby (smuggled into the dorms after a trip to Florida). Older than many of his classmates and never a serious student, Wayne soon found himself caught up in the real lesson being learned at Calvin: independence. The strict upbringing of the students "made it worse because those who grew up with strict parents, with no dancing, and no movies, when they turned us loose up there we did stuff we never would get away with at home," says Budd (Albert) Bosman, a college classmate who also grew up in Fort Lauderdale. The pranks were mostly harmless, particularly by today's standards: Water balloons tossed out of dorm windows onto professors' heads; breaking curfews.

Though he would leave after little more than 3 semesters, Wayne would make his own legend first. There was a rift between the two private colleges in western Michigan, Calvin College in Grand Rapids and Hope College in nearby Holland. Ever the organizer, always thinking big, he created his own brand of detente by holding a joint campus party in a rented American Legion Hall after a basketball game. During another particularly rowdy party, someone tried to get the alligator to imbibe. But the critter "couldn't handle the scotch," as Wayne recalls and died. He borrowed a friend's station wagon to use as a hearse, persuaded a seminarian to preside over a funeral, and took over the chapel to hold proper services for Baby. In February, Budd Bosman was invited not to return until his study habits improved. Wayne left to save the college the trouble of asking him to do the same.

Wayne loaded the car with his possessions, asked Budd if wanted a ride to Florida, went to Chicago to pick up Dick Molenhouse, and headed south. When they arrived in Fort Lauderdale, the three of them landed a job with Harry, helping him build a church. At the time, Harry was paying his workers $2.50 an hour. But to Wayne, business was business, and he talked his father into paying him and his friends $5 a hour.

Without being in school, serving in the Army looked unavoidable. Wayne warned two of his friends, Ed Meehan and John Tomlinson, that if they didn't get organized, they were going to get drafted and spend two years wherever the government wanted them to go. Always working angles, Huizenga suggested instead that they join the Army Reserves, spend six months in the service, then do the weekly meetings and once-a-month day-long training that the Reserves required once back in Fort Lauderdale. Even then, Meehan remembers that his friend wanted to go into the garbage business, that his cousins were in the business in Chicago and had done real well.

After the Army, Wayne returned to Florida where his father was working for a life-long friend, Herman Mulder, who owned garbage hauling operations in Chicago and Florida. An investment in a concrete plant in Peru had gone bust so Harry worked the Miami business with another friend. Meanwhile, Mulder had been having problems with his three-truck Pompano Beach operation. A manager had been stealing from him. Was Wayne interested in a job? Wayne protested that he knew nothing about managing a garbage business, but Mulder insisted he'd learn. Building houses certainly didn't appeal to Wayne. With no better prospects, Wayne took the job as manager of the Pompano Carting Co. He rode the routes, hired workers, and made sure the garbage got picked up.

With a real job, at least now he could accomplish his other goal. During his years of working in Chicago, he'd gotten reacquainted with Joyce

VanderWagon, whom he'd known in high-school at Evergreen Park. They married September 10, 1960 in Chicago. Theirs would also prove a difficult relationship, mirroring some of the pattern set by Harry and Jean. Joyce's father, who'd made a tidy sum in the coal business, would become Wayne's first backer in business. Indeed, the relationship Wayne had with his father-in-law would stay intact even after the marriage disintegrated.

Hauling garbage is a tough business. It's hard, dirty, sweaty work, with cut-throat competition and customers who demand service while often being late paying bills. Little more than a month after he was married, Huizenga tangled with the wrong customer. He was working a route in Pompano around noon on October 11, 1960, radioing the office to check some addresses, when Thomas L. Millwood, a Hillsboro Beach police officer and electrical contractor, complained his trash wasn't getting picked up. Huizenga, brash and cocky, retorted that the bill probably hadn't been paid and noted the garbage can didn't have a sticker to show the account was current. Millwood insisted that he'd paid the bill. Huizenga started to walk to the truck to radio the office and check when Millwood insisted that Huizenga himself pick up the trash. Huizenga refused. The verbal barrage escalated. Millwood threatened to escort Huizenga off the property and grabbed his arm. Huizenga turned and grabbed the man's crotch, and according to Millwood, twisted his testicles. Millwood, much bigger than the slight Huizenga, easily pinned him until the sheriff's deputy arrived. Millwood delayed filing a complaint for more than a month. Huizenga was charged with assault and battery and arrested on December 29, his 23rd birthday, and released on $500 bond.

The case of the State of Florida vs. Wayne Huezenger (the spelling was later corrected) commenced on September 12, 1961. On the advice of his attorney, Huizenga waived a jury trial. Though his attorney argued self-defense on the logic that Millwood had touched Huizenga first, and Huizenga denied assaulting Millwood, the court sided with Millwood's version. Huizenga was found guilty of assault and ordered to pay $100. He appealed the conviction, but the judge upheld the decision. Millwood later pressed a civil case and was awarded $1000 in damages in March 1962. Huizenga could be tough.

GARBAGE GANGBUSTERS

If the adage "one man's trash is another's treasure" was true for anyone, it was true for H. Wayne Huizenga. At the time he plunked down his father-in-law's cash in early 1962 for Wilbur Porter's ailing truck and a smattering of accounts, Broward County was booming again. Connie Francis had just made Fort Lauderdale famous (or infamous) in the 1960 movie *Where the Boys Are* and air conditioning was making Florida's summers tolerable. In addition to the flood of retirees eager to spend their golden years in the sunshine, came a collection of people seeking to work as store clerks, bank tellers, waitresses, and managers in what was emerging as an early example of a service economy. The population boom that had started in the 1950s turned into a virtual explosion of growth for Fort Lauderdale and Broward County in the 1960s. For much of the decade, developers built more houses in Fort Lauderdale than any other city in Florida. The city built a baseball stadium off Commercial Boulevard to host spring training games for the New York Yankees. Fort Lauderdale, Pompano, and the new towns in west Broward strained against their borders as the demarcation lines of mango groves and live oak hammocks between them disappeared in ever-widening concentric circles of urbanization. In the mid-1960s, Fort Lauderdale topped the list of cities compiled by the U.S. Department of Commerce experiencing the fastest economic growth in the nation.

Huizenga dismisses credit for his success, particularly in this era, as simply being, "in the right place at the right time." While there's no disputing that Broward County in the 1960s certainly fits that bill, that doesn't quite explain how Huizenga was able to grow his business from a single truck in 1962 to more than 40 trucks in 1968 with a major slice of the garbage hauling contracts in Broward County and the local municipalities, plus an operation in Key West and for a brief time, Tampa. After all, there were other haulers in Broward County area who didn't go on to build multimillion-dollar empires. "Wayne grew because he worked the hardest and had the clearest vision," says Harold Carter Jr., whose father owned one of the competing garbage companies, All Service Refuse Co. "He knew what was coming in the future in terms of growth. Wayne learned back then how to leverage money, how to use income from one operation to buy another operation. He lived very simply and every cent he made he would pour back into the business."

Harry took over managing the Pompano Beach operation for Mulder while Wayne focused on growing his own business. Again, with help from John VanderWagon, his father-in-law, he bought a new truck and he started selling. "There were a lot of other people soliciting business so you had to get there first and you had to convince people that you were the one that was going to get the work because the guy would have five cards in his hand," Huizenga remembers. "We got most of the work. And we kept the work, too." That first new customer, the Cadillac dealership, he notes, was still a customer years later.

As the business grew, he needed help. Through the Fort Lauderdale Christian Reform Church, he and Joyce befriended Bob and Judy Balfoort, who are also of Dutch heritage. They'd moved to booming Broward County from Holland, Michigan. Over a card game one evening, Wayne offered Judy a job. He had one employee at the time, a truck driver, and one office staffer and he needed extra office help. She was working as a pediatric nurse and he offered her better pay. She started working for him in the summer of 1963 at the double-wide trailer on Dixie Highway which served as an office for Southern Sanitation and later, also for Broward Disposal. "He was always there before anyone else and he was always the last one to leave and inbetween he just did everything," she remembers. "He did a lot of phone calls, a lot of driving. He knew this neighborhood like nobody else did. In Broward County, he knew where every store was, he knew where every new business was opening up."

At the time, garbage was being handled by a master contractor, Associated Independents Inc., which had agreements with six local haulers, including Pompano Carting. Each of the operators had an assigned territory. But with the contract up for renewal, the individual operators saw a chance to get out from under that arrangement. With the county commissioners unhappy with Associated's contract, the county decided not to renew the agreement with Associated and instead reached agreements with each of the local haulers. Associated Independents fought back, suing the county and each of the haulers, including Pompano Carting, which listed Wayne Huizenga as president at the time. Associated charged the county commissioners with interfering with employment contracts with the haulers and the companies with violating those agreements. The haulers hired an attorney to fight the case.

About this time, Huizenga left Pompano Carting to start his own business. The case itself, as it wound its way through the courts over the next two years with suits and countersuits, would become ancillary to the real effect. By not renewing the contract with Associated, Broward County limited the independent haulers to a particular residential area, but allowed them to solicit commercial customers in the rest of the county for new business. By splitting up the contract among six haulers, the rights to those franchises became valuable business assets. After a year or so of his own business, Huizenga bought out his former employer, thus getting the residential contract that Mulder held and the right to solicit more commercial accounts. Finally, the county's decision would set the independents out on their own, and eventually, Huizenga, with his voracious appetite for acquisitions, would later buy many of them out.

With his young company already adding new customers and trucks at a quick pace, Wayne Huizenga needed more bodies. His father worked in the business, living in the trailer and tending the trucks. So in 1964 when Whit Hudson, a tall, lanky young man who'd been dating his sister, Bonnie, on and off for years, asked for a job, Wayne hired him—on one condition. "I don't care if you marry my sister, you either work or you're out of a job," Wayne told him.

It worked out. Harris W. (Whit) Hudson had moved from Tennessee with his parents to Florida in the 1950s. Poor, they'd lived in a one-room apartment in Fort Lauderdale. Hudson freely credits his success—a waterfront mansion in the Las Olas Isles section of Fort Lauderdale across a canal from Huizenga's home, a 112 foot yacht and a net worth estimated at $100 million—to his brother-in-law. Still in the garbage business with operations stretching from Florida's east coast from Fort Lauderdale to Melbourne, he says the lessons from those years apply today.

Hudson worked every aspect of the small operation and learned, often the hard way, H. Wayne Huizenga's rules for doing business. "The most important thing to him at that point was the customer and I don't care what you did, you'd better do right by the customer. No matter what it took and no matter what it cost you. Because if you lose that one customer you're going to lose more customers," Hudson says of those days. All they had to sell, Huizenga would constantly remind him, was service. If that meant getting up at 2 A.M. because a dumpster was on fire or blocking a driveway, or running a route yourself because drivers called in sick or didn't show up, that's what you did. "The most important thing to him was to keep that customer happy because that's your whole base." Huizenga often repeated that 1 unhappy customer would tell 10 people and then you'd have 11 unhappy customers.

The other cardinal rule was cleanliness. Huizenga demanded the garbage trucks be cleaned and painted. A truck in the shop for welding had to be at least spot painted before it was let out on the street. The third rule: no surprises. He wanted to know about problems and demanded communication. Hudson also learned that the hard way. One Saturday afternoon in the mid-1960s, a truck being delivered went under a bridge that was too low, damaging the truck. Hudson decided not to say anything about the incident to Huizenga until Monday morning. Big mistake. Huizenga leveled him. The problem could have been solved on Saturday. Monday was too late. Huizenga isn't a screamer, but when angry, his voice gets hard and eyes go flat. His entire countenance changes. "He knows your weak points and he knows how to get to you," Hudson says.

It was in these years, too, that Huizenga honed his own business skills. "He never stopped," Hudson says. "From the day I met Wayne until today, he's never changed. He's always working, always going. He has a goal for everything, there's a reason that he does what he does. If he meets you and there's something he wants from you, I'm not saying monetary, but maybe he wants some information from you. There's something that Wayne's always working for."

Huizenga applied his prodigious energy and intensity—as well as his father-in-law's capital and bank loans—to growing his garbage business in south Florida in the 1960s. Speaking in his characteristic "we," Huizenga pondered what made him succeed. "I've always been in the right place at the right time. I really don't think that we do anything different. I don't think we're unique, we're certainly not smarter than the next guy. So the only thing that I can think of that we might do a little differently than some people is we work harder and when we focus in on something we are consumed by it. It becomes a passion," he says. On a vacation to the Bahamas in the late 1960s, Hudson remembers his brother-in-law checking out the back alleys of Nassau, looking at garbage containers and saying "we've got to get these guys going." Within weeks, Hudson was in Nassau trying to sell containers.

Back then, Wayne Huizenga was constantly looking for new angles, new ways to make money. He realized early on that the real money in garbage was in renting containers—the dumpsters behind every bar, restaurant, store, dealership, and commercial business in the area. He'd haul dumpsters in a trailer behind his Chevy and when he signed up a customer, would roll off a container then and there. That philosophy of "renting things" would carry through other business ventures: portable toilets, water coolers, parts-washing machines, videotapes, even stadium seats. "To me sports is a rental business and it's an entertainment business," he'd say years later. "And it does everything I've ever wanted to do in life, and that is rent things."

He also learned about loopholes, finding ways to get into business others might consider closed. Haulers holding city contracts had the rights to pick up residential and commercial trash. But there was one area that was exempt: Construction. During a trip to Chicago, he'd seen what were called "roll-off" containers, huge bins used at construction sites. So he bought a used one and took a bunch of containers down to Florida, driving the truck himself. "We used that to grow the business because we could go into anybody's territory. Construction work was open anywhere. So we did a lot with those large containers in the construction business and we focused on areas, mainly the city of Fort Lauderdale where anyone could pick up. We competed head to head," he adds. "Anytime a new restaurant opened up, there were five or six guys trying to get the business. We beat the competition most of the time and that's how we grew faster than the rest of them. We had good, nice equipment, but we were out there getting the business. We had salesmen on the street when nobody else had salesmen." In the beginning, he was selling, Harry was selling, Whit Hudson was selling, and Wayne's stepfather, Casey Jones, (his mother had remarried in 1960) who was also working in the business, was selling. Even as the business grew, Wayne Huizenga didn't slow down. "I worked 20 hours a day bar none. All the time. And I never drove main streets. I always drove the alleys and the side streets trying to find out what was happening."

He and Joyce lived modestly, first in a rented duplex, then in a small house in Pompano, and finally a modest ranch home. Friends from this time remember the intensity. "He had phones everywhere, even in the bathroom," remarks Garo Kalpakjian, who lived in the same Pompano Beach neighborhood of cement-block ranch houses as Wayne did in the 1960s. "It was constant work." He'd take phone calls during pinochle games and "he was as busy in his world then as he is today," adds Mariann Kalpakjian, whose cousin, Judy, worked in the business. It was a low money time in life, with pot roast dinners and picnics for entertainment. In later years, they played golf and tennis and Garo remembers Wayne being competitive, taking lessons on occasion to improve his game, but able to lose gracefully. Garo once kidded him about the Chevy he drove. "Why don't you buy a Cadillac?" he teased him. "I'm not in a Cadillac situation; when I can afford a Cadillac, I'll buy a Cadillac," Huizenga told him.

He worked connections, always returning phone calls (a practice he still has today) and trying to get an edge. At the land auction in the new development of Coral Springs, he bought a lot so he would be able to say he was a homeowner when bidding for the business. With hauling manure from the harness race track in Pompano Beach a major part of their business, he encouraged his father Harry, to buy trotters until they had about a dozen racehorses.

Some efforts didn't pay off. At the time, a number of garbage operations around the country were adding pig farms, with the idea that edible garbage could be separated and cooked and fed to the pigs. In the mid-1960s, Casey Jones suggested they start a similar operation. In typical style, however, Huizenga wasn't content with just a few pigs. They built a pig farm with concrete pens and a raised walkway, and at the peak, had a few hundred pigs. He was always proud of what he did, friends and neighbors remember, and would often take his two sons, Wayne Jr. and Scott, and his friends' children, out to see the pigs. As a diversion for youngsters, it worked fine, but it didn't turn out to be much of a business. "That wasn't one of our more successful ventures," Huizenga smiles ruefully. "It didn't work out very well. In fact it didn't work out at all." The pigs weren't breeding well and some had contracted a disease, though not from the garbage, Huizenga insists, because other operations were doing the same. Though veterinarians from various universities were consulted, the cause wasn't found. The pigs were slaughtered or sold and Wayne gave up any pretense of being a farmer.

CAPITAL CRUNCH

With the business growing so rapidly, Wayne Huizenga found himself in constant need of capital. Containers and trucks were costly. With routes being added every four to six months, that meant another truck at $30,000 or so also had to be added. In addition to his father-in-law, other relatives helped in advancing money or guaranteeing notes. His mother's brother helped as did his Aunt Tena, who'd returned from Africa and worked as a nurse. "I'd borrow four or five grand from her and make payments and I'll tell you what, if you were 24 hours late, she was on the phone," he laughs. He also went from bank to bank to borrow money, with bankers uniformly turning him down, not willing to finance a garbage truck, until he met Jim Fowlkes.

Now 80, Fowlkes was a Virginia native who had 20 years of banking experience when he moved to Florida in 1955. He landed a job with First National Bank of Pompano, then switched to become a vice president of Deerfield Beach Bank. Wayne Huizenga had been a customer of the bank when he applied for a loan of $7,000 in 1963 to finance a truck. Fowlkes checked him out, decided he was a good risk, and made the loan. "He was scared to death when he signed the papers," Fowlkes remembers. "He was just nervous because he'd never borrowed that kind of money and never needed that kind of money." As Huizenga bought more trucks, the bank financed the trucks, and when he started buying waste containers, Fowlkes arranged for loans for those, too. "He could always look you in the eye with those beautiful blue eyes," Fowlkes says, in his slight Virginia drawl. "I don't guess we ever sent him a past due notice on anything and we did a lot of financing for him."

When Huizenga's credit line got high, an aunt in Chicago guaranteed it for him, Fowlkes remembers. But then Huizenga's growth outstripped the bank's ability to lend. Huizenga had reached limits of the amount the bank could loan to one customer. Fowlkes told him the bank couldn't loan any more money. Huizenga remembers being stunned. "I didn't understand why, I couldn't figure that out. We'd never missed a payment. How could you not loan us any more money?" But Fowlkes introduced him to another, larger bank in Pompano Beach, and Huizenga got loans from that bank as well.

Even with payments stretched out as long as possible, cash flow would get tight at times. Huizenga or his father would borrow $1,000 or $2,000 from local finance companies to make payroll, pay it back then borrow it again. He'd call Bob Balfoort, Judy's husband, who is a gentle soul, a school teacher, but stands about 6 foot 4 inches, big-boned and intimidating. "He'd call up and say 'Big guy, I need you to get some money, we need some cash flow,'" Balfoort says. So he'd trudge off to bars and restaurants and collect some of what was owed. Judy remembers juggling bills on occasion. "Maybe one month this bill wouldn't get paid so they could pay this bill and then they would play catch up the next time. It was always like that in the early years, but he always met his payroll." Sometimes that meant going without a paycheck for himself or Whit Hudson. Huizenga would advance salaries to drivers and give time off when it was needed. He paid well and had little turnover. "He was always interested in keeping his employees happy because he never wanted unions to come in," Bob Balfoort notes.

Despite his father's experience with near-bankruptcy, Wayne Huizenga never feared borrowing money, or at least so it appeared. "I think we were probably more afraid than people knew," says Wayne. "If you're afraid and you have doubts then people don't want to invest with you either."

Trucks and containers were the tools for growth, loans from family and banks were the fuel, but Huizenga needed a "vehicle," and that's where buying other businesses became important. Within three years after building his operation from the single truck purchased from Porter, he'd bought out Herman Mulder's three-truck operation in Pompano Beach, cutting his father in as a third partner and buying from another Dutch family from Chicago, the Vandermolens, a garbage hauling business in Key West called Florida Disposal. "Back in those days we didn't have any cash, so we needed terms," Huizenga says. "Those were the ultimate leveraged buyouts—the seller carried the paper." For both Mulder's and Vandermolen's companies, he put a percentage down and paid the balance over three or four years.

Harry went to Key West to run that operation, managing it from a storefront where the locals went to pay their bills. He became a familiar figure in the small island town. "Everybody liked Uncle Harry," says his son. "You couldn't find anyone who didn't like Uncle Harry."

In addition to expanding to Key West, Wayne was also buying operations closer to home. In quick order, he bought out Neely's Waste Removal and Ace Refuse Service, two local haulers who had once worked under the same Associated Independents arrangement that Huizenga started managing for Mulder in 1960. With those acquisitions, he gained their lucrative county franchises plus equipment and commercial customers. With a friend of his father's, he tried a start-up operation in Tampa, but pulled back after a year to concentrate on the opportunities in booming Broward County. "We were doing things in the 1960s that were really on the edge, with our routing and with our computers, with our containers, with the acquisitions," Hudson says. "No one was acquiring anything here at all. These people were going broke. They didn't know how to manage anything, they were not handling the politics. And at Wayne's age, in his 20's, he's telling these guys that are 50 or 60 years old how to run their businesses."

Wayne's willingness to borrow made the difference over competitors who wouldn't or couldn't, Hudson contends. "That's why Wayne stepped ahead of all these people. The first thing he did was get the relationship with banking and with politicians."

Working the politics was something at which Wayne Huizenga would become a master. He honed the skills in the 1960s, appearing regularly at county commission and city commission meetings regarding his contracts, getting on a first name basis with the powerbrokers and politicians in Broward County and in Florida, establishing contacts he would retain for decades. "When you have a city contract you have to work with the whole city structure, starting at public works and working your way up to the city manager, if it's a city manager government, or the mayor, and then work with all the commissioners," Hudson explains. "Your constantly getting calls from them, that there's a complaint here or this or that. Then you're working to tweak that contract all the time and to maintain the contract." But working the politics would take on a whole different connotation in the 1970s as federal regulators began investigating and civic leaders began challenging the lock that Waste Management, through Huizenga's base, had on garbage contracts in Broward County.

While growing his garbage companies route by route, customer by customer, Huizenga's persistence and tenacity paid off. Wayne Huizenga just didn't give up. But along with his reputation as a tough competitor, he could also show compassion. Tom Sette remembers. A heavyset, blustery, gentle bear of a man, Sette ran a competing garbage business in Broward County during the 1960s. It was a small operation, five trucks at the time, and he was doing mostly residential contracts in the town of Lauderdale-by-the-Sea.

Sette pulled in to the lot where he parked his trucks at 6 P.M. one night in January 1962, and found Huizenga had been waiting there for two hours for Sette to return from his route. It was before Huizenga had bought the truck from Porter and he was looking to get into the business. "I want to settle down here and I heard you want to sell," Huizenga told him.

"No," Sette answered. "I got my daughter on a kidney machine and it's costing me $96,000 a year just to keep my daughter alive. I need this business." Instead of leaving, Huizenga stayed and talked for a couple hours about the situation with Sette's teenage daughter. A month later, Huizenga had started Southern Sanitation. Sette met up with him at the county incinerator one trip and told Huizenga that if he was going to sell to anyone, he'd sell to him, but he just wasn't in a position to do so then. "Don't worry about it," Huizenga told him. "We had a relationship," Sette says. "Other contractors were cutting throats and he and I, never." Sette is certain that Huizenga never went after his contract because of the situation with his daughter. Huizenga says he competed with Sette as with other haulers, but Sette is convinced otherwise. His daughter is now 41 years old and has had a kidney transplant. "He was part of my life 'cause he could have rubbed me out," Sette adds. "You know when Waste Management started, they had big money behind Waste Management. But he never, never came into my territory."

MOB RUMORS

As Huizenga's companies grew, so did the rumors. Since the mid-1950s, the American public had already been witness to a number of investigations of organized crime involvement in the waste industry. The most famous of those were hearings held by Senator John McClellan in 1957 which focused on Mafia involvement in the garbage industry in suburban New York. The hearings revealed how mobsters, through trade associations and corrupt unions, had created a monopoly in the garbage hauling industry through methods of intimidation, including murder. Haulers considered stops as "property rights" retained by a company even after a customer moved. Haulers who violated property rights by taking another company's "stop" were penalized by the association. "Whip" companies would raid the customers of firms who didn't abide by the rules. One of the tactics was to pick up garbage from customers of the offending hauler for next to nothing, in order to "whip" the company back into line. In McClellan's concluding statement, he noted that more than 46 known organized crime figures were affiliated with the private garbage industry in the two suburban New York counties examined.

The McClellan investigation certainly wasn't the last. "Traditionally, New York City has been the hub of organized crime activity in this country, thus more investigations of its involvement in the waste business have occurred there than elsewhere."[1] A Rand Corp. researcher once identified 14 different investigations of racketeering and the waste industry in the New York area since 1956.[2] So as the New Yorkers retired to Florida, they brought their impressions of the garbage business and its unsavory ties with them. Those impressions would help fuel the rumors about the garbage business in south Florida.

---

[1] Alan A. Block and Frank R. Scarpitti *Poisoning for Profit: The Mafia and Toxic Waste in America.* William Morrow and Co., New York, 1985, p. 67.
[2] *Ibid.*

Investigations over the years by securities regulators, the Federal Bureau of Investigation, state attorneys and other law enforcement agencies never revealed anything to taint Wayne Huizenga with the brush of organized crime. But that didn't stop the swirl of rumors. "My whole life I grew up with that," says Huizenga. "Even when I was here in Fort Lauderdale before Waste Management, I grew up with 'Oh, you guys are part of the Mafia.' I've confronted that all my life. It is what it is. There's not much you can do about it. That's the perception."

It didn't help that during the late 1960s, there were a lot of new operators from New York with Italian surnames entering the business in south Florida. Given the number of legitimate businessmen who, while on vacation in Florida, would try to think of an angle to open up an operation in that sunny clime, it was natural for underworld figures to think the same. It seemed an easy stretch for organized crime types to set up garbage operations in Florida. A 1973 report by the Florida Department of Law Enforcement focused on shady operators in Dade, Palm Beach, and Pasco counties. "Later on there would be more and more of the Italians coming down here from New York," Huizenga adds. "But they could never get organized down here like they were up there. Now maybe they organized amongst themselves, but they could never get the blond-haired guy, so to speak, and get anything organized. There were rumors down here after our business was getting to be a pretty good size. There'd be rumors about some guy from New York set up down here and the people would say, 'oh boy, stay away from him, he's a bad guy' and so forth. But, you could never prove it. We never had any problems. Maybe we were too big for them to try to do anything to us." During the mid-1970s, Huizenga and his second wife, Marti, used to eat occasionally at a waterfront Italian restaurant until a friend mentioned that it was rumored to be a mob hangout. "When I heard that, whether it was true or not, forget it, we weren't going back there."

The infiltration of mobsters into the garbage business in New York and New Jersey, Huizenga would always insist, was not reflective of the industry in the rest of the country. The vast majority were small, independent, mostly family-run businesses often established by immigrant families, many of them Dutch. "People get hurt by that," Huizenga says of the rumors. "There's a lot of good people in the industry and their kids come home from school with tales and so-and-so said you're part of the Mafia, that kind of stuff. It was never that way. I don't miss it, I'll tell you that. I certainly liked the Blockbuster business a lot better than the garbage business because of the image thing." Unfortunately, the speculation, fueled by nothing more than the fact that he was successful in the garbage business, would cling to Huizenga even after he left the industry. It would waft after him, like the pungent smell that lingers after a garbage truck goes by.

CHICAGO CONNECTION

While Wayne Huizenga was riding the wave of growth in south Florida, the family business in Chicago was changing under the direction of Dean Buntrock. A native of Columbia, South Dakota, of Norwegian and German descent, Buntrock came from a prosperous family by the standards of the area. His father was the town mayor for 25 years and owned and operated a hardware and farm implement store, where Buntrock worked after school while growing up. Round-faced and bespectacled, he was quiet by nature, bordering on shy, not particularly athletic and a solid student. He attended St. Olaf College in Northfield, Minnesota, where he met B.J. Huizenga, the eldest daughter of Pete Huizenga, Wayne's uncle. After a stint in the army, he married B.J. two days after her graduation from St. Olaf. They moved to Boulder, Colorado, where Buntrock sold life insurance, earning $25,000 in his first and only year at it. "He has a poker face, doesn't talk and people trusted him—and he sold insurance like mad," says B.J.

All three of Harm Huizenga's (Wayne's grandfather) sons by his first wife died young, Tom at age 43, Siert at age 54, and Pete at age 47. When Pete died September 1, 1956, his widow Elizabeth turned to her son-in-law, Dean, to take over the management of the complex web of partnerships known as Ace Scavenger Service that now had to support three widows. B.J. claims that her mother demanded that the other partners let Dean come in to work the business, or threatened to remove her share. B.J.'s brother, Peter, was just a freshman in college, but Dean checked with Peter first to make sure he'd be welcomed by his brother-in-law. Peter endorsed the plan and Dean and B.J. moved to Chicago.

The Ace partnership at the time operated some 15 routes with total annual revenues of about $720,000. It also had a large interest in an incinerator that had been built in partnership with a group of Chicago garbagemen. Arrow Disposal, which had been Pete's company exclusively, had two trucks. Though the businesses had steady cash flow, there wasn't much left after payments to partners. He realized, as had Wayne Huizenga, that growth was key.

While learning the fundamentals of the business, Buntrock met Peer Pederson, then a young lawyer who had represented Pete Huizenga. Pederson was just the sort of legal eye that Buntrock needed to help guide the company's growth. Pederson would later become a board member of Waste Management and serve as a director for more than 20 years. The friendship forged with Buntrock would serve as the springboard by which Pederson would become friends with—as well as legal advisor to and often co-investor with—Wayne Huizenga and the other early Waste Management executives and their nexus of business deals.

It was Buntrock who would usher garbage hauling from being merely a scattering of businesses into an industry. In 1962, he helped form the National Council of Refuse Disposal Trade Associations out of three smaller, already existing regional groups, and became its first president. The organization was intended to provide a voice for private haulers as a growing national consciousness would start to focus on waste disposal, and later, environmental issues. That consciousness—and accompanying regulation—would provide the impetus behind the changing nature of the refuse business.

Meanwhile, Buntrock, intent on expansion, borrowed $250,000 to buy some garbage routes from Herman Mulder in Chicago and traded them for a Milwaukee operation and a small Chicago hauler, Wheeling Disposal. The Milwaukee business, dubbed Acme Disposal, became the only unionized company in the area in 1963 when the local Teamsters union successfully organized the drivers, helpers, and mechanics. Faced with having to pay higher wages and benefits, Buntrock looked for other ways to compete. Instead of operating with two-man trucks, Acme experimented with running one-man trucks, and despite initial protests, the innovation stuck.

Through national trade association meetings, family connections, Chicago trips and Florida vacations by Dean and B.J., Wayne Huizenga kept track of his cousin's husband's innovations in the garbage industry. He consulted with Buntrock on buying roll-off containers for construction work and borrowed other ideas as well. He sent Whit Hudson, who was running operations at that point, to Milwaukee one winter to look at Buntrock's one-man-truck operation. At the time, Huizenga's companies were running trucks with two and sometimes three men. "It's impossible," Hudson told him. "I'm telling you, get up there and see it," Huizenga retorted. So Hudson spent a week freezing in Milwaukee, and when he returned, they implemented a one-man-truck operation. "The big thing with Wayne is, if you don't believe it, go see it yourself. That's what he taught me to do—go investigate it yourself because it's going to be your decision."

While Buntrock was developing the Chicago and Milwaukee companies, and Huizenga was struggling to keep up with the pace in Florida, other Huizenga family members were drawn to the business. Cousins started or bought into garbage hauling companies in Grand Rapids and Kalamazoo, Michigan. Another, Harry Huizenga, moved to Orlando, Florida (where he was dubbed, appropriately enough "Orlando" Harry to distinguish him from the other Harrys) and got into the garbage hauling business there with his two brothers-in-law. Many of these operations would later become the first acquisitions by Waste Management. For his part, Orlando Harry played a role early on in Wayne Huizenga's business, buying the Pompano Beach business from him in 1963, then selling it back to Wayne, and buying back a portion of the residential routes in 1965.

So intertwined was the Huizenga family with the garbage industry that Peter Huizenga was prompted once, through Wayne, to reply to a newspaper article that had appeared in the Fort Lauderdale News. In the late 1960s a letter to the editor appeared (a copy of which was kept for more than 20 years by Wayne Huizenga's first banker, Jim Fowlkes) which explains the family connections:

To answer the question raised in the headline of your recent article, "Who Raises Garbagemen?" I wish to give you a little family history.

My grandfather Harm Huizenga immigrated from the Netherlands in 1896 with a strong back and a weak sense of smell.

For a profession, he chose being a "garbageman" and spent the rest of his days in that occupation. Before he died, he raised four sons, all of which were garbagemen.

Those four sons begot 16 children, including seven grandsons (of which I am one) and nine granddaughters.

Of those seven grandsons, six have chosen the "garbage" business as their principal occupation, and the seventh is still in school.

Seven of the nine granddaughters married men who are also principally engaged in the "garbage" business. It all adds up to 17 garbagemen, given this country by one immigrant couple.

Rest in peace, grandpa, you've done your share.

H. Wayne Huizenga
Pompano Beach

While proud of his business, Huizenga could also have fun with it. In the mid-1960s, Southern Sanitation trucks started sporting slogans like "This Truck has Bad Breath" and "We Cater Weddings" and "Free Snow Removal." But his singular focus on work and building the business was wreaking havoc at home. He and Joyce separated on June 15, 1966. But with no hope of reconciliation, Joyce filed for divorce less than two months later. Wayne Jr. was four years old, Scott was just a year old. In the divorce papers, as was customary then, she claimed that Wayne exhibited extreme cruelty. In truth, she was married to a driven man who didn't tolerate weakness in himself or others.

The divorce filing gives an indication of Wayne Huizenga's hallmark intensity. During her testimony, Joyce gave details of her husband's work ethic: 12 hours a day, 6 days a week, for the past four-and-a-half years. "He has no hobbies. He usually either watches television, reads the paper, goes to bed, or works," she said. He was unsympathetic to her difficulties during pregnancy, seemed disgusted and impatient at her migraine headaches and nervous condition, which she blamed on the tension in the marriage. Wayne would humiliate Joyce in front of others and complain openly about being married, according to a friend who testified. Wayne's stepfather, Casey Jones, testified on Joyce's behalf, corroborating accounts of that treatment. "Wayne is not a demonstrative or affectionate man. He is very busy. He works all the time. They are two different people. He has made her very unhappy," he said. "He has put Joyce down so many times—humiliated her to the point of tears."

Wayne did not contest the divorce and agreed to pay alimony and child support of $370 a month, continue payments on her 1965 Mustang, and pay life and health insurance. The house was sold to Southern Sanitation, with Joyce getting $750, half the proceeds. She disclaimed any rights in the businesses at her father's insistence.

It was the divorce from Joyce, oddly, that would forge Wayne's most important partnership in business. After the divorce, Joyce's mother felt awkward about being so involved with Wayne's business, and urged her reluctant husband to sell his interest. It was Peter Huizenga who is credited with coming up with the solution. VanderWagon traded his interest in the Florida businesses and his obligation on the notes by exchanging them for the Arrow disposal business, plus some cash and notes. Buntrock then negotiated to buy an interest in Wayne's companies (with Wayne and his father both giving up equal amounts of shares) while the Huizenga family trust also bought a small stake. This became the start of Waste Management.

For Huizenga, the connection was a lifeline, offering the opportunity to get new credit lines just as they were needed most. The Chicago companies, as well as his aunt Elizabeth, would guarantee additional notes. But hooking up with Buntrock also prompted Huizenga to formalize some of the internal workings of the company, implementing budgets and office organization systems. The men's personalities and business styles complemented each other. Buntrock's methodical demeanor balanced Huizenga's aggression. "Wayne is a great dealmaker, but Dean is a great businessman," says B.J. of her ex-husband. From this start, Buntrock would fashion his idea of creating a national, and later, international waste disposal company into a reality. The impetus for dramatic growth wouldn't come until a few years later. But the spark was already lit. Says Hudson, "The chemistry was there to build the company." And build they did.

2

Garbage into Gold: The Early Waste Management Years

The partnership with Dean Buntrock provided fuel for Huizenga's growth drive. With new signatures available—those of Buntrock, his cousin Peter Huizenga and his aunt Elizabeth—to guarantee loans, he was able to ride the building boom gripping south Florida. "There was stuff going up all over, Galt Ocean Mile, all those apartments and condos along the beach. All you had to do was just be aggressive and go after that work," Huizenga says. Business was tough, margins tight, and competition fierce, but Huizenga made sure that he was the first to show up to open new accounts, since the first step to keeping business was getting it. "We didn't make much money. We were just bent on growing and we did it and ended up gluing it together somehow." He began to step up the first of his many acquisition strategies, buying out more of his competitors in Broward County, snapping up three in short succession. By the end of the 1960s, Waste Management Inc. of Florida had five offices in south Florida—and revenues of more than $3 million.

For his part, Buntrock viewed his partnership with Huizenga as a step to a larger goal. The companies operated independently for a time, though the men collaborated on some ventures. Early on, Buntrock recognized Huizenga's business intuition as being at times uncannily prescient. On a trip to the Bahamas to sell a garbage truck, they had made the sale and were set to leave when Huizenga told Buntrock that he thought they should stay over, that he didn't feel right about the $5,000 check they'd received. The next morning, they went to the bank to get the check certified. Two days after they returned to Fort Lauderdale, the bank went under. He also witnessed Huizenga's gift of persuasion when they were buying a garage and the seller came in on a Sunday morning, wasn't happy about the price, the terms, or that he'd had to give up a Sunday morning to negotiate—but he took the deal.

Soon after the partnership had been created, Buntrock suggested consolidating the companies, tapping the equity markets by going public and buying up other garbage companies to create a nationwide trash-hauling behemoth. Huizenga was less sure, and characteristically, went back and forth on the prospect.

Necessity and a change of heart forced the issue. Strapped to make payroll and meet other current needs, Huizenga in 1970 turned once more to his Chicago connection. He needed $100,000. Peter Huizenga and Dean Buntrock approached the president of a small, local bank who they knew. They had no collateral left and the bank president made the loan based on the signatures of Buntrock, Peter, and Wayne Huizenga. "We were really strapped and it was the last bank financing we could do for him," says Peter Huizenga. "If anything had gone wrong we would have all gone under we were so stretched financially."

Going public seemed the only ticket to additional financing. Finally, Huizenga agreed to go ahead with an offering, but on one condition: He wouldn't move to Chicago. The idea was to split the country and let him manage the South from his base in Florida, while Buntrock and others handled the North and corporate operations.

Wall Street had already become enamored with the great growth exhibited by what would become Waste Management's major competitor. Tom J. Fatjo, Jr., a 28-year-old accountant from Houston, Texas, was the catalyst for the fundamental change in, and consolidation of, the fragmented garbage industry.[1] He had bought a garbage truck in the mid-1960s and by 1968 had four trucks, $1 million in annual revenues, and an ambitious partner, Norman A. Myers. They hooked up with Louis A. Waters, a Harvard Business School graduate and in July 1969, bought control of a New York Stock Exchange listed company, Texas-based Browning-Ferris Machinery Corp., merged the garbage-hauling business with the public company and changed its name to Browning-Ferris Industries, Inc. (BFI).

Using stock and cash, Fatjo and Waters traveled across the country, buying up other trash-haulers in a race to become the first nationwide garbage company. One of the companies they approached was Waste Management. In March 1971, Peter and Wayne Huizenga took a break from the preparations of Waste Management's own public offering and flew to Houston to

---

[1] Harold Crooks describes this in his two books on the garbage industry, *Dirty Business* (James Lorimer & Co., Toronto, 1983) and *Giants of Garbage* (James Lorimer & Co., Toronto, 1993).

meet with Fatjo and Waters. They were picked up by helicopter, flown around to various sites and then to BFI's offices at the top of a bank office tower in downtown Houston. It was a meeting both Huizengas still remember. "We're operating out of this little dinky two-story building in Chicago and these guys are operating out of this big tower and doing everything with flair," Wayne Huizenga recalls. They dined in a private club on the same top floor as BFI's offices and talked about the possibilities being offered by joining up. The Huizengas flew back to Chicago, intrigued but not convinced.

Neither Wayne nor Peter were enthusiastic about going with BFI. The proposal included making Buntrock a vice-chairman and Wayne a vice-president, a prospect that didn't appeal to Wayne Huizenga. Talks continued with executives from BFI, getting so far as having one of their executives meet with Huizenga in Florida to check out his operations. The deal was getting close, though negotiations on price were continuing. Huizenga flew back to Chicago that night where he was staying at the Buntrocks' house. "That night we had lots of discussions about should we do this thing or shouldn't we," Huizenga says.

The next morning, Buntrock asked Huizenga what he thought. "Where Wayne was always arguing for doing the deal, you could tell the next morning that he wanted to argue against it," Buntrock says. "I saw all the positive reasons for doing it but still the negative was always wondering if we could have done the same thing or maybe even better on our own." Huizenga told him he'd just as soon not do it. Buntrock concurred.

They went to Peer Pederson's office that morning where BFI executives Waters and Fatjo were waiting. "OK, are we ready to get going?" Pederson asked.

"Well, Peer, Wayne and I have something we want to talk to you about," Buntrock told him. They went into another room where Buntrock and Huizenga told Pederson they weren't going to do the deal. "You're kidding," Pederson said at first. ("Peer thought we were crazy," Buntrock says.) When Pederson saw they were serious, he said, "okay, fine. You don't want to do it, we won't do it."

Says Wayne Huizenga, "None of us, Peter, myself, Peer, Dean, none of us were a thousand percent convinced we should have done it. And Tom Fatjo, Lou Waters, those guys were very professional. They handled things like real pros. They didn't rant and rave or any of that kind of stuff. They were real gentlemen all the way through. I think I learned something from that experience. They didn't get what they wanted, but they handled themselves in a real professional manner." But now that they were not destined to be allies, and though Waste Management was a fraction of BFI's size at the time, they would become great rivals in a cut-throat competition to build their companies. The race was on.

FACING THE COMPETITION

In the early 1970s, the trash industry was in a frenzy with BFI and other competitors—SCA, Sanitas, and Canadian-based Laidlaw—as well as new-comer Waste Management, all vying to buy well-managed garbage companies in high-growth areas. For Dean Buntrock, the courtship by BFI had broadened his horizons as he realized that what he had envisioned as a $100 million company had the capacity to be a $1 billion company. For Wayne Huizenga, the agreement to stay in Florida and manage the South was quickly revised as he geared up to take on responsibility for spear-heading Waste Management's acquisition drive.

To manage Southern Sanitation and the other Florida companies, Huizenga approached Earl Eberlin, an assistant city manager in the city of Hollywood, Florida, to become the regional manager for Waste Management of Florida. Eberlin had overseen the solid waste program in one of the largest and fastest growing cities in Broward County. The decision didn't sit well initially with Whit Hudson, who had wanted that position. But Huizenga thought Eberlin better suited for the job and family ties didn't get in the way of business decisions and told Hudson so.

Eberlin was concerned about nepotism since Huizenga's father and brother-in-law were both working at the company. Huizenga assured him that he would have complete control and an adequate training and transition time. Intrigued, Eberlin signed on, figuring he could always return to civil service if necessary. The day after Eberlin joined, Huizenga left for Chicago. An experienced manager, Eberlin quickly took charge, and talked with Huizenga by phone whenever necessary, on a nearly daily basis initially. But he and Huizenga laughed for years about the "training period."

Huizenga took pains to introduce his new manager to others as his "partner," a courtesy Eberlin still values. And Huizenga made another offer that former employees remember—a $500 payroll-deductible, no-interest loan to buy Waste Management stock. Though a gesture of appreciation for their hard work, the offer also accomplished one of Huizenga's primary motivating strategies—ensuring others' economic interests were aligned with his. Employees would work harder if they felt like owners, and would therefore make his ownership stake, as well as theirs, more valuable by their efforts. But as another Waste Management exec notes, "if you're not treating that person properly as an individual you're not going to get any benefit out of throwing them $500 in stock. Somebody else could have given them the money, but he put the two together." Ownership became a central tenet of Waste Management, which encouraged all of its employees, from clerical workers to secretaries to truck drivers, to become shareholders through stock purchase plans, while stock option incentives were adopted for managers.

Meanwhile, preparing Waste Management for a rapid ramp-up, other key executives were hired. One of the newcomers was John Melk, 35, a Milwaukee native and salesman with Heil Co., which sold trucks to garbage haulers. His good looks, air of confidence (with just a hint of vanity) and smooth manner would prompt Huizenga to describe him as a "marketing guy," a label which to Huizenga not only defined Melk's skills but also his role.

Don Flynn, on the other hand, was a "numbers guy," a certified public accountant trained at Marquette University who was on a partnership track at Arthur Andersen & Co. Flynn learned the garbage business ledger sheet by ledger sheet. A senior manager of the accounting firm's small business division, he and his staff reconciled the records from the various companies that were knitted together to form Waste Management in preparation for its first public offering.

Others were hired in preparation or shortly after the public offering who would play key roles in growing Waste Management. Phil Rooney joined as Buntrock's assistant and would be appointed president in November 1984. Tim Casgar, who had an undergraduate degree from Harvard and law degree from Stanford, joined as general counsel. Drawing from the industry association he had helped create, Buntrock recognized the importance of public relations and image and hired Harold Gershowitz, who had been executive director of the industry lobbying group, the National Solid Waste Management Association, to fill that role.

Waste Management needed size to make a successful stock offering, and also needed complete control of a large landfill. Buntrock turned to a long-time contact, Larry Beck, whose Atlas Disposal worked the south Chicago suburbs and owned a small stake in the Calumet Industrial Development (CID) landfill outside Chicago, the rest of which was already owned by Waste Management from the time of the Ace Partnership that Buntrock had managed. Beck, whose father was an immigrant from Denmark who'd started hauling ashes in Chicago's south side, had started his own company in 1953. He traded his company for Waste Management shares and became a vice-president and director.

Though Beck is often referred to in company literature and press reports as a "co-founder" of Waste Management, Huizenga would privately take exception to that description, always one to bring somebody else down a peg if he thought they were "big-dealing" themselves. Huizenga thought of him as the first acquisition because Beck wasn't in on the three years of sweat and planning to put Waste Management together. Indeed, the fact that Buntrock brought Beck in as an equal irritated Huizenga for years. "Larry was very loyal to Dean," explains Peter Huizenga. "Dean called him a founder but he was no more founder than the man on the moon. He was an acquisition. Dean was putting Larry Beck in the same classification as Wayne and Wayne would get livid over that. It caused a relationship problem between Wayne and Larry. If Wayne could have seen Larry as a lesser species and that was his position, then they could have had a better rapport."

Larger brokerage houses in New York wouldn't touch the Waste Management offering because of the reputation of the garbage industry. A regional firm, Chicago Corp., did the initial underwriting. With the taint surrounding the garbage industry, securities regulators scrutinized the offering for months before it went forward. At the time of the offering, Waste Management Inc. had posted 1970 revenues of $10 million and net income of $688,000. For each share, buyers were holding an amalgam of the original company owned by Harm Huizenga, Acme, plus the Ace Partnership, ownership of the Calumet Industrial Development (CID) landfill outside Chicago, Atlas, and Waste Management of Florida Inc., essentially Wayne Huizenga's collection of companies.

Harm Huizenga, Wayne's grandfather, would have been proud. He was mentioned by inference, if not by name, in the first annual report issued by Waste Management Inc. which noted that the public offering of 320,000 shares of stock traded over-the-counter June 17, 1971, had ranked "as perhaps the single most important event in the company's 78-year history." But another event of significance, which would help shape Waste Management and that of its counterparts, had already occurred April 22, 1970. The first "Earth Day" celebration was orchestrated by a new force in the U.S. political landscape—the environmentalists who highlighted the importance of "ecology" and protecting the environment. That same year, Congress created the federal Environmental Protection Agency, adding a new acronym, EPA, to the regulatory lexicon, while counterpart agencies on the state levels were also being established. Passage of the first Clean Air Act had already shut down many garbage incinerators across the country.

Meanwhile a host of new regulations, such as the Resource Recovery Act, which required the federal government to establish guidelines for waste disposal, were adopted. To the eternal frustration of some environmental groups, most notably Greenpeace, which would target Waste Management in an "Encyclopedia of Misdeeds" nearly two decades later as Public Enemy No. 1, the very adoption of strict federal and state laws for waste disposal and treatment would contribute to the industry consolidation and Waste Management's success. The thicket of regulations required companies of the size and scope of a Waste Management, with its greater resources—and as important, political, corporate and regulatory contacts—to respond.

The clock was ticking, BFI was getting bigger and the race more heated. The initial offering by Waste Management at $16 a share netted the company about $4 million. Being a publicly held company conferred credibility and opened additional credit lines. But infinitely more important than the money raised was that the stock gave Wayne Huizenga another currency to use besides cash to buy companies. It was a currency with a measurable value and, through increases voted by Waste Management's board (to ten million authorized shares by February 1972) an ample supply.

The men began honing their strengths into a formidible team. Buntrock became president and was the strategist. Huizenga—who viewed himself as a partner and never as second—took the title of executive vice president, and was the dealmaker. Don Flynn acquired a reputation on Wall Street as a finance wizard as Waste Management's rapid growth would be mirrored in its soaring stock price and dizzying multiple. John Melk scouted for potential acquisitions. In an old, beat-up chartered Mitsubishi MU-2 twin-engine propeller plane, Wayne Huizenga, together with Don Flynn and John Melk, joined on occasion by Dean Buntrock and others, embarked on a deal-making journey that would last a lifetime.

GROWTH BY ACQUISITION

First attempts often aren't indicators of later success. That was certainly true for Waste Management's initial acquisition attempt in the summer of 1971 as a public company. They'd targeted a company in New Orleans, Louisiana, a contact of Buntrock's. "That was Dean's deal because Dean and A.J. were friends," says Huizenga, in the casual, almost automatic score-keeping on deals and deal-making that he's adopted over the years.

The deal in Louisiana was spoiled because of timing and an age-old adage: too many cooks. An entire entourage, Buntrock, Huizenga, Flynn, Melk, and other executives had flown down to meet with the owner. "We had to wait 90 days after our public offering before we could do acquisitions so we had to keep that deal on ice for a fairly long period of time," Buntrock remembers. "BFI came in and took that away from us."

Melk recalls of that first effort, "We didn't do very well. We fiddled around and negotiated and negotiated and really we weren't ready to make the deal. We were still thinking too tentative and too small. We were not willing to pay the price that needed to be paid to get that deal done. It was not a good decision but it was our practice run."

From that, Huizenga learned an important lesson that infused his deal-making strategy—*work fast to get the deal done*. The strategy suited Huizenga's personality, which does nearly everything on one speed—fast. Often, Melk would lay the groundwork and make the initial contacts. Huizenga and Flynn would do the heavy negotiating and close the deals, later followed by attorneys to wrap up legal details. Others brought deals in because of contacts, but it was that duo or trio of Huizenga, Flynn, and Melk who usually handled negotiations. Huizenga's boyhood friend and an early acquisition, Dick Molenhouse, along with a team of operations managers and accountants would analyze the business and give a rundown on prospects. There wasn't time for a lot of deliberation. Melk remembers hiring, then firing, a guy brought in to analyze deals who was too stuck on ratios and details.

The contacts that Buntrock, Huizenga and Melk had cultivated during their years in the industry became invaluable, both for the companies they decided to try to acquire and for those they decided—for a variety of reasons—to avoid. Huizenga reiterated his resolve not to buy companies in southern New York or northern New Jersey because of the Mafia involvement in the industry there. "We didn't do business there because of that. We didn't want to be tainted with that."

Indeed, that was one of Huizenga's initial conflicts with Buntrock, who'd gotten some favorable reports on an outfit in New Jersey and wanted Huizenga to take a look. Huizenga objected, "No way, we're not going in there." Buntrock told him, "Well Wayne, you feel so strongly about it, you go visit the company that wants to be acquired by us. You go visit them and see how you feel and when you come back and you're excited about it or you feel differently we'll do it. If you don't want to do it, then we won't do it."

"I spent two days with these guys driving around, listening to them talk and came back and said, 'no, we're not going to New York and New Jersey.' And for as long as I was there, we never went to New York or New Jersey," Huizenga says. "Yes, we did buy a business in northern New York, in Rochester. That was fine, we didn't have any problems."

And though there were suspicions of Mafia infiltration of garbage companies in other parts of the country, Huizenga contends the vast majority of the problem was contained in the metropolitan New York area. "That's just not the way it is in Iowa and Tennessee and all those places." Through industry sources, they'd occasionally hear about operators moving from the Northeast to elsewhere. "You never knew for sure but there were always these question marks," Huizenga says. "We just stayed away from those guys."

There were plenty of other clean, well-managed, mostly family-owned companies to choose from. Learning from the first mistake, Huizenga had taken the lead in snapping up companies in Toledo, Jacksonville, and his cousin Harry Huizenga's operation in Orlando, among others, in 1971. The intensity ratcheted up measurably the following year.

After the initial acquisitions, Huizenga realized they had to focus on three things. One was acquiring companies that had a disposal site, a landfill, not just the trucks, routes, and municipal and commercial contracts. Controlling landfills was key to controlling Waste Management's destiny. They didn't want to be in a position where local municipalities or competitors would own the landfills, raise the dumping fees and they'd have no choice but to renegotiate contracts or eat the additional cost. Plus, controlling landfills, as Huizenga had recognized from his early days in Florida, generated another revenue stream as other haulers had to pay to dump their loads. It was one of those keys to the business, akin to his early insight that renting the containers was where the real money was in the garbage business.

The second priority, gleaned from Huizenga's spectacular run of success in Florida, was to move heavily into the fast-growing Sunbelt states by targeting companies in the Carolinas, Florida, Georgia, Louisiana, Texas, and California. They also targeted the suburbs of metropolitan markets, areas of rapid development, and new tract homes dotting America which promised plenty of new customers. That also differentiated them from competitors, most notably BFI, which concentrated on getting footholds in bigger cities in the early years.

Third, and perhaps most important, was the precept espoused by both Huizenga and Buntrock that they had to get good people. They weren't buying companies, they were gaining people. They could buy all the trucks and equipment they wanted, what was needed were owners who would continue to feel like owners and work as top-notch managers.

It was a heady time, boarding the plane before dawn or flying the night before to a site for a breakfast meeting, then zooming off to another city for lunch, and meeting over dinner in a third, often pretending to return to the hotel after the late-night sessions, only to head to the airport and take off for still another destination, grabbing a few hours of sleep on the plane, to be ready for another target the next morning. "You'd get a phone call and the guy'd say, 'I changed my mind, I think my wife and I are just going to stay' and boom, turn the plane around and fly back and convince them or put them back into bed and then on with the next one," Huizenga says. "I tried not to use the telephone much. We'd make the extra effort to jump on the plane and go talk in person rather than try to get it resolved over the phone. I like to look someone in the eyes when I'm doing a deal. I don't know if that's good or bad, but that's just the way we are. Maybe it doesn't make them feel better, but it makes me feel better." Indeed, that "doing business in person" philosophy would stay with Huizenga throughout his career.

The pace was exhilarating and exhausting and weeded out those not suited to the intensity—and the personal cost—of a massive ramp-up. "That was seven days a week for everyone," Melk says. "We had our manager meetings on Sunday mornings because everyone was working on Saturdays. I'd bring a list of 28 companies and we'd go through the pricing, then get on an airplane and go out and do 'em. It wasn't grinding. It was exciting."

The intense effort generated the stuff of legends, landmarks that would be repeated often in the press to explain the incredible growth. In the 10 months between March and December 1972, Waste Management bought 133 different businesses. At the 1972 National Solid Wastes Management Association convention, "we had almost like an acquisition booth," Flynn says. "We were talking to people for four days and taking business cards and asking how many trucks they had."

Competition was fierce as the other publicly held companies, particularly BFI, were angling for many of the same local haulers. At more than twice the size of Waste Management and with more experience in deal-making, BFI was also more aggressive on the price being offered. "They were much larger than we were and everywhere I'd go it was just the reverse. Like in Fort Lauderdale, I was always the first one on the job," Huizenga says. "Well, everywhere I'd go to try and buy a company, those guys were there before me. So we had to sell."

More often than not, what Huizenga was selling was himself and the experience that he, Buntrock, and other Waste Management executives brought to the table. Huizenga hammered repeatedly on this home-grown advantage. Tom Fatjo at BFI might have bought a truck and routes but he'd started out with the purpose of parlaying the business into a financial maneuver by taking it public. "He didn't grow up in the business like we did," Huizenga would tell them. "Hey, you're better off being with us. We know the business, those guys don't. They might know how to buy companies and they might know how to raise money on Wall Street, but they don't know the business."

NEGOTIATING STRATEGY

Through this, Huizenga developed a deal-making strategy and style, though he didn't recognize it as such at the time. Since these deals were mostly being done with stock, his position was that he wasn't buying a company as much as selling Waste Management's paper, and he wouldn't sell for less than he thought it was worth. In growing the company, Huizenga felt his job was not to dilute the value of that paper by giving away too much of it, more than the earnings of the target company warranted. Huizenga paid for current, not potential, income and figured that if the seller was right about the future prospects, he'd recoup the benefits like everyone else, through Waste Management's increased profitability and rising stock price.

In making a deal, Don Flynn notes, they nearly always pegged a price, not Waste Management shares. That way, if a deal was worth $1 million, they paid $1 million and not $1.5 million if the market ended up sending Waste Management's shares higher before the deal closed. "He'll never leave anything on the table, he's a tough negotiator," Flynn says. "He's fair but if he thinks it's worth a million, he isn't going to pay $1.1 million. I've always said he'll negotiate your last nickel out of you and then he'd turn around and give you a dollar. He's a tough negotiator but then he's such a generous person."

Huizenga adopted a negotiating stance that really involved little negotiating, at least on price. Instead, he concentrated on other issues—the tax advantages of taking stock instead of cash, the comfort level with management, that the owners could stay on and run their businesses pretty much as they had in the past only with the resources and clout of a big company behind them. He spent a lot of time courting and setting up the deal, would stay with it and then try to close it quickly. "Wayne wanted to get the deal done," Flynn says. "He wasn't going to come back three times in order to get a nickel off the price, but he wanted to get the best deal he could that day. Deals don't improve with age."

Huizenga understood the pride and sensitivity that the owners had in their businesses. He took pains, as did Don Flynn and John Melk, not to insult them. He wouldn't offer an outrageously low price and then negotiate up to a more reasonable level. He started out with what he thought was a fair price—even if the other side didn't think so—leaving himself maybe 5 or 10 percent negotiating room, and then stuck to that offer. An owner might insist that the price offered was too low, that the business was going to make more money in a few months. Instead of denigrating him and saying it would never happen, the Waste Management team would simply say what they thought the business was worth. If they liked the owner and liked his business, they would visit again later to see if they could get closer on price. In some cases, an owner might be reminded that by that time, Waste Management may well have already established a presence by purchasing a competitor in the area and may not be as interested. As Waste Management grew larger, the clout of competition became a more powerful argument. It was as much the art of persuasion as the art of the deal.

Years later, his brother-in-law, Whit Hudson, would describe the negotiating style Huizenga developed and would transfer from his experience buying garbage haulers to striking deals for portable toilet, bottled water, and video store companies. Though a very tough negotiator, it's akin to a form of seduction. "I've seen a lot of people that, Wayne will rape them, but they're still friends," Hudson says. "I don't mean rape them. Wayne gets a good deal for himself or he gets a good deal for the company, but maybe they are trying to screw him or I mean everybody tries to get the best they possibly can. It's funny. Wayne always ends up with the best. But they're always friends. No matter what he does, he's fair about it. But he gets what he wants and he leaves you with that feeling that 'I really didn't get screwed. I got, I guess, what I really deserved.'"

His sense of humor and solid business sense smoothed the way of many negotiating sessions. "We did what came natural," Huizenga says. "Browning-Ferris paid more than we did almost everywhere we went. And in hindsight, they were probably right because they had a high multiple and if you gave a guy another one or two times earnings it didn't make that much difference when you were making acquisitions with a forty or fifty multiple stock. But that wasn't the way we looked at it. We didn't take the position that it was only paper. We really believed that our stock was worth what it was worth. Our whole strategy was to pay what we thought we should be paying. We convinced the people to come with us based on the fact that we knew the business better."

That familiarity with the garbage business helped win over people like Sam Harris. In 1958, Harris had started working at a small garbage company his stepfather had purchased in Brevard County, Florida. The space race between the United States and the Soviet Union was just getting started and the company lived off the growth of the space program in Cocoa Beach and surrounding towns. The company was doing $1 million a year by 1973. But spiraling gasoline prices made Huizenga's pitch more appealing. At the time, other competitors, SCA Services and Browning-Ferris, had also been in contact with Harris and his stepfather about buying the company. His stepfather wanted to take the deal with SCA, which was offering cash instead of shares because he didn't really trust the stock. But Harris persuaded him that they should sell to Huizenga and Waste Management instead. Besides the tax advantages of taking stock, "I knew that Wayne knew what he was talking about," Harris says.

While Huizenga wouldn't pay for potential—"Sam, I have to buy what's real" he told Harris at one point—Harris felt comfortable with Huizenga's attitude about servicing customers, growing the business, and reaching that potential. The executive from SCA had turned Harris off by talking about moving six surplus trucks elsewhere after the acquisition. Huizenga, on the other hand, understood that Harris felt he needed those trucks for back-up. Within a year of selling to Waste Management, the company bought new trucks (and kept the back-ups) and expanded the routes.

Harris learned first hand that Huizenga keeps a promise. Huizenga told Harris that if he got the contract for the city of Melbourne, the largest in Brevard County, he'd get a bonus. It took Harris five years to snag that contract and when he did, the Waste Management regional managers said they knew nothing about any promised bonus. But the news got back to Huizenga, and two weeks later, Harris received a check in the mail. "Wayne is a man of his word," Harris says. But Huizenga also kept managers like Harris from getting too self-assured, telling him at one point that he'd left some money on the table in bidding the Melbourne contract.

Harris also remembers another point about his deal with Huizenga. Just before the contract was signed, including a clause for Harris to continue as manager of the company, Huizenga called him aside. Privately, he asked if Harris had cut any special deals with local politicians or was paying anything under the table to local bureaucrats. Harris assured him he had nothing like that going. Huizenga warned him not to get involved with anything questionable or illegal. "You're hired," he told Harris and only then was the employment portion of the contract signed. "I don't understand the things people say about him because I know what his instructions were to me," Harris says. "Wayne was always very honest." After the sale, state investigators came by twice within a four-month period to query Harris on whether he had been coerced or in any way forced to sell. Harris assured them it was quite the opposite, that they had been looking for someone to buy.

From these years come some of the "war stories" of Huizenga's deal-making. As the corporate attorney during the early years, Tim Casgar witnessed a fair number of deals and remembers sitting with Huizenga in a prospect's office in New Orleans. They'd left at 4 A.M. in the Lear jet to get there by 6:30 A.M. because the garbage business starts early. It was a hot, muggy day, and the owner's office was above a transfer station where garbage was dumped and reloaded to take to another site. A deodorizer system went off every 20 minutes just as the smell was enough to make one gag, cloaking the stench in a cloying, sweet smell. By the end of the day, Casgar was nauseated, but Huizenga sat unperturbed, taking in the smell all day, waiting to get the deal done.

"He's willing to take the time to negotiate," Casgar says of Huizenga. "Just like sitting in this guy's transfer station all day long, he had to have patience." Casgar would watch in admiration as Huizenga could switch from talking about sophisticated market concepts to the nitty-gritty of the garbage business.

They worked out of Waste Management's headquarters, then a white, two-story building on Jorie Boulevard in the Chicago suburb of Oak Brook. They were never expansive in spending money on offices or overhead. The planes, a chartered turbo prop and later a Lear jet, were tools for getting deals done and the company off the ground. "When people say to me how can you justify the cost of a private plane, there probably would have been ten or 15 acquisitions that we never would have gotten done (without it)," Huizenga says. "So how do you place a value on that?"

Sometimes deals were done literally on a fly-over. Once while flying back from the east coast, Huizenga, Flynn, and Melk were passing over Erie, Pennsylvania. They'd just met an operator at a convention and Huizenga suggested landing to say hello and get negotiations started. They ended up getting the deal signed that night. "We gave him a jet plane ride afterwards," Huizenga says. "Took him out to the airport and let him go on this charter plane we had."

In buying a Chicago garbage outfit, owned by a Dutch family, Huizenga was invited to join them for dinner and then to sing around the piano afterwards. "With my voice, it was not a good situation, but you've got to do what you've got to do," Huizenga laughs. In negotiating with the old-line Dutch families that ran much of Chicago's garbage business, Huizenga's own heritage was often a plus.

Many friendships were forged during those deal-making years. One long-standing and notable example, which would play a role in Huizenga's later venture in Blockbuster, was with George Johnson. A lawyer in South Carolina and a member of the state legislature, Johnson, his brother, and another friend decided to go into the garbage business. They competed with Waste Management for about two years, but needed $100,000 every month to grow. When Waste Management called about buying the company, Johnson flew to Chicago to meet Buntrock and Huizenga. He and Buntrock hit it off right away. Huizenga visited him in Spartanburg and "negotiated a deal with us in typical Wayne fashion. Funny, cutting jokes and then we got down to the deal and we made a deal and became friends." Johnson was hired as a consultant and his contacts proved valuable when South Carolina's governor became ambassador to Saudi Arabia when Waste Management was bidding for a major contract.

It was during this time that a long-standing joke arose among many of Huizenga's colleagues and friends about his attitude toward deals. No matter what the circumstances, terms, or ultimate price—even if to others it appeared he'd made a killing—Huizenga would always complain about a deal, that it could have been better. "There are those of us who think that

Wayne never feels that he made a good deal," says Peer Pederson. "He always feels that he paid too much or that he left too much on the table."

"Wayne always keeps the carrot far enough out in front of him and he never really wants to catch it," says Buntrock. "That's his personality. He's never satisfied." Now directing Waste Management as a $10 billion corporation, Buntrock freely gives credit to Huizenga in shaping the company in its formative years. "There were so few things that we ever set out to do that didn't get done and for the most part, of the many individuals in the company, you have to give Wayne credit for that. He would make whatever personal commitment it took to accomplish that goal."

It was during one set of negotiations in this period that Huizenga got some advice that he remembers, but did not heed. Meeting with the owner of a garbage company in Washington, DC, he was selling hard that Waste Management was going to be the better, stronger company for this owner to join. It was just the two of them sitting in his office and Huizenga still remembers the conversation.

"'Wayne, I'm going to sell my company to you instead of the other guys for one reason. It's a reason that's good for me that probably isn't going to be good for you,'" Huizenga remembers the man telling him. "'I can see it in your eyes that you want this company, that you're going to make this Waste Management thing grow. But let me tell you something. You're making a big mistake in life because you do not separate your business life from your personal life. You have to separate the two.'"

Reflecting on his success—and that conversation—more than 20 years later, Huizenga still puzzles over this counsel. "I've never been able to do that. To me, my business is my life. Maybe I should have done more of that [separation] in my life," he says. "I believe in what I'm doing and I go after it and that's all I think about all the time. I wake up in the morning thinking about my business. I've never understood how someone could separate their business from their personal life because everything I do is so intertwined. I entertain my business people, I entertain the employees. To me it's all related. I know other people can leave and forget about it [the business] and the next day worry about it. I can't do that. I don't know how one separates the other."

"UNCLE DAD"

When Wayne Huizenga needed additional office help for Southern Sanitation in late 1968, he advertised the position in a local newspaper. Among those who answered the ad was Marti Goldsby, 26, a pretty, honey-blond woman, married, with two young children. Born in San Antonio, Florida, a small town north of Tampa, Marti was the eldest of three children. Her mother was a strong, level-headed German Catholic who, in her daughter's words, "just persevered to get it done." Her father was a barber and a watchmaker and when she was just 12, entered a Veterans Administration hospital. Marti took care of the house and her siblings and started working as a janitor at her school to help with the bills. Her father was in the hospital for six months. The early lesson in responsibility and maturity stayed with Marti.

After she married, she and her husband, Bobby, who worked as an inspector for the U.S. Department of Agriculture, moved to Pompano Beach in 1963. Their son, Ray, was just an infant. She got a job at a local brokerage house and worked there until their daughter, Pamela, was born in June 1968. Later that year, she hired on with Southern Sanitation, working in the double-wide trailer that served as an office, doing billing and clerical work.

Even then, she noticed characteristics about her new boss that she liked then and still remembers. "It was tough making the payroll in the early days of Southern and he was out there with those guys and those trucks and standing on the running board telling them how great they were, and it wasn't B.S." And how, even though divorced, he took pains to see his two sons, routing trips through Chicago whenever possible to take them to dinner or spend a weekend with them.

Then, in August 1969, Marti's husband Bobby was killed in a car-train accident in South Carolina. With no savings, she had to borrow money for the funeral from the company. "I've always given my children all the credit," she says, for helping her through that difficult time. "I don't know what I would have done without the kids. But you knew you had to take care of them." She continued working at Southern Sanitation and about nine months after her husband's death, "Mr. Huizenga" asked her out for a date. "I was petrified," she says. "Because I wanted to go out but I knew I wouldn't work for him if we dated." The first date was a trip by boat, his 31-foot Chris Craft, to a waterfront restaurant with a salesman who was visiting from Alabama. There were more dates until it got to a point that she knew she had to find another job. She waited until she thought he was on a plane before giving her notice to Whit Hudson. But Huizenga called from the airport, learned she had quit and was upset about her decision. "I can't worry about dating and falling in love and what happens if either of them sours, either I'm not doing a good job or we don't continue on," she told him. "I need a job with my children."

She took a job with Reynolds Securities, the local brokerage house she had worked for before joining Southern Sanitation. They continued dating for three years, while he and Dean Buntrock were laying plans for the public offering of Waste Management. Working for a securities firm, she knew the demands required of running a public company and advised against going through with the offering. She remembers going to the manager at Reynolds and asking if the firm could handle the offering and being told that they didn't handle anything small like that. "I've often thought it would be so fun today to bump into him and say, 'aren't you glad you passed this up?'"

Huizenga moved to Chicago after Waste Management's public offering in 1971 and they continued their relationship through phone calls, letters, and his trips back home. The distance actually helped cement the relationship as they realized they wanted to be together either in Chicago or in south Florida. And though she doesn't like to think of it this way, it was Marti who closed the deal. "I don't think he was that interested in getting married. I mean, here's a woman with two little kids. He was divorced with two children. We'd probably still be dating if I hadn't said, 'I have a life, I have children, I have to look at my future.'"

They opted for a simple wedding, flying with John Melk and his wife, Jan, to the Dominican Republic where they were married in April 1972 in Santo Domingo. She and her two children—Ray, 10, and Pam, 4 (later adopted by Huizenga)—moved to Chicago, first to a small condominium, then to a large house in Oak Brook on an acre lot with a creek behind it. Wayne Jr., 11, and Scott, 8, moved in with Marti and her children for nearly a year.

Having worked for Huizenga at Southern Sanitation and for a brokerage firm, she recognized the challenge facing her new husband. "I understood what he had to accomplish. I thought it would be fun for the kids and I to keep track on the calendar when Daddy was home. Well, after about 32 days had gone by without having dinner together, I thought 'this is not a good game.'" When he stopped in to get a new batch of shirts, the kids, at Marti's prompting, would call him "Uncle Dad" as a joke because he was never around.

The absence of Wayne made it Marti's job to meld the two families, a task that wasn't easy. The boys had been instructed by Joyce to call their stepmother "mom" but it was a difficult adjustment, particularly with their father traveling so much. Having a nice big bedroom in a house with a huge lot and snowmobiles and boats didn't make up for missing their mother. "Marti-Mom made the best home she could, but this was all new to us," says Wayne Jr. After several months, the boys moved back with their mother. "We missed Mom intensely. We had been with her all of our lives. It was mostly the three of us. And Mom had gone through a lot of back operations and I used to go and do all the shopping and I'd cook for my brother. We were a team."

In Marti, Wayne had found a partner for his personal life. "He knew I was independent, he knew I was strong, he knew I was opinionated and we just took each other for what we were." He had found someone who understood when he wanted to go look at trash containers on their way to her brother's birthday party, or years later, spend Sunday afternoons visiting Blockbuster stores in south Florida. As busy as he was, she kept herself equally busy, raising the children, and later volunteering for charities and local community work.

After two years in Chicago, Wayne was eager to move back to Florida. "With his commuting around the north, he may not see sun for days and days at a time and it just didn't bode well," she says. "He decided that he would do the sacrifice. If we moved back to Florida, he would commute. But at least he knew he had this every weekend," gesturing to the outdoors and the brilliant Florida sunshine.

Though earning a modest salary of $54,000 as vice chairman, Waste Management's public offering had made Huizenga a millionaire. Instead of returning to their ranch house in Pompano Beach, they bought a 1925 Spanish-style home that juts into the Intracoastal Waterway with water on three sides. Huizenga himself wasn't crazy about the house because it needed a lot of work. But Marti, who had always wanted to restore an old home, would get plenty of practice on the house that had weathered two hurricanes in its first three years. They added bedrooms, an office, and a courtyard and pool area used for entertaining. They bought two adjacent properties and expanded the grounds to include a tennis court and additional garage where Huizenga keeps his collection of classic cars, a hobby-turned-business that Marti introduced him to on his 50th birthday with a 1937 Rolls Royce. Even after his multi-million-dollar fortune ballooned into the $1 billion mark, they opted to stay in the Casa Fiore, valued at upwards of $2 million but still modest compared with their means.

The Huizenga house is a home, the kind of place where a visitor is apt to see a plastic pork-chop dog toy on the tiled floor, where paperwork is piled on a kitchen counter with the morning newspapers spread over the butcher-block island in the kitchen. It is filled with momentos from family and friends and memorabilia, including framed newspaper and magazine stories about Blockbuster and the sports teams, along with family photographs of ski trips, vacations and stuffed marlin trophies.

Keeping his promise, Wayne would leave on Sunday afternoons or evenings for Chicago or a business destination, and return Friday evenings to spend weekends, whenever possible, in Florida. Some aspects of those years still weigh heavy on him. "We worked extra hard to make it (the success of Waste Management) happen, but we paid the price for that," he says. "If I had to do it over again and as I advise Wayne Jr., spend more time with your family than I did. Your kids grow up a lot quicker than you think they do and all of a sudden, you look back, you haven't spent the time with them."

The song "Cat's Cradle" by the late singer and composer Harry Chapin, which describes a father too busy to play with his son, with the refrain "we're going to have a good time then, Dad" still causes a jolt. "That hits me every time I hear that song because that's me right to the T. That comes back and hits you real hard and I wish I'd have spent more time with them. I never saw my kids play Little League ball. I never went to a PTA meeting. Marti did all that stuff. The only play I ever saw was when our daughter Pam one time was in a play. I missed all that stuff with all the kids. That's not good and I wouldn't advise anyone to put that much into it." Yet, whether he intended it or not, in building Blockbuster, key executives would make similar sacrifices, albeit for much shorter periods and for most, without the long-distance commute.

A Good Motivator

While building his reputation as a dealmaker in Waste Management's early years, Huizenga was also exercising another strength—motivating people. "He was a good motivator and a good driver," says Buntrock of that contribution by his partner. "It's his personal drive. He creates an aura of excitement. He has a tremendous sense of humor and he's fun to be with."

It was Huizenga who insisted on having a managers directory made that would fit in a shirt pocket so that while traveling the country buying garbage haulers, he could easily contact a local manager to grab a quick lunch or dinner or even a chat by phone from the airport, a practice he encouraged other executives to follow. Equity ownership was key in keeping motivated the newly acquired owner-managers, many of whom became "paper millionaires" overnight, but it was creating excitement and fun that was a Huizenga specialty.

Early on, Huizenga recognized an opportunity to instill a sense of pride, ownership, excitement, and enthusiasm among Waste Management's burgeoning management team. The annual industry convention by the National Solid Wastes Management Association had already become an event around which many haulers planned family vacations. So Waste Management began hosting an annual managers' meeting a few days before the convention, inviting managers as well as their spouses. The idea was to make it a special and memorable event. "He viewed the convention as a thank you for people who worked extremely long hours," says Ron Shufflebothem, former Waste Management public relations director and organizer of many of the events. "He felt if you just gave someone a raise, they would fight over a new piece of furniture but if you brought your wife along to the convention, she could share in the pride of what we were accomplishing."

It was Shufflebothem who learned first-hand a classic "Wayne-ism" in planning the meetings. "For a nickel more, you can fly first class," Huizenga would tell him. In practice, that meant attention to details like ordering enough food so that the last to arrive had the same fare that the first had enjoyed. No matter how great the meeting or how much was spent on a corporate reception, if they ran out of shrimp or had just crumbs left on trays, Huizenga's theory went, the guy who came in just a half-hour before closing would only talk about the cheap bastards who hosted the event. Another rule was not to keep guests waiting in line. "You didn't stand in line for food or drink and you had the same fare available at closing as at opening," Shufflebothem says. "I learned that from Wayne."

Always, Huizenga paid attention to extra details to make the meetings special. One year at the Omni hotel in Atlanta, he and Dick Molenhouse arranged to have the Waste Management logo inset into the ice at the skating rink that linked the shopping mall with the hotel. It was done at night, so the next morning, it was a surprise for the Waste Management managers and their wives. It was another way of fostering a sense of community and pride among people who were engaged in what was viewed by society as the lowliest of professions. "We were the proudest, most egotistical people you ever met," laughs Ron Shufflebothem. "There wasn't anything we couldn't do, and no one could do it better than we could."

At Huizenga's insistence, instead of plain notepads, the company provided binders bearing the Waste Management logo. Pens, cups, caps—anything that could be inscribed with the Waste Management logo—were given to managers and their wives. He once ordered 5,000 baseball caps to be given away during the industry convention in New Orleans. Caps bearing the Waste Management symbol flooded the city and within hours, even the strippers on Bourbon Street were wearing them. At one of the last managers' meetings, held in St. Louis, the company staged a dinner dance and the women received a gift from Tiffany's. "He loves the gimmick side of business and that's a real motivator," says Peter Huizenga. "A lot of people in business don't really understand how Wayne accomplishes things. It's not just beating people down with his blue eyes or the power of his personality. You're doing things for people. You establish a kind of court of love and you want to get your employees to the point where they'll die for you."

Wayne treated the owner-managers at Waste Management as partners. His friendliness was contagious. He would walk into a convention hall or meeting and within seconds, introduce himself as "Wayne Huizenga," never, "Wayne Huizenga, vice-chairman," notes Dick Molenhouse. Indeed, long-time friend Molenhouse has another explanation for Huizenga's skill in motivating people: "Time. Wayne always took time. If you called Wayne, he would somehow find time to talk with you. He doesn't care if you're a truck driver, a helper on a garbage truck, or a laborer in a landfill or the paper picker, Wayne will take the time to talk with you."

Heeding the lesson he taught Whit Hudson early on about seeing things for yourself, Huizenga was eager always to get out of the office and to go size up a situation in person, whether it was a potential acquisition of a company or landfill, or a division having problems. Once there, he'd talk to the drivers, bulldozer operators, and office workers as well as the managers, to gather information.

He could be impatient if others didn't agree or see things his way, a trait that mellowed but didn't disappear in later years. "I think early on if you didn't agree with Wayne on something that seemed self-evident, then he'd just sort of dismiss you," Peer Pederson says. "Now he wouldn't do that, though he might feel the same way." In dismissing others, "he'd just sort of write you off. Then you wouldn't get involved in anything he had any authority over. Some people tended to be intimidated by Wayne. Maybe they didn't give him the information they should have given him because they were afraid of him."

Still, those who have worked with Huizenga say he used his contagious enthusiasm and power of persuasion, much more than intimidation, to motivate employees and resolve difficult situations. "He can create the atmosphere that excellence comes out of it," says Fred Weinert, who held various posts including vice-president of international. "He gets the most out of his employees. He was good at acquisitions because he knew how to treat people. He would study or think about the other side of the table a lot and he may change his opinion from one day to the next because he's thinking more about the other side of the table. The great word in Spanish for this is "simpatico."

Huizenga's skills could transcend language and culture, as Weinert has witnessed first-hand. When Waste Management was closing a contract for the city of Cordoba, Argentina, in June 1981, Weinert (as the project manager) and the company's attorneys were still negotiating over a clause in the agreement to provide waste disposal services for the city of one million residents. In a centuries-old Spanish-style town hall with white-washed walls, tile floors, and dark, heavy wood, Huizenga met with the city mayor. The mayor was concerned about a clause that allowed Waste Management to reopen the contract for reevaluation for currency devaluations or other extraordinary events. Huizenga assured the mayor that the clause would not be invoked for the length of the agreement. The attitude at Waste Management was that the company would cover those types of contingencies in its price and would abide by the contract.

"He knew the mayor had to be kept reassured so he gave the mayor reassurance," Weinert says. "Now the cost of that reassurance was going to be my problem but to close the contract, that's what mattered." Waste Management might have given up a little on the contract and adopted more risk, but Huizenga's attitude was that in the long run, it would be a good contract. "It's just the opposite of what you hear about Wayne, that here's this tough guy. He took the position that my 'team might have their feet a little bit in cement and I'm going to loosen them a bit to get this thing done.'"

In the prop plane heading back to Buenos Aires, Huizenga asked the pilot to fly over the city. "Fred," Huizenga said casually as he looked out the window, "I'm not sure you have enough trucks in the bid." Weinert didn't say anything but a knot formed in his stomach that stayed until the day of the startup when indeed, there were enough trucks after all. There was probably not any other comment that Huizenga could have made that would strike more fear into an operations manager at Waste Management—and he knew it. "He kept the level of tension up to make sure the startup was going to be very smooth and it was," Weinert says. Huizenga was adept at motivating different levels of employees, keeping managers anxious, tense, and a little off guard, and slapping drivers on the back because that's all he could do, he couldn't really create tension with them.

That ability to motivate employees and his recognition of what was important to someone else—whether a truck driver, a manager, a garbage hauler anxious about selling his business, or a mayor of a foreign city—would help guide Huizenga in building not just one, but two, billion-dollar empires.

3

Waste Management: Regulatory Woes and Industry Triumphs

By the start of 1974, Waste Management revenues had been growing at a 35 percent clip annually and now totaled $132 million, and its shares had already split twice. Buntrock, Huizenga, Flynn, and the rest of the Waste Management team had been building credibility in the company and themselves. The company had reached a milestone on October 25, 1973 when it became listed on the New York Stock Exchange. For Wayne Huizenga, who in little over a decade had parlayed one garbage truck into a company with a market value of $144 million and personal holdings of $2.5 million, it was a particularly sweet sign of success—and conferred additional responsibility. "Through all the years I was with Waste Management, we had to deal with Wall Street and you learn," Huizenga says. "But, the biggest lesson I learned is that if you say you're going to do something, be darn sure you do it."

It was during this time that Waste Management had come to the attention of Chuck Lewis, a young investment banker at Merrill Lynch's Chicago office. Despite the reputation of the garbage industry, he'd been reassured by the credentials of the company's accounting firm and legal advisors and had checked with attorneys in town about environmental and anti-trust issues. But another point also provided some reassurance: Waste Management executives had said they wouldn't buy any outfits in New York or New Jersey. It was in part because of that promise that Huizenga stuck to the rule about not buying any companies in that part of the country. Lewis would become a long-time friend and advisor to Huizenga and other Waste Management principals and earn Merrill Lynch millions of dollars in fees through financings arranged for Waste Management, Blockbuster, and a nexus of other companies spawned by the dealings of these men.

Though Waste Management was in a full-scale race to snap up garbage haulers and landfills and continue the company's growth, it couldn't control events in the Middle East—or the impact on the U.S. economy by the 1973 oil embargo. The oil shock reverberations and economic suffocation in turn strangled the stock market, and with it, Waste Management's stock. "I sat in my breakfast room with my wife and a legal pad and figured out my net worth was like minus $1,000 or something," Melk remembers.

Waste Management was no stranger to controversy. Federal, state and local regulators, as well as the press, would delve into anti-trust violations, environmental problems and political corruption cases involving Waste Management subsidiaries and employees over the years. The scrutiny would be a constant and show the underside of a company whose very business invited controversy, but it didn't slow its steamroller success.

As it was preparing for its public offering in September 1970, the Illinois attorney general sued the local trade group, the Chicago & Suburban Refuse Disposal Association and its dozens of members, including three company subsidiaries, for an elaborate scheme to divvy up the Chicago market. The association paid $50,000 to settle the case in April 1971 without admitting or denying guilt. Nearly a decade earlier, in 1962, the state of Wisconsin had named Dean Buntrock and Acme Disposal, a company in which Buntrock held a minority interest, in a civil case brought against a group of haulers alleging use of intimidation tactics and threats in the Milwaukee market. The allegations were denied, but the Milwaukee Circuit Court issued an injunction against such actions by the firms. The case was dismissed in 1970 when Acme became part of Waste Management. In January 1971, Acme began a garbage collection contract for Milwaukee. In 1973, the state of Wisconsin sued a Waste Management subsidiary for attempting to fix prices. After two mistrials, the hard-fought case went to trial in July 1975 and resulted in a $4,000 fine.

In addition, a contentious bidding contest in Hollywood, Florida, in 1975 resulted in a nasty dispute between the company and the city over Waste Management's reputation. Waste Management was the low-bidder for a three-year contract. But the then-city manager directed the police department to investigate Waste Management. The resulting report outlined allegations of organized crime connections, monopolistic practices, customer allocation and price-fixing, illegal lobbying, and sabotage, vandalism, and threats to competitors—even the supposed use of aliases by high company officials. The scope of the report was later broadened to include SCA, and also cited allegations of organized crime connections and similar violations.

Faced with the reports and a challenge by SCA that Waste Management's bid wasn't to specifications, the city in September opted to keep its municipal service. But copies of the police report had been leaked to the press and to other cities and investigative agencies. In October 1975, Waste Management sued six city officials and police officers for defamation, noting that the report was based on untrue and unsubstantiated information and had harmed its business. By March 1976, the city agreed to settle the suit by requesting that all copies of the report be returned. The reports and police notes were burned in a bonfire at the fire training school.

SEC PROBES FOR MISDEEDS

But those actions paled to the far-reaching, 14-month probe launched in November 1974, by the Securities and Exchange Commission (SEC). Prompted by the complaints of a disgruntled hauler, the regulators first "went through every acquisition, all of the individuals involved with the company, looking for a Mafia connection," says Harold Gershowitz, former senior vice-president of public affairs. The SEC investigation requested documentation and listings of every company acquired and interviewed and deposed many of the former owners as well as company employees and officials. Examiners looked into possible market manipulation, and inquired as to whether misrepresentations had been made by Waste Management executives about stock performance in negotiating to buy companies for shares. They examined the company's accounting practices, particularly the poolings of interest with acquisitions. (A pooling, as opposed to a purchase, calculates the acquired company's results as if it had historically been part of the overall operation. Critics contend such accounting can inflate actual performance.) Again, investigators came up with nothing.

But, investigators weren't finished. The company was asked to conduct its own internal survey of managers regarding political contributions. It was Huizenga's job to instruct Waste Management's divisions to respond to the survey. Two instances surfaced. One was a $35,000 contribution by Norman Goodhead, a politically well-connected owner of a recent acquisition in Toronto, to the Progressive Conservative Party of Ontario. The expense had been improperly capitalized over four years. The propriety of the contribution itself came under scrutiny by a Canadian Royal Commission, which cleared the company of any wrongdoing.

The Florida situation was more troubling. A landfill in Florida, one of Huizenga's original companies, routinely made cash contributions to local politicians from an off-the-books fund characterized by investigators as a secret slush fund. The money totaled about $40,000 over the past three years. Although cash donations were not illegal, anything run out of a cash account by the very nature of its unaccountability, looked suspicious.

In a deposition on Thursday, July 3, 1975, in Washington, DC before two attorneys for the Securities and Exchange Commission, Huizenga—on advice from his attorney Peer Pederson—took the fifth amendment on questions relating to political contributions and his acquaintance with certain south Florida politicians and city officials. (A state grand jury in Broward County had just weeks earlier returned an indictment against a city commissioner of Cooper City for soliciting a bribe from a lobbyist for Waste Management of Florida. The commissioner would be convicted to two years in prison. Charges against the lobbyist were dropped before the case went to trial after a key witness changed his testimony.)

The SEC probe had put Waste Management under a shadow with Wall Street, and the uncertainty of the outcome dogged the company. The SEC was threatening to withhold registration statements and the company wouldn't have been able to hold its annual meeting. "That would have killed us," Huizenga says. "Everybody would assume the worst and the stock would have tanked." On March 26, 1976, Huizenga and Earl Eberlin both signed consent decrees. In signing, they neither admitted nor denied fault, but promised not to violate securities laws in the future. "There was never a finding that Wayne Huizenga did something wrong, that's what people don't understand," says Harold Gershowitz former vice president of public affairs. "Wayne signed for the company."

That consent decree—and Huizenga's taking of the fifth amendment—would haunt him for years. As he built Blockbuster, media reports would reference the consent decree, and some would cite his testimony as well, as signs of a nefarious side to his character. "I got pressured from a lot of people, saying 'what's the big deal, signing the consent decree you're not admitting anything, go ahead and do that.' So I did it," Huizenga says. "As far as the company was concerned, that was probably the right thing to do. As far as I'm concerned, I'm suffering with that for 20 years now. I wish I had never done it."

But out of one of Huizenga's worst moments in his life would come one of his greatest friendships. Representing Waste Management in working out the consent decree with the SEC was an attorney out of Pittsburgh named Carl Barger. Huizenga was just learning how to golf and they'd go golfing together, sometimes to the Casa del Campo resort in the Dominican Republic. Barger's love, besides Pittsburgh, law, and golf, was baseball. Fourteen years later, Barger would play a key role in his friend's decision to pursue a major league baseball expansion franchise.

INTERNATIONAL MARKETS AND NEW TECHNOLOGIES

The push by Waste Management into international markets in 1975 that resulted in a watershed event in the company's history, began with a much smaller horizon. Waste Management's anemic stock price prevented it from making acquisitions without having to give up too many shares, so Buntrock was looking for other ways to expand. "I kept hearing about this big contract in Saudi Arabia and I made calls on that and sent four of our people there to see what this was about," he says. "It wasn't a decision 'now we're going to go international.' It was a decision based on 'this sounds like a great contract.' It was a half-billion dollar contract to clean a small city. It didn't end up being that, but that's how it started."

Saudi Arabia was awash in petro-dollars in the mid-1970s and in hurry to modernize hospitals, hotels, sewage treatment plants—and garbage collection. Peter Huizenga, Don Flynn, and John Melk made the first scouting trip in July 1975. More trips by other teams rounded out details. By October of that year, Buntrock and Wayne Huizenga traveled to Riyadh, Saudi Arabia to hand carry a bid. It was Melk who shepherded the bid through the convoluted process, helped by connections with the right Saudi prince and partner. A contract was finally signed January 31, 1977 for $243 million, which was $64 million more than the company's revenues the previous year. An advance payment of 20 percent was a tremendous cash infusion for the company, and word of the contract sent Waste Management's shares above double-digits for the first time in two years. A team headed by John Melk, Phil Rooney, Fred Weinert, and other Waste Management executives would oversee the massive contract, from hiring workers from India to building housing, buying and shipping trucks, equipment, and supplies, down to shoes for the workers. The contract in Riyadh would be followed by joint ventures in Argentina and Venezuela. Waste Management lost the Riyadh contract in 1982 to BFI, but gained another Saudi contract in Jeddah.

While Buntrock directed the push into international markets, Huizenga focused on the domestic front. During the stock market slump, Waste Management had spent nearly two years revising its operations, moving trucks and equipment. "We were ready to go," Huizenga says. "Browning-Ferris [BFI] hadn't done any of that in that period of time. Everything we did from 1975 on, all that incremental revenue, fell right to the bottom line because we were lean and mean. That wasn't the case at BFI. They didn't get themselves in position."

By then Huizenga and Waste Management were pursuing another strategic direction—one that was quite profitable, but also by far the most problematic of Waste Management's ventures. "We knew that if we wanted to be in the waste business we wanted to be in all aspects of it," Buntrock says. In 1975, the company formed Chemical Waste Management in preparation for a new line of business.

Government regulation drives the refuse industry and no aspect has been driven more in the last 15 years than the chemical waste business. One key regulation adopted in 1976 was the granting of "interim" status to existing sites that generated or managed hazardous waste while the EPA evaluated them before issuing final permits, a process that could take five to ten years. As of November 1980, all new sites would have to go through the longer permitting process. Clearly, this was a market window.

With EPA surveys in hand, Huizenga, Flynn, and others pursued acquisitions. The prospective business was more complex than garbage hauling, the universe of landfill sites smaller, and competition against BFI stiff. The company already had a test laboratory at its Calumet landfill. "We were probably in the business before we knew we were in the business, because we just looked at it as another piece of waste to dispose of in our landfills," says Huizenga. In the quickly changing regulatory landscape, however, that approach would be at the heart of Waste Management's challenge—and problem—in managing its controversial new line of business: The question became whether chemical disposal was indeed "just another piece of waste" or if it was an entirely different sort of business, one requiring more centralized control and greater in-house development of treatment and technologies.

But management of ChemWaste was never Huizenga's responsibility. His job was to make the deals to get the business going. In 1977, a team including Huizenga acquired the company's first major site in Emelle, Alabama, approved by the EPA shortly thereafter to dispose of polychlorinated biphenyls (PCBs). (The 350-acre site was purchased from a partnership that included the politically well-connected son-in-law of then-Governor George Wallace, a point local residents claimed smoothed the way for the permitting process.) Other sites were bought in Vickery, Ohio; Lake Charles, Louisiana; and Kettleman Hills, California. "It was a very, very complicated business and we had a very difficult time for years getting the proper person at the top to manage it," says former general counsel Steve Bergerson. "But Wayne and Don Flynn equally saw the opportunity and went on a real quick campaign to acquire these sites while they had interim status and really knocked the socks off Browning-Ferris. In a year and a half, we built up a national network of sites unlike anyone else."

During this time, Huizenga encountered one of the few deals that, try as he might, he just couldn't get done. He was interested in acquiring OHM Corp., based in Findley, Ohio. The company, started in 1969 by James

Kirk, his father, and three brothers, took a different tack in the hazardous waste business. Rather than transporting the waste to landfills, the strategy was to treat it on-site. At the time Huizenga approached the company, it had about $20 million in sales. "Wayne stopped in and didn't right up front say he wanted to buy the company," Kirk remembers. "We, being young and neophytes in the industry, didn't understand and thought he just wanted to be friends. We talked for five or six years about various opportunities." But Kirk was leery about the replication of the cookie-cutter garbage business philosophy in the hazardous waste industry. In his view, the business was different and every project unique. But he was impressed with Huizenga's approach. He'd seek Kirk out often just to visit. When Kirk was on a job site in New Orleans, Huizenga would go to see him there. "That in itself is unique to Wayne," Kirk says of the extra effort Huizenga would put forth to make contact. "Wayne was always very personable. It was always a deal, but he made it enjoyable. If we would have sold, we would have sold to Waste and to Wayne just because of the kind of person he was."

A solid friendship between the two men developed. Mixing business and pleasure, the families vacationed together on Huizenga's yacht, the Sun Dream. "I tried to acquire him—never did get the deal done," Huizenga says. "I'd get furious with him that he wouldn't do it. But we always stayed friends through the whole thing." Kirk says he never saw Huizenga get angry during the discussions. He thinks they'd still would have become friends even if he had sold, but refusing to do the deal may have strengthened the relationship. "It kept him coming back." They remain good friends—Jim Kirk and his wife were guests of the Huizengas' during the 1995 SuperBowl. OHM went public in 1986 and has become a $350 million company.

Meanwhile, looking for new ways to treat hazardous waste, Waste Management considered a technology used in Europe in which ships at sea incinerated chemicals at extremely high temperatures. Wayne Huizenga arrived in the Netherlands in August 1980 to approach Ocean Combustion Systems about buying such a ship, the Vulcanus. But the owner already had a deal underway with another company and told Huizenga he was leaving for Paris for the weekend. Casually, Huizenga asked him where he stayed in Paris, what he did, his favorite restaurants. Later that day, Huizenga caught a train to Paris and waited in the hotel lobby. When the ship owner saw Huizenga, he was stunned, and asked him what he was doing in Paris. "I'm here to buy the Vulcanus and I'm not leaving until we get it done," he told him. It wasn't the first or the last time he'd use that line to make a deal. They stayed a few days in Paris and began negotiations, then went back to the Netherlands to finish the deal.

Former Waste Management attorney Steve Bergerson, who flew out to handle the legal work, remembers being amazed at Huizenga's ability to get this deal done in such a short time. "This upstart American was dealing with two German shipping lines, turned it around and got it for same price," he says. "I would have thought it was impossible for an American company not in the shipping business [to do the deal]."

The next growth prospect was to go nuclear. ChemNuclear, one of two companies handling disposal of low-level nuclear waste, had its corporate headquarters near Seattle, Washington, and its main disposal facility in Barnwell, South Carolina. That in itself, Huizenga saw as part of a fundamental management problem. After courting board members, large shareholders, and the company president, management balked. The addition of ChemNuclear would increase Waste Management's total revenues by only about 10 percent, press reports said at the time, but would be a toehold in the nuclear waste-disposal business—a potentially huge market.

Instead of a friendly deal, Waste Management ended up doing a hostile takeover, making a $15 a share tender offer. Once the company was in play, Huizenga refused to budge on the price despite pressure from the arbitrageurs on Wall Street who were used to reaping escalating premiums in a hostile bid. Meanwhile, Huizenga, Flynn, and other executives waited the deal out in a Seattle hotel for three weeks. When it was finally done in October 1982, at $121 million in cash and stock, Huizenga and Flynn were at a meeting with members of management who were still trying to negotiate. "Don't they know we own them?" Flynn mentioned to Huizenga.

Waste Management moved the company's headquarters from Seattle to Columbia, South Carolina, about an hour from its main disposal site, taking only three executives from the headquarters team, and replacing the 120 headquarters staffers with a fraction of that number. Over many long days, Huizenga oversaw the transition, planning organizational charts, and thinking about how the new business should be managed. "What impressed me the most about working with Wayne is his patience and focus," says Michael Cole, now president of Chemical Waste Management, who assisted Huizenga on the ChemNuclear integration into Waste Management. "No matter what you're working on, no matter how many things he's got going on, he focuses right then and there on the issues at hand and the people at hand. Despite the fact that a lot of times he knew where he wanted to go, he always gave people an opportunity to talk about what they were doing and why they were doing it." Huizenga's other strength was his attention to detail, his sensitivity to the acquisition of a smaller company by such a large corporation. He worked to build relationships with the community on a corporate and personal basis. Waste Management built new administration buildings in Columbia and Barnwell, and met with local politicians who were worried about the effect of a corporate giant in their backyard. Huizenga brought the Sun Dream to Hilton Head and invited the local powerbrokers and new managers aboard. He insisted that Chem-Nuclear have its own Christmas party and helped plan details of that event.

ChemNuclear would be Huizenga's swan song for the company he had helped found. It was during the transition of ChemNuclear into Waste Management that Huizenga told Cole of his plans. Huizenga had been staying at Cole's house. They'd gone out for pizza and Huizenga had been working on an acquisition on the phone. When he hung up, he turned to Cole and said he was planning to retire. "The company's getting big now and it's not as much fun for me anymore," he told Cole. "I need to know that I have the opportunity to do things that are going to provide big gains for the company. I need to be able to take risks that are going to put me in a position that I can make or lose $1 million in any day." It was time for others to run Waste Management, he'd done his job in helping to build it.

END OF A PARTNERSHIP: HUIZENGA MOVES ON

The difference in personalities between Dean Buntrock and Wayne Huizenga—and their management styles—is reflected clearly in their corporate lairs. Within the maze of Waste Management's low-slung campus-like setting in Oak Brook, Illinois, Buntrock's office is an inner sanctum in an executive wing, accessible only by passing through the office of his assistant, and with a sliding door that he activates with a switch. Standing guard outside his office are trophies from his passion for big-game hunting including a huge grizzly bear tagged in Canada and a Marco Polo big horned sheep in Russia. His office is sparsely decorated, just a small family photograph on a credenza behind a desk devoid of paperwork. "Dean likes to hunt and be CEO," is how one associate sums him up.

Wayne Huizenga's office at the top of Blockbuster Plaza in downtown Fort Lauderdale reflects his exuberance. His office door is usually open to a central hall on the executive floor, with his assistant's office off to the side. The cherrywood credenza is crowded with a collection of family photographs—Harry and Jean, his granddaughter, friends, a picture of him and Marti (plus one of him with supermodel Cindy Crawford). Large portraits of his children hang on the wall above his desk. Models of his planes and awards from civic and humanitarian organizations line the shelves, along with his own collection of treasured trophies—the commemorations of his deals. "Wayne is motivated by money and unbelievable financial success, but he is much more motivated by the hunt, the excitement," Buntrock says. Indeed, but Huizenga is interested in only one kind of quarry—green.

For 15 years, the two men worked together to build an industry power-house. Buntrock's quiet, introverted personality and more conservative approach complemented Huizenga's enthusiasm and aggressiveness. Huizenga is more direct and forceful, Buntrock more contemplative. They used each other as sounding boards to test ideas and strategies. "Probably the fun and the greatest part of working together was doing analysis because Wayne really liked to analyze every situation and every deal," Buntrock says. "Part of his thought process was having a good argument on both sides. He did not want you to agree with him because that interrupted his thought process. He liked the discussion, the argument, and he could really take either side equally effective. Years later, after doing this a lot of times, I used to enjoy saying once in a while in the middle of one of these arguments, 'I agree with you,'" Buntrock chuckles. "This would be very disruptive because then he would probably move to the other side as gracefully as he could anyway."

Like any business partnership, while profitable, it could be problematic at times. "Wayne's a little aggressive from an acquisition, risk-taking mode and Dean may be a little more conservative than Wayne is," says Don Flynn. "I think Wayne always wanted to grow faster and Dean was more concerned with can we manage it. Whereas Wayne would rather buy it then figure out how to manage it." Or as another associate puts it, "Wayne was the spark plug."

Some actions of Buntrock's were a continual source of frustration to Huizenga. The elevation of Larry Beck to equal status was one. But more fundamental was Waste Management's initial ownership structure and the financial rewards conferred to Huizenga and the core group of executives. "Dean wasn't really that concerned about ownership and felt that ownership would always take care of itself," says Peter Huizenga. "He was more motivated by how are we going to put this company together and how are we going to take advantage of opportunities in the environmental field much more than what he was going to get out of it. Dean was always interested in making money, but there's a certain shyness when making money and equating it to negotiating tough wars. He was always very reluctant to talk about himself and what he would get out of it. He just didn't think that was the thing you should do. Wayne wasn't so motivated. Wayne wanted to establish that there was sufficient ownership there for him to spend his energy and talents on building it up. Wayne started out with Herman Mulder (the first garbage company he managed) without ownership and said 'this isn't working, I'm never going to make it this way, I've got to become an owner.'"

Huizenga measures success by personal gain as well as company results, and while Waste Management officers were entitled to stock options, he didn't think it was enough. "This was all new to us and I think that it always bothered Wayne that we didn't take care of ourselves personally a little better in putting the company together in (granting) options and warrants particularly," says Buntrock. Even years later, Huizenga would bait Buntrock on the issue. "Dean, do you know what you're doing? You have got the greatest success story in the world and you haven't stopped to figure out where you fit into it," he'd tell him, as Peter Huizenga recounts the conversations. "Dean, you've created more value and more wealth for other people than anybody else in the history of the world and what have you gotten out of it? Dean you should be a multi-billionaire and what do you have to show for it?"

"I guess Wayne's position was like he ran Blockbuster," says Peter Huizenga. "'I want my interest up front. I want everybody to know that when I go into a deal what my interest and position is and then the salary doesn't matter because I have an ownership interest.' Dean's position on that was that you've got to be Caesar's wife—we should pay a market compensation and you do not use company property for personal use. Just the difference in philosophy, everything's going to come out right. Wayne is more, 'what difference does it make, small potatoes in comparison to our contribution so big deal.'" (Indeed, while Huizenga says he was always careful to reimburse for personal use of company property, his side deals at Blockbuster with his private companies, while disclosed in proxy statements as being at market rates, would garner mentions in the press.)

But it was one particular similarity, not a difference, that over the long run caused a split. "They are both instinctive about profit opportunities. They both team build and attract good people, they probably wouldn't think they're similar but they are, that's why they worked together well for a long period of time," says Don Flynn. "But eventually they both had to be number one. And there really isn't room for two number ones."

"Wayne never liked being second fiddle," says Peter Huizenga. "As close as he was to Buntrock, there was always a love-hate relationship that continues up until today. Wayne never particularly enjoyed being second to Dean. Now Dean kept working at trying to make Wayne feel comfortable in that position, but Wayne never was. Wayne always wanted to be the boss (but) he respected Dean and he respected Dean's counsel," he adds. "Dean won't talk about these issues, but they had a lot of knock-down drag outs. Wayne was the only one that really would challenge Dean. Dean didn't like people challenging him or his leadership. I think there's a competition there that will never resolve itself."

Cognizant of Huizenga's sensibilities on the subject, Buntrock purposely never published an organizational chart for the top tier all the while that Huizenga was at Waste Management. While it was clear that Buntrock made the final calls, he didn't see a need to hammer that point internally. And indeed, neither he nor Huizenga acknowledge much conflict. The situation "worked because Wayne was very, very respectful of me and my position and I was equally respectful of everything he brought to the marriage," Buntrock says. "I don't think either one of us had ego problems. We didn't have philosophical differences. That doesn't mean we agreed on everything. I suppose I could come up with some examples of differences but I don't think Wayne and I ever had a disagreement in public or in front of any of the other officers. When I say disagreement, we didn't agree on lots of mundane things, but if we had serious differences, we handled those privately. I viewed him as a partner."

At one point, there was discussion about creating a co-CEO job, but Huizenga would end up leaving before that ever materialized. "I never looked at myself as number two," Huizenga says. "As far as I was concerned, we were partners and that's the way we started out in the early days and I had no problem with Dean being CEO and me being president."

As the years wore on, Huizenga tired of the commute from Florida to Chicago and by 1979 began talking to Buntrock about leaving the company. He would never consider returning to Chicago. (As his friend Chuck Lewis says, "Wayne is messianic about south Florida.") In an effort to accommodate him, Buntrock offered to move Waste Management's executive offices to Fort Lauderdale. It would be too expensive to move the entire company, but he figured a core group of executives could manage from Fort Lauderdale as well as Chicago. He and Don Flynn bought houses in the area and Waste Management actually opened an executive suite just north of Fort Lauderdale.

What happened next is a matter of interpretation. Some top executives were reluctant to leave Chicago for Fort Lauderdale, and, according to Huizenga, kept pushing for better relocation packages, for the company to pay for private schools and other perks. The demands and the attitude, plus the inconvenience of the frequent trips to Chicago, made the whole process not worth it, he says.

In addition, however, Buntrock says it was Huizenga's own wavering and his dislike of the bureaucracy of big organizations that killed the move. "The company got to be a certain size and Wayne doesn't like working through layers of people," he says. "I think it became more frustrating and it wasn't as much fun." Even after moving the core executives to Florida, "Wayne still was uneasy and I wasn't comfortable that he was still going to stay with the company long term. I became concerned I'd have the corporate offices in Florida and Wayne may still leave." It was difficult to carve out an area of responsibility that was meaningful or exciting for Huizenga to manage out of Florida, as Huizenga made it clear he no longer wanted to be away from home five nights a week. "We used to sit out on his dock or outside his house and he'd say he was tired, he was not having as much fun, maybe he wasn't cut out for this. We talked about how he could make it more fun again and it was during one of those conversation I said 'okay, I'm not going to talk you out of it anymore.' Up until then, I'd say, 'well, let us think about it some more we'll talk about it next week.'" (Huizenga says if the company had been based in Florida he would still be there. "I was in love with that company and I would have stayed." His cousin, Peter, says that Wayne mentioned after he left Waste Management that if anything happened to Buntrock, he'd be willing to come back but only as CEO.)

In 1980, Huizenga began his transition out of the company, relinquishing his position as president and chief operating officer and reducing his involvement in the day-to-day operations, but retaining the title of vice-chairman and still heading the company's acquisition team. As he prepared to leave in 1983 after overseeing the integration of ChemNuclear into Waste Management, he and Buntrock would butt heads again, this time over his severance package. Huizenga initially wanted $500,000 a year for five years, arguing that he'd done a lot for the company and had never really gotten what he was due, even though his salary in 1983 was $475,000 and he held stock and options then valued at more than $23 million.

But Buntrock never understood that attitude and felt as strongly that he was setting a precedent with Huizenga. The severance was set at $330,000 through 1989. For years, Huizenga would throw that up to Buntrock as well. "When you look at what other executives got out of companies when they left, they got a lot more than what I got," Huizenga says. "When you are one of the founders that put together a company of that size in that period of time I think that more should have been done."

The competition and rivalry between them continued even after Huizenga left Waste Management. The last incident involved the hiring of Greg Fairbanks as chief financial officer for Blockbuster in 1992, who had been chief financial officer of Waste Management's international division. Buntrock was upset with Huizenga for raiding one of his officers. Huizenga contended that Fairbanks would have left anyway, since Waste Management was moving its international offices. "They have detente," is how Peter Huizenga sums up the relationship between Buntrock and Huizenga now. "They might not be friends, but they have a love for each other. They can't pal around, but they have such admiration and mutual respect for each other, they've been through too much."

As Huizenga was preparing his exit, others of Waste Management's original group of executives were preparing to leave also. Larry Beck retired in 1983. Huizenga had already told his brother-in-law Whit Hudson of his plans and that if Hudson wanted to team up on new ventures, that he might consider retiring also, which Hudson did in 1982. After Waste Management moved its international headquarters from London back to Oak Brook, John Melk in 1984 decided it was time to exit. Though his official retirement wasn't until a year later, by early 1983, Huizenga was already on his way out when Waste Management's biggest crisis hit.

DIRTY BUSINESS: "SEWERGATE"

By 1981, Waste Management's $772 million in revenues had boosted it past rival Browning-Ferris Inc. to become the world's largest waste disposal company. From a negligible amount in the mid-1970s, the chemical waste disposal business was kicking in more than $125 million annually to Waste Management's revenues by the start of 1983, but would become the source of the company's biggest problems. "It started out not being a problem," Huizenga says of the chemical waste business. "But remember in the early days the regulations changed so much. When you're the biggest you're the example all the time. I'm not making excuses, some of the things we did wrong."

Indeed, this growing revenue stream became increasingly complex. Controversial by its very nature, the new business of managing hazardous waste was being done against a backdrop of shifting regulations, changing science, and the nation's mounting alarm over pollution and an alphabet soup of toxins like PCBs (polychlorinated biphenyls) and dioxins. Contamination of communities like Love Canal, New York, and Times Beach, Missouri, were horrors that struck a collective nerve.

Misjudging the broad support by the public for a greener, cleaner, less-polluted environment, President Ronald Reagan's administration became embroiled in charges of gutting the EPA and hamstringing its enforcement of hazardous waste regulations. A barrage of media coverage about the agency in the fall of 1982 and early 1983 laid bare sordid allegations of sweetheart deals, political favoritism, or special treatment afforded corporate polluters. Meanwhile, Congressional inquiries into what had been dubbed "Sewergate" focused on tales of paper-shredding, erased computer disks, and cover-ups that led to a contempt citation and eventual resignation of EPA Administrator Anne Gorsuch Burford.

Amidst all this, investigators and reporters focused their attention on the nation's largest waste hauling and chemical waste treatment company—Waste Management Inc. On Monday, March 21, 1983 a front-page story in *The New York Times* with the headline "Giant Waste Company Accused of Illegal Acts" laid bare a host of charges of illegal dumping, and deception, omission and flagrant violation of environmental laws at a half-dozen landfill sites around the nation. An article the next day in *The Wall Street Journal* cited "the company's top management consciously and by deception or omission" tried to hide shipments of dichlorobenzidine (DCB) to the company's landfill in Illinois without the proper permit in order to please a customer with which the company had a $4 million contract. The company was also accused of benefiting from EPA favoritism in getting a ban on liquids in landfills lifted and burn permits for the ship Vulcanus, citing the role of an EPA consultant and former regional counsel whose law firm represented Chemical Waste Management. (At least five congressional inquiries at the time also focused on the issue as to whether the lawyer wielded influence on behalf of his firm's private clients. A Justice Department report in August 1983 found no violations of law by his actions.)

Reaction by Wall Street was swift and severe. Within 48-hours, Waste Management's shares plunged 20 points, marking the biggest drop in market value for a company in the history of the New York Stock Exchange—$1 billion. Huizenga flew to Chicago to caucus on the company's response. On March 23, Waste Management acknowledged that there had been some violations of reporting requirements and that it had discovered PCBs in storage tanks at its Vickery, Ohio, landfill site but denied the rest of the claims and hired an Illinois environmental prosecutor to investigate and report his findings to the board of directors.

Meanwhile, Buntrock, Flynn, and Gershowitz met with investors in New York at the Helmsley Palace and throughout Europe to answer questions and concerns and promise the result of the special report would be shared with the investment community. Within six weeks, the stock had recovered to an all-time high. (The report to the company's board of directors acknowledged "serious noncompliance with environmental regulations" in some instances, but characterized most violations as "technical"—failures to fill out paperwork. While the Waste Management's operations had not contaminated groundwater, the report said, the company had acquired sites in which actions by previous owners had done so.)

Throughout the spring of 1983, Waste Management continued to be hammered by a barrage of media reports about hazardous waste violations. But the focus also brought into sharp relief and public prominence an ugly side to its success. Stories in *The New York Times, Washington Post,* and elsewhere recounted questionable business practices at Waste Management subsidiaries, citing civil lawsuits, indictments, and grand jury investigations into political payoffs, predatory pricing, and price-fixing conspiracies, and chokehold practices to disadvantage competitors.

In some circles, Waste Management looked like a corporate thug. The environmental group Greenpeace targeted the company in 1987 in a highly critical report, later expanded to an "Encyclopedia of Environmental Crimes and Other Misdeeds," a 285-page litany of allegations of environmental violations, antitrust actions, and detailed descriptions of political contributions and influence. Greenpeace plainly states that it is opposed to Waste Management's very existence, that an "unholy alliance" of waste haulers and government officials have helped entrench the "myth of safe disposal" and that a company that profits so handsomely from garbage and toxic waste disposal has no interest in reducing it, which the environmental organization contends is the only real solution.

Moreover, Greenpeace claims that fines, including over $45 million in environmentally related penalties and settlements assessed Waste Management between 1980 and 1990, have merely become a cost of doing business. "To create an empire the company has mixed business acumen and foresight with strong doses of deception, corruption, and monopolism," the report states, citing antitrust lawsuits or investigations in at least 17 states and that Waste Management, its subsidiaries and employees have paid more than $28 million in fines or settlements (including out-of-court settlements) for bid-rigging, price-fixing and other violations from 1980 through 1991, the date of the updated version of the report.

The garbage business essentially is a local business, subject to local conditions and ripe for conspiracies that can make it a dirty business. "We went to painstaking efforts to have policies and procedures that we called our PAP manual and everyone had to follow it and we made everyone sign that they read it," Huizenga says, noting that employees throughout government agencies and various industries violate rules and regulations. "You've got rules and you've got policies, but from time to time, people get caught up in whatever they're doing and they violate that. It's not what you want to happen and you hope it never happens. You have the same in any business. I don't mean to make light of it but those things happen. And when you're a new company and you put so many strangers together in such a short period of time, it's hard to follow up on all that stuff. After you're 20 years old and after you've got your professional managers in there and so forth, then it's a little different again, but we put a lot of different personalities together in a short period of time."

State investigators and prosecutors are often overwhelmed by the complexity of antitrust cases, and the FBI and federal prosecutors are often not interested because of the limited scope of the cases, which lack national impact. Nonetheless, by 1987, the activities of the industry had prompted at least eight federal grand jury investigations of waste haulers. The *Fort*

Lauderdale News/Sun-Sentinel published a series in December 1987, called "Titans of Trash" outlining the political influence and checkered regulatory history of both Waste Management and Browning-Ferris Inc. in south Florida and elsewhere. (The series would hit as Huizenga was already ramping up his next major corporate challenge at Blockbuster.)

The antitrust investigation that would hit closest to home was an extensive probe undertaken by federal and state authorities in south Florida in the mid-1980s. Browning-Ferris had started to compete aggressively in the state and that prompted prices in areas where there was competition to drop. That made investigators suspicious about high rates in Miami and parts of Broward County being charged by United, a Waste Management division acquired in 1980, and a competitor. A grand jury indicted two Waste Management managers on charges they participated in an elaborate scheme to allocate customers over 14 years. (The case would result in convictions for both men, though the conviction of one was reversed on appeal. He pled no contest rather than undergo a new trial.) In addition, the Florida Attorney General filed two related civil cases.

Though Huizenga's name surfaced during the state attorney general's investigation, nothing ever linked him to the conspiracy. "We looked and we talked to a lot of people over a long period of time," says Jerome Hoffman, director of the state's anti-trust division. "He has been investigated and investigated and investigated and [investigators] have never had any evidence to show he'd been involved in any of this personally. If he knows what's going on he's done a tremendous job keeping himself insulated. I don't think there's ever been a credible statement to that effect, that 'I conspired with Wayne Huizenga.' At this point, you have to believe him."

Likewise, a study commissioned by Waste Management in 1992 by the law firm of O'Melveny & Myers and later headed by Secretary of State Warren Christopher took pains to note that while there had been two bribery convictions of local employees of Waste Management subsidiaries, neither the company nor any of its subsidiaries had been charged with public corruption. Likewise, the company's antitrust charges stemmed largely from "isolated misconduct of a few individuals." Waste Management's operating divisions have been convicted or penalized in only six criminal cases amid the hundreds of locales it operates, the study noted. (Although each of those cases would spawn civil antitrust litigation and that figure does not include cases in which "no contest" pleas were entered or settlements reached in civil cases.) The study was in response to a highly critical and well-publicized report that same year by the San Diego District Attorney, which relied extensively on the Greenpeace report and *Sun-Sentinel* series.

Greenpeace and other environmentalists would be proven partially correct in one fundamental aspect of Waste Management's business. Its rapid expansion into toxic waste landfills and dominance in the business would eventually backfire by the early 1990s because of market dynamics. As ChemWaste's prices for disposal and treatment rose, producers of toxic wastes found it advantageous to reduce the amount generated and find alternative disposal methods. That would contribute to the management challenge facing Buntrock.

As Waste Management grew from $1 billion when Wayne Huizenga left in 1984 to $10 billion by 1994, its business became much more complex. By 1992, it had changed its name to WMX Technologies to reflect the sophistication required of its new lines of business. It had spun out but kept stakes in four separate publicly traded companies, including ChemWaste, with the intent of separating the controversial and volatile toxic waste business from its core trash collecting operations. WMX was essentially operating as a portfolio of environmental services companies. But its once-skyrocketing stock price languished as the company changed from a fast-growth dynamo to a complex and mature business, and though revenue and earnings increased, results did not meet investors expectations. In 1994, WMX shifted strategies again, bringing two of its portfolio companies back into the fold, and has undertaken a massive internal strategic examination. Although still a shareholder, none of that was the worry of Wayne Huizenga, who was long gone by that time. He'd done his part of the bargain, making the deals and growing the company. Managing it was the headache of Dean Buntrock and the rest of the Waste Management crew. Wayne Huizenga had other challenges awaiting.

4

Wayne's Companies after Waste Management: Toilets, Lawns, Bugs, and Water

In the azure waters off the coast of Australia, the 43-foot white fishing boat swelled with the waves. An ebony streak leaped in the distance as a giant marlin snatched at the bait. In the chair, Wayne Huizenga braced himself as the huge black-billed fish fought against the line, racing across the ocean surface first in one direction, then another. He played out the line and hauled it in, waiting while the fish exhausted itself and was finally reeled to the boat. After a video camera got it all on tape, the leader was snipped and the fish disappeared into the blue depths.

The videotape would show it was close, but there was no proof that Huizenga had gotten an elusive grander. He'd been coming to Australia now four years in a row, fishing for a grander, a black marlin over a thousand pounds. It's considered unsportsman-like, and in Australia very nearly a sin, to take a marlin under that size as the game fish need time to reproduce.

On his first fishing trip to Australia in 1983, Huizenga had enjoyed the sport so much he wanted to return the next year aboard the Dyfken, captained by Peter Wright. The boat was already booked. But something like that never stopped Huizenga. He asked the captain about the odd name of the boat, which was dubbed for a point of land in Australia discovered by a Dutchman years ago. The owner of the boat, who was also a Dutchman then living in London, had named it that after the discovery by his countryman. Huizenga called the boat owner in London who at first didn't want to sell, but after a few months, relented. Huizenga bought the boat and called Wright. "I'm coming back," he told Wright. "Squeeze me in."

He went back three more years in a row. On the last trip, Wayne Jr. caught five black marlins, the largest in the 900-pound range. On that same trip, his father caught one that was close to grander size, but he'd never be sure. "It was a goal to get a grander, to get a thousand pounder," says Wayne Jr. "And one of the few that he has not realized." Not just then, anyway.

*   *   *

After leaving Waste Management, Wayne Huizenga tried to take a year off—and couldn't. With his pal John Melk also retired, they set out to have some of the fun and take some of the vacations they'd missed during the intense years of building Waste Management. Melk wanted to buy a sailboat but had never sailed. Huizenga advised he try it out before investing in a boat, so the two of them and their wives went to the Virgin Islands for a week of sailing school. Characteristically, Huizenga insisted that he and Marti take the front V-berth even though it was more uncomfortable. With sails catching the wind and the boat heeled over just right on a gorgeous day in the Caribbean, Huizenga asked the captain where they were going. The captain nodded to a small island in the distance. "How long is it going to take us to get there?" Huizenga asked him. "Oh, three, four hours," the captain replied.

"You've got to be kidding! If we had my boat we could already be there and be doing something!" was Huizenga's response. That "doing something" might be renting motorbikes or fishing or swimming. "The guy has a little excess energy," Melk laughs of his friend's proclivity toward "doing something." (But of the four, only Huizenga passed the sailing test.)

After the sailing experience, Huizenga took up something more his speed, racing formula cars during a week at the Skip Barber Racing School in Sebring, Florida, with Marti, Wayne Jr., Pamela, and Scott, as Ray was working on a fishing boat off Australia. There was time for a few more trips aboard his 91-foot yacht, the Sun Dream. Once while anchored off St. Johns, Huizenga hired a local band, then zipped around the bay in his Cigarette boat to the small sailboats moored in the bay, inviting the other boaters to join the party. "He made sure that everybody had a good time— it was a fun evening," remembers his friend Norm McCarvill, who was one of six guests with the Huizengas for that trip. "Wayne likes to experience lots of things in life. He likes to try things but he doesn't want to do it all on his own. He wants to give those moments of excitement or pleasure."

With the pressure of commuting to Chicago gone and his home base now in Fort Lauderdale, there was also more time for the society set. The islands of east Fort Lauderdale, lined with palm trees and mansions with million-dollar yachts docked outside their doors, are a world away from the sprawl of south Florida. Tour boats ferry gawking tourists along the waterways, past the opulent homes of the rich and, for the most part, marginally famous. (Back then, Huizenga's house was better known than he was, as the set for the 1983 Burt Reynold's movie "Stick." As Marti Huizenga notes, it was a terrible movie, but the Huizengas got a shar-pei dog and a friendship out of the deal.)

Not as stuffy as the "old money" crowd in Palm Beach, the Fort Lauderdale set is a meld of inherited wealth and self-made millionaires, with a circuit of fund-raisers for diseases and causes good for tax deductions and business contacts as well as the reward of giving. But a real sign of arrival is membership in the exclusive—and secret—CSYC, better known as the Chicken Shit Yacht Club, reserved for the wealthy who do something stupid in boating. During one Columbus Day regatta, a tradition in south Florida in which hundreds of boats sail or motor across to an island offshore Miami for an overnight stay, those rafted up to the Sun Dream were treated to filet mignon (for 15) and a seven-piece orchestra and guests didn't stop dancing until 5 A.M. On that trip, Huizenga was inducted as commodore of the CSYC, dressed as a giant rooster and forced to do a chicken dance.

New Deals: A Collection of Service Companies

He tried playing more tennis and golf but clearly with the "been there, done that, let's go" attitude of Wayne Huizenga, retirement just wasn't going to work. Within weeks, it was back to his first love—making deals. In his last days at Waste Management, Huizenga had urged Buntrock to adopt another strategic direction and broaden the company to include more services. Among the companies suggested were portable toilets, lawn care, and pest control. Waste Management had looked at all three and Buntrock had rejected them all, except for pest control, which he thought might be a possibility.

Huizenga had disagreed, believing that portable toilets and lawn care were better strategic fits. Portable toilets would work because the Waste Management trucks that serviced the roll-off containers at construction sites could pickup and drop off the toilets at the same time. Lawn service had more synergy than pest control, he believed, because it required the same kind of "outdoor" worker—a point with which Waste Management regional managers who had been surveyed for their opinions had agreed. "You come and you pick up the garbage and you're gone and no one sees you," Huizenga once said. "It's the same thing with spraying the lawn. You spray it and away you go. But once you start having pest control a different type of person has to go inside the house. Well, Buntrock just thought 180 degrees. He didn't believe that at all and so even though all the regional managers thought that they should go into lawn care and not pest control, Dean disregarded that advice and went ahead on his track of going into pest control and not lawn care." Huizenga had wanted Waste Management to acquire a St. Louis lawn care company called Evergreen, but Buntrock wasn't interested. Buntrock thought the portable toilet business was too fragmented and small on which to spend much corporate energy. With Buntrock uninterested, Huizenga figured the businesses were fair game. He asked Buntrock if he could use the information gathered by Waste Management to put something together himself. Buntrock gave the okay. Huizenga was on his way.

Not far from where he'd gotten his start 20 years earlier, Wayne Huizenga opened an office in Pompano Beach for WACO, or Wayne's companies. (The name was changed to "Huizenga Holdings" when he realized that it was being pronounced "whacko.") But Huizenga wanted a partner, certainly not for the financing, but for the doing. He had already started cultivating that relationship with a young accountant he'd hired in 1981, Steve Berrard.

The man who would play a key role in helping Huizenga carry out his strategy both for his private companies and later for Blockbuster grew up in Fort Lauderdale as the son of a maintenance engineer turned restaurant manager. Berrard was devoted to his parents but his relationship with his father was never very good and when his parents divorced after he graduated from college, it became particularly poor. Captain of his high school football team, he envisioned becoming a lawyer but with law school enrollment soaring, opted for a career in accounting instead. After graduating from Florida Atlantic University, he began working for the Fort Lauderdale office of the accounting firm Coopers & Lybrand. He'd been there four years and was just 25 when another accountant who had done some work for Huizenga recommended Berrard as a bright young guy who'd be just right to work for his private companies. It was 1981 and Huizenga was already laying groundwork to leave Waste Management. Berrard was brought in initially on a contract basis to straighten out the affairs of Harry Huizenga, who at that point owned a small garbage company and a few other investments. But in addition to being smart, creative, hard-working, and good with numbers, Huizenga recognized in the six-foot, mustachioed Berrard the qualities he valued most: a dogged determination and unabiding loyalty.

Huizenga approached Berrard about a job. "I'm making $30,000 a year, I'm going to make partner, why would I give that up?" he told Huizenga.

"What are you going to make when you become partner?" Huizenga asked him.

"Well, you get a salary for life."

"Well, you know, you're right," Huizenga told him. "You don't want to work for me."

"What do you mean by that?"

"If all you want to do is work for a paycheck then you're not the kind of guy that I need to get done what I need to get done."

That gave Berrard pause. Huizenga offered him a salary of little more than what he was making and a car. Berrard was still unsure, but the prospect and challenge of being in business rather than just auditing it, intrigued him. After negotiating with Huizenga for six months, he ended up with less than Huizenga had offered him that first day, but with a promise to be a 5 percent partner in everything. (It was a handshake promise that Huizenga has abided by; Berrard is a partner in real estate deals and the baseball team.)

In Huizenga, Berrard found a boss, a partner, a mentor, a friend, and, he admits, a father-figure. Fourteen years after that meeting, Berrard in his new role as chief executive officer of Blockbuster would reflect on the depth of that relationship. "I pride myself on being a devoted individual to whatever I do and I take everything very personally," he says. "If someone asked me to cut my wrist for Wayne Huizenga, I would have cut my wrist for Wayne Huizenga." Over the years, others would struggle to describe their relationship, the best analogy being that of an apprentice to a master, and in this case, it was in the art of dealmaking and entrepreneurship.

LESSONS IN THE ART OF THE DEAL

The lessons began early. Huizenga invited Berrard and his wife to join him and Marti on a trip to the Virgin Islands. Though it was never said, Berrard is sure the invitation was in part to see how he conducted himself outside the office, to make sure he wouldn't be an embarrassment to his new boss.

His first day on the job Berrard went to Palm Beach to examine the financial controls on the small garbage company owned by Harry Huizenga. The president handed him a pair of overalls and told him to ride the trucks for a few weeks before giving advice on finances. That first week, Berrard also got a lesson in Wayne Huizenga's ability to retain his roots. Berrard met him at his waterfront house in Fort Lauderdale and they drove up to Route 60 to central Florida to check out a small garbage company near Kissimmee that Huizenga thought was a possible acquisition. The office was a two-story wooden shack with a plywood and sawhorse table with a bare light bulb. The bathroom was literally a hole in the floor with a bucket beneath it. "I'm thinking, this is the number two guy at Waste Management, he's got all this money, I'm here, we're going to build a business together and look what the hell we're dealing with here," Berrard recalls. But he watched in amazement how after just an hour or so, it was like the guy had known Huizenga for 15 years. They didn't end up buying the company, but Berrard learned a valuable lesson in approach.

The second lesson in dealmaking came in buying the portable toilet business, Port-O-Let International, a Jacksonville, Florida, company that did business in about 25 states. Dispatched to negotiate the deal, Berrard got a dose of the Wayne Huizenga school of deliberation. Berrard negotiated and negotiated, would call Huizenga and each time, his boss would say, "well, let me think about it."

"That's when I first learned that Wayne's never satisfied," Berrard says. "I'd call Whit [Hudson] up and say 'you got to be kidding.' And he'd say, 'get used to it.'" The next morning, Huizenga would send him back to negotiate again, as many as 16 different times.

Finally, they reached a price that was acceptable. But the lesson wasn't over yet. In buying hundreds of garbage companies, Huizenga had perfected his technique. To close the deal, Huizenga, Berrard, Whit Hudson, and an attorney named Ronnie Fieldstone flew to New Orleans to meet with the owners, the Leopold family, in their attorney's office. There was still a question of about $100,000 cash in a bank account that the Leopolds insisted that they retain. Some might view $100,000 as not a huge amount to forfeit in a nearly $4 million deal. But Huizenga believed he was paying for all the assets, and if the Leopolds wanted to take the cash, then they could take the bills that were due the next day and the week's payroll as well. It was a fundamental business rule and one he didn't budge on: Don't let anyone take the cash out of the deal. He was going to get that $100,000.

"That's not part of the deal, the $100,000 comes to us," Huizenga told them.

The Leopolds said no. Huizenga looked down at the table. "Okay boys, let's go home," he said. The room was stunned. No one moved or said a word. "Let's go, I said," Huizenga repeated, and he and the attorney started stuffing stacks of paperwork and franchise agreements into their briefcases. With that, they left the room and walked down the hall. Berrard turned to him, "Wayne, are you crazy? Over $100,000?"

"They're never going to let us get to the elevator," Huizenga replied.

Just then, the door opened. "Uh, Mr. Huizenga, maybe we can work something out," the Leopolds' attorney said. Huizenga and his crew were invited back in and the deal was signed. Huizenga got the $100,000. "He knew how to play that particular game and that's just classic of him," says Whit Hudson. "He knows what he wants and he knows how to get it."

But the most important lesson Berrard learned during those first years was one of trust. With the Port-O-Let deal done, Huizenga was already considering entering the bottled water business. He liked the idea of renting the coolers. The constant cash flow was like renting containers in the garbage business. Huizenga left for a vacation in Australia with instructions to Berrard that if he found anything while he was gone to go ahead and buy it. Berrard hopped in his car, tooled around Florida for two weeks to various cities and towns, looking up bottled water companies in the Yellow Pages. He called them, usually getting a wife or daughter acting as a dispatcher who would tell him where the truck was and he'd go meet with the owner, introduce himself as being with Port-O-Let and ride the routes.

He was laying groundwork, knowing that no one was going to sell immediately. Before he left town, he'd give the same spiel: That he wanted to do business and would rather do it with them than compete against them and that he planned to put a 1-800 ad in the Yellow Pages in the next edition so he'd at least be in business. After his two-week jaunt, he hadn't gotten anyone to sell, but on a Friday afternoon, the owner of a Fort Myers bottled water company called and said he'd heard Berrard had been canvassing the state looking for acquisitions, that he was going to a closing but if Berrard paid him $1,000 more, he'd sell to him instead. So Berrard drove to Fort Myers, cut him a check for $16,000 and within a week had bought three companies, including a fairly sizable one doing about $500,000 a year. He'd been in contact with Huizenga by phone. When Huizenga returned, he asked Berrard to take him out to see the companies. "He walked around, he looked, he met all the people. He got back in the car, we drove all the way back across Alligator Alley, he didn't say two words to me," Berrard remembers of that two-hour trip from Fort Myers back to Fort Lauderdale. "I'm thinking, 'I've really screwed up here.'" As they pulled in the parking lot where they'd left Huizenga's car, his boss looked over at him and said, "it was a damn good job."

That was it. Berrard had survived the test. Because of Berrard's foray through Florida, Huizenga Holdings bought 16 water companies out in the following eight months, going from zero to the thirteenth largest bottled water company in the nation. It was sold to Clorox in 1987 for $26 million, garnering a $16 million profit in three years. (But true to form, Wayne Huizenga would mention to his cousin, Peter, that even this deal he shouldn't have made. "He sold it for more than anybody else in the history of the world sold a water company," Peter Huizenga laughs. "He got an incredible price for it and is still crying he sold it too cheap.")

In doing one of the bottled water deals, Berrard learned another favorite Huizenga technique. In performing the due diligence—something for which Huizenga was a stickler—they'd found some points on which they'd been misled. Because of these issues, Huizenga for weeks had intended to cut the deal by $2 million from $5 million. But he hadn't yet said a word. "Wayne would wait and this guy would have this money already spent and we're just about to sign and Wayne would say, 'I just need to step out and talk to you for a minute,'" remembers Berrard. Privately, Huizenga outlined the reason for cutting the price. "Instead of saying anything too soon, he waited just until the very end. Because if he'd said it too soon, the guy could have shopped it around. This way, the check is on the table and the guy's looking at that check, but there's also another check in the bag for $2 million less."

In all of this, Berrard was encouraged to participate and share in the after-deal assessments, the self-critical analysis, Huizenga always did. He was also observing Huizenga's real key to striking deals—his approach. "His first rule of thumb was you've got to get on their side of the table and try to figure out what they really want." In one deal, the owner might stay on as a consultant for four years when he's not really needed. In another, the owner wanted to stay on as chairman and have an office. "He didn't have any role, but what was important to him was not the purchase price. He didn't want to be home everyday. He wanted to come to the office. For all the other employees there, the guys who ran the company, that was their worst nightmare. They wanted a change, they wanted someone new to come in. But Wayne said no. His sense was we could probably buy this for a half-million dollars less because what the owner really wants is a place to put his coat, sit down, and be able to say he's going to work every morning. That's not what I would have focused in on."

By watching, he also began to learn Huizenga's method of sizing up the other side. "The first thing about sitting down and negotiating with somebody is you're both there for the same thing, but you don't know how to get started," Berrard says. "So Wayne would always start somewhere else and he'd talk about what he'd read in the paper or something. In 15 minutes instead of holding on to the end of the table waiting to start haggling about something, by now they're the best of friends, they'd share, 'yeah, I was there, did you ever go here?' Now I never start a meeting off with what we are here to talk about. I always start off with something different, because after a few minutes, you also get a sense of what kind of mood that person's in, if they're nervous, then you got to key into that."

One way to break the ice was to use the sessions to learn more about the business they were interested in buying, which in part, was out of real interest and in part, a style of negotiating. "If they were talking about widgets at 8 o'clock in the morning, he'd be an expert on widgets by 8:15 because he'd ask you penetrating questions," Berrard says. "So at 8 o'clock, you're talking to a guy about widgets, at 9:30, he'd be talking about sanitary toilets, by 11 o'clock, he'd be talking about bottled water, and these were guys who were driving their own trucks. These were guys who took the day off from their route to come explain how they built their business and because he was an entrepreneur himself, because he had driven the truck and fixed the truck, he could just zero in. He used to say to me, 'here you are with your three-piece suit, you don't know a damn thing about the business. So now you're going to go tell this guy what his business is worth?' Well fat chance that is going to be received with any kind of patience or tolerance, so you got to learn about the business, you got to talk to them about it and it's a great way of disarming people."

GROWING BUSINESS AND ADDING VALUE

From portable toilets and bottled water, Huizenga with Berrard's help kept expanding the horizon. He already had a sizable investment in Florida real estate, involved as a partner in about $110 million worth of shopping centers and office buildings in Fort Myers and Fort Lauderdale with developer Terry Stiles. (Despite the fickleness of Florida's real estate market, Huizenga has been a steady partner, Stiles says, even when the market tanked in 1990–1991. "He might have complained about a crummy deal but he lived up to and beyond the obligation. I have said to him 'I have 200 employees here that directly owe you their jobs.' A lot of guys would say terminate them, not him.")

As he had proposed at Waste Management, Huizenga got into the lawn care and pest control business, buying a majority stake through a series of stock purchases in 1986 in TruGreen, the second-largest player, and snapping up a smattering of pest control companies throughout the state. He also bought a local dry cleaning and laundry chain. Key in many of these acquisitions was keeping management on and motivated, the same as during his Waste Management days.

But as Berrard would learn, making the deals was only the start. Growing the business and adding value was the main object. Soon after buying Port-O-Let, Huizenga and Berrard held a meeting with the company managers from around the country. Huizenga kept asking them what they needed to make the business better, to improve the image, to grow the customer base. Nearly every manager asked for new trucks and new toilets. Berrard was keeping track of the requests and blanched when he realized that, for a company for which they'd paid $3.6 million, they were already looking at $2.5 million in capital requests. He thought to himself that it would never happen. At the end of the meeting, Huizenga said, "okay, let's get those toilets."

Shocked, Berrard asked him why they were doing this. Berrard laughs now, "I thought I was going to have a coronary."

Huizenga's response sums up his attitude toward running a service business. "First of all if you're going to build a service business, that truck is riding up and down the street and it's got your name on it and that toilet sitting in a yard somewhere's got your name on it," he told Berrard. "If it looks like hell and it's beat up and it's dirty, that's what people think of your company. And take that a step further. If your employees drive around in those junky, dirty trucks that aren't repaired and aren't clean and if they have to service those dirty, broken down toilets, they don't feel compelled to do a very good job. What we've accomplished is zero. I know the numbers are the numbers, but I'm going to tell you right now this company is going to be worth three times the money a year from now because of its inventory."

"You know, we didn't have to commit to all that," Berrard told him. "We could have done it in stages."

But Huizenga knew that getting a kick start as a new owner was important and making the commitment sent a strong message to the managers. "First of all, I told them I was going to do it, so we're going to do it. You're right, but just trust me."

Before they'd bought Port-O-Let, Berrard had done some due diligence by riding the routes, just like he'd worked a garbage truck in his first days. After Huizenga bought the toilet business, there'd be Sunday mornings when Berrard would be awakened by a phone call from Huizenga telling him he'd been by a yard and trucks or toilets needed cleaning. Learning about the industry and its players was a basic but cardinal rule, and that meant joining trade associations and attending conventions. "I've been to more pumper and dumper shows and lawn care conventions than any man I know," Berrard laughs.

In addition to the lessons on deal making, growing a business, and the demanding pace set by Huizenga, Berrard was also learning about his boss' loyalty. In 1983, while Huizenga was in Australia, Berrard's second daughter was born nine weeks premature. Huizenga called and told him to get whatever medical care was necessary, that he'd pay the bills. As it turned out, insurance covered most of the cost, but Huizenga kept his word, and Berrard received a big bonus that hadn't even been discussed. The Rolex watch on his wrist is another reminder. At one point, Berrard had been working hard to close a deal with a pest control company up in Melbourne, Florida. Flying back to Fort Lauderdale on the day before Christmas Eve after just signing the deal, they passed over Lantana, Florida. At the time, the *National Enquirer* and Generoso Pope family used to host an elaborate Christmas display with the world's largest Christmas tree. Toying with the idea of landing to go see it, Huizenga asked Berrard the time. "I don't have my watch, it's broken," Berrard told him. "Can't you afford a new one?" needled Huizenga, laughing. "Yeah, I just haven't had the time to go get one." The next afternoon on Berrard's desk was a box with a Rolex watch "worth half my net worth then" replacing the Timex he'd owned. With it was a note, "Thanks for a good job, but more importantly here's so you can keep track of time."

With his stable of service companies growing, Huizenga needed more help to manage them. Sometimes he saw potential and hired it, figuring he'd find a way to channel it. That was the case with Don Smiley, a tall, dark-haired salesman who knocked on his door one day.

Few people bear so apt a surname as Don Smiley. Even in repose, the corners of his mouth turn up in a smile. It is sometimes sardonic, sometimes supercilious, sometimes a salesman's professional smile, and sometimes out of genuine amusement but "Smiley" as Huizenga dubbed him, was always smiling. He grew up in Wisconsin and after graduating with a degree in broadcasting from the University of Wisconsin at Oshkosh, began working for a paper company in sales. He transferred to south Florida and then landed a job as marketing director for the Honda Golf Classic. While making the rounds of foundation members, the wealthy bastion of south Florida, to try and sell them a sponsorship, he got to the "H"s and very carefully practiced the proper pronunciation of Huizenga before knocking on his door. "That helped because there's not many people who pronounce his name right," laughs Smiley. They compared their Midwest backgrounds and Huizenga quizzed him on his plans to market the golf tournament. Smiley told him he was new on the job and hadn't figured it all out yet, but outlined a plan to sell sponsorship packages. Huizenga was so impressed with his presentation and his detailed follow-up that after the tournament, he asked if Smiley wanted to work for him, selling bottled water or marketing other products. Taken aback, Smiley politely declined the offer, saying he wanted to stick with the tournament.

A few months later, Smiley landed a job with a company doing professional golf tournament management and figured he was set, doing a job in a sport he enjoyed. But he kept in contact with Huizenga, and remembers being impressed that every time he spoke with him, "it was always, 'we, we, we.' It was never an 'I.' It's not 'I bought this, I bought that,' it was 'we've done this and we've done that.' He had such a way of describing and envisioning the concept of acquiring businesses that had relative qualities and synergies which we would build and possibly sell. He was so sincere and confident in what he was talking about, it just grabbed you." Finally, during one of their conversations, Smiley told Huizenga he wanted to come work for him in marketing and sales. Also joining the team Huizenga was assembling were two recruits from Coopers & Lybrand, Joe Burke and Rick Rochon, who were buddies of Steve Berrard. After Berrard left the accounting firm, he'd call Rochon at least once a quarter for nearly five years about joining Huizenga Holdings. Set on a partnership track, Rochon kept turning the invitation down but the possibilities sounded intriguing enough that after one of the calls, he finally hired on. He'd later oversee Huizenga Holdings, including the business end of Huizenga's sports teams.

SMALL DEALS—BIG CHANGES

For the small business owners and entrepreneurs who sold their companies to Wayne Huizenga, it certainly wasn't business as usual after the papers were signed. T. Edward Benton had co-founded Colony Cleaners with three partners in 1958. By the early 1980s, it was serving three counties and was one of the largest dry-cleaning companies in Florida with a network of routes, 30 outlets, and a uniform and linen rental division. He'd gotten to know Steve Berrard as Coopers & Lybrand was the company's outside accounting firm. When one of the partners wanted to sell out, Berrard made the introduction to Huizenga. Over four months in 1985, the sale was negotiated in a process that Benton describes as "a pleasure" as neither Huizenga nor Berrard ever went back on their word and tried to change the deal. (Why would they—Huizenga put up $1 million in cash, $2 million in notes, and the company had $1.5 million in cash the day he took it over.) Benton and another partner retained a small equity stake with Huizenga. "His attitude about growing the business was really exiting to us," Benton says.

Quality and service were paramount. During the affiliation with Huizenga, the company grew its market share in all its lines of business and expanded by buying another company in Palm Beach County. While the bottom line was the scorecard, Benton says Huizenga also looked longer term. He supported the company's profit-sharing plan and improvements to facilities for the benefit of employees and having the infrastructure, both human and physical plant, to handle the growth. "When you grow that fast and acquire so much, some people think you can't do that and still have a heart," Benton says. "I've seen too many times where it was 'do the right thing.'" In 1987, the dry cleaning and uniform rental businesses were sold, with Benton and his partner benefitting handsomely from their association with Huizenga.

While acting essentially as a venture capitalist for entrepreneurs, Huizenga was no passive investor as Kevin Gowen can attest. At age 29,

Gowen left a job as an industrial chemical sales manager in June 1982 to start his own company to wash automotive parts. From a small warehouse in Tampa, he began leasing machines called a "man's kitchen sink" with a pump that circulated mineral spirits to clean greasy parts and he'd service the machines every four weeks. The big gun in the business was Safety Kleen, but Gowen adopted a different philosophy, targeting larger customers like car dealerships rather than individual gas stations. In 1983, he landed a key account at Walt Disney World servicing attractions like the Pirates of the Caribbean and the EPCOT pavilions, and that contract lent credibility.

With the company growing quickly, investors pumped in $400,000 in August 1983 but Gowen bought them out a year later because they were too controlling, wanting to approve all expenses. By 1986, he had a $1 million line of bank credit but needed additional equity financing and sold 25 percent to an investment company and closed the deal in two weeks on May 1, 1986.

Meanwhile, while leafing through some information on Safety Kleen as part of his continual review of service companies with possibly compatible businesses, Buntrock had learned that its biggest competitor was a company in Florida and he called Huizenga. On May 14, 1986, Gowen got a call from Steve Berrard, wanting to know if he could make the time to meet with someone who was interested in investing in the company. Gowen explained he'd already closed a deal and warned it was a capital intensive business. Berrard persuaded him to give Huizenga an hour.

That hour with Huizenga turned into four hours as Gowen, who'd grown up in Hollywood, Florida, talked about south Florida and business experiences, and how he, similar to Huizenga, had sold units in the morning, serviced them in the afternoon, and built them at night. Huizenga asked if he could approach the new investors and buy them out, paying them $1.1 million for their $1 million stake a month later. At this point, Sparkle Parts was doing $3 million in revenues and had six branches, four in Florida, and one in Atlanta and Washington. By November 1986, Huizenga asked Gowen about buying control, but wanted him to retain a small equity stake and stay on to manage the company. The deal closed in April 1987 with Gowen holding a three-year contract and a 9 percent interest.

By the time Gowen left in 1990, the company had grown to 11 states and $7 million in revenues. Although Huizenga's attention was focused on Blockbuster during this time, Gowen learned valuable lessons. The first was about budgets. Unlike his previous investors who wanted to approve every expense, Huizenga's concern was making sure Gowen was budgeting adequately to meet growth projections. Huizenga believes in investing money to make money, but that has to be supported by detailed budgets. "He wanted to make sure the numbers were real," Gowen says. "If you were to need $1 million, will that accomplish getting the goal of $10 million in sales and if it's $1.5 million, then count that $1.5 million toward the bottom line. He'd say, 'don't just give me the number, what drives that number? What does that number truly mean? Are these numbers credible?' Credibility was very, very important. Wayne never had a problem investing money in a company as long as there was, at the end, a return on that investment." That attitude stayed with Gowen, who has adopted the same stance with the owners of small companies in which he's invested. Too often, he says, entrepreneurs underestimate their need for capital to adequately grow their businesses and once they have to go back to their venture capitalists for more money, they've damaged their credibility.

During those years, Gowen also picked up other valuable business pointers. One was about synergy. Since Sparkle Parts already had trucks servicing customer sites, it could take on other business like picking up lacquer thinner and radiator coolent from dealerships, earning as much as $100 a drum. Another was to expand into a new service area by buying an existing company rather than starting from scratch. He checked out seven smaller competitors along the east coast and bought four. Doing that, he learned to pay as little cash as possible and when issuing a note, to ensure there was a right to reduce it for misrepresentation. "It was constant synergy," Gowen says. "From the time (he) came in 1986 until 1990, our office space didn't grow. We just added stuff for our employees to do. He always taught me to maximize." When Gowen's contract expired in March 1990, he sold his remaining stake to Huizenga for exactly what had been promised. But competition got tougher as Sparkle got bigger and the company was sold to competitor Safety Kleen in March 1995 in a break-even deal.

S&L TROUBLES

Over the years, Huizenga had gotten to know J. Edward Houston, a politically prominent attorney in south Florida and former bankruptcy court judge. Houston joined Barnett Banks in 1978 and three years later became president of its largest subsidiary, Barnett Bank of South Florida and led it through a series of acquisitions that built it into a $2.5 billion asset segment of the bank. Huizenga began investing in a few real estate deals with Houston. Huizenga had also served as a board member of the subsidiary for a short while and it was through Houston during the mid-1970s that he met Alberto Finol, a wealthy Venezuelan industrialist who would become an investor and franchisee in Blockbuster.

When Houston approached Huizenga about backing him in a deal to buy a small Miami-based savings and loan, it sounded like a good deal.

New laws had given thrifts broader lending powers, including the making of commercial loans. South Florida Savings and Loan Association was a $51 million institution started in 1980 and was profitable. The other investors Houston approached were also experienced businessmen including Leonard Farber, who had made his money on the rapid rise of strip malls along south Florida roadways, and John Anderson, a former banker who'd parlayed an expertise in hotel financing into developing hotels. Houston resigned from Barnett Banks in August 1983. Three months later, Huizenga, Farber, Anderson, and a fourth investor from Jacksonville, Martin Stein, each put up $1 million, to buy South Florida Savings with Houston as chief executive.

The idea was to develop a boutique institution, catering to wealthy residents of south Florida with an emphasis on private banking. The S&L opened tony offices in prime locations on Brickell Avenue and Las Olas Boulevard. But for Houston, boutique didn't mean small. He outlined plans in press reports to build a financial juggernaut via acquisitions of other S&Ls, a 40-office finance company and a statewide title insurance firm.

But soon there were clashes over the direction and speed of South Florida's growth with regulators with the Office of Thrift Supervision. Houston rubbed regulators the wrong way. His grand plans and emphasis on fast growth raised suspicions. Regulators complained that salaries paid to bank officers were above the norm and a business plan demanded was never submitted. The thrift financed its growth through brokered funds, paying high interest rates for deposits and making extensive real estate and construction loans, eliciting more concerns by regulators over the level of commercial loans.

Meanwhile, Houston also tangled with some of the thrift's board members over the direction and fast growth of the institution. "Ed Houston wanted to be a Barnett Banks quickly and there was conflict between me and Ed Houston," says John Anderson, whose background in banking and real estate led him to challenge Houston on decisions and question the bank executive more closely than the other directors."I'd take Houston on in some of the board meetings." During the debates, Wayne Huizenga began increasingly to side with Anderson. The experience, unpleasant though it would be, fostered a lasting business relationship between Anderson and Huizenga. "It forged a mutual respect for the way we would approach problems," Anderson says. "Both of us were very involved in the details of what went on."

With Florida's real estate market deteriorating and pressure from regulators mounting, it became clear to Anderson, Huizenga, and other board members that drastic action was needed. Surprised at the level of animosity between Houston and the regulators, it also became clear to the board members that only with Houston's resignation did they stand a chance. Houston resigned in May 1986. Meanwhile Anderson and Huizenga devised a plan to divide the thrift's assets by setting up a company to acquire the non-performing real estate loans at book value. To Huizenga, who proposed to bankroll much of the deal, Anderson and the other board members, this seemed like a good solution. South Florida Savings would get a cash infusion and shed the bad loans. Without pressure from regulators and with time on their side, the thrift directors, who would also be the directors and owners of the new company, could wait out the downturn in Florida's real estate market, absorb the risk, and ride any upside. They'd figured it'd take five years to at least break even. But regulators were chary about the proposal and insisted on extensive appraisals. Board members contended there wasn't time to have the appraisals performed and because they were making the bank whole on the loans, they didn't understand the need.

With no formal response to the plan and facing a stalemate, the directors began untangling the real estate problems piecemeal. Anderson, Huizenga, and the other directors spent hours trying to salvage the real estate deals. Huizenga himself took over the lease—after getting three appraisals and approval by regulators—on the South Florida Savings branch office at 901 Las Olas, the graceful Spanish-style two-story red-tile roof building with a courtyard fountain, which would become the home of his holding company and later the launchpad for Blockbuster Entertainment Corp.

But it was all too little, too late. Regulators moved in on March 25, 1987 and took control of the $175 million institution. It was the thirteenth S&L seized that year by regulators. News accounts in the paper cast the directors as villains, with statements from anonymous regulators about "greed" and jumbo CDs fueling real estate speculation. The bank was folded into another institution, which was then bought by Southeast Bank, the largest bank in Florida at the time, but within three years would be taken over by regulators also.

On two separate sweeps, investigators looked for wrongdoing by the directors. The first probe lasted 18 months and the second began in 1990, just after Huizenga's profile was raised because of his buying an interest in the Miami Dolphins football team and stadium. (John Anderson believes that the second investigation was no coincidence coming on the heels of that publicity.) But there were no director loans, no self-dealing, none of the flagrant abuses that had plagued the scandal-ridden savings and loan industry. "If the government felt it had a case against these individuals, they would have filed," says Miami attorney Michael Katz, who represented the directors. "Everything (investigators) raised we answered with documentation to show these directors did nothing wrong and were not responsible for the losses and the government did not file suit." But it was a costly experience, with Huizenga and other directors each losing their $1 million investment plus attorney fees, untold hours and taking a drubbing in the local press.

"Old Pals" and More Deals

Although Huizenga was out of Waste Management, he certainly wasn't out of deal making. Out of his continued contacts began to evolve what would later become dubbed the "old pals" club in the press, a nexus of current and former Waste Management executives and directors with interlocking investment ties. They are friends but even that has a competitive dynamic, more like a friendly rivalry at times, from the planes they own to what they do for fun. "Wayne is a sensational water sports guy," says Peer Pederson. "I was a lifeguard and I swam competitively in high school and I can swim better than he can, but he can do water-skis and he can ride on a garbage can top or he can ride on a rocking chair and I've seen him do it. He can't scuba dive the way I can but he can do those other things that I can't even begin to do."

One of the first "old pals" deals was by Peer Pederson, brought to Huizenga and Buntrock while they were still in Waste Management. It was for an oil tanker investment in 1979 that still pains Pederson, who keeps a photo of the barge on a wall near his desk. Rising interest rates, oil prices, and increasing difficulty in refining oil in the United States sunk what should have been a great deal into a loss of $11 million, good for not much more than tax write-offs. Pederson says neither Huizenga nor Buntrock have ever said a word about the loss.

Hotels in Florida also held allure for the group. The first was for the Marriott Harbor Beach, a 645-room oceanfront luxury resort in Fort Lauderdale being developed by Rahn Properties, the hotel development company in which John Anderson, whom Huizenga had gotten to know through South Florida Savings, was a principle. Huizenga, Buntrock, Pederson, and Melk invested with Rahn. In December 1985, the same group bought the landmark Pier 66 hotel in Fort Lauderdale from Phillips Petroleum which had developed the 256-room Fort Lauderdale resort on the main causeway to the beach. It looked like such a good deal that Huizenga wanted to do that investment himself, but didn't since he had partners involved in the Marriott Harbor Beach. At the time, Pier 66 was only one of a few unionized hotels in Broward County. As part of the sale, the new owners fired the hotel employees and rehired only a portion of them, prompting the union to file an unfair labor practices charge against both Phillips and the group. The employees were fired because they had employment and settlement agreements with

Phillips, Anderson says, noting that the union lost its case in an appeals court decision. "We did everything by the letter of the law."

Though a bad deal for the union employees who lost their jobs, it turned out to be a bonanza for the new partners. They bought the hotel for $46 million and spent $13 million adding 125 rooms, a restaurant, and a cafe. In August 1987, they sold a 91 percent stake to a real estate syndication group for $79 million, a substantial gain for the group in less than two years. The real estate syndicators in turn sold it to public investors, who bought limited partnerships in the hotel totaling $111 million. But as the real estate market hit the skids, the investors ended up being the losers. In a pre-packaged bankruptcy proceeding (in which terms are worked out before a bankruptcy filing) to avoid foreclosure, the hotel in 1993 was resold to the same investment group of Huizenga, Melk, Buntrock, Pederson, but also adding Don Flynn, Steve Berrard, and Rick Rochon, for $32.5 million—less than half what they had sold it for—and they immediately invested $4 million to refurbish it.

In real estate deals, "he's an excellent partner to have because he does leave you alone," Anderson says. "Wayne is first and foremost a negotiator so he negotiates his position up front and after that we provide the necessary financial details." Anderson got a first-hand experience with Huizenga's formidable memory for business details. In one discussion about a deal, Huizenga brought up a point about how a particular partnership should have been distributed and recalled it had been negotiated over the phone on a Christmas Eve five years earlier. Anderson told him he was wrong, but later checked the papers. "He was right. And it was my business and I should have known."

While Huizenga was a conduit for real estate deals for the other "pals" including Buntrock, Waste Management proved a ready buyer for some of the businesses Huizenga had assembled and grown. Port-O-Let was operating well, but Huizenga knew it would be much more efficiently run with less cost as part of Waste Management. Duplication in storage, delivery, and collection could be eliminated if combined with Waste Management's decentralized operations. But he had to convince Buntrock of that. While Buntrock was visiting for the Miami Grand Prix in 1985, they hovered over the race by helicopter. Buntrock was staying in Boca Raton, about 70 miles north, and on the way home, Huizenga kept needling him about the opportunity he'd lost. "Remember that business you never wanted to go into?" he asked Buntrock. "Well look down there. Everywhere you see a blue portable toilet that's ours."

As they flew north, Huizenga would point out sites and tell Buntrock, "count them over there Dean, on that job. There would be 20 or 30 of them on that job. Then we'd go a little further and I'd say count those down there." Construction was brisk in Broward and south Palm Beach and there were lots of blue toilets. "You missed the boat," he told Buntrock. "Wherever there's construction, you have to put these big dumpsters out for construction. There's no reason why when a salesman goes out to try to get the job for the construction debris, he signs them up at the same time for the portable toilet."

Buntrock told Huizenga to send him the numbers on Port-O-Let, that he'd take a look. He agreed with Huizenga that Waste Management should buy it. As for how it was to negotiate against his former partner, Buntrock says, "it's terrible." He and Huizenga took themselves out of the negotiations, letting Steve Berrard and other Waste Management executives handle it. A deal by a former insider could well prompt scrutiny, a point Pederson as a director of Waste Management raised. "We had to be very careful that it was an arm's length transaction and we got independent, outside appraisals because I didn't want anybody ever to sue us or complain that we did a sweetheart deal with Wayne which we certainly didn't do," he says.

The sale price wasn't disclosed and while some press reports would note the connection with Huizenga, there weren't any special considerations, he says. "Believe me it was arm's length. It wasn't an easy transaction," Huizenga adds. "There were a whole lot of people there at Waste Management that wanted to see how that thing was going to be handled and everybody put their two cents in there to make sure Wayne didn't get any extra, that's for sure." Berrard, who says it was one of the toughest deals he'd ever done, concurs.

With lawn care, Huizenga had bought into TruGreen in 1986 with the express idea of making a quick sale to Waste Management, but Buntrock still had no interest in the lawn care business. That changed by 1987 and after losing out on a bid to buy the largest lawn care company, Buntrock turned to Huizenga and Waste Management in August 1987 bought Tru-Green to enter the market. "That was probably the luckiest thing I ever did for me and not good for Waste," Huizenga says with slight smile. Two years after he sold, much of the nation suffered first through a drought, then through a flood, which cost the company both customers and money. "After two years, Dean said the heck with this, we're out of this business. They lost money both years on that and it was just a fluke."

But a bid by Waste Management for the largest lawn care company, ChemLawn Corp. and some well-timed stock buys in early 1987 by some of the "old pals" caught the eye of investigators for both the Securities and Exchange Commission and the Federal Bureau of Investigation into possible insider trading. No charges were filed as a result of either investigation.

A shareholder lawsuit against Waste Management in 1987 prompted a six-month inquiry by a committee of three outside Waste Management directors who retained a former deputy director of the SEC to assist in its examination. The committee looked at 19 purchases of ChemLawn stock by Buntrock, his family, Peter Huizenga, and two other Waste Management executives which netted them close to $1 million total in personal profits. The committee concluded that there was no violation of law nor any breach of fiduciary responsibility. Although the executives purchased the shares over two years while Waste Management was intermittently considering—and rejecting—ChemLawn as an acquisition candidate, the committee reported in February 1988, that it had found no purchases were made when the acquisition was in progress or by anyone who knew at the time of purchase that Waste Management was actively considering a bid.

But the transactions left a taint in the press. Articles, including a scathing editorial in *Crain's Chicago Business* before the committee's report raised the prospect of a conflict of interest by Waste Management insiders in the murky area of securities law and insider trading. A letter to the editor by Waste Management senior vice-president of public affairs Harold Gershowitz noted that the executives had bought ChemLawn stock while Waste Management had been rejecting a diversification into lawn care. "The excessive zeal with which you mischaracterized their motivations is unfair, reckless, and damaging to individuals who have not—and would not—do what your editorial falsely alleges." But Crain's was unrepentant and in another editorial February 8, 1988, called the committee's report a "whitewash of charges of insider trading from an accommodating committee of Waste Management outside directors. . . . At a time of intense scrutiny of corporate America—when discretion and judiciousness among America's elite managers are so desperately needed—Waste Management insiders decided to grab for the extra buck. And business is the poorer for it."

While not a Waste Management insider, Wayne Huizenga told SEC investigators that making an extra buck—though not because he had inside knowledge of Waste Management's bid—was what prompted him and his family to buy ChemLawn shares in February 1987 just days before Waste Management made its tender offer. At a voluntary deposition before two SEC attorneys in Chicago on March 24, 1989, Huizenga testified as to the chronology behind his sizable purchases—the exact amount was not disclosed—of ChemLawn shares. His deposition to the SEC and a summary of the committee's report as recounted in *The Wall Street Journal* in February 1988, illustrate how Huizenga, as well as family and friends, can profit handsomely from his knowledge of the deal flow.

Wealthy men like Wayne Huizenga and the "pals" don't have to look for deals—deals look for them. By January 1987, Huizenga was working on a concept to take his collection of service companies, the pest control, lawn care, bottled water, and parts washing operations public. The idea was to use the stock to buy more companies in these areas—a repeat performance of Waste Management. By this time, Don Flynn was in the process of planning to retire from Waste Management and with Buntrock's okay had already started working with Huizenga on what they had dubbed Newco or Mega Company, later known as Service USA. Huizenga knew Flynn's credibility on Wall Street would help the venture. Flynn had put up $1 million in good faith money for the new company, though he and Huizenga were still working on how to structure the deal with the minority partners in the lawn care and other companies.

On January 22, Huizenga, Flynn, and Berrard met at Merrill Lynch's office in New York to talk about the prospects for Mega Company. Over lunch, Chuck Lewis, who'd flown in from Chicago, and other investment bankers had brought up to Huizenga, Flynn, and Berrard the idea of acquiring ChemLawn. The collection of service businesses Huizenga had brought to them were too small to be very interesting, a total of $50 million in revenues or so. In the hot and heavy takeover days of the late 1980s, Chem-Lawn looked like a prime target. Rather than taking the service companies public, Merrill Lynch recommended offering a takeover bid for the largest player in the lawn care business into which Huizenga could then merge his service companies. That didn't appeal to Huizenga because there didn't seem to be enough of a stake for him in the deal. In Mega Co., he and Flynn would end up with about 70 percent of the company. As a leveraged buyout, ChemLawn would require more financing from Merrill Lynch and, to his way of thinking, he'd be doing all the work and end up with just 20 or 30 percent. Huizenga turned down the idea.

Not deterred on his idea for Mega Co., Huizenga flew to Chicago for another meeting with Merrill Lynch executives on Tuesday, February 3. The night before, he had dined with Buntrock, who didn't like the concept of the company Huizenga was trying to put together and thought it was too small. Huizenga mentioned to Buntrock that Merrill Lynch had talked to him about ChemLawn. Buntrock repeated that he'd never liked the lawn care business. It was too cyclical, too fickle, the same arguments he'd made to Huizenga when shooting down a lawn care deal for Waste Management a few years earlier. Buntrock dropped him off at a restaurant where Flynn was having dinner as Huizenga was staying at Flynn's house.

At the meeting the next morning at Merrill Lynch's offices on the 55th floor of the Sears Tower, he and Don Flynn were set to talk about Mega Co. when investment bankers again made a pitch about the prospects for Chem-Lawn. "Merrill Lynch made the push that this was really something and in their opinion was really undervalued and that somebody was going to do something with this thing and they wanted to be the ones to do something with it. It was insinuated that if we didn't do something, they'd find some-body to do something." After hearing out the 20-minute presentation, Huizenga made it clear that he still wasn't interested—it was too big a deal. Discussion turned again to Mega Co. As Huizenga was leaving, Chuck Lewis asked if it was all right to bring up the ChemLawn idea to Buntrock. "You can ask Waste if you want, but I'll tell you right now, I had dinner with Dean last night. There's no interest at all," Huizenga told him.

Over lunch that day with John Melk and James Kirk, his friend and chairman of Ohio-based OHM Corp., Huizenga talked about plans for his service company, and mentioned what Merrill Lynch had said about Chem-Lawn and that he thought it might be a good stock play. He didn't know if Melk or Kirk acted on the tip. Later that afternoon, Huizenga reluctantly visited the Blockbuster video store that Melk owned and had been pester-ing him to see, a visit that would begin the deal of his life.

Discussion of ChemLawn as an acquisition target by Waste Management had been picking up steam since January. The lawn care company had been identified back in 1985 as a potential target and sporadically discussed through 1986, but ruled out at an October board meeting. Through 1986, Buntrock, his second wife, Rosemarie, and Peter Huizenga bought shares for themselves and two family trusts. Buntrock bought his last 2,000 shares in November 1986 bringing his family's stake to 35,000. Peter Huizenga bought 2,000 shares in December, bringing his total purchases since July 1986 to 6,000 shares. (He invested because ChemLawn was a service com-pany and looked undervalued, he says, and that during that time, Waste Management had decided not to acquire the company.)

In January and through early February 1987, Merrill Lynch suggested to Waste Management that ChemLawn was an acquisition target. "Buntrock is annoyed that Merrill Lynch is pressuring him to make an acquisition. He thinks Merrill Lynch is going to put ChemLawn 'into play' regardless of what he does," *The Wall Street Journal* cites in its summary of the commit-tee report.

Busy with the Blockbuster deal, Huizenga didn't act immediately on the information he'd received from Merrill Lynch about ChemLawn. He bought his first shares of ChemLawn on February 12. "You just get more and more comfortable, that you know, Merrill Lynch is going to make something happen there. And, even if Merrill doesn't, someone will," he told the SEC attorneys. "Based on the conversation and the comments that Merrill made, it was apparent to me that company was going to be put into play or something was going to happen." Coincidentally, on February 12, Don Flynn met with Phil Rooney and Dean Buntrock and now strongly en-dorsed a Waste Management takeover of ChemLawn, according to *The Wall Street Journal*.

By Tuesday, February 17, rumors about a takeover of ChemLawn were building, with speculation that a company from Europe was going to make a bid. Berrard kept getting calls from executives at TruGreen, the lawn care company in which Huizenga held a majority stake, about industry speculation on a takeover. "The rumors kept coming and coming," Huizenga said in his deposition. "After the Merrill Lynch meeting, I thought this was coming a lot faster than I would have thought it was coming. But, I said, let's go buy some. And there wasn't much downside risk, being in the lawn care business. We kind of knew what we thought the value of the company was. When we bought TruGreen, we thought we stole it and we thought that ChemLawn was undervalued and that it was a good situation to pick up some dollars." Huizenga bought additional shares that day through two different brokers. The next day, Marti bought shares as did Huizenga's mother, Jean, at his suggestion. "She sits home all day and watches television and I told her, why don't you buy some of this stock. Just to give her something to do. She watches the ticker (stock quotations) all day long." On February 23, Huizenga bought more shares as did his mother. His sister, Bonnie, also bought shares. "The rumors kept coming hot and heavy from the TruGreen guys that something was going to happen. And we just felt that something was going to happen fairly quickly there and we decided to take a bigger position."

On the evening of February 25, Huizenga got a call from Buntrock. Waste Management the next day was going to announce a tender offer for ChemLawn. Buntrock had called to let him know so he wouldn't hear about it somewhere else first, saying it looked like they'd now be competitors. "I was stunned," Huizenga told investigators. "I was trying to think what that meant now with Waste Management and us competing, because I know Waste Management is an acquisition-oriented company and I was trying to just put all that together in my mind as to what it meant." He says he didn't discuss with Buntrock then or later why his change of mind regarding the lawn care industry. "I had no idea that they were even looking at the company. Flynn never said anything to me."

On February 26, Waste Management announced a cash offer of $27 a share for ChemLawn, a substantial premium over the previous day's closing price of $17.75. The next day, it sued ChemLawn seeking an injunction against enforcement of anti-takeover laws that had been adopted by the state of Ohio. The battle got ugly, with ChemLawn preparing documents to fight Waste Management. The purchases of ChemLawn shares by Waste Management officials had been properly disclosed in proxy statements but the news was picked up by the press. Waste Management increased its offer to $33 a share, then to $35 a share. ChemLawn was acquired by EcoLab Inc. of St. Paul, Minnesota, for $36.50. ChemLawn suffered through the same weather-related hits that Waste Management had with TruGreen after buying it from Huizenga. Both companies ended up being sold, Eco-Lab sold ChemLawn to Service Masters, and Waste Management sold Tru-Green to the same company.

"We dodged the bullet and we got beat," says Flynn, assessing the deal eight years later. "We took our run and we got into a bidding war and they bid it up to a point where we walked." The allegations of insider trading "was all silly. Dean owned some ChemLawn stock. If we'd thought of it, we'd have had him sell it before we made the offer. When most of them bought that stock they had no idea that it was anything that we would ever buy." Flynn was neither a buyer nor a seller of ChemLawn shares and says he "didn't have a clue" that Wayne Huizenga had bought shares.

"There were allegations that we had inside information, but we didn't have any inside information," Wayne Huizenga says. He would testify before a U.S. attorney in Chicago who looked into the allegations, but the case was never pursued. "We went through lengthy investigations and they just dropped it. I had no idea that Waste was even interested in that business and I still don't know today what made them decide to go after ChemLawn." At $36.50 a share, Huizenga, his mother, and sister, as well as others who may have bought the shares on his recommendation, doubled their money in a few weeks.

Lucrative though it was, ChemLawn was only a stock play for Huizenga, and would pale in comparison to the number and magnitude of the deals that lay ahead. A few years later, he would note that dozens of deals passed by the "old pals" members every week. "We could do two deals a day if we wanted." He, Flynn, Melk, Buntrock, and Pederson, joined occasionally by others, acted as a de facto screening committee for the group, turning each other on to what they thought were good deals. "We've been together over 20 years. We've been together so long it's a different level of confidence. If you say you've got a deal for me, I'll say send me a bunch of stuff. If Don Flynn or Peer Pederson or Dean Buntrock says they've got a great deal, I'm pretty confident it's a good deal."

As the deal-machine kicked into high gear, Huizenga would find less and less time for fishing trips. As exciting as it was, trolling for a grander off the coast of Australia would have to wait. His son Ray explains the attraction of fishing for marlin compared with other game fish. "The black marlin can be running and streaking across the surface and rushing towards the boat—a little more violent, serious and dangerous at times, which adds to the fun." But it was while trolling for business and not for pleasure that Wayne Huizenga, though it wouldn't appear so at first, was about to snag a grander.

5

Video Venture: Taking Charge of Blockbuster

Riding the elevator to the penthouse suite of the Marriott Harbor Beach Resort in Fort Lauderdale, Wayne Huizenga wondered what it was that his friend Melk wanted to talk about. Melk liked staying at the oceanfront hotel, particularly since he had an ownership stake along with Huizenga and other partners and one of the bennies was that he didn't have to pay for the suite, an attitude that Huizenga found amusing. It was a glorious, sunny December day in Fort Lauderdale, but Huizenga knew that Melk wasn't visiting just to escape the brutal winter winds of Chicago. This had to be about a deal, of that Huizenga was sure. The two men had done hundreds of deals together in building Waste Management and, like any good partnership, they knew each others' strengths and weaknesses. In the four years since they'd left Waste Management, they'd run dozens of deals by each other. Some of the ones Huizenga would invest in, Melk would take a pass, and vice-versa.

For his part, Melk had prepared for the meeting. Numbers were what turned Huizenga on, he knew, and he was going to give him plenty of good numbers. This video store deal looked real good. He wanted his friend to join in an investment, maybe just a franchise, maybe something bigger. "I want you to look at this," he told Huizenga. "This is one fantastic deal. This is really an exciting deal." Scanning the pages quickly, Huizenga threw the folder back on the coffee table with scorn. "You know I get 20 of these a week," he told Melk. "Come on, John. A video store? I'm not interested."

To Huizenga, who rarely watched movies and didn't own a VCR, the video rental business held absolutely no appeal. It brought to mind sleazy joints in bad neighborhoods. Even if the industry was becoming more legitimate, to Huizenga, it had all the markings of a fad. It was dependent on a technology that might soon be obsolete, too ethereal for his taste. He liked real businesses, services that people used: lawn care, pest control, bottled water. Give good service and there'd be no reason for them to go elsewhere. With that philosophy, he'd been assembling his own collection of such companies he was planning to take public.

Melk checked his irritation at his friend's reaction. He changed the subject and shelved the projections in his briefcase. But he knew Wayne Huizenga well enough to keep up the campaign. He was convinced this was the right business for them and that Huizenga was the right guy to run it. He enlisted Don Flynn, who was still chief financial officer of Waste Management, to help him. Melk knew that Huizenga respected Flynn's acumen with finances and his involvement would carry some weight. The two friends kept up the pressure. "I know you're not high on it but you ought to take a look. That video store makes a lot of sense," Flynn would say when he and Huizenga talked.

Melk was so persistent, so unrelenting, that Huizenga told his wife, Marti, that he knew he'd have to visit the store sometime, because Melk just wouldn't give up. On one of his periodic calls to Huizenga, Melk learned from Marti that he was in Chicago. Huizenga had gone to see his friend, Chuck Lewis, at Merrill Lynch, on February 3 about taking the service companies public. Melk insisted that Huizenga look at the store before he left town.

Indulging his friend, Huizenga relented. As he toured the store on Lombard in suburban Chicago, Huizenga felt that twinge of excitement, that sixth sense that told him this was a really good business and could be a great deal. "I walked into the store and you know, wow! What a difference! And that's where our slogan first came from. Tom Gruber (a McDonald's executive hired in late 1987 who spearheaded Blockbuster's marketing drive) came up with the slogan, but it was based on what we said when we first went to see the store—Wow! What a difference!" Melk then called Scott Beck, who showed Huizenga around the store and went through the numbers and explained his territory. He had stores in Chicago, Atlanta, and Detroit and rights to Milwaukee, Minneapolis, and St. Paul.

BLOCKBUSTER: THE BEGINNING

Scott Beck had grown up a bit of a rarity—a rich man's son with lots of confidence but also plenty of drive. His father, Lawrence, had retired as one of the founders of Waste Management. Scott was enrolled at the University of Arizona in Tucson, but decided to take some time off. He bought a BMW motorcycle and cruised through the country for 16 months. He ended up enrolling in Southern Methodist University in Dallas because it had a study program in England and Beck had always wanted to go to school in London. While in London, he stayed at John Melk's house. Melk headed up international operations for Waste Management.

After graduating, Beck founded Pace Investment. He invested money for clients in limited partnerships and other investments. In October 1985, Beck got a call from a stockbroker friend in the Los Angeles office of Bear Stearns about a video store opening in Dallas. The broker said he was going to buy the company's stock and suggested that Beck take a look, too. An avid movie renter, he instantly recognized the store's appeal and its market potential. "It was like IBM and McDonald's had opened a video store." Wandering around the store, he bumped into Sandy Cook who was restocking shelves, and started pestering her with questions. She asked if he was a competitor. He said no, but he was an interested investor.

Sandy Cook was a video buff who had wanted to open a video rental store. But not just any video store. What coalesced into the Blockbuster concept was a combination of her disappointment with limited selection at small stores, the personal pride of her ex-husband, David Cook, and the stubbornness of a small, local video store chain owner who reneged on a deal to sell his company.

By 1985, the videocassette recorder was well on its way to becoming a standard entertainment appliance for the average American household. Prices for VCRs had been dropping since their introduction a decade earlier, making them no longer a plaything for the wealthy. By then, 28 percent of U.S. "television households" had a VCR and that number was expected to more than double in five years. The format known as video home system, or VHS, had beaten out Sony's Betamax as the machine of choice in the marketplace. And Hollywood had called a truce in its epic legal battle against the tide of technology as it realized the lucrative new revenue stream the machines produced.

No longer were VCRs merely tools of "time-shifters" who wanted to record episodes of "Hillstreet Blues" or "Family Ties" to be watched later. Ever since George Atkinson had started a video rental club in 1978 in Los Angeles by running ads in the *Los Angeles Times,* thousands of video stores had sprung up to satisfy the demand by Americans who wanted to watch prerecorded movies, but not plunk down $49.95 per tape to build a library of films. "The VCR and the prerecorded videocassette set hearts on fire in entrepreneurial breasts all over the land, Americans from every imaginable walk of life cracked open their nest eggs, remortgaged their homes, and put the arm on their parents, siblings, and in-laws in order to become the proud proprietors of Video Castles, Connections, Corners, Hutches, Huts, Palaces, Patches, Places, Shacks, Sheds, Sources,

Spots and Stations. It was as if someone had hung a classified ad in the sky: "Retail Oppty.-Lo cash/EZ Startup."[1]

Video retail specialty stores blossomed from 7,000 outlets in 1983 to an estimated 19,000 by 1986. Lured by the prospect of building traffic and a few bucks per transaction, supermarkets, convenience marts, music stores and book shops began offering videos for rent. These two factors—the ease of entry into the business and the proliferation of video rental outlets— would haunt Blockbuster from its inception and later spur Huizenga to grow the business at breakneck speed.

Into this industry milieu in 1985 stepped the Cooks. But David Cook wasn't an undercapitalized entrepreneur trying to make a killing in the latest business craze. He *had* money. Cook had taught himself to write computer programs for business applications just as the power of computers was being harnessed for more and more business uses. He started writing real estate programs in 1978, then created a new program for the oil industry. David P. Cook & Associates rode the oil boom and by 1982 had five offices, 85 employees and hundreds of oil company clients. In preparation to go public, he hired Kenneth W. Anderson who had experience as a chief financial officer with several large, publicly traded companies. The offering on February 1, 1983 netted $8 million for the renamed Cook Data Services.

Then the unthinkable happened. Just weeks after the offering, the Organization of Petroleum Exporting Countries slashed the price of oil. The impact on the oil industry—and Cook Data Services—was devastating. Overnight, clients couldn't pay their bills and wouldn't return phone calls. The company went from solidly profitable to a loser in a sick industry. As the oil industry tanked, so did the stock of Cook Data Services. Adding insult to injury, a shareholder lawsuit was filed accusing the company and directors of fraud for not warning investors that OPEC might cut prices. "We were incensed but that didn't make the lawsuit go away," Cook says. The suit was settled in 1984 for $1.5 million.

With no end in sight to the oil industry doldrums, Cook and Anderson hunted for other ways to deploy the company's cash. One deal that showed promise was a company that used bar code tag technology to identify herd animals, hence the name Amtech for "animal management technology." But Cook and Anderson saw promise in applying it to other business uses like railcars and toll roads and funded it with $500,000 over the next two years. (Later, Amtech would become an exit for Anderson and Cook.)

---

[1] James Lardner in *Fast Forward—Hollywood, the Japanese and the VCR Wars*. W. W. Norton & Co., New York, NY, 1987.

They were still scouting for opportunities when his ex-wife, Sandy Cook, suggested opening a video store.

What David Cook had needed was the right concept. And though Sandy Cook didn't have a business background, she intuitively sensed that if a small video store could do well, a bigger store would do even better because of the additional tapes that could be rented and the customers they would draw. The idea of a superstore also appealed to David Cook's ego—he didn't want to do anything small. As they developed other aspects of the concept, Cook found a site at Skillman and Northwest Highway in Dallas, in a free-standing section of a strip shopping center fronting the busy intersection. The site offered great visibility and potent demographics—lots of affluent young renters in apartments and townhouses. "I know Dallas well enough to know that the single best site in Dallas has got to be that intersection." It is still one of Blockbuster's most successful stores.

Cook approached a local video store chain about becoming a franchisee. He wanted to test the concept of a superstore and suggested the required franchise fees be waived because of his additional investment. When the owner balked, Cook offered to buy the company for $2 million. But the next day, the deal fell through when the owner demanded $4 million. This time, Cook balked. He couldn't see shelling out that much in shareholder money for a video rental chain with three company stores and some franchisees. They'd have to go through the learning curve themselves.

So Cook Data Services began a metamorphosis into a video rental chain. Sandy Cook researched titles, looking at 30,000 titles over six months before coming up with a basic inventory of 10,000 tapes organized around 30 categories. Meanwhile, David Cook locked up the site in June 1985. The next month, the company sold David P. Cook and Associates, its only operating subsidiary, to a group of investors, including members of management. Now Cook Data Systems was committed to the video business. Sandy designed the store's interior with bold blue and yellow colors, floor to ceiling windows, oak trim and bright lighting. She devised the torn-ticket logo and the name, Blockbuster. "I didn't like it at first, like the first hour," Cook remembers. "The more I said it, the better it sounded." The seeds for the company's later diversification were sown early: when the company changed its name in May 1986, Cook deliberately chose Blockbuster Entertainment Corp. rather than the more limiting Blockbuster Videos, because he could see the name could work for a host of company subsidiaries.

Some industry innovations that Blockbuster got credit for—like the "live" display meaning the movies were actually on the shelves—were simply a matter of practicality. There was simply no way to service a store with 8,000 videos in the old method of customers having to bring empty boxes to clerks to see if the movies were in stock. And unlike the industry norm, Blockbuster didn't charge a membership fee. Cook didn't want customers to not come to the store because they felt they had "invested" with another chain. Blockbuster's policy against renting X-rated films, which garnered pluses in the press and was later parlayed into its "America's Family Video Store" slogan, wasn't because of any moral high ground by David Cook, but rather because "while we don't care if people watch pornography, we just don't want to sell it to you." The timing was right as the video industry was shifting from adult renters to a large kid and family rental business. "A lot of families came to our store only—not because of the selection and not because of the long hours and not because of the convenient check-out and the three-day rentals—they came because they didn't mind their kids running around the store because they wouldn't see any garbage."

Other innovations, like the store's computer system, were key to its initial success. The system used a bar code scanner to read key data from each rental tape and from the member's card. Within seconds, the computer calculated the rental amount. (Initially, it was $3 for 3 nights per tape. Cook decided the company would eat the sales tax in order to speed checkout so clerks wouldn't have to make change.) Returned tapes were also run through the scanner and any rewind or late charges were added to the customer's account, which would be recalled and settled on the next transaction. The strong inventory control system detailed the number of times each tape was rented, generated a daily summary report by store, and held a wealth of data on the demographics of Blockbuster customers and what tapes they rented. It would be years before Blockbuster would start to mine this field to better manage its tapes and select inventory for stores. But it lent some depth to Blockbuster's "story" and was a point later burnished for the benefit of Wall Street and the media on occasion.

Everything that could go wrong with opening the first store did. Construction delays postponed the opening from August and organizing 8,000 video tapes the first time was a nightmare. Finally, by October 19, 1985, all was ready and the doors to the first Blockbuster video rental store opened. They had spent upwards of $800,000 to develop this first store, including the computer systems. That was a big chunk of change, and David Cook was nervous about the reception it would get. The first day was better than either of the Cooks could have imagined. Working behind the counter, David Cook could hear customers' comments as they wandered among the shelves lined with brightly colored movie boxes, displaying an entertainment selection never before available. Customers mobbed the membership counter and clutched three and four tapes in their hands—and they weren't leaving. A line formed outside to get in.

Among the throng of customers the second day was Scott Beck. It would be one of those chance meetings that changed destinies for both Cook and Beck. Customer number 91 in Store A would become Blockbuster's largest franchisee and play a pivotal role in the company's history and in the lives of David Cook and Wayne Huizenga.

Skeptics and Short-Sellers

After talking with David Cook, Scott and his father decided to invest. They formed a partnership and bought 9 percent of Blockbuster's stock over the next 60 days. That got the attention of Cook. But Beck saw more possibilities as a licensee and embarked on a two-month study of the industry. He visited other video rental chains, including then-major players such as Las Vegas-based Major Video, which would become a target of Wayne Huizenga's just two years later. But while Beck was pretty sure about going with Blockbuster, he made up his mind on New Year's Eve. As he'd learn later, New Year's Eve is one of the biggest video rental nights of the year. Beck stopped by the store to take a look. There in front of the store was a stretch limo and inside was David Cook, telling his girlfriend that she'd have to go to a party without him, that it was simply too busy for him to leave. Anyone with that type of commitment to the business, Beck thought, was the right person to go with.

In early 1986, Cook and Anderson were laying the groundwork for what they already were planning to be a major video rental chain, perhaps as many as 1,000 stores nationwide. They hired personnel, including executives for finance, operations and administration. They spent $3 million on a distribution center which Cook designed. The center took tapes from distributors, repackaged them in plastic cases, coded and packed them by categories. The system allowed an entire store inventory to be packed and shipped, down to the toilet paper for the restrooms. "The real story isn't the store," Cook says. "That's the end of the story. The real story was all the stuff behind the scenes that allowed us in eight hours to send a store out to Atlanta." Anticipating growth, but never dreaming of how much, Cook designed the distribution center so three stores could be loaded in 24 hours. That capacity would be key under the frenetic pace set by Huizenga later, in which a Blockbuster store would open every 17 hours.

With the computer systems and distribution center, Cook felt he had a jump on the industry. But he needed help expanding. "We could deliver a store a day easy, but we couldn't finance a store a day." To Cook, granting licenses to broad stretches of territory seemed the ticket. He didn't charge up-front licensing fees, but instead charged for services, such as site selection and royalties for the computer system. He and Anderson looked for deep-pocket investors who could bankroll the buildout. Huizenga would later criticize the license agreement as being too loose, but as Cook notes, those easy terms were needed to get investors to risk their money on a new concept. Cook approached the Sanchez family of San Antonio, which had struck a fortune in the gas business and had invested in Cook's original software company. The Sanchezes put up the money for territory including San Antonio and Cook and Anderson set up and managed the stores. Through his investment firm, Beck started selling limited partnerships and convinced two of the Waste Management "club," Peer Pederson and John Melk, to invest. On August 25, 1986, Beck opened his first franchise store at 10 A.M. in Marietta, Georgia. A store owned by Sanchez opened one hour later in San Antonio, central time.

Word of mouth and the stores themselves attracted other licensees, people like George Baker, former president of Kentucky Fried Chicken, Fred Montesi III, who had just sold his Memphis-based family-owned grocery store, the largest in the state, and was looking to invest in a new business. A San Antonio attorney, Raymond Schneider, walked into the Blockbuster store owned by the Sanchezes in September and became an instant convert. "I literally had dreams about that video store and thinking about how I could run it," he recalls. "I had a senior partnership in the second-largest law firm in San Antonio and making, in my experience then, a lot of money. I was so captivated I gave it all up." Schneider worked connections to raise money and within four months had snapped up licenses for much of Florida—another event that would lead Huizenga, who initially wanted a franchise in Florida, to invest in the parent company.

By now, the $8 million kitty held by the fledgling Blockbuster Entertainment Corp. had dwindled. Cook needed money to expand. A plan to meet with Ross Perot, the mercurial founder of Electronic Data Systems and investor, foundered. Preliminary talks with Cox Cable proved fruitless. Cook and Anderson decided it was time for another stock offering. Anderson knew Clinton Allen, a senior executive with Advest Inc. The Connecticut-based brokerage firm decided to handle the offering.

Blockbuster had a good "story" for Wall Street. The proliferation of video stores was a concern but the concept was fresh. Cook and Anderson were hoping the offering would net as much as $18 million after fees. But the stock market was queasy. Anderson watched with concern as the market weakened over the summer. And he and Cook also noted that the short position in Blockbuster's stock was growing.

So began the involvement of "short-sellers" with Blockbuster, a force that would dog Blockbuster and Huizenga for seven years and which Huizenga took delight in crushing whenever he could. Short-sellers are the yin to the yang of Wall Street. They're the pessimists, the ones betting that a company's prospects aren't as good as they seem, that the bubble of an "over-valued" stock will burst. Short-sellers essentially sell borrowed stock. If the stock price falls by the date they have to deliver, they can buy it at a lower price and pocket the difference. If the stock price rises, they have to buy the stock at a higher price and get "squeezed."

Then, in the world of Cook and Anderson, came an event nearly as catastrophic as OPEC cutting the price of oil. In the September 1, 1986 edition of *Barron's,* the well-read "Up & Down Wall Street" column questioned the Blockbuster concept and sneered that with the vast proliferation of video rental outlets, the last thing needed was yet another, even if it was a "Superstore" concept. Moreover, the article underscored the big fear: "Building a retail store and arranging to stock it with thousands of cassettes doesn't strike us as horrendously difficult. Any measure of significant success by Blockbuster doubtless would entice others to do likewise and we well could see the emergence of a chain of Box-Office Boffo Stores, slightly bigger than Blockbuster's, staying open slightly longer hours and with slightly more inventory. And Boffo would begat who knows how many others."

The negative article on top of a shaky market cratered Blockbuster's stock offering. Selling a smaller number of shares at a reduced price brought in just $4 million. "The Barron's story was the single changing point in my life," Cook says. The article set in motion a chain of events that would cause Cook and Anderson to lose control of Blockbuster and for Huizenga to take a fledgling video store chain and build it into a powerhouse that would prove the doubters wrong.

HUIZENGA BUYS IN

On a two-and-a-half hour flight back to Fort Lauderdale, Huizenga looked at the numbers, the projections, and the industry background Beck had given him. The more he looked, the better Blockbuster looked. It was a rental business and a service business, both of which Huizenga understood, and had plenty of cash flow, which he liked. But now he was in the role of a convert trying to sway the skeptics. His top lieutenant, Steve Berrard, didn't hide his dismay. "I did everything I could to defeat the premise that this was a real business," remembers Berrard. At one point, Berrard told Huizenga flat out, "We should not be doing this. This is not a good business for us. It can't be true. It's too good to be true and there are deals like this all over the place." Over breakfast at The Chemist Shop, a drugstore and coffee shop on Las Olas Boulevard, Huizenga tried out the idea on his two other assistants, Rick Rochon and Joe Burke. Neither said much, not as sure of their relationship with the boss as Berrard, but they made it clear they weren't enthused about this new venture. "Hell, if the numbers are half this good, it's worth a look," Huizenga told them.

On Thursday, February 5, he and Don Flynn, who still owned a house in Boca Raton and spent a good part of his time in Florida, flew to Dallas. Melk met them from Chicago. With Scott Beck as intermediary, David Cook and Ken Anderson showed Wayne around a few stores and visited the distribution center. Huizenga recognized the distribution center as key to the company's growth. He liked the systems and organization. Over dinner that night at the Energy Club at the top of a Dallas office tower, they discussed possibilities. Huizenga initially wanted to be a franchisee. But a good chunk of the territory in Florida was already licensed. So he decided instead to invest in the company. They hammered out the parameters for a deal.

Meanwhile, Anderson had done his own checking on Huizenga and Waste Management. "We actually had some concerns in the process of negotiating. The minute you hear "Waste Management" you think about the garbage business, and when you're in the garbage business, you think of the Mafia and we actually had some concerns about that." He was reassured by the fact that Merrill Lynch was Waste Management's investment banker, but he also checked with friends at Houston-based competitor Browning-Ferris. The word back was that "they're tough and they're good, but they're clean." It wasn't the last time that Huizenga's background in the garbage business would raise questions in the video industry.

But the deal struck over dinner began to unravel the next day. The company didn't have directors and officers insurance, meaning the new directors with their sizable net worths could be personally liable. There were issues over the number of warrants that would be granted. The lawyers were insisting that more time had to pass for more due diligence before a change of control could take place. In truth, both sides were having a case of cold feet. "Anytime you're committing $18 million for something and you're talking from their side, you're nervous. You're saying hey, that was too easy, maybe there's something we don't see here," says Cook. "And from our side, we're saying I'm not sure we need these guys, they're pretty tough bastards."

Huizenga, Melk, and Flynn broke off the meeting. Huizenga flew back to Fort Lauderdale. He didn't need Cook, Anderson, or Blockbuster as much as they needed him—and he knew it. Sure enough, within hours, he got a call from one of the company's directors, Clinton Allen, asking if they could meet again. Both Beck and Allen had worked on Cook, convincing him that $18 million was too much money to let details stand in the way. The group chartered a Lear jet from Dallas and flew to Fort Lauderdale. They met Sunday at the offices of Huizenga Holdings, a gracious two-story Spanish-style building with a fountain and courtyard that seemed more suited to a hacienda than the soon-to-be headquarters to build a billion-dollar company. There, they worked out the parameters of the deal again. "I remember coming out of that negotiation thinking that Wayne was smart and one step ahead," says Clinton Allen. "That negotiation was us reacting to Wayne rather than him reacting to us. He does deals like a chess player. He's always two to three moves ahead of whomever he's dealing with."

Learning from his experience at Waste Management, Huizenga was going to make sure that the money and credibility his group was infusing were adequately compensated. The structure of the deal they made that day—plus the options Huizenga would earn later as chief executive and by all three as directors—would vault them from being mere millionaires to mega-millionaires. The group would invest $18.5 million in three stages for 1.2 million shares of Blockbuster stock, and would be granted warrants, or rights, to buy an additional 1.7 million shares, half at $17 and half at $21 a share. The deal gave Huizenga and his group 60 percent of Blockbuster's stock and Cook and Anderson would give up control. They and the Becks would put their stock in a voting trust, to be voted the way Huizenga's group saw fit. Cook could sell, but Huizenga had control. "He's a tough, hard-nosed business guy, but that's okay, he was always fair," Cook remembers of those negotiations. "He was a solver. It's like he's got a goal and he tries to run around this way to it and if that doesn't work, he runs around the other way and he finally finds a way through, but, as long as he reaches his goal who the hell cares how he got there. But he always gets his goal." More than seven years after he ceded control to Huizenga, Cook got a call in the summer of 1994 as the fate of Blockbuster's merger with Viacom hung in the balance. The caller, a broker, wanted to know whether Cook thought the deal would fly. "I said the only thing I can tell you is that Wayne always gets his deals so that's what I would bet on."

On Tuesday, Huizenga and two of his lieutenants flew to Dallas to begin working with lawyers on the details. Huizenga was ready to fly back to Fort Lauderdale, leaving his assistants to finish the task before an announcement would be made. But word was leaking out about the new investment group and the stock began to trade at a heavy volume with a rising price. Beck, watching with concern, called Cook out of a barber's chair and sent an associate to head off Huizenga at the airport. With a fairness opinion and voting agreement worked out that Wednesday afternoon, they announced the deal.

As Huizenga was signing the final papers, he did something so characteristic that it still makes his friend Melk laugh. After putting down the pen from signing the papers, he looked up at Cook and asked who was the biggest competitor. "Major Video," Cook replied, citing a video rental company based in Las Vegas which had also embarked on a superstore concept. That night, reminicent of the pair's Waste Management days when they'd fly at night to get on with business first thing in the morning, Huizenga and Melk flew to Las Vegas just for a "get acquainted" meeting the next morning with Major Video founders Gary Moore and Hank Cartwright.

Huizenga would later court Major Video over more than a year and acquire it in what would be one of the most important but problematic deals in Blockbuster's history. But the seeds for that deal were already being sown the day he invested in Blockbuster. "Wayne is a relationship guy," marvels Clinton Allen. "Part of his genius is this. He's great at setting up an acquisition. He sets it up like an artist sets up a painting. Instead of picking up the phone and saying 'I'm Huizenga and I want to buy you,' he stopped in and visited them. Why did he do that? It's all part of the way he works. He gets to know them and when he comes back, it's not as an outsider but with some kind of personal relationship."

On Friday, February 13, when the Blockbuster agreements were all drawn up and the legal work done, Huizenga chartered a second Lear jet to bring his son, Wayne Jr., his father, Harry, Steve Berrard, Joe Burke, Rick Rochon, Don Smiley and other friends and associates to the closing. Even though Huizenga viewed Blockbuster as an investment, it was a pretty big deal even by his standards. They celebrated with bottles of Dom Perignon on the flight back home.

MANAGEMENT CLASHES

The celebration was short-lived, at least on the parts of Cook and Anderson. It didn't take long for friction to develop between the new controlling shareholders and entrepreneurial managers. Suggestions became directives which met with resistance and resentment. There was nothing "passive" about these investors. With Flynn still chief financial officer of Waste Management and Huizenga overseeing his collection of service companies, Melk became the liaison. Huizenga dispatched Rick Rochon to Dallas as well to become steeped in the financials. Melk set up an office in the exercise room off of Cook's office and started to learn about the business. Cook thought Melk arrogant, condescending and without a clue of what made video rental tick. Melk viewed Cook as a computer nerd and a neo-phyte in business.

Beyond personality clashes were deep differences on business funda-mentals. Both the original management and the new investors recognized the same pressure: with nothing proprietary, Blockbuster's concept could be copied. But they responded to it very differently. To roll out the concept quickly, Cook wanted to concentrate on building company stores in the Dallas area and license everything else out, planning to buy the licensed stores back later for stock. "There's a concept out there that Wayne came in when there were just 19 stores, that this was a little bitty chain and he took it to some great heights. We might have had actually 19 open or some-thing, but when he actually took over we had a whole lot more than that, and a whole lot more in development."

But to Huizenga, licensing gave away too much territory with too little oversight and control. It rubbed against his very grain of running a busi-ness. Huizenga took the licensing agreement home and read it. "I'd never read a licensing agreement in my life, and didn't know anything about fran-chising, so I wasn't trying to be an expert," he recalls. "I couldn't under-stand why in the heck we had that franchising thing worded the way it was worded. That was probably our first confrontation."

Licensed stores didn't contribute enough to cash flow and earnings to make much of an impression on Wall Street. "I was of the opinion that Wall Street had seen enough franchise companies," says Huizenga. "Franchise companies come and go every day. If you really want to do something, you have to build some mass. And the only way you are going to build mass is if you own these stores."

Repeatedly, Huizenga made this point with Cook. "Why should we let somebody else build these stores? Why don't we build them ourselves?"

"We don't have the money," Cook answered.

"Then we'll get the money. We'll put in more money if we have to," Huizenga replied. "But why let somebody else run these stores? These stores are gonna do terrific."

"We don't want to do that. We're just going to build up a lot of debt and we're going to get in over our heads and why should we have all that debt?" Cook believed the only thing that could make Blockbuster stumble was debt and he wasn't willing to borrow until he felt the company's cash flow could handle the payments. But Huizenga and Melk were adamant and pressured Cook to stop the licensing program.

Cook wasn't the only one chafing under the new investors' demands. Anderson's conservative financial bent was uncomfortable with the ag-gressiveness of Huizenga's group. "I was skeptical," Anderson says. "They claimed they were gonna get that stock up to $100 a share in two years."

There was also friction over Huizenga's strategy of acquisitions. Huizenga knew he couldn't quite duplicate the rapid-fire deal-making machine that had propelled Waste Management into an industry powerhouse. There were only a few chains worth acquiring, but he was intent on buying mass where he could.

The first Blockbuster acquisition target was St. Louis-based Movies-To-Go, a chain run by Jim Ellis and his three brothers. As a college student, Ellis had hooked up with a top executive at General Dyanmics Corp. who had provided backing for his first video store, which opened in June 1981. One of the pioneers in the business, Ellis was also one of the most aggressive, growing off of cash flow to 29 stores by early 1987, mostly in St. Louis and Chicago. Movies-To-Go was the second-largest privately held video store chain (not counting franchise stores) in the country at the time.

Acquiring Movies-To-Go would accomplish three things for Huizenga: it would give Blockbuster critical mass in an area, it would give the company needed management depth so long as the Ellis brothers signed on, and most important, it would give Blockbuster immediate profits. Blockbuster had lost $3 million in 1986 and this acquisition would help change that picture. Finally, a more minor consideration, the deal would remove a competitive threat that was encroaching on Scott Beck's territory in Chicago.

John Melk made the introduction, meeting Ellis in the TWA Ambassadors Club in St. Louis and then inviting him to Dallas. But it was Don Flynn who headed up the negotiations. Ellis remembers being polite, but feeling insulted by the first offer, floated by Melk, then meeting with Flynn four or five times before the deal got done. Young, confident, and with an operation at that point bigger than Blockbuster, Ellis knew these guys would be fierce competitors, but that didn't mean he was going to capitulate, either. He'd been advised by lawyers and friends not to do the deal. "We didn't need them. He needed us and maybe Wayne had never been in that position before," Ellis says. "Wayne was under the gun. He had $3 million in losses in 1986 and he had to produce results."

There had been virtually no real acquisitions in the video industry, so there was no benchmark. "It was basically our price and their terms," Ellis remembers. Huizenga flew up on a Saturday with his father, Harry (who walked the store off, measuring square footage) and Joe Burke, who did some number crunching. Huizenga wasn't happy about the price. But the deal closed in May 1987, valued at roughly $17 million in cash, stock, and warrants. "There was no question that Wayne made it clear that he was not happy with the final outcome of our deal," Ellis recalls. Indeed, after many years and acquisitions within the industry, Ellis was still on record as garnering a top price for a video store chain. Flynn heard grief for years about the Movies-To-Go deal. "The company really needed an acquisition to give it some more substance before it could go out and do other things," Flynn says. "That wasn't a bad deal, I don't think. Maybe it wasn't the greatest deal in the world."

But tough negotiator Huizenga doesn't like to have the tables turned and Ellis paid for driving a hard bargain. After working for Blockbuster for nearly two-and-a-half years to build the company, Ellis decided he'd had enough and resigned in January 1990. But only half his options—rights to buy stock at a favorable price, the key to Blockbuster's compensation plan—had become vested. Although other executives would be granted consulting contracts and other arrangements to continue allowing options to become exercisable, Huizenga felt no such obligation to Ellis. A week after he'd announced his intentions to leave, Ellis checked with Huizenga about the options and was told he wasn't entitled to any since he'd already resigned. He was forced to forfeit half his options, which cost millions.

The incident would be noted by other Blockbuster executives as an example of how tough Huizenga could be. Ellis didn't volunteer information about the incident, but does confirm it. "Wayne felt I was paid my due," Ellis says. "To my knowledge, I was singled out and I didn't think it was fair." Ellis says he's never brought it up to Huizenga, who is a neighbor in Fort Lauderdale. "It's never come up between us," he says. "He knows the score and I know the score."

While the Movies-To-Go deal was being negotiated, friction between the groups at Blockbuster was growing more pronounced. Huizenga knew tensions were rising. Cook complains that Melk was constantly giving suggestions that didn't display any understanding for the industry, at one point suggesting that the stores sell Godiva chocolates since their upscale audiences were the same, a notion that struck Cook as absurd. At one particularly contentious meeting, Don Flynn suggested that store managers had to be responsible for budgets. Cook was furious. The only thing store managers had to manage was personnel, that was the way he had designed it. "Why don't you take enough time to at least see what we do before you tell us how to do it," he told Flynn. "It was a very bad meeting," Cook says later. "We all kind of broke out of there and went to our corners." For his part, Huizenga keenly watched Cook's reaction when Flynn or Melk spoke. This young executive was proving to be quite problematic.

For Anderson, the Movies-To-Go acquisition was the last straw. He was convinced Huizenga was going to cheapen the Blockbuster concept by acquiring these smaller store chains. Meanwhile, the tag technology company, Amtech, was in need of more capital. Huizenga refused to fund it any further and agreed to sell it to Cook and Anderson for what Blockbuster had invested in it, about $1.5 million. Anderson resigned in mid-March.

Cook stayed on at Blockbuster as chairman for another month. But finally, Cook had had enough.

The phone call came on a Sunday night in April 1987. It was nearly 10 P.M. on what had been a quiet evening of just watching television with Marti, the rare relaxing kind of time Huizenga had missed during his years of shuttling to Chicago during his Waste Management days and were becoming more infrequent as he geared up for his next venture. It was a tranquil evening, or at least as tranquil as it got for Huizenga and his perpetual deal-making machine. Even now, as he sat in one of the thickly-upholstered chairs placed between the sets of French doors, he had briefcases open on the tile floor around him. That tranquillity would be shattered with this phone call, which would thrust him back into the limelight and the pressure cooker of running a public company. It would prompt him to again court Wall Street into believing a vision. And it would challenge him to draw on the experience, talent—and some of the bare knuckles tactics—honed in building Waste Management to grow a company past the $1 billion mark in less than half the time it'd taken to get Waste Management there.

But now, all Huizenga knew was that he had a problem. An $18 million dollar problem. The caller was David Cook. "You're the chairman," Cook told him. "I want out." He was leaving to join Ken Anderson at Amtech. Huizenga had little appreciation for the technology, but Cook and Anderson parlayed it into a successful public company.

Huizenga tried to convince Cook to stay. Huizenga had his own stable of service companies—pest control, lawn care and bottled water—that he was weaving together and preparing to take public. He was in the midst of talking with underwriters about Service USA. He didn't need this headache with Blockbuster now.

But Cook was adamant. He was convinced that Huizenga, Melk, and Flynn were going to cheapen the Blockbuster concept by acquiring other video rental chains and saddle the company with debt in their hell-bent drive to expand by building company stores. He'd learned the hard way about letting someone else control his business and wasn't about to repeat the mistake. Blockbuster's stock had already more than doubled since Huizenga and his group had bought into the company. Cook was going to cash out while he could.

Huizenga hung up the phone, then quickly dialed the home of Steve Berrard. He'd already earned Huizenga's trust by managing his collection of private companies and had proven a quick learner in the Huizenga school of dealmaking. Now he'd have a new role as Huizenga's chief lieutenant in building Blockbuster into a $2.6 billion public company—and in seven years, would land a spot as a top executive of one of the largest entertainment companies in the world. Huizenga told Berrard to pack a suitcase. "Get ready," he told Berrard. "We're going to Dallas."

* * *

Huizenga had hoped to find other management before Cook had exited. Now he had no choice. He had to take over as chairman. He hoped to make the transition as smooth as possible. Huizenga asked Clinton Allen to stay on as a director. Allen readily agreed. A big, jovial bear of a man, who loves fishing, Allen would come to count Huizenga as a friend. (His New England accent still puts an "r" at the end of the name, pronouncing it "High-zinger.")

Huizenga also tried convincing Cook to stay on the board as a director and founder. "David, why don't you be like Colonel Saunders of Kentucky Fried Chicken? You'll always be known as the founder of the company." Cook refused. "I'm getting out," he said repeatedly. Years later, Cook readily admits that Blockbuster would never have grown to the scope it did under his leadership. "I suspect we'd be at 2,500 stores right now. I would never have gone out and acquired the chains he did. I would never have done the job he did in acquiring market share. I wouldn't have done it. Wayne has a history and it's probably as successful as anybody in business of acquiring companies. He's a magician. I mean he is the best there is at that. He did a far better job of expanding Blockbuster than I ever would have."

On April 23, 1987 the day that Blockbuster posted its first profitable quarter of $397,000, Cook was gone. Before he left, he held a meeting to brief employees about the change of management. It was awkward and uncomfortable, particularly for those loyal to Cook, but also for Huizenga. "I'm leaving," Cook told them. "This guy's your new chairman. His name is Wayne."

6

Fast Forward: Building the Blockbuster Management Team

The crowd was abuzz the second day of the 1988 Video Software Dealers Association convention at the Las Vegas Hilton. From its start in the early 1980s as a potent grassroots force to counter Hollywood's determination to take a cut of rental revenue, the organization had mushroomed. Now roughly 12,000 representatives of the video industry gathered at this annual event. The meetings had grudgingly become recognized as a marketing opportunity by Hollywood, which feted the legions of video store owners with parties and celebrity visits. This year, comedian Jay Leno provided laughs, singer Natalie Cole crooned over dinner, and impressionist Rich Little acted as the master of ceremonies for the awards banquet. Stars like Angela Lansbury, Shirley MacLaine, and Chuck Norris visited the exhibition floor. Baseball legends Willie Mays and Pete Rose were on hand. Jeffrey Katzenberg, then-chairman of Walt Disney Pictures, had given the keynote speech.

But the real curiosity the morning of Tuesday, August 9, was about this new upstart video chain, Blockbuster, and its chairman, whose name no one could pronounce. H. Wayne Huizenga was already rewriting the script used by the small entrepreneurs who'd built the industry. In the 16 months since he'd taken the helm, Blockbuster had acquired two other video store chains and now totaled upwards of 250 stores. In April, it had announced plans to swallow another industry big gun, Las Vegas-based Major Video, with 175, mostly franchised superstores. Who was this guy, who had bought up small garbage companies and formed them into the colossus Waste Management? And was he planning a repeat performance in the video industry?

Into the convention hall filed Blockbuster executives, easily identifiable with their uniform dark suits, white shirts, and ties amidst the polo shirt and polyester crowd. Huizenga took his seat in the middle of the front row. He was curious himself what his marketing executive, Tom Gruber, was going to say. Less than a year ago in enticing Gruber, an 18-year McDonald's marketing veteran, to join the fledgling video chain, Huizenga had appealed to his ego by predicting that one day soon, Gruber would be addressing this very convention, that Blockbuster would grow that fast and become a force to be reckoned with that quickly.

As the lights dimmed, Gruber stepped on-stage. His presentation was slick, complete with video clips and slides. The idea had been to compare marketing hamburgers and marketing videos, but it turned into a lengthy commercial about Blockbuster. He hammered on Blockbuster's kids and family theme. He showed a television ad, an industry first, with the "Wow, What a Difference!" slogan. He compared the bright, clean look of Blockbuster's stores to pictures of dirty, dingy, unkempt outlets. But the clincher was showing huge head shots of Ray Kroc, the legendary McDonald's leader and pioneer of the fast-food industry, and H. Wayne Huizenga and comparing them as titans of American business.

The murmuring in the crowd grew to an audible hiss and several audience members walked out. Who were these guys, anyway, to threaten to drive them out of business? Tell them how to run their stores? Huizenga was embarrassed, more so as the animosity grew palpable. Some Blockbuster executives cringed, and some recently acquired newcomers, longtime figures in the video industry, took off their company badges. It was all so blatant, this chest-thumping that wouldn't go over well in the industry.

Trade publications would say later that Gruber's speech had given a wake-up call to video store operators. Some competitors would later cite that speech as part of the impetus to improve their business and customer service. But at a reception that night, with the buzz still mostly negative, Huizenga worried a bit. Maybe he should have toned Gruber down. Maybe they shouldn't have done this at all. They'd revealed a lot of their hand on the marketing front, but it was too late. Blockbuster and Wayne Huizenga, through Tom Gruber, had thrown down the gauntlet to the industry. The McDonalds-Blockbuster comparison was affixed. Huizenga's reputation as taking on the video rental industry was cast; there was no going back now.

BUILDING THE BLOCKBUSTER CHAIN

In April 1987, when founder David Cook made his quick exit, taking much of the top management of the fledgling Blockbuster chain with him,

Huizenga still had no intention of running Blockbuster full-time. "I'll put myself in as chairman for awhile, and then we'll find the right person," he kept telling Melk.

But Melk had other ideas. "We never looked for the top guy. He may have, but I never did." Getting Huizenga in to run the show, Melk saw from the start, was what Blockbuster needed to realize its potential. There was never any question about which of the three investors would take charge. Flynn was still chief financial officer of Waste Management. And though Melk had been the point person, the liaison who had learned about the industry and had plenty of management and business experience, he didn't consider the top job for a moment. "He's much more suited, much more capable, and much more high energy and obviously could do a much better job," he says of Huizenga. "I'm sure I could have run the company, but I don't think the company'd be any billion dollar company."

One of the first things Huizenga realized he had to do was understand the industry better. "Okay, now that we're in this deal, I guess we'd better learn a little bit more about the business," he told Melk. Usually a stickler for thorough research, Huizenga had taken comfort from the fact that the Becks were involved as franchisees and hadn't done as much due diligence as he might have otherwise.

Huizenga and Melk boarded the Lear jet and, borrowing a page from their Waste Management days, flew around the country visiting video stores. Aside from Major Video, most operators insisted that the superstore concept wouldn't work. This was a hit-driven business. The latest releases drew customers into the store, so why waste the floor space and pay rent and inventory costs to maintain a library of 8,000 to 10,000 tapes? "Everywhere we went, everybody said that the superstores don't work," Huizenga recalls. "Yet, we'd get on the plane and we'd look at our numbers and we saw big stores do work."

While gathering feedback from the industry, Huizenga had to exorcise doubts of his own. What he initially saw about the business didn't reassure him. In May, he met with a group of investors, big holders of Blockbuster stock who had gotten in during the David Cook days. Chick Martin, who'd hired on during the Cook-Anderson era, was handling investor relations along with a myriad of other tasks. He arranged for a breakfast meeting at The Mansion on Turtle Creek in Dallas. Among the investors was Tom Marquez, a Dallas heavy-hitter who was one of the early employees of Electronic Data Systems founder H. Ross Perot and had made a killing riding the rise of EDS and other companies. Blockbuster would turn out to be another bonanza, but the tone of the first meeting with Huizenga was far from comforting. "I'm introducing them to Huizenga and he looks at these guys in the eyes and says 'You know if I knew what I know today I wouldn't have invested in this deal,'" Martin recalls. In his experience in investor relations, this meeting was supposed to reassure investors in the new management. Huizenga's words were hardly encouraging. "This is a great concept, but right now there isn't the muscle to build it," he told them. "Frankly, I think the stock is overpriced right now." Then he laid out plans to grow the company and make it worth the stock price it carried—and then some. Marquez still remembers the meeting. "All the things he said he was going to do, he did." He remembers Huizenga as a man with "incredible common sense, practical, no-nonsense, and one of those guys with no artificial barriers. Absolutely fearless." Huizenga vowed to Marquez and the others, "If I screw up, then call me." Says Marquez seven years later, after Blockbuster had been sold to Viacom, "How many times did I call him? None."

Then a few weeks later, Huizenga called Clinton Allen in early June. He was worried and wanted to talk with Allen, who'd been a director for a while. "I think we made a mistake," he told Allen. "I just got some numbers here and I think we made a bad mistake. The business just tanked." They didn't realize it at the time, but spring and fall are soft months for the video rental industry. In the spring, people are spending more time outside and in autumn, they're watching new television series. But to Huizenga, it was as if the bottom had fallen out. "Maybe it's a fad," he said to Allen, voicing his own fear. "Maybe we should get out of it." Allen didn't understand the pattern either, but he did his best to reassure Huizenga. "Let's let it settle down and watch and see what happens," Allen answered. A few weeks later, the numbers were back on track.

In July, Huizenga held a franchisee meeting after his first shareholders meeting as Blockbuster's new chairman. The Blockbuster crew—about 100 employees and franchisees then—boarded a rented yacht and cruised down the Intracoastal Waterway and through the maze of canals (which has earned Fort Lauderdale the moniker Chamber of Commerce types like to use as "Venice of America") and paused in front of Huizenga's graceful, Spanish-style waterfront home. Though Huizenga still harbored doubts about Blockbuster, he hid them well from franchisees as he outlined his growth plans for the company. Fred Montesi III, who'd licensed the Memphis and Nashville areas when Blockbuster was managed by Cook and Anderson, recalls that first meeting. "I remember we came out of one session and we were at Marriott Harbor Beach hotel and every pay phone was tied up because everyone was on the phone calling their brokers to buy more stock because we were absolutely convinced this was the best thing that could ever happen. We had two stores and were doing great but the absolute consensus was that if you want to make money beyond the stores, then invest in Blockbuster stock."

Meanwhile, for the Blockbuster executives who had joined under David Cook, the transformation was immediate and total. "Within very short order the thing went from being a fast-growing business to a light speed type of business," recalls Chick Martin. He was impressed that Huizenga, along with Melk and Flynn, provided their home phone numbers with instructions to call if necessary. A genial man with an affable smile and helpful demeanor, Martin quickly discovered an aspect of his new boss that others who had worked with Huizenga already knew and new hires would soon find out. "He's the only man I ever worked for that never really was satisfied with what you do for him," Martin says. "He's always like, 'well, you did a great job on that, now do this.' The guy's very tightly wound."

Executives like Martin, who had a smattering of experience in a number of areas, such as information management and investor relations, were all of a sudden in charge of several of them. One of Martin's first tasks, at Huizenga's directive, was to come up with a monthly summary, the "Blue Book." It was a synopsis of the business, from the films Blockbuster was renting to the number of stores and where they were. Huizenga needed the information so he could tell investors and Wall Street what was going on. After their fact-finding trips visiting other video store chains, Huizenga and Melk had come away convinced that the naysayers about superstores were wrong, and the "Blue Books" buttressed that belief. "One day it just sort of dawned on us. Blockbuster had the best concept out there," Huizenga says. But it didn't take him long to recognize the downside of that revelation. "We better hurry up and develop this thing before somebody else figures out that what everybody is saying isn't right. And so, you know, we had to move quick."

BUILDING A MANAGEMENT TEAM

"Entrepreneur" is an over-used label for a broad range of business talent. If "inventors" are on one end of the spectrum with "implementors" on the other end and "innovators" in the middle, David P. Cook and H. Wayne Huizenga exemplify the two extremes but meet in that middle. Cook is an inventor and an innovator. Huizenga is an innovator and an implementor. Ray Schneider, the San Antonio lawyer who worked with both of them as a franchisee, says of Huizenga, "He's a real good guy to take other people's ideas and build on them." Indeed, Huizenga takes companies, technologies, and systems created by others and envisions new ways to manage them, connect them and leverage their strengths. As Scott Beck, the initial conduit for his involvement in Blockbuster once told *New Miami* magazine, "It's not so much that anything Wayne touches turns to gold. He only chooses to touch those things that, through his level of intellect, he understands have a high probability of being able to turn into gold." Huizenga knew the key to Blockbuster's success was growth—at nearly any cost. The company needed to open new stores, buy existing chains, consolidate operations and build enough mass in markets to support advertising and create a loyal base of Blockbuster card-carrying customers.

Huizenga stepped up his education on Blockbuster, commuting to Dallas often aboard the Lear jet. Rob Castleberry stayed on as a senior vice-president of operations to handle the day-to-day decisions. He and Chick Martin were about the only executives remaining from the Cook-Anderson days. Huizenga sent Steve Berrard and Joe Burke to Dallas to be temporarily based there. Part of their task was to get financials and projections in order, to crunch numbers until they were comfortable with the growth trajectory. He would need these for Wall Street, for internal planning and for his own assurance. Within weeks, he and Don Flynn convinced a reluctant Berrard to take the chief financial officer job at Blockbuster. After a week of back-and-forth, Huizenga had walked in Berrard's office and simply told him, "Here's the deal. You're going to be the CFO and you're going to move out to Dallas and you can come back once you get the company moved back here." Huizenga made Joe Burke the corporate controller.

Huizenga realized what he knew: He knew how to grow a business by acquisition, manage fast growth, and set up regional operations. He knew how to make deals; and he knew how to court Wall Street, but he didn't know retailing. Didn't know the video business. Didn't know real estate, site selection, or consumer marketing. Didn't know franchising. But at least he knew that he didn't know. One of his first priorities was to set about to find executives who did—and to convince them to share his vision.

He needed special expertise for marketing. Huizenga hadn't dealt with a consumer products company before. Waste Management hadn't needed to concern itself with "marketing" in the traditional sense of slick television commercials and brand awareness. And the companies he had concentrated on developing during his post-Waste years had been similar types of service businesses, the kind of luxuries-come-necessities that others were willing to pay for if you did the job right. Blockbuster presented a different challenge. Intuitively, Huizenga knew Blockbuster had to become a brand, had to differentiate itself from the swarm of mom-and-pop video stores and small chains that characterized the industry. Still, he saw it primarily as a rental business, akin to how he viewed Waste Management. Instead of renting dumpsters, he was renting video tapes. That view would eventually evolve as Blockbuster did, from a rental company to a retail company to an entertainment company, but Huizenga's initial instinct was correct—its core business would remain, essentially, rental.

(Left) Wayne Huizenga's yearbook picture from Pine Crest School, 1955. Even in high school, he showed an inclination toward business and sports.

(Right) Wayne played center for the Pine Crest Panthers, the first football team fielded by the private school. He won a contest to name the school teams the Panthers. He would use that same name for his professional hockey franchise, one of three professional sports franchises he owns.

(Below) Wayne played baseball throughout high school. This photo was taken in his senior year. Though a good third baseman, Wayne was better at football, says his former coach, Bill Munsey. Football was and remains Wayne's favorite sport.

WAYNE HUIZENGA
Chicago, Ill.
Baseball 1, 2, 4
Basketball 1
Student Council 4; Treas.
Football 1, 4
Sand Spur 4
Yearbook 4, Bus. Mgr.
Monarchs 1, 2

Baseball

FIRST ROW: Wayne Huizenga, Bill Rosse, Mike Starling, Mike Clark, Tito Auger, Chuck Schmidt, Jack Patterson, Dick Holman. SECOND ROW: Cliff Hogan, Joel Samuel, Roger Hailes, John Leech, Craig Campbell, Buck Beiser, Jack Fike. THIRD ROW: Jim Pengra, Jack Cummings, Pete Fernandez, Jim Anguilo, Ellis Adler, Nick Eman, Bill Swart, Coach Bill Munsey.

(Left) Left to right: Wayne along with Dean Buntrock, co-founder of Waste Management Inc., Wayne's brother-in-law Whit Hudson, Arnie Myer, an executive with Heil Co., Wayne's father, Harry Huizenga, Harry Harrenberg (on bulldozer), and Bill Post (a Southern Sanitation employee) participate in the ground-breaking for the Resource Recovery Plant/Solid Waste Reduction Center in Pompano Beach in 1970. The plant used a then-innovative method of treating garbage by compacting it into pellets, allowing metals and other materials to be recycled.

(Below) Less than three years after going public, Waste Management Inc. shares began trading the New York Stock Exchange on October 25, 1973 under the symbol WMX. A New York Stock Exchange official shows the ticker tape to Dean Buntrock, co-founder and chairman of Waste Management, and Wayne Huizenga, co-founder and vice-chairman along with Harold Gershowitz, president.

(Left) Wayne Huizenga and Dean Buntrock on a Waste Management truck in the 1970s. The partnership they forged created an industry powerhouse. Their hands-on experience in the garbage business won over many of the small and medium-sized companies they sought to acquire in a race against Browning- Ferris Inc. and other competitors to dominate the industry. When Huizenga officially left Waste Management in 1984, the company was generating over $1 billion in annual revenues and was the industry leader.

Wayne with friend and business partner John Melk in a Blockbuster store. Melk retired from Waste Management in 1984 after spearheading its international expansion. In February 1987, he convinced Wayne to visit a Blockbuster video store near Chicago that he owned. Skeptical at first, that visit helped convince Huizenga, along with Melk and Don Flynn, then-chief financial officer at Waste Management, to invest in Blockbuster.

On April 27, 1989, Blockbuster was listed on the New York Stock Exchange—the second such company Wayne Huizenga brought to the NYSE. With him are two New York Stock Exchange officials. Wayne's father, Harry (not shown) traded the first 100 shares.

Blockbuster prided itself on being a family-oriented business by mandating that it would not offer X-rated videos—and the "Blockbuster Kids" helped promote this philosophy. The theme was introduced in 1988 by marketing executive Tom Gruber (left) whom Wayne had hired to do for the video industry what McDonald's had done for fast food. Another McDonald's veteran, Luigi Salvaneschi (not shown) oversaw Blockbuster's rapid rollout. The former McDonald executives, "family" marketing theme and clean, brightly-lit stores helped affix the nickname "'McVideo" in its early years.

In November 1989, Blockbuster celebrated that it had 1,000 stores with a banner stretched across its headquarters in Fort Lauderdale, Florida. In 1987, when Wayne bought into the company, there were just 8 company owned stores and 11 franchised stores. During its fastest growth rate, a new Blockbuster location opened every 17 hours and by 1994 it had over 3,700 stores in the United States and 10 foreign countries. With Wayne is his father, Harry, with whom he shared the company's success. Harry was a partner in a number of Wayne's businesses.

At the last Blockbuster shareholder's meeting on September 29, 1994, some of Blockbuster directors stand behind a table laden with momentos from some of the 110 deals done since Huizenga (far right) bought into the company in 1987. From left are director John Croghan, Steve Berrard, director, president, and chief operating officer, director John Melk, and director Clinton Allen. Not shown is director Don Flynn.

Opening Day of the Florida Marlins, April 5, 1993. Wayne Huizenga's expansion team takes the field against the Los Angeles Dodgers in its inaugural game at Joe Robbie Stadium. Bringing baseball to south Florida made Huizenga a hero to area sports fans. Here, Wayne Huizenga greets Dodgers manager Tommy Lasorda as part of the pre-game festivities. The Marlins won that first game 6 to 3.

At the Florida Marlins 1994 opener, Wayne Huizenga waves to the crowd as Marlins president Don Smiley (far left) applauds, along with Marlins partners Steve Berrard, second-in-command at Blockbuster, brother-in-law Whit Hudson, Wayne Jr., and father, Harry Huizenga. The season was marred by a bitter baseball strike that cost the sport and the Marlins dearly.

Wayne Huizenga confers with Don Shula, coach of the Miami Dolphins football team. Huizenga bought 15% of the Dolphins and half of Joe Robbie Stadium in March 1990, which ushered him into the world of professional sports team ownership. He bought the rest of the team and the stadium in January 1994, and by that time, also owned the Florida Marlins baseball and Florida Panthers hockey franchises. His approach, to treat sports like any other business, didn't wow his teams' fans but that didn't change his philosophy.

Family has always been paramount with Huizenga. He and his wife Marti have four children, Pam (left) and Ray (center) from Marti's first marriage, and Scott (far left) and Wayne Jr. (far right). Despite the demands of his business life, he made time for the family, which became easier as the businesses grew more successful, as opposed to the early days of Waste Management when the kids teasingly called him "Uncle Dad" because he traveled so much.

Wayne and Marti enjoy their waterfront Fort Lauderdale home. For his 50th birthday, Marti bought Wayne a 1937 Rolls Royce. That started one of his few hobbies—collecting antique cars. But characteristically, he'd turn even that hobby into a business by extending a line of credit and investing in cars expected to appreciate significantly in value.

As a teenager, Wayne enjoyed fast cars. After retiring from Waste Management (notice cap with company logo) he took a course in racing cars at the Skip Barber school in Sebring, Florida, in 1985 and took along family members. He'd treat some Blockbuster executives to a similar experience years later.

(Top) The pending merger of Viacom and Blockbuster announced in January 1994, which played a key role in the successful acquisition of Paramount Communications Inc., had become doubtful by the summer of 1994 because of Viacom's lagging stock price. At the Allen & Co. investment conference in July 1994 where this photo was taken, Huizenga and Steve Berrard (standing, left) meet with Frank J. Biondi Jr., president and CEO of Viacom (standing, right) and Sumner Redstone, Viacom's chairman.

(Left) Blockbuster's size and influence as an entertainment giant conferred recognition by Hollywood on both the company and its chairman, Wayne Huizenga. At the 1995 Superbowl, hosted by Miami in Joe Robbie Stadium, supermodel and actress Cindy Crawford gives Huizenga a hug—one of the perks Huizenga enjoyed by being a force in both Hollywood and in the world of sports.

Fishing for marlin off the coast of Australia is one of Wayne Huizenga's favorite past-times. In April 1986, he's pictured standing next to a black marlin caught by a friend. Huizenga's goal was to catch a grander—a black marlin over 1,000 pounds. That's a goal he hasn't yet realized, though he's arguably caught, or helped create, two in his corporate life through Waste Management and Blockbuster and has embarked on a third with Republic Waste Industries.

Wayne Huizenga standing in front of Blockbuster's world headquarters in downtown Fort Lauderdale—a visible symbol of success for a hometown boy who started out with a trash hauling business in 1962.

Huizenga also embodies a rare combination for an entrepreneur. While they may be brilliant inventors or innovators, entrepreneurs often lack the skills to be good managers and the business acumen to turn an idea into a very profitable venture. They envision, but don't trust others to carry it out. Huizenga does both. Though he finds the building more creative, more fun, he has a solid grasp of business fundamentals. "He's an operationally oriented person who also has a forte about doing deals and making the transactions happen," says Melk. "He's not just a deal-maker." Moreover, Huizenga was not only willing but eager to delegate and tap the expertise of others. In building Blockbuster, Huizenga knew what kind of management talent he'd need—and what it would take to get it.

MARKETING THE MCDONALD'S WAY

On September 29, 1987, Huizenga met with Tom Gruber at the Marriott Harbor Beach Hotel. Gruber sports chestnut brown hair combed to one side and gray-green eyes behind aviator glasses. He was born and reared in Minneapolis where his father owned a modest-sized advertising agency. After his graduation from the University of Minnesota, he worked for an agency and soon joined McDonald's. He traveled the world for the company and lived the life of a globe-trotting, confirmed bachelor while preaching the fast-food giant's obsession with family and wholesomeness. The turning point in his life was when he married in 1977 and later had two children. He had come late to family life, and that conversion—along with the 18 year inculcation by McDonald's—seared him with a single-minded zeal for "family" marketing that would appeal to Huizenga, but annoy other Blockbuster executives.

It was at this breakfast meeting that H. Wayne Huizenga got his first lesson in consumer marketing. Eager to tap the brain of a marketing exec, Huizenga asked Gruber to lay out what a marketing department should entail. On back of a place mat, Gruber drew up a marketing department structure, borrowing liberally from McDonald's. The boxes, he explained, were for a senior vice-president of marketing, a vice-president of advertising plus a promotions, public relations, and merchandising office. The video rental industry had focused its nascent marketing efforts on merchandising, emphasizing new titles. Gruber told Huizenga that the key wasn't to copy a marketing department from other video chains but instead, focus on image, à la, McDonald's. "He saw that as a plus not only because of the expertise, but because of the news value on the Street, particularly on Wall Street," Gruber says. Indeed, comparing Blockbuster to McDonald's would become an easy analogy for analysts and reporters to understand.

"We can't afford all those people, you're going to be the guy that does all that," Huizenga told him. "You know that, right?"

"Yeah, but I'm going to need those people soon," Gruber replied.

"What I need is a program here that can establish a marketing structure that is capable of moving a small company to a very big national company and possibly an international company in a short period of time."

"What do you mean by a short period?"

"Well, in a couple of years," Huizenga said.

"You're not going to do this in a couple of years," Gruber shook his head. "It took McDonald's years to do this. I'm showing you a marketing department that exists 28 to 30 years into the thing."

"We have to move fast because we have nothing exclusive," Huizenga told him, a refrain that would become a constant spur to the company's frenetic growth. "Anybody can duplicate this so we've got to be out there. We've got to be out there first with the superstore because if somebody comes in across from us it's going to be harder. We've got to establish this thing called Blockbuster and it's got to mean videos. Will you do it?"

Huizenga didn't even wait for an answer before asking "show me how you'd do it." The one-hour breakfast stretched to two while Gruber took another placemat and mapped out a plan for launching a brand, following the plan he'd used in launching McDonald's in 14 countries. He started with the store as the "package," then adding radio advertising, movie theater advertising, and then television. He even showed him how franchisees contribute to advertising programs in the McDonald's system. "He never interrupted. He just listened," Gruber recalls. "He was just enthralled, absolutely, because he could see in what I was saying exactly what he wanted to do, but now he was seeing how to do it."

Huizenga then painted a picture of Blockbuster's future for Gruber. This was the guy he wanted. Now he had to convince him to take a chance on a small company with big potential. Money would be a big part of the attraction, but Huizenga knew the key was to appeal to Gruber's ego. "You know what the VSDA is?" Gruber shook his head no.

"The VSDA is an industry group, there are 25,000 video stores in this country and many of them belong to the Video Software Dealers Association. It's like the National Restaurant Association, and it's a big deal. You come here, and you'll be on stage at the Las Vegas Hilton addressing the VSDA probably as key note speaker because this company is going to be that important to the industry." That prediction, like so many others made in the early months of Huizenga's taking charge, would come true in short order.

The next day, Gruber met again with Huizenga. Gruber would have to take a 60 percent pay cut to work for Blockbuster, and Huizenga had to sell him on the potential for Blockbuster's stock options. For Gruber, who had worked under the legendary Ray Kroc, who had steered McDonald's to become the dominant force in fast food and reshaped America's eating habits, the similarity of the two men, at least in one aspect, was clear at that second meeting. Though their paths to corporate dominance were quite different, "ultimately they became just motivators," Gruber says. "Wayne does have that ability to sit down one on one or with a group and talk about whatever he's talking about, whether it's a sports program these days or whether it's Blockbuster or it's service or a new design and he gets you so excited about that, so motivated. That's what he did to me that day in that conference room; he got me motivated about this company, about what it was going to be one day. And I was convinced although I felt he was way out of line in terms of projections. But if the projections were only 25 percent true, this was going to be a big deal and it was going to be fun." But Huizenga's projections on the stock would more than come true.

SCOUTING FOR NEW BLOCKBUSTER LOCATIONS

Eager to get Blockbuster's name known in his hometown of Fort Lauderdale, Huizenga asked Don Smiley, who'd done marketing and sales for his water and other private companies, and his father, Harry, to scout for Blockbuster sites in south Florida and get some stores open. With absolutely no experience in retail, site selection, or video rental, Don Smiley and "Uncle Harry" cruised south Florida in Harry's silver Cadillac and with the help of a real estate agent, plenty of maps, and demographic information, soon opened 10 company-owned video stores.

But Huizenga realized that he needed an expert in site selection and construction. Huizenga turned to Tom Gruber, whose years of launching McDonald's internationally had yielded valuable contacts. Gruber suggested another McDonald's veteran, Luigi Salvaneschi.

An Italian immigrant who started as a crew member at one of the first McDonald's stores, Salvaneschi had worked his way up to become an expert in real estate. Nicknamed "the professor" by the Blockbuster crowd, he waxes philosophical at times, a harkening to his training at the Vatican's Lateran University, from which he holds a doctorate degree in law. He emigrated to the United States in 1959 and started working at a McDonald's restaurant in Glen Ellyn, Illinois. He was sent by Ray Kroc in 1961 to manage a McDonald's store opening in California, became involved in developing new sites in 1964 and in 1969 was put in charge of the company's real estate acquisition department. From 1969, under his direction, McDonald's growth mushroomed during this period with the opening of more than 5,000 stores. He'd joined Kentucky Fried Chicken in 1983 and was moving into a comfortable life as a consultant and academic.

At Huizenga's request, Gruber called Salvaneschi, who insisted that he was happily retired and teaching at the University of Louisville. Gruber convinced him to visit Fort Lauderdale since there were no Blockbuster stores in Louisville. Salvaneschi met with Huizenga, but wasn't convinced. "The more he said no, the more Wayne wanted him," Gruber remembers. "Luigi wasn't playing hard to get, he really meant it, he really didn't want to come. That made Wayne want him more." Finally, after much discussion, Salvaneschi agreed to do some consulting. At a seminar in Dallas, attended by company execs and franchisees, Huizenga asked Jim Ellis, founder of the first video store chain Blockbuster had acquired, Movies-To-Go, what he thought about Salvaneschi. It was typical of Huizenga to test an idea and seek opinions. After all, Ellis was no neophyte in the business, having opened 28 stores and currently managing a region and boosting Blockbuster's expansion. "Do what you have to do, but hire this guy," he told Huizenga. That was Huizenga's thought exactly.

The day after Christmas in 1987, Huizenga and his wife, Marti, went to their new house in North Carolina. She insisted and he indulged even though he hates going to North Carolina in the winter. He loves it in the summer, but there's nothing to do in the winter except ski, and if you want to ski, he believes, you might as well go to Colorado. He brought his three or four briefcases and kept going over Blockbuster's numbers. What he saw convinced him that the old retailer's saw about "location, location, location" was right. Blockbuster needed Luigi Salvaneschi and Huizenga was determined to hire him. He called Salvaneschi on December 30 and told him he wanted to come see him, that he'd meet him at 8 A.M. for breakfast the next day. (That meant leaving the house on New Year's Eve day at 5:30 A.M. to get to the airport and to Louisville by the appointed hour, while he was supposed to be on vacation with his wife. But Marti was used to his intensity.)

They met at the Executive House East near the Louisville airport. "What do you want to talk about?" Salvaneschi asked.

"Luigi, I've come to hire you on a full-time basis and I'm not leaving until you say yes."

Salvaneschi instantly refused. "Oh no, there's no way I can do that. I'm already retired and my wife's not feeling that well, and I've traveled all my life and I want to spend time with Lenore. We're starting to get older now, it's not fair that I haven't been around."

"Two years," Huizenga told him. "Just give me two years."

"No, I can't do that."

Breakfast stretched into lunch with the two men still talking. Huizenga explained how he got into the company and didn't know what to do, didn't know about real estate, didn't know anything about retailing. It was classic Huizenga. He was being genuine, but he was also deliberately playing on Salvaneschi's sympathy.

"I don't know anything about locations. So can you give me a hand?" he asked Salvaneschi, who again refused.

Then Huizenga took a yellow legal pad and started illustrating the concept he had in mind. How many stores they would open, what those stores would contribute to earnings and how those earnings would be reflected in a rising stock price, and how the stock would split and then keep rising—and how much the options Salvaneschi would be granted would be worth under various scenarios. Salvaneschi still has the yellow sheet of paper. "He came up with a figure at the end that was of course outstanding," he recalls. "And it came true to the letter, actually better." Besides the prospect of the enormous wealth generated by the options, the prospect of helping to build the company also intrigued Salvaneschi. He viewed it as more than just building a company, but of helping to shape an industry. As much as Huizenga and Gruber, perhaps more, he believed in Blockbuster's family orientation, that he could help clean up a sleazy industry and create a de facto video library, which appealed to his sense of culture and education. "I was really enticed by the concept. He knew I could help. I knew I could help."

As 5 P.M. approached, Luigi asked wearily, "Wayne, how long are we going to go through this?"

"I'm not leaving until you say yes," Huizenga repeated.

Finally, Salvaneschi said he'd discuss the offer with his wife. Over New Year's Eve dinner, they talked and he called Huizenga the next day. "Okay, I'll come on board." But at the outset, Salvaneschi made it clear that his tenure would not be long.

ATTRACTING OTHER TALENTED MANAGERS

Other members of the management team were added via connections with Huizenga, Salvaneschi, Gruber or through headhunters—and sometimes by visiting Blockbuster stores. One of the early hires was Gerry Weber, who had been in the liquor business in Fort Lauderdale and sold his interest after a falling out with his partners. He'd met Huizenga at a few charity events around town. A music and movie buff, he'd been to a few of the south Florida stores, knew that Huizenga was trying to build Blockbuster, and made a cold call to him in the summer of 1987. He told Huizenga he'd liked what he saw and wanted to put his retailing background to work for Blockbuster. Huizenga told him, "We don't know what you're going to be doing and we're trying to figure this out on the fly. But, come on board and let's figure it out together."

Weber remembers that his family's reaction was initially less than thrilled about his new job. Huizenga's past in the garbage business loomed once again. "I went home to tell my wife and she told some family and they said, 'Gerry's going to work for a video store chain? What is he, nuts? Has he taken leave of his senses?' Then, 'Well, he's going to work for Wayne Huizenga. Wayne, who? Well, you know, he's one of the founders of Waste Management. Oh my God! Waste Management. You mean those mob people. Oh my God, he's going to work for the mob!' It was unbelievable, the reaction. Contrast that with, three or four years later, the attitude of, 'You work for Wayne Huizenga? Great! You're with Blockbuster?' You'd sit on an airplane and somebody'd see your luggage tag and say, 'You're with Blockbuster,' and they immediately want to bond with you. They pull out their wallet and pull out their Blockbuster card. It was amazing. Everywhere you went, people were pulling them out."

Weber joined the team that Huizenga was putting together, which included people from a broad range of backgrounds with fast-growth companies: Taylor Devine, who'd helped roll out Mrs. Fields Cookies stores, Gerry Geddis, hired from Radio Shack, Doug Kinney, a franchise attorney, had already been hired by John Melk, Bob Guerin, had headed up the Wells Fargo armored car division before joining Waste Management in 1978 as a regional vice president in Atlanta, and joined Blockbuster in March 1988. Phil deMena, who'd worked with Salvaneschi at Kentucky Fried Chicken, came aboard in August, 1988. Ron Castell would be hired a few months later from competitor Erol's Inc. and become known within Blockbuster as "Mr. Hollywood" because of his studio contacts.

Though it was expensive for a small company, Huizenga believed in having the management talent in place to handle the growth. "If you're going to grow fast then you need to put people out into the field. So we were hiring people way ahead of the curve." Still, Blockbuster's meteoric growth never quite allowed the hiring to keep pace. "Hire the best people" became a company mantra. "When you move quickly, it's hard to bring in people that you have confidence in, that are gonna be able to have the experience to go through building up something so quick," Huizenga says. "It was different than what we did at Waste Management. At Waste Management, we acquired companies that had management. But here, we had to build."

As the company's blistering growth churned through a series of division, regional, and district managers, Huizenga would often tell Salvaneschi, "We need good people. Pay for people because it is the best investment any company can make anywhere at any time." With a company that would telescope 20 years of events into 7, Huizenga needed executives with initiative, resilience, energy, plenty of endurance—and an ability to work with him. "The analogy is driving a stagecoach," says Rob Castleberry, who, while not hand-picked by Huizenga, stayed on long enough to observe his style. "The driver has 12 horses and the reins in his hands. He can totally let the horses run or he can keep them tight. The way he drove the stagecoach is that he allowed each individual horse to run at their pace without being restricted, yet he had his fingers on the pulse."

Many of Blockbuster executives, and especially those who broke into the "inner circle" grew up middle-class, often from the Midwest. "The profile of his group," says Clinton Allen, "is that most were football players or went to school on scholarships and they didn't have a nickel as kids. That's the kind of people he trusts and feels comfortable with. They're extraordinarily devoted to Wayne. And there are times you have to be devoted to Wayne because he tests you. With him, you have to give up a lot to be on the team, have to go places and do things at times when no one else is doing it, and take time away from your family. It's tough. There's no such thing as a nine-to-five employee or director. It doesn't work that way."

As Blockbuster's headquarters were being consolidated in Fort Lauderdale through 1988 and into 1989, it would soon be the end of the ride for Castleberry, Martin, and others who didn't want to leave Dallas. Blockbuster's frenetic pace would wear out more than a few executives and field managers. But, one of Huizenga's main concerns had been met. He had his team in place, and with that team, he would reshape an industry and build a Blockbuster of a business.

OPTING FOR OPTIONS

To grow the company as quickly as he wanted and to the size he envisioned, Huizenga knew he needed management depth. But Blockbuster was a small company with just $43 million in revenues at the end of 1987 and couldn't afford high-buck executives. Further, Huizenga believed that to keep executives working for the benefit of shareholders, you had to make them think like shareholders. The answer lay in what had worked so well at Waste Management and had become a key part of executive compensation elsewhere in corporate America: stock options. So powerful are options that top executives can make many times their salaries with these lucrative stock-based incentives. They must be held for a certain period of time before they become effective and can be exercised. Provided the company's stock price has risen in that period, the executive pockets the difference between the option price and the current selling price of the shares.

One difference, however, is that while many companies reserve options packages only for top executives, Huizenga believed in spreading stock incentives from the top throughout the executive ranks, and throughout to employee ranks as well. Blockbuster's board of directors voted in 1987 to adopt an options program and options became the core of compensation at Blockbuster. Many executives took pay cuts, some as much as 60 percent, to join Blockbuster, but they more than made up for it in the options. Huizenga was also careful to tie options to job titles. When Steve Berrard once questioned that, Huizenga told him he'd done so deliberately to avoid executives "coming down here and kissing my ass two days before we're going to make an option decision. If you're good enough to have the title and be here then you're good enough to get the options."

Leading by example and so confident that he could build the company and work the stock to make a return for shareholders, including himself, Huizenga took just $1 a year in salary for the first three years of his chairmanship of Blockbuster, instead opting for options. In addition to his investment of $17.5 million in Blockbuster stock and warrants, the options granted a spectacular return for his yeoman efforts—with his holdings valued near $600 million when he stepped down as CEO seven years later.

Many executives take pride in the number of jobs their companies create, the number of people employed. Huizenga takes pride in the number of millionaires Blockbuster created within its executive ranks. In addition to the handsome returns earned by shareholders, the lucrative option packages made millionaires of more than a dozen Blockbuster executives.

For entrepreneurial types such as Jim Ellis or Barry Rosenblatt, who had started chains absorbed by Blockbuster, the stock they accepted as part of their buyout packages, plus the options, preserved the feeling that they were working for themselves. "I wasn't working for Wayne," says Ellis. "I was working for the stock." For those groomed in more traditional corporate cultures, the options helped spur an entrepreneurial spirit in the company. "We all had pretty good stock options and we all were pretty independent, so I didn't mind telling the guys in Fort Lauderdale that they were full of it and I really needed something and I wasn't concerned about getting fired," says Chick Martin. "Wayne understood that if you surrounded yourself with a bunch of guys that he could give some financial independence to through the stock that they could be really good managers."

The excitement at Blockbuster's headquarters at 901 Las Olas Boulevard about Blockbuster's soaring stock price was contagious. "There were two ways Wayne kept us going: by example and the stock was going up like a rocket," remembers Doug Kinney. "We all had options. We used to go down the halls high fiving. It was exciting and exhilarating. We were working seven days a week, 52 weeks a year, but no one cared." Phil deMena recalls a conversation in late 1988 with another Blockbuster executive, Bob Guerin. "I hadn't been there but six months and Bob was talking and his eyes got real big and he said, 'Phil, we're all going to be millionaires.' It was like all of a sudden it came on him and he realized it was going to happen because when we opened new stores up, the volumes went off the scale. We had so many stock options and the buy-ins were so good that you just knew that if you kept your nose to the grindstone and did your job, we were all going to end up as millionaires."

The distinction between bonuses and options programs is that with a bonus, an executive who meets certain targets is awarded a certain amount of money at yearend. With Blockbuster's option program, only one-quarter of the shares granted could be exercised every year, creating a perpetual "golden carrot" for executives. As Huizenga knew well, that helped Blockbuster executives keep up the incredible pace. "That's what keeps people on their toes. That's what keeps them on the airplane at midnight, is the stock going up." For Huizenga, it comes down to a basic human trait, "Greed. Greed. We all have greed. Some days you'd say, 'if I could have $5 million, I'd be the happiest person in the world.' Then when you've got 5, you'd want 10 and there's nothing wrong with that. I mean, if it's the only thing you live for, then there's something wrong with it. But there's nothing wrong with wanting more."

To keep his tired tigers happy, all Huizenga would have to do is remind them of the rewards. "You can come in on a Monday morning and these guys are all tired. They've been working Saturday and they've been working Saturday night, and Sunday they sat home and watched the football games with their briefcase in front of them. And they may feel they've been working hard, but if you want to have fun around lunch time, get them all in and start talking about how much money everybody's made and boy, they get big smiles on their faces real quick."

October Crash

As he was gathering his team to take on the industry, Wayne Huizenga was also doing one of the things he does best: wooing Wall Street. He spoke often with his friend and long-time advisor Chuck Lewis, an investment banker at Merrill Lynch's Chicago office. He and others who had followed Huizenga at Waste Management were watching eagerly what he would do with Blockbuster. Regional analysts were picking up on Blockbuster and Gary Jacobson, an analyst with Kidder Peabody, became the first analyst with a major brokerage house to become a Blockbuster believer. Though there was skepticism at first, Huizenga wowed Jacobson and others with prospects of growth for Blockbuster and consolidation in the video industry.

It helped that Huizenga was a known commodity on Wall Street. Although Waste Management had suffered its share of controversies, it had delivered top notch earnings and stock performance for the Street. "We've never missed a goal," he boasts of the record of his tenure at Waste Management and Blockbuster. "It takes a long time to build credibility and Waste Management built credibility. There were a lot of things people didn't like about Waste Management, but not the stock price that's for sure." Ensuring that analysts understood and liked Blockbuster's "story" was important. A strong stock was crucial to Huizenga's plan. It provided the impetus for the option packages, the acquisition strategy, and the company's growth.

Meanwhile, the company buildout was eating up a lot of cash. At $500,000 a store (later reduced to roughly $360,000), a lot of capital was needed to keep the growth curve on track. Huizenga had already speeded up the second and third infusions that he, Melk, and Flynn had promised to put in with their stock purchases. By August 1987, the three were already in for $18 million. And he had arranged for a $10 million loan from a Miami bank, which initially had wanted Huizenga's personal guarantee, but then relented.

But Huizenga wanted to go to the public market with Blockbuster's story. Through the summer and into fall of 1987, Blockbuster prepared for a stock offering. On September 21, another *Barron's* story appeared, questioning the video store concept and the proliferation of outlets. Huizenga shrugged off the article. He wasn't about to let that deter him. The first "road show"— at which companies planning a stock offering present their case to institutional investors and brokerage houses—was set for November 5.

So confident was Huizenga about the offering, he went on a photographic safari to Africa with Marti as part of a Young Presidents Organization trip, a business world pow-wow attended by heavy hitters in the world of industry and finance. But even in the wilds of Africa, word filtered back about the dream-shattering 508-point stock market crash on October 19, 1987. Several of the participants on the safari left right away, others cut the trip short. Huizenga refused to do either, even after Marti asked about doing so. He knew there was nothing he could do the next day or so that couldn't wait a week. "We should have come home," he reflects years later, but not because of Blockbuster's pending offering. "We could have done some great bottom-fishing about that time."

The market was much too hostile for a company with an unproven track record and scant earnings. Huizenga wasn't about to shave the offering price and sell Blockbuster stock cheap. With Blockbuster stock knocked down to $13.75 a share from $32, there was even talk about taking the company private, which Huizenga ultimately decided not to do. Some advisors, like Chuck Lewis from Merrill Lynch, suggested slowing down the growth. But Huizenga wouldn't hear of it. Speed was Blockbuster's weapon in the industry and he wasn't about to jeopardize that strategy.

Some of a rich man's best assets are his rich friends. During his Waste Management days, Huizenga had made plenty of rich friends in the United States and abroad. Huizenga decided to hit up some of them for a private placement of Blockbuster's stock.

Chicago attorney Peer Pederson put in $2 million. Chuck Lewis invested $250,000 and got five other colleagues at Merrill Lynch to raise a total of $1 million. Huizenga also called his long-time partner, Dean Buntrock, chairman of Waste Management. He called his father, Harry, and his sister, Bonnie. With those phone calls and others, he sold one million shares of Blockbuster stock netting $8.4 million after various expenses.

It was a mixed blessing for Huizenga. He'd clinched the money needed to keep Blockbuster on its expansion plan. But now he had his friends on the hook as well. Family members, friends, even his wife Marti, would note years later that this was a turning point for him. "He felt such a sense of responsibility to the people who invested their money, that friends on his judgment and his word, were investing a great deal of money," says Marti. Indeed, that commitment may have driven Huizenga to build Blockbuster even faster than had the public offering gone through. "Who knows if that hadn't happened," she adds. "I think it still would be what it is today, but maybe not in the same time frame."

That sense of responsibility would deepen as word got around Fort Lauderdale about Huizenga's latest venture. Friends, former teachers, and high school buddies were betting their money on Wayne. One thing was certain: Any doubts he had were vanquished. Says Clinton Allen, the director whose investment company, Advest, had been one of the scheduled underwriters of the tanked offering: "He became a Blockbuster believer. He really committed himself when he took money from family and friends and plunked money down himself. That's when you knew he was in it up to his neck."

BUILDING A BRAND

"Fast" is not fast enough to describe Blockbuster's growth in its initial three years under H. Wayne Huizenga. Every month brought announcements, deals, store openings. At the end of 1986, Blockbuster had 19 stores. The number of company and franchise stores would balloon to 133 by the end of 1987 and 415 stores by the end of 1988 and then 1,079 stores by yearend 1989. Luigi Salvaneschi and his team of district and regional managers oversaw operations and site selection. Soon there was a new store opening every 48 hours, then 24 hours, then 17 hours, along with stores from acquisitions that had to be converted. (Huizenga promoted Salvaneschi to president in June, 1988. Before he'd made that change, he'd stopped by Steve Berrard's house one Sunday to break the news. Though Berrard's title was chief financial officer, Huizenga viewed him as a partner, an ally and a potential successor even then, and didn't want this event to alter that relationship. Berrard says he told Huizenga the decision was fine by him.)

Huizenga kept abreast of operations, but left the details to others, mostly Salvaneschi. He knew he could get people to manage that end of the business. "I firmly believe there's two sides to a house. You've got one side that's running the business. You've got the other side that's doing acquisitions and developing the business," Huizenga says. "If one person tries to do both, it doesn't work. So I spent my time not dealing with the day to day, but dealing with all the stuff that has to be done, whether it's raising money, whether it's dealing with the Street." Huizenga's team was working like it was supposed to, making the company a success story he could take to Wall Street. And a key part of that message, Huizenga knew, would be conveyed through marketing.

Under Gruber's direction began efforts to build the Blockbuster brand. "Blockbuster was an adjective that we were trying to make into a noun," says Gruber. Along the way, he had to educate his boss, who had little marketing experience and at first didn't appreciate the enormity of what Gruber was trying to do. It was an amazing rampup of a brand and a company image, from ground zero to a national awareness within three years. "It was tough," Huizenga says of his education in marketing. "I give all the credit to Gruber. And I suppose it was very frustrating for Gruber in the early days dealing with me, who didn't know anything about it."

With experience in rolling out the McDonald's brand internationally, Gruber drew heavily on his experience with the fast-food giant in creating Blockbuster's image and marketing programs. He quickly developed a radio commercial and a few months later, a television spot. Blockbuster registered trademarks like "America's Family Video Store" and its torn-ticket logo. And Gruber's fixation on the children's market led to the creation of a "Blockbuster Kids Clubhouse" and a cast of characters, including "Player," "Slo-Mo," and "Rewind" to appeal to the vast children's video rental market. Though seemingly a small step in the company's development, that connection with Blockbuster and "family" entertainment would prove important to Huizenga, who would see it as a building block for later endeavors. Gruber's insistence, bordering on obsession, with "family" image became a point of frustration and at times derision for other Block-buster executives. But he found a backer in Huizenga, who never wavered on the "no-X" policy instituted by David Cook, not even when acquiring other chains for which X-rated films constituted as much as 15 percent of revenue. The hit to revenues and profits was often initially even greater given the "sandwich effect" in which patrons would place the porno flick they were renting between two non-X films to conceal it and rent all three. Huizenga was convinced that Blockbuster's stance would win out in the long run.

Garnering press attention was another strategy, and Gruber hit pay dirt in early 1988 with the company's "Youth Restricted Viewing" program, which took the company's "no-X" policy one step further by reviewing and restricting the rental of videos deemed inappropriate to children under age 17. The program garnered widespread press attention, including mention on national networks, and kudos from the White House to movie critics Gene Siskel and Roger Ebert.

But that early victory didn't signal smooth sailing for other suggestions. One of his first battles with Huizenga was over plans for the 1988 annual shareholders meeting. Gruber wanted it to be a splashy affair, an event, like McDonald's, which used it not just as a perfunctory meeting to review company financials and corporate affairs, but also as a marketing forum. "We're in showbiz," Gruber would tell Huizenga. "No, we're not, we're in the service business," Huizenga would answer. He wanted the shareholders meeting to go straight by the book, a business-like, no-nonsense session like those Waste Management held. Waste Management kept its annual meetings as low-key as possible, as they were often opportunities for protests by environmentalists and critics of the company. Besides, what was the sense in spending all this extra effort and money? Gruber argued his point for days, weeks.

Finally, when he saw his argument going nowhere, he opted for another strategy. He contacted Chuck Lewis, Huizenga's friend from Merrill Lynch's Chicago office. "Chuck, you know I've exhausted my ability to get to Wayne on this and maybe you can," Gruber told him.

Lewis promised to call Huizenga, then arranged to have a videotape of the McDonald's annual meeting sent to him. Huizenga called Gruber into his office in early February. "Know that meeting we've been talking about? How about doing it?"

"For next year," Gruber replied, knowing what went into these productions.

"No, for this one," Huizenga told him.

Gruber was stunned. He had just 27 working days to pull this off. Gruber's "staff" of just three finished the television commercial, the jingles, songs, new logo, the Blockbuster Kids uniforms, and got ready for a show, a really big show. Gruber would meet with Huizenga periodically to review major segments of the package. Huizenga liked the songs, giving a tape of them to Marti to play in her car. But he hadn't a clue of what went into that first meeting, Gruber says. "We spoiled Wayne because he just thought this is what marketing people do. They do this stuff and they can get it done overnight."

At Blockbuster's 1988 annual meeting at the Pier 66 hotel—an area landmark Huizenga now part-owned near where he taught water-skiing as a teenager—shareholders and franchisees were treated to a full-blown preview of Blockbuster's marketing clout. From the darkened stage, the screen showed movie stills and a deep booming voice declared, "The stage is set. The time has come. Innovation. It started with innovation." The intro was to a video about the history of the movie industry, from Charlie Chaplin to the "talkies" to modern Hollywood and the VCR. Shareholders got a peek at the yet-to-be released television commercial, "Wow! What a Difference!" and a review of the favorable press generated by the Youth Restricted Viewing program.

The flash and splash had its desired effect: Blockbuster's vast potential had been demonstrated to its shareholders, franchisees, the press, and the analysts who attended the meeting. "We were acting much bigger than we were and we were projecting an image that was far larger than life," Gruber says. "We were operating on a shoestring. We didn't have a marketing budget yet we were pretending we did. We weren't on TV, yet we were acting like we were. I showed a television commercial we hadn't even run by August (1988). We introduced these Blockbuster Kids as if they were going to be the new McDonald's characters and there was no place for them to go. We didn't even have the uniform."

Huizenga basked in the audience's glowing comments after the meeting, and in the favorable press attention and analysts' reaction. But while the 1988 shareholders meeting raised Gruber's esteem in Huizenga's eyes, he still had to check and balance Gruber's big marketing plans against what was still a small company budget. "I give Tom Gruber a lot of credit for standing up to Wayne in those early days," says Don Smiley, who'd moved over from Huizenga's private companies to take a marketing spot under Gruber for two years. Fortunately for Blockbuster, Gruber was confident enough in himself and his job to withstand the relentless Huizenga decision-making process. Gruber understood, as Smiley says, that "just because (Huizenga) asks a million questions and just because there were spirited debates doesn't mean he didn't give you the rope that you needed to do your job. But he wanted to know why."

Huizenga and Gruber waged battles often, over coupons, promotions, use of television, but mostly over budgets. (Blockbuster's marketing budget would grow from $5 million in 1988 to about $100 million in 1992.) With a tone of exasperation that even Gruber now admits bordered on being condescending, he'd explain again and again his marketing programs to Huizenga. "Wayne would listen, where another chief executive would throw you out," Gruber says.

Gruber also began efforts to polish the public image of his boss, to push him into being more of a public persona. Gruber even wanted to submit a pitch to the television show, "Lifestyles of the Rich and Famous," focusing on Huizenga's Florida home on a prized peninsula property on Fort Lauderdale's waterways ("just across from Jackie Onassis' Florida home and Elvis Presley's former 'Blue Hawaii' Florida residence"), his two planes (the G-II with its 24-karat gold ashtrays and fixtures and his backup Lear jet) and his 50th birthday party (for which his wife Marti, bought a 1937 Rolls Royce). But Huizenga resisted those efforts. He wanted the focus to be on the company, not on him. That resistance to being a public persona would erode over the years as Blockbuster's success multiplied and the purchase of sports teams thrust him, uncomfortably at first, into the limelight and bestowed celebrity status, particularly in south Florida.

One of Huizenga's roles, as he saw it, was to tone down and channel Gruber's exuberance. "There's a fine line in marketing and hype," he says. "And I don't want to be known as a company that hypes itself because hype lasts one quarter and if you don't deliver, hype doesn't mean anything after that, right? Marketing the product is something else again but we wanted to be careful that we weren't singing the praises of Blockbuster and then not being able to deliver."

IMPROVING OPERATIONS

Delivering was the worry Huizenga had handed off to Luigi Salvaneschi and his team. With the company growing at a breakneck pace, Salvaneschi found that not only did he have to lay the groundwork for site selection and development, but also for operations. He worked a store in Cincinnati for a few days early in his tenure and was appalled at the few controls and lack of procedures. Improving operations was a message he would carry often in his spiral notebooks to Huizenga during marathon meetings that covered three or four pages worth of jotted notes and just as many hours. Gerry Weber and other Blockbuster executives and even franchisees were often amazed at the level of detailed knowledge Huizenga had about territories, even down to individual stores. He and Marti spent many Sundays visiting stores, and he often dropped into stores while in cities or towns doing deals. (On their way to a birthday party for Marti's younger brother, Huizenga stopped at a Blockbuster store in Fort Lauderdale. Marti's comment was that at least it beat going through alleys and looking behind stores at garbage containers to see which company had the customer.)

But Salvaneschi was privately frustrated that Huizenga wasn't more concerned with operations. And though usually an appearance by "Wayne" had the effect of boosting morale among the troops, at one presentation to store managers in early October 1989, Salvaneschi remembers, it had the opposite effect. Accustomed to addressing the owner-managers at Waste Management with their lucrative stock option packages, Huizenga couldn't relate as easily to the different breed of rank-and-file store managers at Blockbuster. In his speech, Huizenga emphasized Blockbuster's stunning stock market success and scarcely mentioned the backbone of the business, the video stores themselves. "He talked to them about the stock and he stuck to the stock all the time. He made some remarks concerning the work of the managers in the stores like not being so important and he really left some negative feeling." And at the last board of directors meeting Salvaneschi attended before he retired, he warned Huizenga that the company had to be more responsive to customers and not as obsessed with Wall Street. "I think this company is too much development and financially oriented and I think the customers are suffering and you need to put more emphasis on the operating of the stores," he said at the meeting.

On one operations issue, however, Huizenga was adamant. At a meeting December 15, 1988, Salvaneschi proposed installing a standardized pay system which would simply bump up salaries of employees a given percentage each year. Huizenga refused. "I want to know," Huizenga told him. "I want to talk about every single employee."

"Everybody? But that'll take days," Salvaneschi responded.

"It's all right. We'll just sit there and talk about every single employee because if we're going to truly review that employee, just writing something on a piece of paper doesn't really get that through. We owe it to them to do that." Huizenga felt this detailed review was important for two reasons: first, word trickled back to employees that "the boss" and top management reviewed their performance and decided their raises. But more vital, in a growing organization, it gave an opportunity for all top executives to learn the strengths and weaknesses of those coming up the ladder, who could be tapped for special projects, an early promotion, and conversely, who wasn't going to make the cut. That practice stayed until the company's growth and sheer size made it impractical for Huizenga and top management to review every individual employee, but the last round he was involved with in 1991 included all employees who earned $25,000 or more.

For Blockbuster executives, "Wayne-isms" ruled. Two favorites, as quoted by Steve Berrard, could be expected to be heard often, "'you don't delegate responsibility, you only share success,' and 'don't tell me all the good things because the good things always take care of themselves. I want to know about the problems and I don't want to be surprised.'" New executives like Phil deMena learned early on. Huizenga can speak for hours without ever using the personal pronoun "I," and he made it clear that his example was to be followed. When deMena wrote a memo using "I," Huizenga summoned him to his office. "Phil," he said. "This is a 'we' company." (Huizenga often told Don Smiley that "'we' is easy to make from 'me'—you just turn the first letter upside-down.")

He sought input, not necessarily consensus, and retained decision-making authority on most issues for himself and Steve Berrard, particularly in the early years. Some seem petty, but for a small company, which Blockbuster was in 1988, every penny counted. Gruber wanted to fly American flags at Blockbuster stores and sent out a memo detailing the source for flag poles and flags. Huizenga called him into his office and Gruber knew from his tone of voice that something was wrong. "This is a decision for the management team," Huizenga told him. Gruber was puzzled, since he had responsibility for the image of the stores, inside and out. "Wayne was seeing dollars, he didn't see much value in it," he says now. Word quickly spread that "Wayne" had nixed the flag decision and Gruber's memo was ignored. A few weeks later, Huizenga summoned Gruber again. "You know that memo you put out about the flag? Well, Marti and I were out visiting stores and I told her what you said about the American flag and the Blockbuster flag and we went and looked at the McDonald's stores and they all have that (a company flag and an American flag.) Marti thought that was a neat idea, thought it looks great and the more I look at it, I think it looks pretty good too. So why don't you put out a memo and you tell them on the bottom you've discussed this with Wayne and we want to do it." The memo went out, and so did the flags.

The task of building and converting stores, staffing regions, and promoting a brand name was so great in those early days, it was easy to be overwhelmed by the amount of work ahead. "There was a tremendous amount of fear permeating the organization," says Doug Kinney, who was handling franchisee relations and development at the time. "Everyone was scared to death to screw up. We were moving so fast with so few resources that you were scared you were going to screw up and get hammered for it. Everything had to move in exactly the right pattern for everything to work and only two people (Huizenga and Berrard) in the organization knew everything that was going on. You were never sure if what you were doing was working at counter purposes to what was happening at the executive level. It was like walking on eggs and you'd get so far, and realize you can't go any further until you talked to Wayne but because of his schedule, it might be two to three weeks before you could talk to him."

Other executives from that period remark how Huizenga's own confidence imbued them with the same. Shortly after deMena was hired in August 1988, at his first meeting with the chairman, Huizenga laid out the goal of having 400 stores, company and franchise, by year-end. It was eight months into the year, Blockbuster was nowhere near that goal and with deMena's experience in real estate, he could see no way that plan could be achieved. He felt himself getting nervous at the prospect of finding and signing that many sites so quickly. But by the end of his hour session, he walked out feeling sure of the goal.

Indeed, Blockbuster ended the year with 430 stores. DeMena then learned another lesson. Calling him into his office in January 1989, Huizenga praised him for a job well done and gave him a bonus in options. But as deMena got up to leave, Huizenga told him, "One more thing, Phil. I asked for 400. You opened 430. That extra 30 stores cost us $12 million. Please remember that the number we ask for is the number we want." Startled, deMena asked how the extra stores had cost the company $12 million. Huizenga explained that the extra cost was in the capital expense to open the stores. DeMena walked out with his head swimming. He'd accomplished a task he'd deemed near impossible, indeed surpassed it, and had gotten praised, rewarded, and chided all in the same session.

Executives, particularly in the early growth years, had latitude on their responsibilities and authorities—within boundaries. "I had heard that once he hired you to do a job he left you alone and I found that wasn't the case," says Kinney. "The question was making sure you had the correct parameters for your decision making. It was a very flat management curve. The buck stopped with Wayne and he insisted on your being able to defend what you did." Two standard questions that executives could be expected to answer in defending their decisions or presenting a plan were: "Why would I do that? What does that do for me?"

Monday-morning management meetings were spirited affairs with strong personalities like Gruber, Salvaneschi, and other experienced executives making their cases and providing input. "The decision process was very simple," Berrard says. "Either Wayne made the decision or I made the decision and I wouldn't make a decision that Wayne wouldn't make." After hearing from the various executives about problems with opening schedules or other issues, Huizenga would, as Berrard puts it, "play Solomon. You put all these people around a table, not everybody is going to agree on everything, but he always lets it come out and then he'd say 'fine, I hear both sides and you go ahead, you do it this way. If it doesn't work we'll try it your way.'" The one quirk some executives remark about Huizenga's decision-making style is that while seeking input, at times the last person he consulted with would appear to hold sway over the final decision.

Though Huizenga kept a firm hand, executives who could effectively argue their case could get him to come around. "Wayne did everything through suggestion, strong suggestion" deMena says. "If you would argue with him and show him your point and why you wanted to do so and so, he would listen and you could change his mind. But it'd better work." He also expected his executives to get back to him if something he wanted to do didn't work. After an all-day meeting July 11, 1988 in San Diego with Barry Rosenblatt as the company was in the process of converting his recently purchased Video Library outlets to Blockbuster stores, Tom Gruber jotted down these words uttered by Huizenga: "Let's be perfectly clear about this, Barry. If I'm wrong, it's your ass." He said it with a smile, but everyone in the room knew he wasn't joking.

THE INNER CIRCLE

The Blockbuster inner circle changed periodically but included Steve Berrard, Bob Guerin, and later Ron Castell, and from Huizenga Holdings, Rick Rochon and Don Smiley. Gruber, while never considering himself part of the chosen few, nonetheless was invited to enough charity events, private parties, and dinners at Casa Fiore to remain in the boss' favor.

Indeed, the charity circuit in Fort Lauderdale for various causes and diseases and political fund-raisers—usually Republican—always featured a Blockbuster table. Huizenga is a staunch Republican supporter and one of the GOP's largest contributors in Florida. A former Blockbuster exec recalls being awed at attending with other execs a "photo op" session with former vice-president Dan Quayle where Huizenga wrote 12 checks for $1,000 each. Executives were invited to all black-tie events (though the political fund-raisers included disclaimers.) "You were expected to go," says Gruber of the charity and fund-raising events. "You really were and after a while, the inner circle went and the others didn't."

Jockeying for position in the "inner circle" became a favorite past-time of some Blockbuster executives. "Never let it be said that Wayne doesn't have an ego because he does and those on the inner circle play up to his ego a lot," Kinney says. "He takes everything that happens in business very personally. It's a personal thing to get a deal done. He has to have a personal relationship with officers. Everything is hard-nosed business but the inner circle of people is where he does his business." Currying favor with "Wayne" could be done by working more hours—if that were humanly possible—and playing up to his ego. But rarely could it be done by sniping at someone else. A complaint about another executive's performance would often end up with Huizenga calling the named person into his office with the accuser having to face the accused as he'd want to know first-hand what had happened.

Those on the "inner circle" also felt his sting. Huizenga's more forceful arguments are saved for those closest to him, as Guerin, Berrard, and a few others know well. "You've got to be able to stick to your guns. If you really believe, he'll know. You'll know because you're not going to stand there and argue with Wayne Huizenga unless you think you're 100 percent absolutely damn sure," says Bob Guerin, who as the liaison with franchisees had one of the toughest jobs at Blockbuster as he was often the bearer of news Huizenga wouldn't want to hear.

To work for or alongside Wayne Huizenga is to learn the art of effective argument, as Berrard knows well. It's a form of mental battle. "You'll go in there all ready, you've got your arguments down and you make your argument and he'll combat you and then all of a sudden he'll jump on your side of the table and take the opposite view and then he'll agree with you. Then he'll disagree with you. If you really don't believe before you walk in there, do not walk in there because you will never get him to agree with you," says Berrard. "If you're convinced and you believe, he'll let you have your way. But you better be right more than you're wrong. He will debate and debate. If you come in there and have a full head of steam on, he'll disarm you, he'll be nice and calm and relaxed. If you go in there passive, man, he'll jump on you and you'll lose your composure. And all he's doing is seeing if you really believe."

One notable instance—and what Berrard says was one of his biggest disputes with Huizenga—occurred in February 1988 and resulted in a formative experience for Blockbuster's development. The computer systems that David Cook had installed were already straining under the company's growth; they were written in a computer language that was not common in the business world. Berrard hired Arthur Andersen as consultants to come up with a better inventory and management information system. The price tag of $16 million for the system was steep, especially for a small company that at the end of 1987 had just $43 million in revenue.

Huizenga was livid. "You've got to be out of your mind. It's almost half of what we did in revenue!" he told Berrard.

To Berrard, getting a better handle on the company's inventory of tapes was crucial for its continued growth. "Wayne," he argued. "These are $50 bills sitting on the shelves. When they get a set of legs and run off, that's the end of it for us. We'll never know where they go. We have plans to open three or four stores every week. How in the hell are we ever going to know?"

But to Huizenga, who was hell-bent on opening stores, spending that chunk of change on information systems was a waste. "For all the money you're spending on systems, we could build 40 stores!" he retorted. His anger building, he slipped into sarcasm. "Now you want to tell me that I'm supposed to give up 40 stores for goddamn computers? Listen, I'll tell you what. I'll solve all the problems for you. We'll just start paying the employees out of the cash register. We'll have all the stuff delivered to the store. We'll just pay right out of the cash register and we won't need all this shit."

Chagrined at the exchange in front of other executives, Berrard nonetheless stood his ground. "Wayne, we can't . . ."

"Hey, listen, Steve. When these little mom and pops that we compete with come to work every morning, that's how they do it."

"Yeah, but we've got 4,000 of these some day. We can't do that."

"Well, then fine. You give me a better solution than tell me I've got to sacrifice building 40 stores for some goddamn systems for you damn accountants."

Berrard was embarrassed. But he knew his boss. And he also knew his argument was solid. Blockbuster would simply not be able to handle the growth without adequate systems. He brought this up to Huizenga again and again over the course of a few weeks. Berrard argued that Blockbuster would need the systems to handle the growth. And he brought up the spectre of how an inventory problem sometime in the future would look to Wall Street. That inventory argument didn't wash with Huizenga, who countered with characteristically simple, but devastating, logic.

"I don't need damn systems to tell me we have too many tapes in the store. Just go in there on a Saturday night. If the damn things aren't rented then obviously you have too many of them," Huizenga told him. Berrard admits even now, it was a good argument. And indeed, for a while, Blockbuster had its managers count tapes on Saturday night and report on Monday morning. But Berrard wasn't budging. He put the argument to Huizenga several times, got input from franchisees who were also complaining about the computer system, and brought pressure from various camps to help make his case.

"He'll argue nine ways to Sunday and some people can't handle the debate," Berrard says. "I can't think but of a handful of times when he's said, 'no, do it my way.'" Since then, Blockbuster has spent heavily in information systems, approaching $20 million some years. As Berrard knew, the systems were vital to track information and help absorb the company's growth and acquisitions. (So good were the MIS systems—along with cheaper labor costs—that seven years later Viacom would decide to shift some administrative functions, like payroll, from New York to Fort Lauderdale after the merger.)

His management mode—summed up in one of his favorite expressions, "don't tell me about the good things, tell me about the problems and I don't want any surprises"—sounds harsh but in a fast-growth environment, he says, is absolutely necessary. "We don't have to spend a lot of time talking about the good things, because you're working so fast the good things always take care of themselves. You have to focus on the bad things. It's tough for your people because they're out there busting their butts, traveling in the middle of the night, making things happen and they come home and as soon as they walk in the door you start talking about some of the bad things. You've got to be careful with that, but yet you don't want to sit there and spend three hours with the guy telling him how wonderful he is and you don't take care of the problems either."

To survive Huizenga's decision-making process, those trained in debate had an edge, but not much of one. "I loved the debate because Wayne was really good, he really made you think," says Tom Carton, who came in as general counsel in October 1988. "It was almost a law school exercise, the Socratic method. He really challenged you to justify what you did. You'd be in and out of Wayne's office three or four times and it wasn't an unusual occurrence to be in a 15-minute debate over a course of action and come out and think to yourself, 'why didn't I think of that?'"

Yet conversely, Huizenga knew when not to argue a point, when shooting down an idea might crush enthusiasm or damage relations. For Huizenga, notes Ron Castell, the common phrase "let me think about it" isn't a platitude. "He actually thinks about it. Usually you blow people off. Wayne will call you up or come to you and say, 'you know that thing we talked about on Friday? I've been thinking about it.' And he could either say, let's try it, or let me tell you what the problem is. It's never like, it's a terrible idea."

Tom Gruber learned that Huizenga lesson early on. Over dinner at an Italian restaurant in Tampa in late 1987, Huizenga and Gruber listened as franchisee Ray Schneider explained to them and one of his partners an idea to have "movie consultants" help customers pick out films in a program he'd dubbed "Professor Video." Gruber picked apart the idea, explaining in great detail why it wouldn't work. Huizenga grew more and more uncomfortable. Though never directly contradicting Gruber, "he made it pleasantly clear that he was upset with the forcefulness with which Tom was attacking my idea," Schneider remembers. The dinner ended amicably, though Schneider, a bit coolly, told Gruber he was going to pursue the idea anyway. Gruber and Huizenga returned to the hotel after midnight and

Huizenga invited him to his room for a drink. Gruber was surprised, since Huizenga rarely drinks, and readily agreed.

"You know, that was a nice dinner and Ray's a good guy, he's going to be a good franchisee and you know who was with him, don't you?" Huizenga asked. "That was his partner. That's the guy, you know, the kind of money man. What you did tonight and what we did tonight, we absolutely won the battle down there, but you know what? We lost the war."

Gruber was puzzled. He'd thought he'd saved Schneider and the company from making a costly error. "What do you mean Wayne?"

"Ray was very proud and very excited about this concept and it seemed like a good concept and he was talking to us as well as his partner, whom he doesn't work for but is essentially his backer. And he laid out an interesting plan and you shot him down like a fighter pilot and you won that battle, no question. But you lost the war," Huizenga repeated.

"I understand and that's a very good and poignant lesson, Wayne, and say no more." They finished their drinks. Gruber went back to his room and Huizenga never brought it up to him again. Huizenga called Schneider the next day and offered him $100,000 to undertake the Professor Video plan. (Gruber was ultimately proven right, as the program, while popular with customers and still a favorite idea of Schneider's, couldn't demonstrate any appreciable increase in revenue. But Huizenga, says Schneider, saw the money as the price of knowledge. "I wasn't being paid for being there. I passed my idea along. I was just a franchisee and he was trying to be respectful of that.")

As Huizenga's team coalesced into a working machine at Blockbuster, the pace never let up. The newly hired were quickly initiated as Phil deMena found. Staying at the Riverside Hotel, four blocks from Blockbuster's offices, he arrived his first day at 8:30 A.M. and was chagrined to find most executives already there. He arrived a half-hour earlier each day over the next several days, determined to beat Huizenga into the office, realizing that "the boss" usually appeared between 6:30 and 7 A.M. Huizenga led the grueling pace by example, and his car was usually the last to leave, often not before 9:30 P.M. That example meant a lot to the other execs. "He didn't set any goals for me to accomplish that he didn't set for himself," deMena says. "He wasn't playing golf while I was working seven days a week. He was right there with me."

The mandate was to fly at night to get the most out of every day. It was an edict more than one executive wife resented. Meetings were often held aboard the Lear or, later, the G-II, and Saturdays and many Sundays were spent in more meetings and catch up. Doug Kinney remembers arriving at 7:30 A.M. one Saturday in the spring of 1988 for a meeting with Huizenga to review memos about franchise deals. Huizenga asked if Kinney could wait, and Kinney had plenty of work to do while he waited. But the meeting kept getting pushed back as Huizenga met with other officers to resolve other issues. "He finally got to me at 10 P.M. that Saturday night and we reviewed the memos for two hours until midnight." Huizenga says he never demanded that his executives work those long hours, and Kinney and others concur. "He never asked me to stay. It wasn't that someone said you have to do this. You were afraid you'd stand out as someone who wasn't giving 210 percent. I felt it was part of my job to be available 24 hours a day, 7 days a week, and to do what needed to be done no matter what it took or sacrifices were made. It was contagious." The incentive was more, much more than monetary. "There was an implied pot of gold and the idea was that if I hang in there, some of what this man is will rub off on me and I will be able to be successful like him."

Nearly every Blockbuster executive has a tale about trying to outwork Huizenga. It became a competition, sometimes bordering on obsession. Carton remembers one time waiting to meet with Huizenga near midnight one night, then leaving as he was still in the office. "I thought to myself, 'I'm going to beat that SOB in' and I pulled in at 5:45 A.M. the next morning and Wayne got out of his car and said to me, 'got here a little late this morning, huh?'" The pace sometimes resulted in some unusual scenes. Florida's frequent summer lightening storms would occasionally kill the phone system at the Las Olas building. That would instigate a mad scramble as Blockbuster executives raced to their cars in the parking lot where they continued working, talking on their car or cellular phones as the rain pounded.

But the relentless pace had a price. Death, divorce and burnout were the byproducts of Blockbuster's blistering growth and Huizenga's driving work ethic. Executives who weren't making the cut would find their "box" of decision-making authority shrinking until they got disgusted and left. In late summer 1988, the pace had already claimed one casualty. Bill Dietrich, whom Gruber had hired from McDonald's, was wearing three titles, director of advertising, promotion, and field marketing, and handling the equivalent of three jobs, which many Blockbuster executives were doing. But the 15-hour days proved too much of a strain, and Dietrich suffered a heart attack August 21, on his first day of a vacation, and died at age 51.

Marriages suffered. Steve and Denise Berrard divorced in September 1990 after 11 years of marriage. Doug Kinney was separated from his wife, who stayed in North Carolina during the early Blockbuster years. "I would go for weeks and not have time to talk to her," he says. He and his wife reconciled after he left Blockbuster and they now live on a horse farm in

North Carolina. "It was tough. I can honestly say that I burned out. By 1991, my brain was fried and there wasn't that much to do anymore. They consolidated my area and I didn't have my job." But Kinney bears no grudges. "I would have worked for Wayne for free. He's an extraordinary person. Just having worked for him gave me a graduate level course in entrepreneurship and how to grow a company."

Over the years there would be a tremendous turnover of area and regional managers, personnel directors, and others who didn't fit in or couldn't keep pace. "One of Wayne's strengths is that he will go find the best possible people that are needed for the business at a point in time and when the need for them is over, those people usually move on by his choice or their choice," says Taylor Devine, a regional vice-president who left in 1991 after a stint in England. When it was time to let someone go, Huizenga would have someone else carry out the task, usually Berrard, Guerin, or in the earlier days, Salvaneschi. Dodging the dirty work of firing someone, Salvaneschi says, wasn't because "he just doesn't like it. I think he's sensitive." That oft-cited ability of Huizenga's to read people, which so many cite as one of his strengths in deal-making, cuts both ways.

Though Huizenga found ways to relieve the pressure on his executives through parties, perks, and extras, he made no apologies for what he was demanding of them. He was asking no more than what he demanded of himself. Even close friends and family members noticed the change. "Wayne lost his smile during early Blockbuster," says his cousin, B.J. Buntrock. "He'd meet for breakfast and ten minutes into the conversation, he'd already be somewhere else." Huizenga would often tell his executives: "Someday we'll have time to have some fun. Right now, this *is* our fun."

7

Deal du Jour: Blockbuster Swallows Up the Competition

Wayne Huizenga was having fun doing what he loves doing most: deals. The deal-making had started in 1987 soon after Huizenga & Co. had taken control of Blockbuster. Clinton Allen quickly realized what being an outside director for a company run by Huizenga meant. In June 1987, his family rented a house in Ponte Vedra, Florida, for a week of vacation. He spent most of the time on the phone with Huizenga, being briefed on Blockbuster's affairs and deals. "My wife to this day calls it the vacation from hell," Allen says. "He was doing so many deals and I was the outside director so I had to approve them." It soon became obvious to Allen that this was not your average board of directors. "It was an active board and that's why Wayne had to keep it small. Wayne couldn't survive in a 15 or 20 board member situation. I would fly to Vegas, fly out to San Diego and so he had outside director the whole way." In addition to the Movies-To-Go transaction and the Video Library deal (which didn't actually close until March 1988), Huizenga was buying back a few franchises and laying the groundwork for later deals.

But the deal-making hit full stride in 1988. In his seven years as Blockbuster's chairman, there would be 110 different deals—from buying video chains to music stores to Hollywood studios. As always, Huizenga would work a deal over and over in his head, looking at all the possibilities, prospects, promises, and problems. But because there were so many deals underway that were so critical to the company's growth at this point, his normal fixation became obsessive. The intensity was so great during this period that Marti recalls laying in bed one night "and I could feel him thinking. And I asked him, 'What deal are you working on right now?' And he said, 'How did you know what I was doing?' And I said, 'I can almost see the rows of figures on the ceiling.'"

Often Huizenga had so many deals percolating simultaneously in various stages that his own executives couldn't keep up. As the director of franchise development, Doug Kinney had one of the most frustrating jobs at Blockbuster. "Every time I'd get a deal worked out, there'd be another deal on the table that would kill that deal," he remembers. Huizenga insisted that Kinney review all transactions with him. The remaining non-franchised territory was a valuable asset of Blockbuster's, and because he had so many deals going at once, Huizenga needed to make sure that something Kinney was doing wouldn't conflict with one he had already made or was working. Kinney was reminded of that edict when he did a three-store deal without Huizenga's approval in early 1988. "You did not need a telephone to hear him from Fort Lauderdale to Dallas," Kinney says. Upon arriving at Blockbuster's executive offices for his dreaded meeting on a Saturday morning, he saw a haggard Steve Berrard leaving Huizenga's office. Anxious to know how much trouble he was in, he asked Berrard how angry Huizenga was. Berrard told him: "'I've been in the barrel for two days. Now it's your turn.'" Says Kinney of his meeting with Huizenga: "He reminded me what the deal was on approving deals. That was where I had pushed his authority. There wasn't one thing that I might do that would not have had an effect on something else. I didn't know better and I couldn't be made privy (to what was going on) because of confidentiality rules."

Huizenga's "Good Guy-Bad Guy" Negotiating Style

Huizenga and Berrard were moving so fast, they nearly lived off adrenaline alone. Just as he had teamed with Melk in the early Waste Management days, now Huizenga teamed with Berrard in building Blockbuster. Huizenga would make the deal, laying out the parameters, and Berrard would wrap up the details. He perfected the "good guy-bad guy" approach with Berrard or the lawyers taking the heat in ironing out details. All the lessons Berrard had learned under Huizenga's tutelage were reinforced full force in these early Blockbuster years. "Any deal we've done probably fits the same pattern," he says. "Tough on price, strong legal agreement, lot of due diligence, but done very quickly. You start on Monday morning and work 18 hours a day, 7 days a week until it's done. He always had this theory that nothing gets better with time." Huizenga held fast to two rules: Don't lose a deal because you're not paying attention to it, and never talk about it until it's done and in writing.

Within Blockbuster, nearly all executives comment about how Huizenga believes in doing a "fair deal," repeating the phrase like an internal mantra. "He has a keen understanding of where peoples' level of tolerance is. Where they will cry uncle and at what point they'll get their backs up and how to approach it to end up having them feel good about the transaction," says Gerry Weber. "It's kind of like romancing someone. It wasn't insincere or calculated to 'now let's just get him and bomp, we'll nail him.' It was 'hey, let's let these people go out with some measure of dignity.' They could walk with their heads held high, winners. And, as it turns out, most of them ended up being winners because they took Blockbuster stock and they made more money on Blockbuster stock than they ever made running their businesses."

Huizenga's reputation as a tough negotiator helped in building Blockbuster. "People say we drive a hard bargain, I don't know if that's true or not," Huizenga says. "To me, the deal doesn't work if one person has to walk away unhappy because you're going to come across that person's path again. I've never approached it that we have to squeeze the last and get the last drip of water or whatever. I've never approached it that way. Maybe I do subconsciously, but my way of talking to our people here would not be to squeeze them to get the last."

Drawing on the style he'd perfected in buying hundreds of garbage companies and later, service companies, Huizenga was no match for entrepreneurs in the video rental industry. Just as in his Waste Management days, he believed in the value of Blockbuster paper. He would offer a price he thought was justified and that price was so right in his own mind, given Blockbuster's rising stock price and increasing competitive threat to whomever he was buying, he wouldn't budge. "We don't move much. We're not the kind that asks for 5 knowing when you want 10 and that we're going to settle on 7½," says Berrard. "We put the best price on the table. We'll always move a little bit. But, I betcha we've never moved more than 10 percent off the price. I've cut it more than I've increased it."

While Berrard by now was used to Huizenga's deal-making style, other Blockbuster executives were getting a ring-side seat in the art of the deal. He rarely would start out talking about the issue at hand, instead drawing on recent news events or tell a joke or a quip, often self-deprecating, to put the other side at ease. Huizenga relied on logic and reason in presenting an argument on why a prospect should sell at his price. "But if logic wasn't working, he wasn't afraid to put the strong arm of economic incentive in same paragraph," recalls Tom Carton, who served as general counsel until he became a Blockbuster franchisee. His biggest negotiating strategy was to convince the other side to do what he wanted for their own good. "Sometimes that was logical and calm and non-threatening and sometimes it wasn't, it was more of a power play." Huizenga would always start with the supposition that his prospect was a reasonable business person who could see the benefits of what he was offering. But if they didn't, he'd tell them the consequences with Blockbuster developing more territory and opening more stores and becoming more of a threat. Says Carton, "Wayne was famous for 'do the deal now for $100, do it tomorrow for $90.' He was very good at that."

Survival of the Fittest: An Acquisitions Case Study

Erol Onoran learned that lesson the hard way. A Turkish immigrant, he opened a television repair shop in 1963 in Washington, DC. By 1980, he had 7 stores in the area servicing and selling televisions and VCRs. He started renting movies in 1980 and did so well he became one of the pioneers in the video rental business. He was innovative, using computers and bar codes and membership cards in his 3,500 square foot stores. Erol's was already a giant by industry standards when Huizenga bought into Blockbuster.

Huizenga paid a visit to Erol Onoran early on in his research foray into the industry. He proposed doing a deal then, but Onoran instantly refused. "They grew and beat me up," Onoran says. "Blockbuster's locations were always better than mine and twice as big as mine. I never take my time and find the right location." He made the mistake of continuing to charge membership fees, while Blockbuster didn't, and was forced to drop that fee. Huizenga hired away his top marketing guy, Ron Castell. As Blockbuster continued to open more company and franchise stores around him, Onoran refused to go public or to sell, especially to Blockbuster. Meanwhile, the debt that Onoran had taken on to build Erol's was taking a toll. As the situation got more desperate, there were few options left for Onoran. At a meeting in Philadelphia at the Four Seasons hotel in late 1990, Berrard remembers Onoran telling him and Huizenga, "I hate you guys. If I could sell to anybody else, I'd sell to anybody else. But right now you're the only one, but there are others that are interested."

Berrard flew back up shortly after to see Onoran again. He was anxious about who the "others" might be and worried that West Coast Video, another competitor, might take the deal. "I was sitting around the hotel and I thought, what would Wayne do. Wayne is going to want this deal done, so I got in my car and it was winter time and it was cold. I took a blanket and I slept in my car. I slept outside of Erol's house in my car because I knew Erol was going to go and sell to somebody else because he hated Wayne and I with a passion." At 8 A.M., he knocked on Onoran's door. "I sat at Erol's house all morning and I worked him over all day long."

But the deal that was finally struck in December for $40 million was held up as regulators scrutinized it for possible anti-trust problems. By the time it was given the okay, three months had passed and Erol's was losing $1 million a month. Berrard told Onoran that Blockbuster was no longer interested. "When I made the agreement to sell the business in November, they brought their people in. They knew everything that was going on and they knew I was losing $1 million a month. They knew how desperate I was." Whereas before, Berrard was calling him four times a day, now he wouldn't return Onoran's calls. Finally, in a room full of bankers and lawyers, Berrard renegotiated the deal. "That's probably one of the toughest things I ever worked on in my life," Berrard says. "I made a lot of phone calls to Wayne because having 30 bankers in a room and all their lawyers telling you we're taking you to court, because you're cutting the price. And I closed the deal. It was tough." The renegotiated deal for 200 stores closed in April 1991 for $30 million in a combination of cash, stock, and debt assumption.

"I got half of what I was supposed to get and the banks got $15 million, each bank got $5 million less," Onoran says. "They're very tough negotiators they'll screw you as much as they can." But to Huizenga and Berrard, it wasn't their problem regulators held up the closing, the only other probable choice was bankruptcy and their obligation to shareholders was to get the best deal. Onoran won't comment on whether he's bitter, but blames his pride more than Huizenga. Would he do business with Huizenga again? "Of course," he says. "If I had sold to them two years before, I would have $60 million more."

The acquisition of Erol's was the key example of the industry Darwinism that Huizenga and Blockbuster brought to bear in the video rental business. Resentment among the small entrepreneurs about Blockbuster and Huizenga grew palpable as Blockbuster continued to buy competitors and roll out new stores. "It was this great corporate chain and ruined what had been a party for a lot of entrepreneurs," says Frank Molstad, editor of *Video Store Magazine.* He cites figures that show a decline of specialty retailers in video rental from 30,000 units in 1989 to 26,000 in early 1995.

The animosity was so great that the Video Software Dealers Association did, and still does, get grief about Blockbuster representatives being on its board of directors even though Blockbuster was invited to join in 1991. Even with all of its growth and acquisitions, Blockbuster would never constitute more than 20 percent of the video rental market, though, of course, it dominated many local markets. "They do such a good job of marketing that it increases rentals in town when they come in," says Tom Adams, a long-time industry analyst. "In every instance, they have grown the market. They advertise more and whip up enthusiasm. It's small consolation to the guy who got squeezed out who was across street, but anyone

Reprinted with permission, *Tribune Media Services.*

who had more than one than location and was nimble enough to react survived and thrived."

Indeed, Blockbuster and Huizenga conferred to the video rental industry a legitimacy and patina of success that, in many cases, benefited some of its competitors. "It's hard to deny, however resentful you might be of Blockbuster, they've really done a lot to improve the perception of the video industry on Mainstreet and Wall Street," says Rick Karpel, a media attorney in Los Angeles and former executive director of the VSDA. That made it easier for smaller chains to get financing and tap the capital markets. The resentment "has subsided as weaker operators dropped out of business and now stronger competitors look at Blockbuster and Huizenga with more respect." Indeed, after Huizenga announced his plans in September 1994 to leave Blockbuster, Ron Alsheimer, who, though he had rebuffed various overtures by Huizenga to buy his 18-store Video Factory chain in upstate New York, remained friendly with him, took out a full-page ad October 3, 1994 in a trade journal called *Video Store*. "Speaking for the more 'open-minded' of video store owners, you have been quite an inspiration," the "Open Letter to Wayne Huizenga" read. "You've not only been one hell of a competitor, but you've been one hell of a teacher. You have challenged those of us who have had to compete with your company to become better operators. You've brought our industry the respect and professionalism it needed."

CABLE PARTNERS: HUIZENGA MEETS JOHN MALONE

To keep up with Blockbuster's growth, Huizenga was constantly scouting for more money. Blockbuster could buy other companies for stock, but it still needed cash—plus additional credibility on Wall Street. And Huizenga knew how he could get both. Already, skeptics were taking shots at the longevity of video rental because of the threat of pay-per-view services that cable companies were starting to offer. So who better to get to invest in Blockbuster than cable companies? The two deals Huizenga would strike with cable companies, with United Cable in April 1988 and Cox Cable in September 1989, would both end up being unwound within 18 months of being struck, but Huizenga got what he wanted out of both at critical junctures in Blockbuster's growth: cash and credibility.

Gene Schneider had started in the cable television business in the 1950s with his brother, Richard, in Casper, Wyoming, introduced to the business by one of its founders and a family friend. By the late 1980s, he had built United Cable Television into the seventh-largest cable company in the United States and his son, Mark, was looking into video rental as a potentially complementary business. Blockbuster's sales volume and its image, along with H. Wayne Huizenga, impressed him. "I could tell he was going to make it a smash hit, the McDonald's of the video industry, and we wanted to be part of it," Mark Schneider recalls. He also remembers Huizenga mentioning that he wasn't sure if he'd ever watched an entire movie. "That enamored me because he wasn't in it to play around with movies, he was in it to dominate and saturate the marketplace."

Talks started in late winter with meetings in Dallas, Fort Lauderdale, and Denver. Finally, in late March, on their way back from a meeting in San Diego, Huizenga and Berrard stopped in Denver, ready to strike a deal. And what a deal. After weeks of negotiation, United Cable was set to invest up to $100 million, up to 40 percent of the company. The first chunk, $40 million, was to be invested immediately and the rest was to come in stages. For Huizenga, who'd been looking for a big infusion of capital after the October crash, this was the answer to that worry.

There was one hitch, however. Before the Schneiders could ink the deal, they had to have the blessing of John C. Malone, president and chief executive officer of Tele-Communications Inc. In 1972, Malone had joined TCI chairman and founder Bob Magness and helped the cable television pioneer build the company into an industry powerhouse, becoming the largest cable television company in the world in 1982. At this point, TCI owned a majority interest in United Artists and after a long courtship, United Cable was merging with United Artists in a complex and multi-stage process. That meant that TCI owned about 18 percent of United Cable, and the Schneiders had to get his approval to make any "material" investments—and a potential $100 million deal was material.

Huizenga and Berrard cooled their heels in a conference room, while Mark Schneider went to see Malone. What was to be a 15-minute, perfunctory meeting between Schneider and Malone dragged on for more than an hour. As the time ticked by, Huizenga grew more worried. He had reason to be.

At nearly 7 P.M., when Huizenga and Berrard walked into Gene Schneider's office, where Mark and another executive, Bill Elsnor, were waiting, his fears were confirmed. Mark looked furious. "Listen guys," Gene told Huizenga and Berrard. "I'm really sorry but we can't do this deal." Another TCI executive, John Sie, had counseled Malone against it, poking holes in the concept of video rental. He had argued that if the Schneiders wanted to get into video rental, they could invest in a chain in Salt Lake City that a TCI subsidiary was establishing as a test of cross-promotion. Mark Schneider countered that Blockbuster was already fully committed to the business and the concepts weren't comparable, but no dice. TCI wouldn't give its approval. (Sie doesn't recall being the determining factor in the Schneiders not doing the initial deal. He adds that he was wrong on his analysis of Blockbuster's cash flow, which he thought was mostly from opening new stores and capitalization of startup costs. Sie had never been a believer in video rental, giving a speech in 1984 at an industry conference about how pay-per-view would soon replace the business. "I was wrong on that," he says now.)

As they sat in Gene Schneider's office, nursing the hurt with a couple of scotches, Huizenga was stunned . . . and angry. But he knew that the Schneiders felt bad. It didn't make any sense to beat them up about the situation. He, and Berrard from his cue, were conciliatory and simply commiserated with them about the circumstances and what a great deal it would have been and how good a partnership they would have made.

The deal dead, Huizenga and Berrard trudged back to their hotel in the midst of a snowstorm, dodging ten-inch snow drifts and shivering in their Florida suits because they hadn't planned on stopping in Denver and hadn't brought their overcoats. "What the hell are we going to do?" Berrard asked.

"Don't worry," Huizenga told him. "We'll get the money. I'll put the money in myself if I have to."

His teeth chattering, Berrard thought his boss was crazy and told him so. The storm kept the plane and the perpetual deal-making duo grounded for the night. The two ate dinner at the hotel. When Huizenga returned to his room, his message light was blinking. It was Mark Schneider. They wanted to do the deal anyway, and they'd get TCI to sign off. Huizenga and Berrard met with them the following morning and worked out a deal, smaller than had been originally proposed. United would buy $12 million in stock and the rights to develop up to 100 stores. As Huizenga recalls, it was that morning that he first met John Malone. The cable titan listened to how they wanted to restructure the deal, and Malone gave the nod. It wasn't the last time that his path and Huizenga's would cross.

Blockbuster's stock was so hot, the Schneiders did a second deal, just five months later, in which it bought warrants from Don Flynn and John Melk. Huizenga had wanted to get the warrants off the books, since Blockbuster's stock was moving so fast that every time the stock price got past the warrant price, the warrants had to be included in earnings-per-share calculations. That was holding down the EPS figure and the price of Blockbuster's stock. Here again, Huizenga's contacts from his Waste Management days proved valuable. He called a friend and former competitor, Mike DeGroote. DeGroote told Huizenga to put him in for as much as Huizenga was putting in. This time, the Schneiders were on the same side of the table with Huizenga. Mark Schneider remembers these negotiations being not as pleasant as the first deal. "It was a pretty hardball thing," he says. "These guys can play pretty rough. I don't mean that negatively. There's no quarter asked or given when negotiating. They take business very seriously. They'll tell you what you asked and no more. You're dealing with someone honest and fair but tough." The warrants transaction infused Blockbuster with another $21.5 million, but years later, Huizenga still marvels at how his friends Melk and Flynn made out on their end of the deal. "They each walked away with $25 million bucks in cash. And they still had all their shares that they bought yet."

For Huizenga, the partnership with United Cable hadn't yielded as much as he'd initially hoped, but it helped. "He wanted an infusion of cash and the credibility of a New York Stock Exchange Company and a cable company was a good tie in," Mark Schneider says. Indeed, United's involvement was an important imprimatur for Blockbuster on Wall Street.

Later, Mark Schneider would have occasion to remind Huizenga of the credibility that United had provided at that critical point in Blockbuster's development. In 1989, when TCI bought the rest of United Cable, the Schneiders exercised an option to purchase United's Scandinavian and Israeli operations, from which they formed a new company, United International Holdings. The Schneiders also wanted to keep the development rights to Blockbuster stores and use that as a base to build their new company. But they needed Huizenga's consent.

For his part, Huizenga saw an opportunity to capture back territory and cash flow. And by playing hardball, he knew, the Schneiders wouldn't press him for other points they wanted, like the rights to develop Blockbuster stores internationally. Over dinner at the Regency Hotel in New York, as Mark Schneider recalls, they made their pitch. But Huizenga wouldn't budge. Irritated, Mark Schneider told him, "You're being a real jerk. When you started out, we were there and you're not being fair." He got up from the table in the middle of dinner and walked into the hotel bar. A few minutes later, his father, Gene, joined him, leaving Huizenga alone at the dinner table. Over drinks, they groused about how unfair and how much of a jerk Huizenga was being. After ten minutes, Huizenga walked into the bar and told them, "All right, goddamnit, I was wrong. I'll sign the consent." Then the three started talking about football.

"He was tougher than a bear and on principle, you don't give away anything in his philosophy," Mark Schneider says. "He doesn't give on a business point. We did not have a clear right (to the consent) in my opinion and he was thinking I'd love to have them back, why give them to the new group. We could have made a compelling argument in court but it would have been very messy. He could have made it very, very difficult for us given our history and he conceded. He had to suddenly feel he was doing the wrong thing so I appealed to his sense of fairness and I knew it was in there somewhere. He didn't apologize, but he did sign the consent."

The other cable partner, a division of Cox Enterprises Inc., would put up $15 million in September 1989 and sign a letter of intent to franchise up to 100 stores. The deal would again give Blockbuster a shot of credibility at a critical time, helping the company recover after a blistering blast of criticism for accounting practices. At this point, Huizenga had gotten a vote of confidence from two of the nation's major cable companies, negating, at least for the short-term, the supposed threat posed to Blockbuster by these entertainment rivals and their pay-per-view potential.

FOWS AND ROWS AND MORE OLD PALS

It didn't take long after Huizenga got involved with Blockbuster for the FOWs and ROWs to come calling. The acronym was a handy code for Blockbuster insiders to denote "Friend of Wayne" or "Relative of Wayne" status. Some—like Hal Gershowitz and Fred Weinert—were friends and associates from his Waste Management days, eager to get in on another Huizenga deal. George Johnson, who had sold his garbage company to Waste Management in 1976 and become friends with Dean Buntrock, heard about Blockbuster, flew to Dallas and had a similar conversion to

Huizenga's. He, Buntrock, and another friend formed a partnership and in the next six years became Blockbuster's largest franchisee.

Other FOWs were contacts from the political spectrum, like former Florida Republican Party chairman Van Poole and his wife, Donna, who have the franchise rights to the state capital, Tallahasee. Huizenga offered the franchise to part of Washington, DC to Marvin Bush, son of former President George Bush. At first, Huizenga was cautious about franchising to family as Wall Street was skeptical of franchise firms that conferred too much territory to relatives. But as Blockbuster became more successful, that concern eroded and his son, Wayne Jr., as well as some in-laws and cousins, became franchisees. Although Huizenga would rarely say to a Blockbuster executive that someone was a friend, word spread quickly. A FOW or ROW might get phone calls returned more quickly—and some executives marked their files—but insiders contend that was all the special treatment granted. Part of Tom Carton's job as general counsel, he says, "was forever checking with Wayne about making sure beyond a shadow of a doubt our arrangements were no more favorable than with anyone else."

"Everyone was a FOW," says Steve Quamme, an attorney and partner with Marvin Bush in the Washington, DC stores. "There was great demand to be a Blockbuster franchisee. Wayne has done business with a lot of people over the years and a lot of people got in because of a previous relationship with Wayne." Quamme and other FOWs and ROWs insist that the only favor bestowed was getting the territory. "After that, it was a standard franchise arrangement." (But for some, Blockbuster provided financing, extending a $2 million credit line, for instance, to Bush's group until other financing could be arranged.)

Indeed, because of the pressure to open stores quickly, even FOWs had to carry out the development schedule. "Wayne doesn't give anything away," says Luigi Salvaneschi. Nor did being a FOW exempt someone from Huizenga's anger if he thought they were taking advantage of their position. While Huizenga was on a trip to Egypt with the Young Presidents Organization in the fall of 1988, Salvaneschi was approached by George Johnson to grant him more territory in the Southeast as his stores in South Carolina had been so successful. When Huizenga returned, he was furious and summoned Johnson to a meeting.

"You took Luigi to the cleaners," Huizenga told Johnson, storming around his office. "You got him to give you all this territory and you don't even have a damn development schedule yet! Do you think you can get away with that?"

"Wayne, give me the development schedule you want," Johnson told him, trying to calm the situation. "I'll sign." (As Johnson's company into the company's largest franchisee, they'd spar over other issues, like the amount of tape inventory purchased, which Huizenga complained wasn't enough.) Sometimes Huizenga had so many deals with FOWs going that Salvaneschi and others were left in the position of finding out—sometimes by accident—that a deal had been struck. In 1989, Huizenga struck an agreement with a friend to install Blockbuster outlets on military bases. Salvaneschi, who had experience dealing with the military, intervened and renegotiated the deal. That Huizenga had made the arrangement without consulting him didn't perturb Salvaneschi. "That's Wayne, that's part of the man. You can't control that. You don't want to. He ultimately lives for negotiations." Huizenga got plenty of opportunities to negotiate in the deal to buy Major Video.

MAJOR MOVE: WAYNE'S "KILLER INSTINCT"

Of all the acquisitions of video store chains Huizenga made in building Blockbuster, the most difficult was the Major Video deal. The courting had begun the night he'd signed the deal to invest in Blockbuster, when he and Melk boarded the plane to Las Vegas to meet with Hank Cartwright and Gary Moore, the founders of Major Video. Major Video had pioneered the "superstore" concept with its first store in Las Vegas in April 1985. At the time of Huizenga and Melk's first visit, Cartwright was skeptical. "We'd started the concept and were so far ahead of them." But as the gap started to close, talks got more serious as both Cartwright and Moore began to understand that Huizenga was a top-notch competitor.

By buying Major Video, Huizenga would add stores mostly concentrated in the West and speed Blockbuster's development schedule by a year. As important in the eyes of many, though Huizenga himself downplays this reason, acquiring Major Video would eliminate a potential No. 2—the Burger King to McDonald's analogy, or closer to home, BFI to Waste Management. The fear was that someone else with greater access to capital than Cartwright and Moore could buy Major Video and duplicate the recipe Blockbuster was using. "That radar flashed on Major Video and it was all over," says Clinton Allen, the Blockbuster director who accompanied Huizenga to many of the Major Video meetings. "If Wayne wants to do a deal, you can be pretty damn sure he's going to do it." (Allen remembers after finishing the Major Video acquisition, they returned to Caesar's Palace, where they were staying, around midnight. Huizenga suggested they split a beer and ordered a Budweiser and two glasses. As they finished it off, Allen stuck a quarter into a slot machine, pulled the handle—and lost. But when Allen returned to his room that night, he laughed that they'd just inked a potential multimillion dollar deal, and all that Caesar's had been able to wriggle out of them was $1 on a beer and 25 cents on a slot machine.)

The negotiations between Huizenga and Cartwright and Moore were unevenly stacked. It was, as Moore puts it, "Wayne being a big wheeler-dealer and us being hometown boys trying to develop a concept. I was more adamant about not selling than Hank was because I wanted to grow and develop the company." But the offer to shareholders was too good to turn down, even if it meant the deal would wreak havoc, as it did, with Major Video franchisees, many of whom were friends or relatives. "Wayne was just so persistent in making this deal happen even with the hurdles and road blocks, that didn't deter him," Moore says. "Had it been anybody else but Wayne the deal would never have been done—wouldn't have been even close. But at that stage in his life, Wayne would have done anything not to have same situation with Waste Management and BFI." (Not long after, as Blockbuster withstood blasts by critics and short-sellers, Huizenga would come to wish there was a strong number two in the industry to help validate and provide a comparison for results.)

In negotiating with Huizenga, Moore got a first-person lesson in the Wayne Huizenga school of deal-making and his attention to detail. The courtship went on for months in Las Vegas, Fort Lauderdale, Dallas, even Wichita. At one point, Huizenga invited Moore and Cartwright to Dallas on a Sunday to see Blockbuster's computer system and warehouse just so they knew what they were up against. After that, negotiations went a lot easier. At one meeting in a hotel suite in Las Vegas, Moore remembers, Huizenga sat on one side of the table with he and Cartwright on the other. Huizenga opened the drapes and the sun bounced off his bald head forming a halo, forcing Moore and Cartwright to squint into the rays while trying to hash out parameters for the deal. Moore is sure he set it up like that on purpose. "His motives are all intentional on what he does," he says.

Meanwhile, in his own camp, Huizenga had to counter nay-sayers. In warning Huizenga against the deal, Salvaneschi noted that he wasn't just making a deal for the company, but with every single Major Video and Blockbuster franchisee since there was virtually no area in the country in which there wasn't a conflict. He thought many of their sites were poor and the concept inferior to Blockbuster. Moreover, at McDonald's, he'd learned to effectively fight a number two and his contention was to just keep battling in the marketplace, keep building and eventually, they'd fall. All the Major Video deal would buy was a string of lawsuits. "It was not going to be profitable enough to go through the hassle," he says. "I'm against that acquisition and am still now. But Wayne had the instinct, the killer instinct."

Indeed, it turned out that reaching the initial deal with Moore and Cartwright would be the least of Huizenga's worries regarding Major

Video. Late into negotiations, trading volume in Major Video began rising, forcing Huizenga to announce April 24 that discussions were underway and a letter of intent had been reached. The trading volume initiated a Securities and Exchange Commission inquiry into insider trading in which Huizenga, other Blockbuster directors and executives as well as those at Major Video, were deposed. No action was ever filed. The Federal Trade Commission also took a look because the deal involved two of the largest chains in the video rental industry, but took no action. But those regulatory skirmishes paled beside the legal battles ahead. "One of the keys to Wayne is his level-headedness and tough-mindedness about doing acquisitions," says his friend Chuck Lewis. "He always balances the natural human tendency to talk yourself into things with talking himself out of things." As the fallout of Major Video continued through 1989 and beyond, Huizenga may well have often wished he'd prevailed in talking himself out of it. "We probably didn't need to do it," he says now. "All the time and effort we spent getting that deal done, we could have just gone on our own." One thing was for sure—it gave him plenty of fodder to negotiate deals.

"Arrogant SOBs": Battles with Franchisees

Two weeks after the letter of intent was announced, Blockbuster held two meetings for Major Video franchisees. The one in Fort Lauderdale went well enough, with Major Video franchisees meeting with Kinney and other Blockbuster reps afterward to start to try and resolve conflicts. But the meeting in Dallas was a disaster. Huizenga made his pitch about Blockbuster's superior system and support, meaning that he wasn't going to budge on conversion costs, higher royalty rates, stricter development schedules or other requirements. But he misjudged a more fundamental reaction. The Major Video franchisees had looked upon Blockbuster as the enemy. Now they were being coerced into not only conceding, but capitulating—and besides, Major Video's system was bigger at this point than Blockbuster's. The primary reaction among Major Video franchisees was "Who were these arrogant SOBs anyway?" Adding insult to injury, when Salvaneschi spoke about Blockbuster's nationwide rollout, he referenced his years of experience at McDonald's on a similar campaign. He outlined how he approached markets in great detail, scouting for sites not only for current needs, but well into the future. "We are going to take over," he told them. "We're going to roll over like a tank."

That set the tone for the rest of the meeting. By the end of the session, many of the Major Video franchisees were livid and resolved to stop the deal however they could. Six banded together in a lawsuit to try to get an injunction issued to stop the sale. The closing was delayed pending a hearing on that issue, while other Major Video franchisees filed a separate suit. The Texas judge ruled in October that the deal could go through, but said he fully expected to see the litigants back in court. He was right. Several Major Video franchisees later sued Blockbuster, some naming Huizenga and Blockbuster officers personally.

What are often cited as Huizenga's strengths in deal-making—his logic, rationality, and lack of emotion—blinded him to the reaction of the contentious Major Video franchisees. "Wayne miscalculated the emotion on the other side," Kinney says. "He was looking at it from a business perspective. He literally believed he would have put them out of business anyway. He believed he was doing them a favor." The irrationality "was very frustrating to him," adds Tom Carton, who came in as Blockbuster's general counsel in October 1988, just as the firefight with the Major Video franchisees was underway. "He was so logical and well-reasoned and in so many cases, knew what the consequences were going to be but for reasons of business planning and strategy he wouldn't articulate that."

Meanwhile, Huizenga called Gary Moore every morning at 6 A.M. to tell him the deal didn't look like it would happen. That, of course, spurred Moore to call franchisees to try and convince them to drop their suits or accept a deal Huizenga was offering. "He knew how to feel people out to find out what your hot button was and what we really wanted," Cartwright says. "I wanted out of (Major Video) and he could see that I wanted out and that gave him more leverage." Huizenga shaved the final price of the deal 10 percent because of the remaining litigation. Even so, Blockbuster's stock was rising so fast that the final deal approved by Major Video shareholders January 17, 1989 was valued at $110 million, more than the original deal.

The cleanup went to Bob Guerin, Doug Kinney, Tom Carton, and a team of lawyers. The task was to convert as many Major Video franchisees as possible to Blockbuster stores while redrawing territories and resolving existing conflicts. Huizenga would not budge on the costs of conversion or Blockbuster's higher fees and royalties. Major Video franchisees could decline to convert, if they desired, but they risked having Blockbuster stores go in across the street. "If Wayne ever got a bad reputation about being a tough guy it was probably with (Major Video) franchisees," Berrard says. "They thought he was unreasonable, wanting them to convert their stores. I don't think Wayne was being unreasonable. He was convinced, as all of us were, that by converting from the Major Video colors and color scheme and systems to ours, their business would be much better. And the better their business is, obviously the better for us. Wayne took a hard line for their own good and obviously for ours as well. This is not a charity."

Though settlements would eventually be reached, the legacy is still so bitter that many former Major Video, now Blockbuster franchisees, won't discuss Huizenga or that time period. One of the few who will, Roger Ellis, says the experience left him soured on doing business with Huizenga. He resented the implied threats, notes, and Huizenga's constant checking of Blockbuster's stock quotation in the middle of meetings. "I don't believe he believes in a win-win philosophy. He believes in him winning and screw everyone else." Ellis finally sold his stores to Blockbuster.

For other Major Video franchisees, Huizenga turned on the charm to finally win them over. Steve Littig, who had Major Video stores in Reno and San Francisco filed a lawsuit against Blockbuster that also named Huizenga and other officers. He and his attorney were videotaping depositions of Blockbuster executives in Fort Lauderdale when Huizenga walked into the conference room, jovial and friendly. (His deposition was scheduled for later that afternoon.) Huizenga invited Littig and his attorney to have a cup of coffee. "My attorneys told me you put everything in this suit except the kitchen sink and it'd made me furious to read it, so I didn't read it," Huizenga told him. "But that's part of business. Let's go have coffee."

Over coffee, Huizenga talked with Littig. Couldn't there be a business solution to this? Who in the company would he feel comfortable talking with? Littig mentioned Scott Beck, Blockbuster's largest franchisee whose stores the company had recently acquired. Littig had known Beck through industry forums and Beck hadn't been named in the lawsuit. Through negotiations with Beck, he eventually sold back his San Francisco stores and kept territory in Reno, Nevada, where, though under Blockbuster's umbrella, he remains one of the last holdouts as a Major Video franchisee.

So good was Huizenga that Littig didn't come away with the impression that the encounter had been calculated. But former Blockbuster attorney Tom Carton recalls otherwise. "We would implore Wayne to pursue that strategy because he was good at it," he says. "He was a master at it. Steve wanted to be a big guy and it would mean a lot if big Wayne would talk to Steve. Wayne was the good guy there and he ended up making some headway."

The Major Video aftermath would take more than two years to wrap up and Huizenga and his crew would use all the tools at their disposal to resolve the disputes. Jack Donson, the Cincinnati attorney who represented the Major Video franchisees in their Texas case as well as many of them in their individual lawsuits, says he was impressed by Huizenga's negotiating skill. "He's able to turn on charm from time to time when he determines that's the technique that serves him in negotiations and be very tough when negotiations call for that." But Huizenga's reputation got to the point, as Carton says, that "some Major Video people would not negotiate face to face with Wayne because they felt if they went in with their wallets, they would come out without it and not know it."

McVIDEO: A STREET STORY

As Blockbuster grew, so did the attention by Wall Street and the media. Huizenga would often be quoted that he wanted Blockbuster to be "the McDonald's of our industry" though what he meant was that he wanted it to be clean and friendly and family-oriented, and insists that, at least on his part, there was no master plan to copy the fast-food giant.

It was Huizenga's investment in Blockbuster that had first caught the eye of the financial community. The infusion of $8.4 million in a private placement after the 1987 stock market crash aided credibility. Sensitive to the need to communicate well with Wall Street, he insisted that Blockbuster open a store in Manhattan, even though it was a difficult market with high-price real estate, because it provided a benchmark for analysts. And even after Blockbuster got big enough to attract coverage by major Wall Street firms, Huizenga and Berrard retained contact with regional analysts like Gary Wirt of The Chicago Corp. and Tim Rice of New Orleans-based Johnson Rice who had covered the company in the early days. "People forget their friends when they get to the big leagues and I never felt these guys treated me differently when they were a multi-billion company and the first day I turned up on their doorstep," Rice says.

As Blockbuster grew, the analogy to McDonald's proved irresistible, particularly as fast-food veterans Tom Gruber and Luigi Salvaneschi began a repeat performance of the rollout of a national brand and the establishment of a standard for a consumer commodity—a video store. Wall Street and the press quickly picked up on the comparison with the Golden Arches. Stories soon appeared in *Forbes, USA Today* as well as the local, regional and industry press, outlining Huizenga's vision for Blockbuster and the changes in the offing for the video industry. The McDonald's analogy didn't always play as well inside Blockbuster. Executives like Weber chafed under the McDonald's image of "consistent mediocrity" and believed Blockbuster could do better than that. There was some grumbling that marketing videos was not the same as marketing hamburgers, no matter how much Gruber copied the McDonald's strategy. Even Huizenga would later say the analogy was overdone—but it was too late. The moniker "McVideo" was affixed.

Blockbuster was moving so fast, it couldn't help but generate additional coverage. Its stock split twice in March and August 1988, and once again in August 1989. Headlines noted the investments by United Cable, later by

Cox and the company's skyrocketing revenues and earnings. With the Blockbuster's hyperactivity garnering a lot of press and Huizenga's good relations with Wall Street, the line that Huizenga toed between marketing and hype was a thin one indeed. "Predictability is what you need," Huizenga believes. "You want to be careful you don't try to say something you can't deliver. It's real easy when things are going well. Some of your people get flippant and some of your people get overconfident in what they can actually deliver and before you know it somebody says something that we can't live up to. So my role here was to always keep these young tigers hungry enough to go want to make something happen but not let them get ahead of themselves on their expectations. That was where my experience at Waste Management came in on how to treat Wall Street."

Despite that, Blockbuster remained a tough sell to institutional investors. Analyst Gary Wirt remembers visiting institutional clients in 1988 with Huizenga, and the portfolio managers being unimpressed by the story. Huizenga's past in the garbage industry bothered some. On a more substantive basis, the institutions worried about the impact of pay-per-view, the proliferation of rental outlets and the high multiple on Blockbuster's stock. Wirt still has an internal memo from one mutual fund portfolio manager who, after listening to a presentation by Huizenga and company managers, wrote to him and called Blockbuster "an exploding cigar and that the cigar was lit."

Huizenga believed that getting Blockbuster listed on the New York Stock Exchange would raise the company's profile in the investment community, particularly among individual investors. "An institution doesn't care, but when you tell the average person, it makes a difference." The implied status also gives employees a boost and helps when a company does business abroad, he contends, and he's counseled other corporate chieftains to list their companies on the NYSE. Blockbuster applied for the listing and after a two-month or so standard review, received approval.

But the ceremony on April 27, 1989 was anything but standard. Huizenga works his executives hard, but believes in rewarding them as well, and here was a chance to share in Blockbuster's success. Landing in LaGuardia aboard company planes, a string of limousines met the Blockbuster contingent, which included executives and spouses. Huizenga, his wife, Marti, and his father rode in a white limo at the lead, with the rest following. They arrived at the Helmsley Palace and enjoyed a catered buffet dinner followed by tickets to the hot show "Phantom of the Opera." The next morning, they were whisked by limos to the Exchange before it opened, where Huizenga was presented with a commemorative plaque. As the contingent walked down to the trading floor, Huizenga was hit by the realization that this was the second company he would guide to a listing on the NYSE. As his father Harry placed an order for the first 100 shares, tears welled in his eyes, which he quickly blinked back. The celebration continued with the executives attending a luncheon at Merrill Lynch's offices while the wives accompanied Marti for a private fashion show in the fashion district. There were more catered dinners and luncheon at "21." Huizenga and his crew would need the respite and the celebration. In just two weeks, the skepticism about Blockbuster would resurface with a vengeance, and Huizenga would face his biggest challenge yet.

Bear Call: Blockbuster Takes a Hit

Through 1988 and into early 1989, Blockbuster and H. Wayne Huizenga seemed unstoppable. The Major Video deal closed in January 1989. Huizenga had announced plans to acquire the company's largest franchisee, which would add substantially to Blockbuster's base of company stores and earnings. These acquisitions and others were being paid for mostly with Blockbuster's hot stock. The shares had already split twice, each time issuing two shares for every one held by stockholders, and zoomed to $33.50 a share from just $5.75 months earlier. Then came the bombshell.

In early May 1989, Huizenga was preparing for Blockbuster's annual meeting. The speeches had already been written and approved, extolling Blockbuster's record and bright prospects for the future. Huizenga expected a triumph at the May 9 meeting, a forum to tell shareholders and visiting analysts Blockbuster's story of the unprecedented growth and profits which were behind its dizzying stock price. It was to be indeed a sweet victory for a hometown boy made good. But Huizenga had one nagging worry. The "short" position in Blockbuster's stock had grown in recent weeks, making it one of the most heavily shorted stocks on Wall Street.

Huizenga had reason to worry. On May 9, the day of Blockbuster's annual meeting, a respected Bear Stearns analyst, Lee Seidler, issued a blistering attack on Blockbuster and its accounting policies. Quoting Biblical verse, the report started off: "Ye looked for much, and, lo, it came to little" . . . Haggai 1:9 and included subtitles such as: "'Have you ever seen a 40-year-old video store?'" Seidler claimed that aggressive accounting practices boosted Blockbuster revenues and earnings and thus the price of its shares. Most of Blockbuster's phenomenal revenue growth was due to one-time sales to new franchisees. Blockbuster had changed its policy for expensing the cost of hit videotapes acquired, spreading the cost over three years instead of nine months, which it had formerly used. In acquiring video store chains, Blockbuster was expensing "goodwill"—the purchase price paid above the actual value of physical assets like videotapes, fixtures, and store leases—over 40 years instead of a shorter, more conservative time frame. All of this he said made Blockbuster's financials look better and enticed investors to buy the stock, boosting its price.

In turn, the high stock price was fueling Blockbuster's growth, since Huizenga was essentially using the company's stock as currency to pay for video store chain acquisitions. In essence, Seidler contended that Blockbuster's performance was a house of cards that would soon come crashing down. "For the last two years, Blockbuster Video has parlayed a combination of real growth and smart accounting into a soaring stock price," he wrote. "Unless the company's accountants have several big, new rabbits in their hats, it will be difficult to continue the pace." Without all the fancy accounting tricks, Seidler knocked a full 50 cents off Blockbuster's earnings per share, claiming that Blockbuster really only earned 7 cents from videotape rentals versus the 57 cents reported in 1988 earnings.

The reaction was swift and furious on both Wall Street and in Blockbuster's executive suite. The shortsellers were in their glory. Blockbuster shares plummeted $5 a share the day Seidler's report became public. Huizenga was enraged. The report hadn't been widely distributed or as yet publicized by the media, but wire services were already carrying summaries of it. That meant most shareholders probably hadn't learned of it yet, but the financial press would be waiting. His lips taut and his flat blue eyes flashing, Huizenga demanded a copy of the report. It was not yet available. With just minutes to go before appearing before shareholders, Huizenga decided not to mention the negative report during the meeting. He didn't want to dignify it or add to its credibility.

That proved a mistake. Afterwards, in response to reporters' questions, Huizenga labeled Seidler's report "ludicrous," and contended Blockbuster followed generally accepted accounting policies. But he'd missed a chance to address the issues head-on. Huizenga's strategy was to let supportive analysts counter the negative report. But Blockbuster's stock continued to fall. A shareholder lawsuit followed, charging that Blockbuster's management had consistently overstated earnings over the past two years to artificially boost the stock price. (The suit would be dropped in October after Huizenga refused to settle.)

What had been seeds of doubt had grown to a full-sized tree. For nearly two years, the Bear Stearns report and questions of accounting would dog the company. Indeed, Huizenga and his crew would have to work harder— much harder—to dispel the shadow that now hung over Blockbuster.

But Huizenga made a quick comeback. The company coincidentally had scheduled a meeting at the New York Society of Security Analysts on May 16. This was Huizenga's chance to recover. He and top company officials, including Berrard, Salvaneschi, Gruber, and directors met at the Helmsley Hotel in his suite the night before to practice their speeches. The other presentations were fine, but no one liked Huizenga's. It was too prepared, too canned. Board member Clinton Allen and advisor Chuck Lewis from Merrill Lynch pulled an all-nighter, mapping out talking points for Huizenga. But when the meeting finally broke after 3 A.M., no one was quite sure what Huizenga was going to say.

The meeting was packed the next day with analysts and a smattering of short-sellers, all eager to hear how Huizenga would defend his company and his credibility. Some of the analysts who were supportive of the company were nervous. Andrew Beja, an analyst with Advest, for instance, had just given a buy recommendation for Blockbuster stock the day before the Bear Stearns report. Would his faith and that of others in Huizenga be rewarded?

After Gruber gave his marketing spiel and Berrard defended the nuts and bolts of Blockbuster's accounting policy, Huizenga took the podium—and met the challenge head-on. The consummate businessman, he decided first to point out the numbers, that Blockbuster's stores pulled in $82,500 a month on average and made 35 percent or over $29,000 in pretax profit. "Here is a store that is paying for itself in less than three years. That is the real issue, ladies and gentleman, the tremendous cash flow these stores have," he said. "I don't care if we use pooling or purchase accounting and I don't give a darn if we use 40 years or 20 years to write off the goodwill. After all, the difference between 40 years and 20 years is only two cents a share this year anyway. The fact of the matter is these stores make a lot of money. We want to own as many stores as we can as fast as we can. I am going to tell you right here and now we will continue to build and continue to purchase or pool whenever we are able and I don't give a damn what Bear Stearns says."

Huizenga looked around the room with his eyes blazing. His anger was evident. "I am not an accounting expert, but damn it, I am a good businessman and I am working this company 15 hours a day, 7 days a week, and I know it is good. I know it is very good." He went on to extol the experience of Blockbuster's franchisees and the efforts of analysts who talked to franchisees, visited stores, and worked to understand the concept. "If the five analysts at Bear Stearns can't find the time or don't have the interest to sit down with management, understand our business, our stores, our concept, talk to our franchisees or visit our distribution center, then I believe that kind of reporting is unprofessional at least and questionable at best. To put it another way, I don't think that report is worth the powder to blow it to hell."

The other Blockbuster executives were relieved. Says Salvaneschi, "It was important that he came on strong. That could have been the end of this company. The stock had fallen and his credibility was on the line." Indeed, he, Berrard, and others believe it was a watershed moment for Blockbuster. "That event single-handedly probably saved this company," Berrard says. Analysts concur. The stellar performance by Huizenga vindicated the buy-side analysts. Beja says that the Bear Stearns' report, while damaging, ultimately proved beneficial. "It cleared up the issue. Rather than whispering behind their backs, it was out front and center." Before, someone could invest in Blockbuster stock and not be sure about the accounting issues. Now they had to examine it. Believers stayed with the company and nonbelievers exited.

Later that year, Huizenga flew out to meet with Lee Seidler at his home on Sanibel Island on Florida's west coast. Riding a helicopter in, he met with his nemesis for an hour-plus breakfast and talked about the accounting issues and the report. Huizenga was trying to test Seidler to see if another report was in the offing. But Seidler had no intention of going back into that issue. He'd done his job, as he saw it, in pointing out the flaws in Blockbuster's accounting policies. The rest was up to the investment community. Huizenga invited Seidler to hire on at Blockbuster but he declined. Seidler stands by his work and denies he was ever a tool for short-sellers. "What we did was cut the growth rate of the stock," he says. The report "got the growth rate where it belonged."

Blockbuster's stock recovered within weeks, and rebounded so well the company did another two-for-one split in August 1989, its third in 17 months. Despite Huizenga's spirited defense at the analysts' meeting, the accounting issue didn't fade quickly. It would be recounted in the media for months, even years, afterwards. "I still bump into people today who say, 'oh yeah, you're the company that had those accounting problems.' We didn't have any accounting problems, but the perception was that we did, because it was in so many papers." In restoring his reputation and that of Blockbuster, he says, "We fought like hell. We were ready to take anybody on." But charges of accounting problems would be supplanted by new threats waved by the shorts: technological obsolescence in the form of pay-per-view and later, video-on-demand. Huizenga had fought one major battle with the bears. But the war was far from over.

GOING ABROAD

In addition to putting out fires on the home-front, Huizenga had other lands to conquer. Almost from the beginning, he had his eye on international expansion for Blockbuster. There were lots of possibilities, as VCR penetration abroad lagged that of the United States and Blockbuster could ride the trend. Besides, it was another good story for the Street. England seemed the natural choice. He and Gruber, who had contacts in England, made a foray there in July 1988. (In typical Huizenga-mode, he suggested flying to England over the July 4 holiday weekend. When Gruber noted the holiday, Huizenga looked puzzled and reminded him that Britain didn't celebrate the Fourth of July.) "We wanted to beat the competition as much as we could and not only that, we wanted to grow in two places at the same time instead of one, and pretty soon it was three or four or five places at the same time," Huizenga says.

But Blockbuster's success in the United States did not transfer to international shores easily at first. Jim Ellis, then Taylor Devine, then later Gerry Geddis, would be designated to go to England to oversee company operations. It was a tough haul. Huizenga, who normally ceded to Salvaneschi in real estate decisions, balked at his choices in London. Huizenga insisted on copying the United States concept as closely as possible. But Salvaneschi argued that the large Blockbuster stores and parking lots of the United States couldn't be duplicated in London's expensive real estate market. Besides, he kept telling Huizenga, in London, people walk. Huizenga countered that argument with his usual logic. "I kept saying, 'Luigi, if people walk, why is it so crowded over here? I mean everywhere you go, it's cars. Everybody's bumping into each other. You can't move. Somebody is driving somewhere.'"

Indeed, the first international Blockbuster store opened in February 1989 in a London neighborhood that was less than desirable and had little parking. Results were disappointing, lending fodder for Huizenga's arguments. He contends that as soon as his prescription was followed, the market improved, though the turnaround was more complex than that. Later that year, the Blockbuster "system" which included franchise stores, opened its 1000th store, a 7,000-square-foot store in Birmingham, England.

Meanwhile, John Melk, who loved living in London where he had overseen Waste Management's venture in Saudi Arabia and other international operations, decided to plow the market as a Blockbuster franchisee. He resigned his post as company director at Huizenga's insistence. (Huizenga didn't want to have any problems with a perceived conflict of interest with a franchisee also serving as a director.) For a time, Melk and Blockbuster pursued parallel development of the market. But England proved problematic for him as well and Blockbuster would later buy out his stores.

To Salvaneschi, the problem lay in the approach. "The market was tackled wrongly. Too soon, too fast and not in the right way," he says. The situation in England wouldn't really change until late 1991 when Blockbuster acquired its largest competitor in the market, Cityvision, which operated Ritz stores. But the foray established a beachhead for the company internationally and boosted the appearance that Blockbuster was bigger than it actually was. By the end of 1990, Blockbuster had reached agreements to open stores in Mexico, Australia, and Japan. Some of the international franchisees would be FOWs, like Alberto Finol, who would develop Blockbuster stores in Venezuela and Spain. Other contacts would come through Blockbuster executives. Tom Gruber's many years of international development for McDonald's yielded a key contact in Den Fujita, who as the joint venture partner for McDonald's and Toys "R" Us, was instrumental in breaking U.S. companies into the Japanese market. Huizenga met Fujita in July 1990 in Hawaii and by October, an agreement for Blockbuster stores had been signed. (Huizenga was so taken with Fujita calling Tom Gruber "Gruber-san" that he adopted it as a nickname for Gruber as well. As for Huizenga, he became known to Fujita as "Wayne-san.")

HUIZENGA AND HOLLYWOOD

Hollywood was akin to a foreign country to Huizenga when he took over Blockbuster. It was Melk who actually spent the initial time learning how the studios distribute films and how the video store operators obtained them. But since Blockbuster was going to be a force in the industry, Huizenga wanted first-hand knowledge. Huizenga's business background didn't impress the studio heads or the execs running their profitable home video divisions. What did a bunch of trash haulers, even if they had built a billion-dollar business, know about Hollywood? And Huizenga's oft-professed disinterest in movies, if anything, fueled the skepticism.

But as Blockbuster opened stores, and made good on its promise to grow, skepticism became grudging admiration, and then fear as Blockbuster's sheer size became an issue. The studios don't sell to video stores directly, they sell through distributors. Blockbuster's leverage wasn't in what it bought, but rather in what it could decide not to buy. Its vast library meant that it could help a studio recover the cost of a poor performer just by buying a copy for each of its stores. Huizenga himself never believed in using Blockbuster's size to browbeat the studios. "We got criticized on Wall Street a lot by (analysts) saying 'you guys are the 800-pound gorilla and you're not buying much better than the little guys.' My attitude always was, what's the big deal. We're going to buy a tape a dollar cheaper and we're going to upset our principal vendor." He preferred the approach of McDonald's where vendors are treated as partners rather than as adversaries.

Blockbuster's rapid growth and nearly equal rapid turnover of executives in charge of buying had ruffled many studio executives. Ron Castell was put in charge of purchasing and retooled the methods Blockbuster used. In addition to smoothing relations with the studios, Castell served as Huizenga's link to Tinseltown. He arranged a tour of the various studios in the summer of 1989. While at Paramount's studios, they visited the set for *The Hunt for Red October,* the spy thriller by Tom Clancy. They went up in the submarine and with Huizenga's eye for detail, he noted right off that even on the balsa wood set, the dials and pressure gauges and other instruments were lettered in Russian. Huizenga went to the set of Star Trek, where he sat in Captain Picard's chair. The visit to the sets gave Huizenga another idea, a reward for company execs and franchisees, and a way to make them feel they were in the entertainment business, an offshoot of Hollywood itself. Huizenga suggested to Castell that Blockbuster initiate an annual event, to be dubbed FAME for Franchisee Annual Marketing Expo. By 1989, Blockbuster was already such a force that Hollywood agreed to sponsor FAME meetings. During the first one in 1989, sponsored largely by Disney, franchisees had the run of Disneyland for an evening after hours. There were theme parties, and a tour of the Warner Bros. back lot, complete with a Blockbuster store inserted into a New York street scene. Though he rarely watched movies and hadn't even owned a VCR before Blockbuster, by 1990, Huizenga was among the top 10 most powerful people in entertainment, named by *Entertainment Weekly* in a list which was headed by Michael Eisner. Huizenga ranked number nine, behind Arnold Schwarzenegger and before Gene Siskel and Roger Ebert.

BECK YEARS

Perhaps no relationship remains as puzzling to many Blockbuster insiders as that between Wayne Huizenga and Scott Beck. As Larry Beck's son, Scott represents a generational bridge between the Waste Management and Blockbuster eras of Huizenga's career building billion-dollar companies. The tensions that arose between the younger Beck and Huizenga were predicated—at least in part—upon Scott's styling himself as a "Wayne in training"—an entrepreneur and a deal-maker. (Beck was once quoted in a magazine article as describing Huizenga as a "deal-junkie," a comment that didn't sit well with Huizenga and which prompted other Blockbuster executives to note privately the same proclivity in Beck.)

He even boasts a few of Huizenga's physical characteristics—short stature, premature baldness, and an air of intensity. He liked loud rock music, fast motorcycles, and embodied a self-assuredness that bordered on irreverence, a trait that Huizenga found irritating. In Huizenga's definition of life, as recounted by Steve Berrard, at age 20, you're born in business, at age 30, you're 10-years-old in business; at 36, you're 16; and so on. By that definition, Beck, who'd started as Blockbuster's first franchisee at age 27 and would sell his stores to the company three years later, was a beginner in business with whom Huizenga found himself having to deal with as an equal.

In building Blockbuster, Huizenga was frustrated by Scott Beck's power and the amount of territory he controlled. Five of the nation's major metropolitan areas—Atlanta, Chicago, Detroit, Minneapolis-St. Paul, and Milwaukee—were under the license agreement Beck had struck with David Cook. Though Beck ramped up his development schedule, opening 106 stores over three years, it was never fast enough to suit Huizenga. "When you're the largest franchisee, there's going to be tension," Beck says. (In a court appearance, he characterized his relationship with Huizenga as a franchisee as being "always a very difficult relationship.") Also irritating to Huizenga was that before he could close the Movies-To-Go and Major Video deals, he had to talk with Scott Beck because of potential conflicts. In short, Beck controlled too much of the company for comfort. Likewise, by early 1989, Beck's constant quest for capital to continue the buildout was getting critical and he'd started talking with potential buyers, including Blockbuster.

The buyout of Beck's operation illustrates how the "old pals" can play serious hardball with each other, as pieced together from interviews and a voluntary deposition by Huizenga before the SEC in an informal inquiry into trading of Blockbuster stock. The inquiry was ultimately dropped. In early March 1989, Huizenga got a call from Dean Buntrock, one of Beck's partners. He wanted Huizenga to know that Beck had gotten an offer, a large offer, from an investment firm and that Peer Pederson, who was in Florida for a golf tournament, had the details. Huizenga was determined to buy those stores and the territory back from Beck. But doing so would prove problematic. "We knew, and I think Wayne knew that we knew, and he knew, that the ultimate buyer and the best buyer was going to be Blockbuster," says Peer Pederson. "Nothing else made sense."

Huizenga sent a plane over for him and met Pederson at the Executive Jet Center at the Fort Lauderdale-Hollywood International Airport. Pederson knew his friend, and his strength as a negotiator. But friendship is one thing. A deal is another. "We can put friendship aside and negotiate real hard," Pederson says. In his meeting with Huizenga, Pederson said that the partnership had an offer for $175 million.

"No way do I think that business is worth $175 million," Huizenga told him. "Not even close." Pederson told Huizenga that the other group wanted to move, and if he was interested, he'd have to act fast. "I don't know if they were serious," Pederson says now. "Wayne never believed it. I'm not sure I did, (but of) course I tried to use that. But, again, I didn't overuse it because I wouldn't deliberately misrepresent to him. You misrepresent once to Wayne, and that's the end."

Discussions continued, but there was little movement to close the gap on price. The most Huizenga valued the business was $80 million to $100 million, tops, and he really wasn't eager to do it at that price. Beck wanted $150 million. "Wayne has a strong personality and is committed to his point of view and likewise we're a strong personality and committed to our point of view," Beck says of the negotiations.

Meanwhile, Huizenga had notified his original partners in Blockbuster, John Melk and Don Flynn, of Scott Beck's intended end run. On March 11, Huizenga, Melk, Flynn, and Berrard met with Scott Beck, Pederson, and two executives from Beck's organization. Huizenga said he didn't believe the projections they'd put together for the stores and repeated that he would pay at most $100 million, reminding Beck that he had the right to approve any transfer of a franchise. At that meeting, there were hints that Beck was considering starting a competing chain to Blockbuster. "I wouldn't even hear of any conversation like that," Huizenga said. "There's no way. You're a franchisee of ours and you're going to stay a franchisee of ours, period."

It was over dinner with Peer Pederson that Huizenga learned more details of Beck's plans—whether a negotiating tactic or a real intent—to start a competing chain. Pederson said they'd sent the franchise agreement to a law firm which had opined that the partnership could set up competing stores in areas outside its Blockbuster territory. Beck had been working on a new concept for even larger stores, up to 15,000 square feet and carrying music as well as videos. "We'll get our own interpretation of the law," Huizenga told him. "Well just have to litigate that." The discussion got heated, and Pederson switched tactics, saying they needed to work this out on a friendly basis and if Huizenga was willing to use stock they could bypass taxes and would be willing to sell for less than $175 million. To Huizenga, it still wasn't enough. He worried that putting out that amount of stock would depress Blockbuster's share price. He hadn't wanted to do this deal for a year at least, and now he was being strong-armed into doing it now. "This was not a friendly meal," Huizenga said. "These were not friendly telephone conversations and these were not friendly dinner meetings. I was really upset with these guys for thinking that they were going to take us head on. They're our franchisee. And they're going to abandon the system and fight against all the other franchisees in Blockbuster and basically try to rip the whole company apart and compete against their fellow franchisees in one market and be a Blockbuster franchisee in another market. No way."

"They were extremely difficult negotiations," remembers Tom Carton, Blockbuster's general counsel, who witnessed many of the sessions. "Scott

Beck and Wayne went back and forth viciously, who said what to whom, when and what was in the agreement."

Blockbuster's rising stock price helped close the deal. By April 20, 1989, Huizenga and Beck hammered out an agreement on the number of shares and by August, Blockbuster stock had risen to value the deal for the 106 stores and territory at $122 million. Beck himself pocketed $28 million, a considerable return for the $900,000 he'd invested, even accounting for the years of intense work. Those shares were worth upwards of $100 million in August 1994.

This acquisition years later would cost Blockbuster dearly in money and public opinion. Drawing on his experience and contacts as a financial advisor, Beck had raised money to build Blockbuster stores by selling limited partnerships. In reaching the deal, Huizenga and Berrard insisted that the transaction be able to be accounted for as a "pooling of interests." (That meant Blockbuster would not have to write off goodwill, or the difference between the fair market value of the assets and the purchase price. There was no way that Blockbuster at that stage in its growth would take the hit to earnings that writing off that much goodwill would generate.) But that meant that while selling the master limited partnership, Beck left out the limited partners who had invested in Blockbuster stores.

The limited partners were outraged but, buoyed by Beck's assurances that a solution would be found, didn't stop the deal. But Charles Howell was more angry—and more desperate—than most. He had been a client of Beck's financial investment firm and one of three partners in the first limited partnership to build Blockbuster stores and felt betrayed. After two years, Blockbuster offered to buy him out for $450,000 in Blockbuster stock, less than the $600,000 he'd originally invested. Howell reluctantly agreed and signed a release promising not to sue. He sued anyway, claiming fraud. In August 1994, a Texas judge ruled that Beck and Blockbuster had defrauded Howell and awarded a judgment of $123 million. Although the original suit did not name Huizenga, nor was he called to testify, the case got widespread press attention and was cited in some media reports as impinging on Huizenga's reputation for fairness. It is on appeal.

With negotiations between Huizenga and Beck so acrimonious, the addition of Beck as vice-chairman and chief operating officer surprised many Blockbuster insiders. About 60 members of Beck's organization joined Blockbuster in the merger, with Beck coming on board two weeks after the deal closed. The latitude Huizenga afforded Beck—negotiated before he joined—shocked executives schooled in Huizenga's management style of control and oversight.

Blockbuster became Beck's laboratory. He set up a myriad of task forces, convened all-day meetings at 6 A.M., spent lavishly on consultants, research and projects like "focus stores" intended to redesign Blockbuster stores to increase customer traffic, but which backfired. "Scott was really playing Monopoly with real money and real people and a real company on the New York Stock Exchange," recalls Tom Gruber. "He was doing all these little things he had read about in textbooks and was going to put them into practice and he had the position, the authority, the company and the money to do it."

The only thing playful about his efforts, Beck says, was a light-heartedness he brought to Blockbuster. "I've always brought to my work a level of intensity and seriousness that has got nothing to do with Monopoly," he says. "But I do bring a certain lighter spirit, play some rock music, am a little irreverent from the Corporate America perspective. I took it very, very seriously." Indeed, the youthfulness and exuberance of Beck and his team fueled the excitement and fast-pace already pumping within Blockbuster.

But with no intention of staying long-term, Beck and his core team of a half-dozen executives began to scout for other opportunities—which ultimately provoked a confrontation with Huizenga. Saad Nadhir, who joined from Beck's organization to head up Blockbuster's international push, left in September 1991 to snag their next big deal, a restaurant chain called Boston Chicken. As more members of Beck's team left to join Boston Chicken's executive ranks, Huizenga grew suspicious, then angry. Beck had promised not to take anyone when he left. Now he was breaking his word.

Beck says the execs who left had helped him build Blockbuster and make a lot of money, and wanted a chance to get equity in a new deal. He says he warned Huizenga early on that they were looking at Boston Chicken. "He was just disappointed when it happened," Beck says. "He felt betrayed and it bothered him." In late December, Huizenga confronted Beck, and ordered him and whoever else planned to leave, to do so sooner rather than later. (Beck left, and just months later joined Boston Chicken, which counted at least six former Blockbuster executives among its ranks. The popularity of chicken restaurants, the management's Blockbuster pedigrees and an overheated market for initial public offerings sent Boston Chicken's stock soaring 143 percent on its first day of trading in November 1993.)

"It wasn't a surprise. It was a disappointment because he said he wasn't going to do it," Huizenga says of Beck's raiding of Blockbuster's management ranks. Both Beck and Huizenga attribute much of the tension in their relationship during that time to Beck's youthfulness. "Wayne and I have had a volatile but very mutually profitable relationship," Beck says. "We're both very strong-willed, both very confident and I'm 20 years younger than him so I didn't bring to the situation a level of maturity that probably would have made it less volatile."

PLANES INC. AND OTHER SIDE DEALS

Even during the intensity of building Blockbuster, his penchant for deal-making led Huizenga into other business venues. A man of few hobbies, he even found a way to make a business out of one of those. After Marti bought him a 1937 Rolls Royce for his 50th birthday, he began collecting classic cars, and soon owned a 1931 Packard, a 1933 Chrysler Phaeton and—after he was awarded the baseball franchise—a 1965 Marlin. They appreciate in value, and that makes him happy. He also created a bonafide business venture in 1990, Classic Automobile Investors, a $1.5 million credit line established with the owner of a classic cars magazine, to buy two Ferraris and a Cobra expected to appreciate significantly.

Some new ventures were borne of risky situations. After negotiating to buy back stores from a Blockbuster franchisee in March 1988, Huizenga and Berrard took off in a blinding, lightning snow-storm from Amarillo, Texas. "All of us were pilots and we couldn't believe they were leaving in this snowstorm to make another deal," recalls Bill Denton, the franchisee. "But they had a deal to make and they made it. Wayne said afterwards that he didn't make any money on our deal because he had to buy a jet to climb through the storms quicker."

Indeed, after that, Huizenga bought a Gulfstream jet. Though he had long looked at planes as a tool for doing business, this time, he decided to get into planes as a business. He hired the pilot who'd flown down the G-II to start up an airplane brokerage business. With Huizenga's already prodigious contacts in business and soon within sports and entertainment, it was a natural.

Just as he liked fast cars as a teenager, Huizenga likes fast planes as a multi-millionaire. When a BAC1-11, a plane the size of a DC-9, once owned by a Saudi prince, became available in October 1989, Huizenga bought it for family trips. The planes are also a form of competition between he and his wealthy friends. After his friend George Johnson proudly showed off his $1.25 million King Air 200, a pressurized turbo-prop, Huizenga congratulated him, then mentioned that propellers made him dizzy. Soon after, Johnson sold the King Air and bought a Lear jet. "If you get a little pompous, he'll prick your balloon," Johnson says.

Unlike many corporate chieftains for whom companies bestow perks like private planes, Huizenga owned the planes personally and charged Blockbuster for usage. Even so, the company never paid full cost. But Blockbuster became a handy client for other Huizenga businesses. Since Blockbuster would buy these services anyway, why not buy them from companies he owned or in which he had an interest? As long as terms were fair, that was only good business. When Huizenga got back into the bottled water business in 1991, for instance, Blockbuster became a client. As Huizenga's ownership of the stadium and sports team expanded, so did Blockbuster's advertising and sponsorship of sports events.

But the biggest side deal—and the one that attracted the most controversy—involved drug screening of prospective Blockbuster employees. Blockbuster was the largest client of Psychemedics Inc., a company that had developed a drug-testing method using hair. Huizenga was also an investor in the company, which was brought to the attention of his "old pals" group of investors from Waste Management by newcomer Clinton Allen, the Blockbuster director. Huizenga bought into four private placements in the tiny $1.7 million company through 1989–1990 and also loaned the company $515,000. Don Flynn and John Melk also participated in the private placements and became directors. But even with their involvement, the stock didn't move much and the company remained a disappointment. Its method of testing threatened and competed against pharmaceutical giants who did more conventional urinalysis testing. Indeed, Huizenga's political connections created a bit of a stir in 1990, when the *Miami Review* reported a lengthy story about then-Florida Governor Bob Martinez urging federal regulators at the National Institute on Drug Abuse to grant federal approval to hair-testing as a form of drug screening. It was suspected he wrote the letter as a favor to Huizenga, a campaign supporter, as Psychemedics was based in Boston and had its main testing lab in California— not exactly a Florida constituent.

Fun and Fame

The intensity of Blockbuster's early years didn't destroy Huizenga's penchant for fun. As with the celebration for the listing on the New York Stock Exchange, Huizenga recognized rewards were needed to keep up the brutal pace. And his ability to laugh at himself showed a new dimension to executives and franchisees alike. At the first franchisee meeting in July 1988, for instance, Marti suggested a "tacky tourist" theme party. Huizenga not only attended, but in full costume, black socks, clear plastic tie, straw hat and all. He regularly donned costumes for all the FAME "theme" parties, from a motorcycle gang member to a 1960s beaded hippie (with hair).

Huizenga has a strong sense of one-liners and timing, and used them often to break the tension, in negotiating or other situations. One time, when deMena was meeting with Huizenga to discuss shuffling offices for the growing number of executives at 901 Las Olas, he suggested that perhaps Huizenga's office could be cut down in size to accommodate another executive. "We could do that," Huizenga said. "But we could also do this!" he added, grabbing the pencil and, with a smile, erasing deMena's office.

At the urging of other Blockbuster executives, most notably Don Smiley, Huizenga in 1988 approved the company getting a skybox at the newly opened $110 million stadium built by Joe Robbie for his Miami Dolphins football team. Though a season ticket holder since 1966, it was from that box, suite 234B, that Huizenga's new business venture into sports would begin. During the 1989 Superbowl, Huizenga was hosting Blockbuster executives, then-governor Bob Martinez and other friends. During that game, Huizenga dropped by Joe Robbie's skybox to say hello. He'd met Robbie at various charity events around town. Talks would soon begin with Robbie that would ultimately launch Huizenga's entrance into professional sports. Little more than a year later, Huizenga would buy half the stadium and 15 percent of the Dolphins. Seven years later, Huizenga would own the entire stadium, the Dolphins, two other sports franchises and would sit in the owner's box while Miami again hosted the Superbowl.

The stadium also gave Huizenga the venue for another event. Don Smiley learned of plans in August 1990 by Raycom Sports to bring another college football bowl game to south Florida, specifically to Joe Robbie Stadium, and they were looking for sponsors. He attended a planning session and reported back to Huizenga, who instantly saw the potential of Blockbuster being the title sponsor. Blockbuster Bowl. It even had a nice ring to it, and it was exactly the kind of big-name event that appealed to him.

At a management meeting, Huizenga broached the idea to the Blockbuster execs. Gruber instantly shot it down. He didn't like sports marketing and besides, it was going to eat up a huge chunk of his marketing budget. But the others signed on, as did Gruber when it became apparent Huizenga was determined to do it. Smiley joined the board of the Sunshine Football Classic, soon to be dubbed the Blockbuster Bowl and worked out details regarding arrangements and fees. The only thing missing were two teams. Most college teams were already committed to the established bowl games, like the Orange Bowl, Rose Bowl, and Sugar Bowl. As Huizenga's luck, persistence and contacts would have it, the inaugural Blockbuster Bowl ended up with one of the most interesting matches that season, with a contest between the Florida State Seminoles and Penn State Nittany Lions and two renowned coaches, Bobby Bowden of FSU and Joe Paterno of Penn State.

The first Blockbuster Bowl on December 30, 1990 was a smash success. Blockbuster's name was splattered across the front pages of newspapers across the country, on ESPN, CNN, and every network sports show. "The Blockbuster game was said and printed more because of that football game than a lot of local store marketing could ever do," Smiley notes. In an impish twist, Smiley cooked up a pregame surprise that shows Huizenga's ability to have fun and laugh at himself. Blockbuster hosted a pregame party for franchisees, families, and friends, about 1,000 in all, featuring its own cheerleaders—top company execs dressed as buxom cheerleaders (with the aid of balloons) including Huizenga. Smiley had gotten Huizenga to sign on by saying other execs had already agreed to do it, then cajoling them to participate because Wayne was going to. A picture of the cheerleading troupe would surface during Huizenga's bid for a baseball franchise, causing a consultant to groan and warn that baseball owners were conservative types and cross-dressing as cheerleaders was not a way to impress them.

Bowl game rules and politicking would prevent Blockbuster from getting another Florida team during its remaining two years as a bowl sponsor, a prerequisite by Huizenga to continuing the agreement. Attendance dwindled for the next two Blockbuster Bowl games. They still were useful in regional marketing. Bob Guerin remembers Huizenga agreeing spontaneously to visit an Alabama franchisee who had only four stores to help whip up interest and excitement by meeting with the local sports press. But the splash of the 1990 game had its desired effect: Blockbuster's name was brought into thousands of homes in America, and hastened its becoming a household word. As Gruber would say, "It was a case of acting bigger than we were."

But Blockbuster was already big—and getting bigger. By the end of 1990, Blockbuster's system-wide revenues, including franchisees, had surpassed $1 billion. Huizenga's credibility and that of his company had not only survived attacks but thrived. Now would begin a new era. As early as October 19, 1988, at a meeting for executives at Luigi Salvaneschi's house, Huizenga had sketched his broader vision for the company. With less than 400 video stores, he was already looking forward to the day when the company would have 2,000 stores and so much cash it would have to diversify into other lines of business. Now that effort would begin in earnest.

8

Don't Hit Pause: Blockbuster in Turbulence

The numbers didn't look good. In fact, they looked pretty sickly. Huizenga stared at the computer printouts in front of him, sighed, and rubbed his eyes. In store after store, region after region, across the nation, the story was the same. Hot movies were cooling on the shelves, classic favorites were collecting dust, customers weren't coming into Blockbuster stores. Instead, they were at home, glued to their televisions as CNN and other networks provided live coverage of modern warfare in the comfort of their living rooms. Even Huizenga had to admit he'd been staying up late to watch CNN. With a months long buildup as the United States had readied for war against Saddam Hussain, and with so much real drama now unfolding in the desert sands of Kuwait and Iraq, who needed entertainment?

It'd been like this for weeks now, right after the first shelling began January 17, 1991. At first Huizenga and his crew hadn't been willing to believe it. It was an aberration, a hiccup. But now there was no disputing the numbers. "We could always respond to changes in the business," says Berrard. "But one thing we couldn't respond to was something that took people away from the stores and from their television sets and that's the alternative of time. We really had to focus on the fact that our business really competes with trying to get two hours of your time. When the Persian Gulf War came, it was astonishing to us. Everybody was so fixated on watching TV, they just didn't come in the stores. Nothing we were going to do was going to change that. The first night the bombing started it was like we dropped off the face of the earth."

Up until now, they'd been so careful in massaging Wall Street's expectations about Blockbuster in keeping with Huizenga's primary rule: no surprises. As Berrard notes, "The one thing that we always prided ourselves

173

on here is we're pretty astute on trying to make sure that we had the Street at least within the relative range of the estimate, that no one was too high, no one was too low. We never gave them the numbers but we would always try to give them some indication of what we felt was a fair range. We tried to help them to build their models, tried to give them the store counts that we were expecting to build, tried to talk them through the strength or weakness of the business. We did a lot of work internally every week based on our business just to make sure we weren't going to disappoint them."

But as the "Gulf War effect" battered the results of restaurants and retail companies, analysts were getting suspicious. Huizenga had held off saying anything, hoping that as the short-lived war wound down, Blockbuster would make up the shortfall. Though results were improving, it wasn't enough to compensate. Now they'd have to break the news and he and Steve Berrard would have some explaining to do. Revenues and earnings would still be up double-digits, but would fall short of analysts' projections. "The Street had been speculating that Blockbuster was affected and the company had been denying it and denying it," remembers Craig Bibb, an analyst with Paine Webber. "When they finally reported it, the stock slid because comps [comparable sales] were down and because they had said repeatedly it wasn't the Gulf War; reaction on the Street was worse than otherwise because [analysts and investors] began to look at other culprits: the video rental fad must be over, then the 'electronic highway' stories started coming out and there were other incremental things to worry about. That started the big negative slide on the stock."

Huizenga knew Blockbuster's shares would take a hit and the short-sellers would score a victory this time, and that burned him. He'd fought so hard to regain credibility, and for Blockbuster's stock to recover after the devastating 1989 Bear Stearns report had raised questions about accounting methods. And earlier, he had vanquished his own doubt, convincing himself about the long-term viability of the video rental business.

Now the doubt came creeping back. But masking the flicker of uncertainty was anger. This was just the sort of stumble that the shorts had been waiting for all along. But Huizenga had no choice. On March 12, Blockbuster issued a carefully worded press release that nonetheless was a bombshell. The company announced that revenue was up 31 percent for the first two months of 1991 over the same period in 1990. But analysts expectations had been anticipating a 40 percent boost in revenues. The market took the news hard. Blockbuster stock, which had split just four days earlier, started trading late because of heavy sell orders and the news knocked Blockbuster shares initially almost $2 a share, recovering to finish down 1⅛ at 12⅛.

But the "Gulf War effect" was just the first of a series of blows to Blockbuster in early 1991 that Huizenga had to handle. Just weeks later, the "technology cloud" that had already started to dog Blockbuster appeared to grow darker and more menacing. Amid much media fanfare, Time-Warner Inc. announced it was upgrading a cable-television system in Queens, New York, with fiber optic cable which would allow it to offer 150 channels instead of 75 channels. Then just days later, another team including Tele-Communications, AT&T, and U.S. West announced a test would be launched later in the year which would allow customers to order from a list of 1,000 movies and special programs whenever they wanted to see them. The media chatter about transforming the dumb television into an "interactive tool" via which consumers could indulge their couch potato inclination to order up the latest Hollywood release rather than drive to the video store, would grow louder and more insistent over the following months. It was a perception that Huizenga would fight hard to dispel, but one whose persistence nonetheless would ultimately help drive him to sell the company less than three years later.

Then the third blow hit. An article appeared in the Friday, May 3, edition of the *Atlanta Constitution,* revealing plans by Cox Enterprises, parent company of the newspaper, to sell its 82 Blockbuster stores and back away from its commitment to build a total of 120 stores by December. Huizenga was irked. He'd been negotiating with Cox for weeks about buying back some stores, but they hadn't come to terms on the price. Now the news had been leaked to the press, perhaps to put pressure on him. Maybe playing hardball had backfired a bit this time, but he wasn't about to back down. At first Cox had wanted to sell or swap some 26 stores in the northeast, Philadelphia and upstate New York, that were doing poorly for stores in Atlanta. But when, as a Cox insider then noted, "we couldn't get their attention," the decision was made to sell all the stores. Huizenga and other Blockbuster officials tried to dispel the rumors surrounding the sale, emphasizing that Cox was exiting because it wanted to concentrate on its other businesses, not because it was unhappy with Blockbuster or worried about the future prospects of video rental. But coming on the heels of the barrage of publicity about new technology, the reassurances sounded weak. (Cox officials declined to be interviewed for this book.)

Regardless of the reason, it was terrible timing for one of the company's largest franchisees—and a cable company to boot—to be pulling out. Huizenga contended it was a friendly disagreement, a matter of price. "Yes, it shaved a point off our stock, but our attitude is that it will come back," he said then in an interview. "If we make bad business decisions, it may not." Huizenga still stands by that statement. "I remember that their announcement that they were going to sell came at the worst possible time," he says. "But if we or I don't think the price is fair then we don't have to buy at that price."

As Blockbuster's stock continued to get hammered, Huizenga knew he'd have to fight back even harder at a forum that would prove most favorable: on his home turf at the company's annual meeting in May. Together with Ron Castell, Steve Berrard, and Blockbuster's new president, Joe Baczko, they worked to fashion a response. But there was a problem, an Achilles heel, that Baczko noted years after leaving the company. With all the bad press and the doubts about the video rental industry being replaced by technology, "during all of this, internally, I'm convinced that almost everybody, believed some portion of it. I may have been the only one who didn't. I just could not see this happening," Baczko says. "I think there was legitimate doubt in the company about the longevity of the video industry and in turn what our position was. The doubt was there because I could see it in how we were articulating our position. We spent two months creating our answer that was going to be delivered at the annual meeting," he recalls. "But there wasn't that conviction. If this issue had been raised with a true founder, then that conviction would have been there. It would have been communicated much more."

The preparation for Blockbuster's annual meeting that year was even more intense than usual. The hours that Huizenga insisted on for practicing speeches and polishing presentations turned into tens of hours. He wasn't about to repeat the mistake of the 1989 meeting and not address the doomsayers head on. This time, he knew how much was on the line, how much depended on his ability to get his message across, to restore faith in the company, in the industry, in his leadership.

MEDIA ATTACKS: BLOCKBUSTER AS "CASKET CASE"

But the bad news bears weren't finished with Blockbuster. On Friday, May 10, just eleven days before the annual meeting, disaster struck again. In his *USA Today* column, financial columnist Dan Dorfman quoted a Los Angeles-based money manager named Pam (Palomba) Weingarten who trashed Blockbuster and its prospects. "It's a casket case," she said. "The video store is going the way of the dinosaur. In three years, it won't be around. People will just dial up movies with their phones." The column noted that the $1.9 billion family of funds Weingarten then managed, the Los Angeles-based Pilgrim Group, isn't permitted to sell short under its bylaws but that Weingarten, through the use of put options, was short 30,000 shares in her personal account. In the column, Dorfman quoted

Huizenga as refuting Weingarten's comments, "Almost shouting at times, Huizenga bellows, 'We're a viable business today; we'll be an even more viable business in the year 2000.' Weingarten's skeptical response: 'The guy ought to rent a film from Blockbuster: It's called *Death of a Salesman.*'"

It was a direct hit. Huizenga, Berrard, and others fielded calls all day from shareholders, analysts, and institutional holders, and reporters who spread the story still further. "You had someone who was grossly misinformed and seems to have all the taint of self-interest," Berrard said of Weingarten, calling her comments "outlandish." As he told one newspaper, "we're a billion-dollar company with no debt and we're supposed to disappear in 3 years? It's almost an insult to readers."

But the skeptics still weren't done. An eight-page missive from Kynikos Assoc. Ltd—Kynikos being the Greek word for "cynic"—dated May 17 made its way around Wall Street with the headline: "Blockbuster Entertainment Corp.—Wow! What Accounting!" In it, noted short-seller James Chanos made the point that most of Blockbuster's earnings were from franchise sales and that when that slowed, Blockbuster would be in trouble. He raised again the notion that the company inflated earnings by not writing off its tape inventory fast enough. And he, like other critics had already been noting, warned of the threats posed by pay-per-view and the maturing of the video rental industry. (The maturing market theory held that as more U.S. households bought VCRs, the "new toy" phenomenon which prompted new VCR-owners to rent a larger number of tapes would wear off as the novelty wore off, and there would be a more stable base of VCR owners as regular customers.)

The well-timed attack wasn't a surprise to Huizenga, who was too-familiar with Chanos from his Waste Management days. "The shorts have been on us from day one, particularly Chanos, who in my opinion has a personal ax to grind," he said in an interview with *CFO Magazine* later that year. "Chanos took on Waste Management heavily in the early days and predicted its demise, and we certainly know that never came to pass." In the article, both Huizenga and Berrard noted that Chanos rebuffed invitations to visit Blockbuster's headquarters. "It was never anything personal from my perspective," Chanos says. "Coincidentally, (he) was involved in two companies we were short over a ten year time span. If anything, Mr. Huizenga's involvement in those companies presented me with a negative from the short-sellers' point of view. He is perceived as a capable manager." Chanos concedes he lost money on Blockbuster, but won't say how much.

The credence afforded Chanos' view and that of other short-sellers in the press would remain Huizenga's biggest frustration during his years at Blockbuster. "There was no reason for him to have the audience that he had," Huizenga contends. "I guess my biggest disappointment was that all the newspapers and magazines had jumped up and were quick to point out all the things that were wrong at Blockbuster just because some guy decided he was going to make some kind of press release. It didn't make any sense and the disappointment was that the facts were never checked. It took us a long time to go back. I can tell you a lot of shareholders sold Blockbuster based on the lies and innuendoes that were out there and then they missed the ride and it cost them a lot of money and I don't think it's right."

The Blockbuster board of directors dinner at Huizenga's favorite waterfront restaurant, Burt & Jacks, the night before the annual meeting was a glum affair, with lots of discussion about the undeserved bad press the company had been getting. Huizenga would say the next day that they'd spent an hour and a half at the meeting and during it, "our directors all of a sudden are all instant PR experts. Sorry guys. It isn't as easy as it sounds." He knew how hard it was to get Blockbuster's story out. That's why he'd hired a public relations firm to try and help do just that. And that was also why he'd spent so much effort preparing for the shareholders' meeting.

So when the lights dimmed on May 21 at 1 P.M. inside the Parker Playhouse, a landmark local theater in downtown Fort Lauderdale, Huizenga was primed and ready for all takers. The standing-room-only crowd of 1,200 shareholders or so was tense, curious about what would be said to counter the barrage of bad publicity. The front of the stage was a mockup of a Blockbuster store with "customers" choosing tapes. A "Quik Drop" slot had been "cut" into the podium.

The mockup fell away to reveal a screen and on that screen, boomed a voice, "This story is true. The names are real. The events are legendary: Blockbuster Rides Again." It was corny, but it set the tone. The introductory video used a Western theme with Huizenga as a trail boss and other Blockbuster executives in Western gear. The video highlighted the successes of the past year: Blockbuster's emergence as the largest renter of video games; Blockbuster stores opening in Puerto Rico and Japan plus agreements in Mexico and Australia; the media barrage generated by the Blockbuster Bowl. But all those accomplishments had been drowned out by the recent press and Huizenga didn't waste time getting to the point.

"We have a lot to talk about today and it's all good, but we do, however, have this cloud hanging over our head. In the last month or so, our stocks have been heading south. The shorts have circled our wagons and we've been getting a bad rap in the press. So let's start right off by addressing these issues head on." Up on the screen flashed the *USA Today* story. Huizenga described Weingarten as "an unknown money manager who has decided that our company is, in her words, a casket case and a dinosaur.

And in just three years she predicted the video industry will not be around. In just three years she says there will be technologies that let people sit at home and dial up movies with their phones and watch whatever they want to watch when they want to watch it. She doesn't know that the dial phone is long dead," he said to chuckles that rippled through the audience. "The rest of her information is just about as accurate." The chuckles turned into a roar of laughter. He permitted himself a quick smile at his own joke, then rallied on.

"Her prediction is wrong. We are not going away, not in three years, and not in 23 years, and not in anyone's foreseeable future." He took care in explaining the difference between pay-per-view, which had been around for several years, but so far gotten a tepid response from consumers, and the yet-to-be-developed video-on-demand technology that was the current media obsession. Blockbuster had hired two sets of consultants to examine the technology issue and analyze the findings. "Our industry may undergo change but I can assure you Blockbuster will be in the forefront of those changes and we're not going to be at the end of the parade cleaning up after the elephants. What it boils down to is that we don't believe there's a threat and we don't believe that the people who think there's a threat know what the hell they're talking about." It was vintage Huizenga, using humor to make his point and mixing plain talk with a tinge of the ire and irritation he felt at being treated, in his mind, so unfairly.

To make sure his point got across, he mailed a five-page missive to shareholders, reiterating what was said at the annual meeting. But Blockbuster's stock would continue to languish the rest of the year. By midsummer, Blockbuster was still one of most heavily shorted stocks on the New York Stock Exchange. And as a *Miami Herald* columnist summarized the situation in January 1992, Blockbuster's stock value dropped 6.8 percent in a year when the Dow Jones Industrial Average advanced more than 20 percent, underscoring the weight of perception over reality accorded by Wall Street.

Internally, it had shaken Huizenga that Blockbuster's stock price had been affected so dearly. At board meetings, talks turned increasingly to diversification plans and the future of the company. Was Blockbuster a retailer, or was it an entertainment company? "I'm not convinced that in itself [the Gulf War] forced diversification, but it did indicate there's a vulnerability," Berrard reflects. "We didn't do a lot of diversification in 1991, but we started thinking about, okay, where are we going to go?" Huizenga's mission to Berrard was three-fold: Focus on the new technology and what it meant; look at opportunities to buffer against events such as a Gulf War and figure out how to position the company more as an entertainment company.

DIVERSIFICATION DISASTERS

The first small foray into diversification wasn't promising. Through a social contact in Fort Lauderdale, Huizenga got the idea to team up on a tour boat operation. But it was a penny-ante deal and ended up in a mess. "That was my idea so I can't blame that on anyone else but myself," he says. Huizenga brought up the deal to the board. It struck some of the directors as odd, a bit out of character for Blockbuster, and some, like Luigi Salvaneschi, thought it was a crazy deal and said so. But the directors didn't go against it. Clinton Allen and Carl Barger both knew of tour boat operations in the northeast that appeared to be doing well. Huizenga wanted it, it wasn't a big deal, and who knew? Maybe there was a tie-in with the tourism market.

But it ended up being a local disaster. It started out as an equity venture in July 1990 with Blockbuster advancing $540,000 and guaranteeing construction of a new boat. Meanwhile, Huizenga had a yacht broker friend scope out the prospects for a nationwide operation. The report back was not promising: too much competition in too small of a business. "The one mistake that I really made there and that none of us picked up," says Huizenga, "the industry wasn't big enough. How much time and effort do you want to spend on an industry that isn't large enough?"

Meanwhile, the tour boat operation in Fort Lauderdale had its eye on developing a barrier island into a tourist spot, sparking an outcry by environmentalists and giving Blockbuster, by association, a black eye. When the tour boat company started answering its phones "Blockbuster Cruises," Huizenga had had enough. Deciding the business prospects didn't look good, he decided to change Blockbuster's interest into that of a creditor rather than an equity partner. Struggling with other debt, the company ended up insolvent while affiliates filed for bankruptcy, and Blockbuster sued the companies and affiliates for defaulting on debt, not paying agreed upon royalties and abusing the trademark and licensing agreement.

The other small diversification deal done in June 1990, to initially develop and operate three Blockbuster Amphitheaters also proved disappointing at first. The plan was to build facilities in warmer-weather climates to have nearly year-round events. A plan to build an amphitheater in south Dade County never materialized, but others were built in Charlotte, Phoenix, and San Bernadino. But three venues wasn't enough to promote a tour or an act and the business wouldn't really take off until November 1993 when Blockbuster teamed with Sony Music Entertainment and Pace Entertainment Corp. and put together eight amphitheaters.

But these were just sideshows. In press reports in the summer of 1991, Huizenga was already musing publicly about ways to redirect Blockbuster's cash flow. All those $3 rentals at stores across the country meant

Blockbuster would have plenty of cash to invest once its store building slowed. "We have the best locations in town," he said. "We've got a plain vanilla box. We can sell shoes there if we want to. Maybe we'll build a music store that's green and white. We could call it Chartbusters." Huizenga wouldn't ever sell shoes, but he would make a move into music little more than a year later. But first, he had to restore credibility in Blockbuster through results and, optimally, deals with high-profile names. The first part of the equation came quickly: Blockbuster's revenues and earnings showed smart increases through the rest of 1991. The second part—the deals with high-profile names—started in late 1991 with an initial foray, a one-two punch, that was brilliantly timed. So brilliantly, in fact, that Blockbuster insiders still joke about the corporate shell-game, the big-stakes bluff, that was played for Blockbuster's benefit.

DUTCH TREAT: PHILIPS AND CITYVISION

Landing in Eindhoven, the Netherlands, Huizenga was back in the homeland of his father, waiting for a car to take him and Berrard to the headquarters of Philips Electronics N.V. They'd left at 2 P.M., flown all night, and in a few hours, would start the trip back. This trip was instigated, like many of the deals would be, by Steve Berrard. It was Berrard who had fretted over the stores in England. The market had been a headache and Blockbuster was still having problems making headway. Berrard had been eyeing Cityvision plc, owner of the Ritz video store chain, the largest in the country. Blockbuster had made three attempts to buy Cityvision over the years, but the stock price had always been too rich.

Then in early fall, Berrard noticed a newspaper article that Cityvision had missed their first half estimate and their stock had taken a heavy hit, and had dropped to less than half its previous level. Berrard called the chairman, who was reluctant even to take the call, feeling, rightfully, quite vulnerable. Berrard went to Huizenga's office, telling him here was their chance to snag Cityvision and cure the problematic United Kingdom market in one move.

But Huizenga was less than thrilled. Cityvision had a bunch of small stores, why would they want to dilute the Blockbuster concept? Berrard hammered hard on Cityvision's 30 percent market share, noted that Blockbuster had been struggling in the market and here was a chance to eliminate a competitor and capture that chunk of the market for themselves.

"I'll give you two weeks to get the damn thing done," Huizenga told Berrard. But he reminded Berrard of his attitude about takeovers. "Wayne had one rule," Berrard says. "You're never going to go after anything and lose. So if we're going to launch a takeover of a company, we've damn sure got to avoid someone coming over the top and taking it from us and suffer the embarrassment of being amateurish."

At Huizenga's behest, Berrard identified the two most likely candidates to challenge their effort. One, a United Kingdom-based company, he wasn't worried about because he didn't think they'd be able to make the deal fly because of potential antitrust problems. But electronics giant Philips Electronics N.V. held an interest in Super Club Retail Entertainment, a video rental and music store chain, as part of a foray into consumer retail markets and were expanding aggressively in the United States. At one point, a Philips executive had even made overtures about acquiring Blockbuster. So Philips could be a threat and could well thwart a takeover of Cityvision.

But where Berrard saw a problem, Huizenga saw opportunity. He quickly recognized courting Philips as a way to achieve both a near-term and long-term objective. "We wanted to acquire Ritz over in the UK, but we didn't have the size to do that deal and it was pretty expensive," Huizenga remembers. "How we think around here is, if we want to do something, we go out and do it and we figure out how we're going to take care of it later. The fact that we don't have the money doesn't stop us from getting it done." In this case, Huizenga had not only thought through the first step, but also the subsequent steps in a classic case of using OPM—Other People's Money—to do a deal.

"There's one thing we can do and that's talk to Philips," Huizenga told Berrard. He suggested Berrard set up a meeting with Jaap VanWeezendork, an executive at Super Club whom Berrard had gotten to know. Through that contact, they arranged to meet Laurens Das, a top executive at Philips headquarters. They left at night and used Huizenga's plane so they could save a day in travel. They could be in Holland and back in 24 hours. Over dinner, Huizenga sketched out the scenario for taking over Cityvision. The bottom line was that Blockbuster was going to go after Cityvision and wasn't going to let Philips take it away. "You have a couple of choices," Huizenga told Das. "One, you can join us, or you can go after it. But we're telling you right now we're not going to let you take it. It might be easier if we do it together." Initially, the idea was to go in as partners to do the Cityvision deal which would add about 800 stores in the United Kingdom to their operations. And there was also talk of the prospect of going into other parts of Europe as partners.

That sounded appealing to Das, who had wanted to establish a relationship with Blockbuster anyway. At Huizenga's suggestion, he arranged a meeting with Philips Chairman Jan Timmer and other top Philips executives. There were more meetings and "through these meetings we just got to liking each other," Huizenga says. "And the fact that I'm Dutch didn't hurt. Jan Timmer and I struck up a great relationship and I trusted him and he trusted me. They decided to put $66 million in because we were under timing pressure to get the tender offer going on Cityvision and he said, 'Wayne, just because I can look into those Dutch blue eyes am I doing this deal.'"

Though it didn't play a major role, Timmer concurs that the common ancestry was a plus. "We are always interested to meet people who come from this small country," he says. "It helped to build a relationship. Although his ancestors had come from there [Groningen province] I recognized some of the traits of the father, of where they come from. Those people are direct, straightforward. They tell you without diplomacy what they have in mind. They are well known for that and that trait was very visible in Mr. Huizenga."

It was Berrard who negotiated the two-way deal. When Berrard left for England to begin talks in earnest with Cityvision executives, Huizenga urged him to take the G-II. He knew Berrard was going to need it. Huizenga warned him again when he left: "Steve, this is a stock deal. I'm not coming up with a lot of cash, I'm telling you that right now." The investment bankers weren't encouraging with Berrard about the prospects for a stock deal. Blockbuster shares, though recovering, were still reeling from the bad publicity earlier in the year.

Berrard shuttled between London and Eindhoven, making 13 trips in six days. He'd negotiate with Cityvision, say he was returning to his hotel, then fly out that evening to Eindhoven to meet with Philips' executives. The sessions with Cityvision's investment bankers and executives were problematic at first. Top company officers were dismissive of Huizenga and Berrard about using stock. Even the investment bankers Berrard first approached weren't hopeful about doing a deal with U.S. securities. But Huizenga wouldn't budge. "No stock, no deal," he told Berrard. "Either you get it done or you come home." After the third discouraging round of talks, Berrard called Huizenga again. "I don't care what the price is you've got to use stock," Huizenga told Berrard. "If Philips puts the money in, the money can go toward the deal," he told Berrard. "But absent that it's stock. We've got a big multiple, we're going to use that multiple."

That boosted Berrard's efforts to get the deal done with Philips, so that the money could be used to offer a half-cash, half-stock deal. "He never wavered," Berrard says of Huizenga. "Unfortunately by now I'd fallen in love with this thing and he was still objective." With a deadline to meet to make the tender offer for Cityvision, Berrard stepped up the pressure on Philips' executives to make their investment. When they hesitated and wanted to do more due diligence on Cityvision, Huizenga and Berrard convinced Philips to buy Blockbuster stock instead, with a right to convert into an interest in Cityvision.

Blockbuster issued a press release November 18 announcing the commitment by Philips to invest $66 million by January 15, 1992. The vaguely worded statement said the electronics giant had the option of acquiring six million shares of Blockbuster stock or develop jointly with Blockbuster "business opportunities in the home entertainment industry." The release quoted Huizenga as noting that an anticipated benefit was that Blockbuster would promote Philips' new Compact Disc Interactive (CD-I) systems and software in its stores. The reaction was immediate, with stories in *The Wall Street Journal, Financial Times,* as well as other national and local press appearing the next day focusing on the move by the $31 billion electronics giant and the vote of confidence a technology and engineering leader was giving to what had been cast as the outmoded, soon-to-be eclipsed video rental industry. Speculation on the vague "joint business opportunities" zeroed in on Philips ownership of Super Club and a possible partnership in music or video stores.

It wasn't until four days later that the true nature of the relationship became clear. The day after snagging the Philips commitment, Berrard made one more trip to see Cityvision's executives. All the while, he'd suspected that they'd been holding out, hoping that Philips or another suitor would come along. In this last meeting, Berrard played his trump card. Philips was in as part of Blockbuster's deal. On November 22, Blockbuster announced that Cityvision had agreed on the terms of an offer to be acquired in a deal valued at $135 million. Philips had the right to buy half the Cityvision shares acquired by Blockbuster or buy Blockbuster stock.

But Huizenga knew from the start what he wanted. He wanted Philips not as a partner in Cityvision, but as an investor, a big-stakes investor, in Blockbuster. What better way to quell the technology fears than to get a technology company to invest?

Huizenga convinced Timmer that Philips was better served by leaving its investment in Blockbuster and taking stock. In April 1992, Timmer agreed. Blockbuster announced that Philips chose to acquire six million shares of Blockbuster stock, and reached an agreement for an option for five million additional shares. "To give Wayne credit, by keeping Philips in here during 1991 and 1992," Berrard says, "really kept the technology dogs out of our backyard."

So important was that perception that Berrard came up with a solution in July 1992 when Philips wanted to exercise its option for additional shares, but didn't have the cash. On their way back from Eindhoven, Berrard suggested to Huizenga that they take a note instead of cash. "Because what we wanted was the perception that Philips was stepping up even more into the company. Here's an electronics company that knew about technology and here they're making another investment in our company."

From the time of the initial deal in November 1991, speculation was rife in the media about Blockbuster buying Super Club, the video rental and music store division owned by Philips. But Philips had stumbled in making the investment, though and had paid too much, the division had been poorly managed and Huizenga wasn't willing to pay the asking price. "The deal with Super Club hadn't been too good," Timmer says. "We were impressed that other people in the same business did so much better and tried to understand what the secret was and we were particularly impressed with their system of control, how they knew what each store was doing and it was something we felt could be taken as an example." He remembers being impressed with Huizenga and Berrard's grasp of the details of the business. "They were well informed about the business they were in. They talked very little about grand design and philosophy. They talked facts and figures and targets. They were extraordinarily precise and had an impressive track record."

The relationship with Philips didn't change Blockbuster's dogfight in the market against Super Club. "We competed with them real hard," Berrard says. Blockbuster finally reached an agreement with Philips in October 1993 to buy Super Club, which consisted of 160 video stores and 270 music stores in the United States for approximately $150 million. Berrard notes it wasn't a dime more than he'd offered two years earlier. Learning from the Major Video trauma, Blockbuster spent six months planning how to integrate the stores with existing franchisees.

As promised, Blockbuster tested Philips CD-I system in some of its stores and reported back to Philips on consumer reaction. Because of internal restructuring and focus on Philips' part, the relationship between Blockbuster and Philips stayed more of an investment than a partnership. "I don't think they got as much out of it as they had hoped or we had hoped and the only thing that made it palatable is that they made a ton of money on the stock," Berrard says.

Says Timmer of the relationship with Blockbuster, "We got out of it what we wanted. I am a great admirer of Wayne Huizenga. He is an example of an outstanding entrepreneur and I have always worked very, very well with him. He is a man with an enormous amount of common sense and that is a quality in rare supply. He is very goal oriented and he has a very sharp mind and he has an instinct for business opportunities." Indeed, it was that very instinct that had led Huizenga to Philips and a deal which went a long way to restoring faith in Blockbuster.

RETAILER OR RENTAL BUSINESS? BLOCKBUSTER'S "SPLIT PERSONALITY"

As Blockbuster skyrocketed through 1990, Huizenga knew he needed to bolster the company's upper management ranks. That need became even more pressing as he and Berrard focused more on strategy and direction. On a strategic level, for years, Huizenga had been hearing analysts and others refer to Blockbuster as a retail company. Few within Blockbuster's management team had retail experience. "So we said let's try to bring in a guy with retail background and let's see if he can help move the needle more than we're moving the needle," Huizenga said.

There were even hints that Huizenga could see his own role lessening in the future. Years later, though Huizenga would insist there was no connection, it would seem more than a coincidence that at the time he appeared to be preparing investors for what might be change in his role in the company, he had been diagnosed in late 1990 with a very early stage of highly curable prostate cancer. Rumors swept through the company that he was ill, and the commonly held explanation was that he had to undergo a hernia operation. He underwent surgery New Year's weekend, after the spectacular inaugural Blockbuster Bowl. Huizenga insists the incident wasn't a factor in his decision to broaden management. Indeed, the only real effect, family and friends note, was that Huizenga gave up potato chips, switched to decaffeinated coffee, and ate more salads and chicken. "He was supposed to be out three weeks and was back to business within days," says Berrard.

It was during a meeting in 1989 with Den Fujita, who would become Blockbuster's partner in Japan and who had successfully launched McDonald's and Toys 'R Us in that tough market, that Huizenga heard of an executive he might be interested in: Joe Baczko from Toys 'R Us. Huizenga liked the idea. Not only would someone like Baczko bring retail experience, but there was terrific marquee value in the Toys 'R Us pedigree for Wall Street.

When Huizenga called him in the fall of 1990, Baczko rejected the notion. He didn't know much about the video business and he wasn't interested. But Huizenga mentioned his relationship with Den Fujita and suggested meeting somewhere. They met in Washington and began a dialogue.

But Joe's wife, Kathy, wasn't interested in moving to Florida. So in late 1990, Huizenga began his courtship of the Baczko family. "Wayne pulled off a fantastic ploy," Baczko recalls. "The first Blockbuster Bowl was coming out and he called and invited us to come down to the Blockbuster Bowl as his guests. Of course the kids were as excited as all heck about coming down here to watch Penn State play against Florida State." It was all first class, Huizenga style. He sent a plane up for them, had a helicopter waiting when they arrived to take them on a tour of the area. During the game, Huizenga took Baczko's son down to the field and he was extremely gracious to Kathy, knowing he had to win her over, had to overcome her hesitation in moving to Florida. The effort paid off. "It was obvious that the company was real, that they had a tremendous amount of enthusiasm, and it was a captivating environment at that time," Baczko remembers. He signed up.

The entry of Baczko into Blockbuster in February 1991 as president and chief operating officer marked a distinct era in the company's development—and a particular challenge for Huizenga. When he arrived at Blockbuster, says Baczko, "I came in to a series of firefights." But while he resolved some problems, his management style fanned the flames of some of those fires into roaring blazes. Though he held a Masters in Business Administration from Harvard University and had worked as an executive for Max Factor and W. R. Grace, his approach borrowed more from his training in the Marine Corps, where he'd served as a sergeant in Vietnam. Impatient and curt, he brooks no fools and doesn't hesitate to say when he thinks someone fits the category. In his 23-month tenure at Blockbuster, by his own count, he would go through 12 vice-presidents, half of whom he fired, with the rest lost through attrition. His emphasis on paring payroll would cost dozens more jobs.

From Baczko's viewpoint, Huizenga's entrepreneurial management style had created a confederation of fiefdoms within Blockbuster. Marketing reported to Tom Gruber. Operations reported to Scott Beck. Merchandising was under Ron Castell. "Not being really an operating person, much of what was going on within Blockbuster, Wayne was just either unaware of or allowed to happen," Baczko says. "There was an incredible amount of money that was being burned and a lot of energy being burned."

Destroying the fiefdoms and establishing control was one of Baczko's first priorities, and he carried that mission out throughout Blockbuster's ranks with zeal. Under Huizenga, a key management concept was that each store was independent. He treated store managers akin to the owners of the garbage companies Waste Management had gobbled up. Within guidelines, managers used discretion in deciding how many new releases to order, on the theory that they knew their customers best. To Baczko, that was non-sense. What did a 21-year-old manager who's going to work a store for a year, maybe two, know about customer needs? One fundamental change implemented was taking control away from the store managers to a regional manager level. That didn't win him points among the store manager ranks. Other unpopular decisions were cutbacks in perks like free movies for staffers and first-class travel for executives.

But those actions just made the troops unhappy. He also cut the troops. Payroll was pared to the bone. At the stores, the only Blockbuster employees customers could find were at the cash registers, which often had lines a dozen or more deep. Compared with Scott Beck's free-spending ways, it was a total culture shock for Blockbuster executives. With some executives, like Tom Gruber, it became nearly open warfare as Baczko gutted the marketing department. Gone was the emphasis on building the Blockbuster brand, as well as the Blockbuster Kids, the Kids Corners, and the family positioning Gruber had created. And Gruber would have been gone, too, if Baczko had had his way. "Joe wanted to fire me in the worst way," Gruber says. "I would have been gone in the first wave, the second wave, but Wayne wouldn't let him."

The contrast between Huizenga's and Baczko's management style was startling for Blockbuster veterans. Huizenga is demanding but rarely demeaning. He makes his point directly, often using humor which could be biting but not malicious. "Originally when we started to have staff meetings the guys would bring up an idea and Wayne would just hammer them," Berrard says. "Not so much to degrade them but to make sure that before you make a statement you think about what you're saying. And you could watch over time, people were tenacious, but they also had a lot of reasons as to why they were saying what they were saying. Wayne would do it first of all in a manner where he'd be joking and laughing, but you know you're getting your shot." That style differed sharply from Baczko's, who acknowledges that Huizenga told him he was too tough on others.

For his part, Huizenga shoulders the blame for the atmosphere that festered at Blockbuster during Baczko's reign. "There is no question that the styles were different but I probably would criticize myself more than Joe," Huizenga says. "Because as tough as Joe was, I'm just the opposite and more easy going. I let things get loose and people doing their own things and Joe comes in and he screws everything down. Right away, he's not going to be a popular guy but that should be blamed more on me than on Joe because if I would have been tougher, Joe wouldn't have had to be in that spot."

But Baczko's tenure was marked by more than just an abrasive management style. He fundamentally saw Blockbuster's business differently. He aimed to turn it more into a retailer, emphasizing the sale of video tapes over its core rental business. He also implemented other changes, like cutting the rental time for new releases to two nights instead of three to allow more "turns" of hot movies, and bolstered Blockbuster's fledgling international expansion. Initially, Baczko's strategy worked. Increased sales of video tapes helped boost 1991 results, with the key retail barometer of same store revenue rising nearly 8 percent. Those results aided the recovery of Blockbuster's lagging stock.

But selling tapes was a thinner-margin business than renting videos and its emphasis blurred Blockbuster's identity. Moreover, Baczko's implementation of a Toys "R" Us mentality—big stores, lots of volume, little customer service—clashed with the views of Blockbuster veterans, particularly Berrard, and with franchisees. "Our business didn't need to be so retail like," Berrard says. "We got ourselves caught in the transition from what we had done so long and so well, to changing the business in an arena that we were never going to be able to compete in because people don't come to our store and look at us as a discounter. All the research we do today, we're looked at as the high-cost provider."

Another split brewing within the company surfaced in the summer of 1992 over a new rating system adopted by Hollywood, the NC-17, or no-children under 17, which replaced the X-rating, and over carrying unrated, uncut versions of movies. Blockbuster had been getting bombarded by postcards from conservative Christian groups urging it to adopt a separate "Dove" rating for family videos and not to carry NC-17.

Internally, Baczko and Ron Castell, along with some franchisees, were pressuring to carry select NC-17 or unrated equivalents. Gruber, "Mr. Family," meanwhile, continued his end-run around Baczko and warned Huizenga that the elimination of Blockbuster's family positioning, in his view, was unhealthy for the company long-term and that only he could settle this issue and preserve Blockbuster's image. At a tense management meeting called to discuss the NC-17 rating, Gruber also brought up that Kids Corners were being taken out of the stores. "They are? Is that right?" Huizenga asked Gerry Weber. It was an uncomfortable moment for Weber since Baczko had ordered their removal. After a few minutes of Weber talking around the issue, Baczko acknowledged that he'd ordered them removed. "That's not our philosophy," Huizenga said. "Our philosophy is family and kids and no NC-17." The decision had been made.

"Wayne was very much a proponent of adhering to the rating system and if NC-17 is an X, then it's clear what we do," Castell says, who admits it provided effective deflection to groups on both the left, who were complaining of censorship (though certainly Blockbuster wasn't preventing other video stores from carrying the movies and indeed, its decision benefited those stores) and on the right, who wanted even stricter screening.

Besides internal turmoil, relationships with franchisees were also fraying under Baczko. Some Blockbuster franchisees had certainly had differences with Huizenga, particularly over the Major Video, Erol's, and other acquisitions. While some franchisees might think of Huizenga as a SOB at times, at least he was a pleasant SOB. His friendly and jocular manner masked his hard-as-steel business approach. In the view of many franchisees, Baczko was just abrasive. "Joe had no franchisee experience," says Bob Guerin, who was put in charge of franchisee relations during the latter part of Baczko's tenure as damage control. "Joe was a control guy. I think more where Wayne had a love-hate relationship, that he admired (a franchisee) for being an entrepreneur but he resented the fact that he couldn't tell them what to do, Joe simply resented the fact that he couldn't tell him what to do. For the most part it was just oil and water with Joe and the franchisees."

For his part, Baczko notes that he inherited a difficult situation with franchisees when he arrived. Because of the knocks in early 1991 with the Gulf War and the attacks by critics and short-sellers, franchisees, their partners and investors were nervous, and angry that the company couldn't seem to get its side of the story heard. Baczko acknowledges that his policies exacerbated existing tensions. "I think the franchisees disagreed with what I was doing in the company, no question about that," he says. But a more fundamental attitude is summed up in his blanket statement that "I have never felt that you could franchise retail."

In addition to tensions within the company and with its franchisees, Baczko also created friction with Blockbuster's biggest supplier: Hollywood. Under Baczko, Blockbuster began to flex its muscles with the studios. He had a retailer's mentality, in which if one supplier didn't give the best deal, you went to the next one. The problem with that approach in the movie business is that movies are a proprietary product—only Disney, for instance, has an animated version of Snow White.

The new attitude "made dealing with Blockbuster an absolute chore," says Herb Dorfman, president of Orion Home Video. "The marching orders were to beat the studios into submission and that was very different for Blockbuster." Relations with Disney, in particular, deteriorated. "It was one of the worst relationships I had in business," says Ann Daly, now president of the domestic video division of Disney. She admits that the problem cut both ways. "We did not do ourselves or Blockbuster a favor and we were equally difficult to deal with." But Blockbuster's attempt to exercise clout didn't work well with Disney. Since its animation and family videos generate more tape sales than for other studios, it relied less on Blockbuster as a customer. Since Blockbuster had never been a primary outlet for sell-through, Disney pursued other ways to compensate for the lost business.

An underlying current was that while Baczko was convinced the studios could be made to bend to Blockbuster's clout, Huizenga feared a potential backlash. Investors in Blockbuster's stock were already skittish about the so-called "window" during which the studios provided movies to the video market before distributing them through pay-per-view or cable. Baczko never saw much of a threat in that, and indeed, he may well have been right. The number of homes available for pay-per-view at the time, even studio executives admit, made it economically unfeasible for the studios to carry out such a move. But Huizenga feared that even the threat of it, though more political than real, could send Blockbuster's stock into a tailspin.

Huizenga was in a box with the Baczko situation. Complaints were growing from friends and franchisees. Tensions were high between Baczko and other Blockbuster executives and even Hollywood studio heads. Yet he couldn't risk Baczko leaving too soon. It would look awful for the Street. As Blockbuster's management split into the Joe-camp, with executives Baczko had hired, and the Steve-camp, with executives loyal to Berrard, Huizenga grew increasingly irritated at the polarization and politicization of the company. In early 1992, he talked to both Berrard and Baczko. "He sat me down and basically told me I was creating a political environment that he wasn't going to stand for and I suspect he told Joe the same thing. It wasn't good for the company. His attitude was, it's going to change or we're all going to be doing something different and I got the message," Berrard says. "I'm not so sure I improved a whole hell of a lot but I was sensitive to the fact that Wayne had a sense that Joe and I had created our camps and I was just as much at fault as Joe."

By his own admission, Baczko was given broad latitude by Huizenga to implement his program. It was part of Huizenga's "no excuses" management style: outline responsibilities, provide the resources, and expect results. But concern mounted within Blockbuster as same store sales, that key barometer in retailing, began dropping in the summer of 1992. Baczko blames a number of factors: the summer Olympics, lousy movies, poor weather. But the change coincided with his strategy of cost-cutting, marketing mix, and other tactics. "We weren't doing as well on a comp basis and were very concerned about what we were going to tell the outside world," he says.

What Berrard did tell the outside world was that the company was in transition. He kept trying to lower the expectations of analysts. Further, while the conflict with Baczko was kept largely out of the media, analysts knew there wasn't harmony in Blockbuster's headquarters. Blockbuster's stock remained resilient during this period in 1992, though strong revenues and earnings reports didn't move it much because of the low same-store sales growth. "We didn't get hurt but we didn't get any credit, either," Berrard says.

In August 1992, Huizenga hired a marketing executive, James Hilmer, formerly of Whittle Communications and a friend of Chuck Lewis. Ostensibly the reason was to determine the reason and a solution for the slippage in same store performance, and restore the company's image-building program. But the real mission was to diagnose the company's management and morale ills. Huizenga had also reinstituted management meetings and was getting feedback from Gruber and other executives.

Meanwhile, although Blockbuster had recently expanded into music retailing, Huizenga and Berrard had resolved Blockbuster's identity crisis and the question of whether Blockbuster was a retail company or an entertainment company. The dogfight retail business with its thin margins held little appeal. Already, they'd begun scouting for acquisitions in Hollywood. From now on, the emphasis would be on Blockbuster *Entertainment* Corporation. The strategy shift also provided a convenient way for Baczko to exit with minimal public relations damage.

"There was never what you'd call a breaker," Baczko says. "Wayne got an awful lot of his feedback from franchisees, from friends of Wayne's and from some people in the company who really should not have been there. And he kept it to himself, his own counsel, so you never knew. You had a lot of rear guard action." Huizenga's "open door" policy sounds positive, but Baczko maintains it helped foster a political environment. "It can be a very constructive thing, if in fact you're not discriminating about what you want to hear or what you'll allow yourself to hear. I think in Wayne's instance, it was one way of keeping his control," Baczko says. "He is always open to gossip and I think that helps him and hinders his company. Looking back on it, I wasn't aware of how much was coming into Wayne from the back door."

On Monday, January 4, 1993, at 8:10 A.M. Blockbuster's top executives gathered for their first meeting of the new year. Without a word, Huizenga passed out an organization chart and a draft of a news release. "Blockbuster Reorganizes for Global Opportunities. President Resigns." The news was met with silence, not surprise. "The future of the company didn't fit Joe's personality and style," Huizenga told the assembled group. He stressed that it was important that no one say anything negative about Baczko to the press. He noted that the press release mentioned a new retail venture that Baczko might enter into with Blockbuster and other investors and it would not serve the company to speak ill of someone who might be a partner. Few present bought the partnership angle, believing it was a convenient way to buy silence and save face on both sides. "Blockbuster is not a retail company," Huizenga said. He noted that the biggest complaint he'd been hearing was that Blockbuster had changed. Service wasn't good. Stores looked different. The company would need to spend more, add more people. The cuts had gone too far and customers resented the change. Blockbuster was going to be focused on customer service and being customer friendly and anyone who didn't agree with the new direction needed to leave.

Repair work within Blockbuster and in its relations with franchisees and Hollywood studios was quickly underway. Ann Daly credits Huizenga for healing the rift with Disney. "We had pursued other ways to make up for that business and that was when Wayne stepped in and said we're going to have a better relationship with this company," she says. Not only did she fly to Fort Lauderdale for a meeting within weeks of Baczko's departure to discuss the situation, but Huizenga, through his dealings with Walt Disney Co. Chairman Michael Eisner after Disney and Huizenga were both awarded new hockey franchises in December 1992, also strove to improve relations.

Internally, Huizenga and Berrard assessed the management ranks. Within months, some of those most closely identified with Baczko had left Blockbuster for other jobs. There was no wholesale bloodletting but there were some anxious times. Knowing he was perceived as a member of the Joe-camp, Gerry Weber followed the strategy of a strong offense being the best defense. "Welcome back," he told Huizenga and Berrard. "You guys walked away from the business literally for these two years, left him to do his thing, and where were you? Somebody had to execute. I tell you what, I guess I had a choice, I either followed Joe's lead, his direction, or he would have fired me. And since you gave him the mandate and gave him the power, it was clear to me that he had your support." Weber stressed that it was Huizenga who had hired him and ran through the diverse management eras that he and other operating execs at Blockbuster had already lived through during its short history: Rob Castleberry, Luigi Salvaneschi, Scott Beck, and Joe Baczko. Weber's words took Huizenga and Berrard aback and saved his job. They gave him the benefit of the doubt, and watched carefully his relationships with regional and field managers over the next few months. Within months, Steve Berrard took over as Blockbuster president and by August 1993, Huizenga had tapped his long-time friend and Blockbuster's largest franchisee, George Johnson, to be president of Blockbuster's newly named "consumer division" which included video and music stores.

Weber sums up the Baczko era at Blockbuster: "Did he enhance our bottom line? Did he add profit to the bottom line? Did he help our stock and everything else? Absolutely. Did it hurt our business? The top line? Yeah, I think during Joe's tenure, our top line was hurt. Morale was hurt." This period still puzzles him. If Huizenga wanted to improve the profitability, there were other ways to go about it. But it was Baczko's Toys "R" Us pedigree and the credibility that had conferred on Blockbuster with Wall Street that had been the draw. "The bottom line is, if Wayne wanted to cut costs he had the group, the infrastructure in place. All he had to do is give us some direction. We're the ones who implemented it anyway. Joe Baczko didn't teach anybody how to cut costs," he says. "Wayne could have, Steve could have asked that of us. But we didn't have the marquee value."

Music Moves: New Diversifications

The Gulf War had jolted Huizenga. By mid-1992, Blockbuster's stock, boosted by the Philips investment, had recovered, but the lessons of the war had not been forgotten. Branching out into other lines of business had become a mandate for Berrard, but it was tricky. "We had to spin a story that would also fly with Wall Street because in the early days of going out and doing all these acquisitions all the doomsayers came right back out and said 'they're running away from the business,'" Berrard says. "I spent the next six months going out and saying, 'no, here's why we did what we did.'"

Huizenga's marching orders were that the new ventures had to be in industries large enough to be a potential billion-dollar business (no more tour boat companies), provide opportunities for consolidation, and relate to entertainment. The first deals Berrard brought in as potential targets were far afield. One was a company that dispensed drugs in hospitals, and rented the dispensing machines to hospitals. It appealed to Huizenga's penchant for rental companies but he nixed it since there was no fit with Blockbuster's core business.

Blockbuster had three key strengths that Berrard decided to build upon. It had a brand name that represented entertainment and fun. It had a retail distribution network that spanned the country and was expanding overseas. And it had a database of 50 million customers with names, addresses, and profile information (though the value of that data base was heavily debated within Blockbuster).

With that criteria, the move into music was a natural. Huizenga had thought early on, as early as 1989, that Blockbuster could extend its franchise in video to include music. Some companies were experimenting with both video rental and music retailing in the same stores, but Huizenga didn't see much sense in that. His view was that a store could never carry enough of either product to satisfy customers and risked losing sales for both. Instead, he wanted to acquire an existing music store chain. One drawback: the thin margins in music retailing, a fraction of those in the video rental business. The key was to develop a new kind of music store, one that would appeal to an older clientele and cut the "walkout" rate—the number of potential buyers who walk in but leave without making a purchase.

To avoid Wall Street knocking Blockbuster's stock because it had diversified too early, before its core video business was built out, Huizenga was forced to wait until Blockbuster was bigger and was turning a positive cash flow. But that didn't mean he couldn't start to get acquainted with the industry and build relationships that would later bear fruit. Throughout 1989 and 1990, he began calling on executives throughout the music retail business. One of those he met with was Stanley Gold, president of Shamrock Holdings of California Inc., the private investment company of Roy Disney, which controlled two music store chains, Sound Warehouse and Music Plus. In the summer of 1992, when Shamrock was ready to sell, Gold called Huizenga, a call that wouldn't have been placed, Huizenga notes, without the prior groundwork. Negotiations culminated on October 19 when Blockbuster announced it had bought the two chains totaling 236 stores in a deal valued at $185 million in cash and stock, vaulting into seventh place among music retailers. (A few years later, Blockbuster would be criticized in some circles as trying to Disney-ize the music retail business with strict dress codes, including prohibitions on earrings and long hair on male employees. Employees who complained to *The Miami Herald* were fired within days of the published article.)

Meanwhile, during one of his trips to Europe during his negotiations for Cityvision, Berrard had visited a Virgin Megastore in the United Kingdom. These stores, usually more than 10,000 square feet, aren't stores as much as music playlands for adults, as much a destination as an outlet to get the latest compact discs. The stores feature separate rooms for classical, jazz, and other music venues, individual listening stations, video viewing points and cafes. Berrard had particularly been impressed by the flashy store on the Champs de Elyses in Paris, and decided joining forces with Virgin in music retailing would enable Blockbuster to make a splash of its own. "I found the perfect music concept," he told Huizenga, who flew out to London to take a look at the store and meet with Virgin executives.

In late September 1992, Huizenga and Berrard met at the Beverly Wilshire Hotel with Trevor Abbott, the second in command to Virgin's mercurial founder, Richard Branson, and Ian Duffell, president of Virgin Retail Group in the Americas, Canada and Asia. "As a person, he was fascinating," remembers Duffell. "He seemed to be totally fearless in the way he approached business but he'd been through the logic a million times over in his own head. His mind was a computer, processing information, but in some ways, he was very naive about business on a day to day basis and was soaking up information to rapidly increase his learning curve."

At that point, Virgin was three months away from opening its first test store in the United States, which was an enticing, but potentially dangerous market as other retailers from England had tried to crack it and failed. Virgin had gotten a Singaporean investor with whom they'd worked with before to help back the project. At the meeting, Huizenga wowed them with stunning Blockbuster's factoids: it was bigger than the next 300 video store chains combined and had more Blockbuster cardholders than American

Express. The Brits were impressed. Here was a partner who was not only willing but eager to back the expansion of the Virgin name in the United States. In the deal announced November 16, 1992, less than a month after Blockbuster announced its foray into music with the acquisition of Sound Warehouse and Music Plus, Blockbuster was to be an equal partner in Virgin's 15 stores in Europe and have 75 percent ownership of U.S. stores (other than the Los Angeles one) which was a three-way partnership with the Singaporean investor. Virgin would retain managing control along with its 25 percent interest. There was no upper limit to the commitment, and each Virgin store cost about $5 million to open. Blockbuster's backing accelerated Virgin's expansion, including the planned opening of what was being billed as the world's largest music store in Times Square in New York in 1995.

But the partnership between Huizenga and Branson wasn't a happy one. Huizenga saw the ventures as Virgin-Blockbuster Megastores, and fully expected the Blockbuster name to be clearly part of the logo and affiliation. When he visited the Los Angeles-area store in early 1993 just before it opened, he was incensed to find that the Blockbuster name was nowhere to be seen. Not on the logo, not inside the store, nowhere. Huizenga felt he'd been taken advantage of—he hadn't committed all those millions just to be a behind-the-scenes partner. The point was to build the Blockbuster brand name and leverage off its database of card-carrying customers.

Berrard, as was often his role, was caught between what Huizenga wanted and what could be done. From the start, negotiations with Virgin had stumbled over the name issue. In Europe, Branson and his team were adamant about not adding Blockbuster since the Virgin name was already so well established. In the United States, they were more amiable, but wanted an example of what Huizenga and Berrard had in mind. A few faxes of examples went back and forth, but nothing suited Huizenga. "No way, our sign should be just as big," he told Berrard. Finally, at an impasse, Berrard handed the baton to his boss. "Wayne," he said, "I think you're going to have to settle this one yourself."

Huizenga and Trevor Abbot discussed the issue again and finally, many faxes later, Abbot agreed to one that while unappealing, would suit the agreement in spirit. "We got the deal done knowing in my heart this was always going to be a problem," Berrard says. Since Virgin had agreed to put the Blockbuster name up in a few strategic locations, Berrard didn't focus in on the issue any more—until the visit to the Los Angeles store.

The store manager was showing Huizenga and Berrard around. "Wayne was livid, just livid," Berrard recalls. "The shopping center owner came up and Wayne just took into him, too. It was a big thing and then of course, around here, you can't delegate responsibility, so it falls in my bailiwick. In the meantime, the guys from Virgin are telling us that none of the land-lords want the damn Blockbuster name up on these Virgin Music stores because it doesn't fit the example of the same store that gives condoms away for nothing."

But Huizenga didn't budge. "Who in the hell knows Virgin. We have Blockbuster stores on every corner. Don't you think when we own 75 per-cent of the store we ought to have our damn name up?"

Berrard admitted that was hard to argue with, but tried to ease the situ-ation with reason. "Steve, I really don't give a damn. We own 75 percent. Do you think our name should be up on the store?"

"Yes," Berrard answered.

"Well, don't you think it should be as prominent as the name of the per-son who owns 25 percent of the store?" Huizenga asked.

"Yes."

"So why isn't it done?"

Says Berrard: "It was like a circle. He was really upset and rightfully so. My argument was, we're out here building Blockbuster Music stores every-where around them. I said, there is a distinguishing mark that belongs to Blockbuster." The argument didn't sway Huizenga, who still considers it a sore point. "I liked those guys and the only thing I didn't like about the re-lationship was the fact that we could never get the logo thing worked out. They didn't have any interest in working the logo thing out. They liked the name Virgin and they wanted to stick with it and of course we were in love with the Blockbuster name and logo and we wanted that all over the stores."

"We exchanged views but we didn't see eye to eye," Duffell remembers. "It created a lot of unrest and he boxed with a lot of people as a result. In his head, he had such a strong equity in Blockbuster that he had everything to gain by it. Fortunately, I wasn't employed by him, so I could go on with what I thought. If I had been employed by him, I might have been a vic-tim." To this day, there remains little or no sign of Blockbuster in or on the Virgin stores.

But though not a stated intention, perhaps Huizenga lobbed his own re-sponse. Through negotiations with Virgin, Berrard had made it clear that Blockbuster's intention was to become the dominant music retailer in America. The two-pronged strategy was to invest with Virgin to develop mega, destination stores, while buying chains with smaller stores to ser-vice the "convenience" or neighborhood markets. The Virgin executives were mollified, since it seemed the small stores wouldn't compete with their concept. Blockbuster hired two design firms. "Then what we added to it were some of the entertaining aspects," Berrard says. "We really got that out of the Virgin relationship."

The Blockbuster Music Plus stores are strikingly similar to the Virgin concept in miniature, too close for the comfort of Virgin executives. Virgin offers a large number of personal listening stations, up to 100, and Blockbuster offered 20 or more. Rack designs and other elements also borrow liberally from Virgin's concept. "Imitation is the sincerest form of flattery, but on other hand it is slightly frustrating," Duffell says. "Someone stealing your ideas encourages you to improve what you're doing." There have also been conflicts over real estate sites, with both Virgin and Blockbuster Music scouting for the best locations, and that's caused more anxiety than anticipated when the deal was struck. The relationship between Virgin and Blockbuster would continue to fray until it was finally severed in early 1995.

The two very different entrepreneurs, Branson and Huizenga, make for an intriguing comparison. Huizenga "seemed to me totally fearless and that's how I see the connection with Richard because Richard is almost identical in those characteristics," Duffell says. "The challenge is more important than the actual process of the deal." And like Branson, "once he's convinced he's going to do something, he's unshakable. They've both got their egos. They like to read about themselves and publicity that benefits the business. The good thing about both of them is that they don't get carried away with it. Many people fail because they believe what they read and believe they can walk on water. They're both great publicists, but have a bit of a wry smile when they read something about themselves."

But they approach business quite differently. Branson has never bought a business, has always built from scratch, and pursues different lines of business because he finds them interesting, like developing an airline or more recently, a condom company and a cola company. "Richard is a classic entrepreneur because he takes crazy ideas and makes them work. We're not in the cola business because it fits the business. It's because he likes the challenge. Strategically, Wayne is much more disciplined, but Richard is more entrepreneurial. When Wayne was diversifying the business, they were all entertainment based businesses. If you asked a business strategist on where he should be with a plan to expand (Blockbuster), he's done a tremendous job. He's soaked up everybody's good ideas like a sponge, kept the good ideas and rejected the bad ones. He's very disciplined in that way."

He remarks about one other incident: He and his wife spent an evening with Huizenga at dinner once. He met up a month later with Huizenga, who asked about his wife by name. "He has a helluva a data bank in that computer brain of his," Duffell says. "He's an interesting, complex character in that he's interested in small details in the personal side of things but on the other hand absolutely ruthless in the business side of things. Once he locks in on something, nothing will stop him from doing it. I think we got on pretty well but I wouldn't like to cross him."

GOING HOLLYWOOD: REPUBLIC PICTURES CORP. AND SPELLING ENTERTAINMENT

In plotting Blockbuster's future, Huizenga and Berrard also turned to Chuck Lewis, Huizenga's long-time friend and contact at Merrill Lynch's Chicago office. In the summer of 1992, Lewis arranged a meeting in Merrill's New York office for Huizenga and Berrard to talk with analyst and investment banker Harold Vogel and James Mason, who had expertise in the entertainment industry. As they sat around a conference table tossing out ideas, Vogel warned about the treacheries of Hollywood. Many a corporate giant has been humbled by Tinseltown, their visions of cinematic grandeur reduced to balance sheet versions of slasher movies oozing red ink instead of blood. Huizenga knew the dangers, but it didn't hurt to hear them voiced again.

One company that Vogel noted was conservatively run and a potentially interesting candidate was Republic Pictures Corp. Founded in 1935, Republic Pictures had a long and convoluted history until 1985 when an investment group headed by Russell Goldsmith bought into the publicly traded company and took over management control. Republic was a "sleeper" with just $17 million in revenues, but an incredible library boasting rights to more than 1,000 films, including many classics. The library would prove ever more valuable in satisfying the voracious demand for programming by cable and broadcast networks. In part by aggressively marketing Republic's library, Goldsmith and his crew had grown the company to $81 million by 1991.

Huizenga's entry into baseball would provide useful contacts. He'd been awarded one of two expansion franchises in July 1991. Goldsmith was also part-owner of the San Diego Padres baseball team. After the meeting with Merrill Lynch, Huizenga made a point of seeking out Goldsmith at the next baseball owners' meeting and recounting the conversation at Merrill Lynch's offices and wondering if they could meet. Since Blockbuster was the largest video retailer and home video was Republic's largest revenue segment, Goldsmith was happy to talk with him. At the first formal meeting in the fall of 1992, Huizenga and Berrard explained to Goldsmith that they were interested in Blockbuster diversifying into software and wondered if Blockbuster and Republic could do something together. "I was interested but unclear how it would work out," Goldsmith says. "It evolved that they would like to buy a minority stake in Republic. We had prided ourselves on having strong relationships with some interesting companies and individuals and this was a way to get additional capital and enhance our relationship with the leading video retailer."

In January 1993, Blockbuster announced it had bought a 35 percent stake in Republic, plus warrants, for $25 million. But Wayne Huizenga, who is rarely content with having a minority interest in anything, had grander designs for Republic—and for Blockbuster. In little more than a year, those plans would squeeze out Goldsmith and much of his management team.

While Huizenga was talking with Goldsmith, discussions were already underway with the Lindners about buying their stake in Spelling Entertainment. The company had been founded in 1965 as Aaron Spelling Productions and gone public in August 1986 as Spelling Entertainment Group Inc., a transaction that allowed Aaron Spelling to cash out $63 million worth of stock, but still keep a majority stake of the company. Through a series of complicated transactions with Lindner-controlled companies, Spelling Entertainment ended up a television production company inside the discarded shell of an oil company.

When Huizenga and Berrard began looking at it, the company was a combination of a formidable library of television shows and movie rights, plus new creative potential if Aaron Spelling and his crew stayed, and environmental liabilities remaining from the Charter Oil days. The environmental claims were a concern in negotiating the deal with the Lindners, as were residual effects of bankruptcy claims from an earlier incarnation of Charter and another Lindner affiliate. But those concerns were mollified by reserves for estimated damages and a pledge by the Lindners for additional coverage.

As with Republic, much of the value Huizenga saw in Spelling lay in the existing library, with rights to television favorites like "The Love Boat" and "Dallas" and movies like *Terminator*. The new cable channels slated to come on line, Huizenga figured, would need programming. The valuation of Spelling's library was close enough to the amount they were willing to pay for the company that Huizenga and Berrard felt comfortable. It was a good deal despite their inexperience in Hollywood. Acquiring a majority stake of Spelling would be another triumph for Huizenga and send a sure signal to Wall Street about his plan to speed the evolution of Blockbuster into an entertainment company.

But there was one key factor remaining. Huizenga had to convince Aaron Spelling to stay. The legendary producer's contract said he answered only to the Lindners. Any change in control meant he could leave. Without Spelling, the company wouldn't be worth near as much. While there was value in the library and in distribution segments of the company, the creative drive, and the engine behind that drive, came from the man whose moniker the company bore.

As Huizenga walked into the home office of the legendary producer, he knew not to hammer on the business details. What he saw confirmed his hunch. The oak bookcases lining the walls held family photos, two Emmy awards—and a lifetime of creative endeavor. On the shelves were bound volumes of every script in which Spelling had ever been involved, episodes of hit television shows from the past like "Charlie's Angels" and "Fantasy Island." After a brief dry spell in 1990, Spelling had come back strong with "Beverly Hills 90210," a popular series carried by the Fox Network about spoiled, rich high-school kids coming of age.

For his part, Spelling had no intention of staying. He didn't like change. "I was flabbergasted at this chain of events," he says. But as Spelling recalls, during the meeting with Huizenga, "the weirdest thing happened. We talked for ten minutes about why he wanted the company and his interest in TV and motion pictures, and I don't know what happened, I just listened to him and totally changed my mind. And I swear to you, I'm not a child and not easily swayed but there was something about Wayne and Steve that was so honest and forthright about what they would do and wouldn't do and they wouldn't interfere with the creativity of the company." The message was exactly what Spelling wanted to hear: We want you to do more and we'll provide the resources for you to do so.

At meeting Huizenga, Spelling was reminded of a conversation he'd once had with actress Bette Davis, when he was casting his first script, a pilot called "Decorator," and looking at tryouts for a supporting cast. Her advice was to watch the eyes: if the eyes reflected back, they were mirrors, but if you could see through to the soul, they were windows and they were looking for windows. "Wayne," says Spelling, "has great windows. They're piercing, right to the soul windows." In this case, Huizenga's "windows" had won Spelling over and moved Blockbuster up another notch in his plan. On March 8, four days after Huizenga's meeting with Spelling, Blockbuster announced it had bought 48 percent of Spelling Entertainment in a deal valued at $140 million.

Analysts took note of the moves by Blockbuster into programming, but kept watching for the next step. For much of Wall Street, the new directions, while interesting, didn't quite answer the question of how Blockbuster was going to put the pieces together. The biggest bet was that Blockbuster intended to develop a cable channel to parlay its acquisitions of the Republic and Spelling libraries and even provide a venue for Huizenga's Florida Marlins baseball team as additional "programming."

But Huizenga was moving cautiously into Hollywood and often warned Berrard about being taken in by the glamour. When Berrard became chief executive officer of Spelling, Huizenga told him, "the first time you read a script, you and I are going to have big troubles." He said it jokingly, but Berrard knew he wasn't kidding. "We're not Hollywood guys so we're going to be like the guys that move into town with a wheelbarrow full of money and everybody's going to have their hands in that wheelbarrow and by the time we get to the end of Rodeo Drive the damn thing will be empty," he'd tell Berrard. "How are we going to avoid that?"

The basic premise was to run Spelling—and eventually, Republic, as Blockbuster would finance a merger between the two—like they ran Blockbuster. But this was Hollywood. "The first meeting I had with one of the top guys, he looked at me and said, 'so how's it feel to have someone working for you that makes more money than you do?' I said, 'well today it doesn't feel real good, but it won't last that way forever.' He's no longer there, obviously," Berrard says. "It was a culture shock for us, but Wayne's first three things were: 'we're not going to do it because that's the way it's done and I don't want to hear that's the way it's done in Hollywood. Because when I look at all these Hollywood companies, none of them makes any damn money and there's a good reason for that.' Two, we're not going to take risks. We're not going to make big budget films because everybody else feels that's what has to be done. Third, we're not going to fall in love. The third thing probably drives the other two. The one thing that gave Wayne a lot of confidence is that Aaron is very conservative and he was a big part of the company and his name was still on the door."

Indeed, Spelling still approved all expense reports on his production groups, an oversight mechanism Huizenga and Berrard liked. Huizenga, who became chairman, along with Berrard and Ron Castell, who became the point men in the transition, borrowed some of Blockbuster's basics, putting in a stock option program, scaling back bonuses and taking a hard line on compensation.

As for Spelling Entertainment, the adjustment to the new owners was a switch from a parent that had been finance-driven, to one that saw the company as a related business. "Our opinion was these guys are in the video rental business," says John Ryan, president of Worldvision, the distribution arm of Spelling Entertainment. "We found out they viewed themselves as being in the entertainment business and once we got to know them, we found they were very much in the entertainment business."

Over dinner at the Manhattan Ocean Club in June 1993, Berrard, Huizenga, Ryan, and Cohen discussed possibilities for new ventures by and between the two companies. With Huizenga's penchant for always thinking big, there was even discussion of Blockbuster buying a network. A more immediate possibility was a cable channel. "Wayne was always interested in finding ways to synergistically grow the organizations so one would help the other so we were constantly pushed to think of ways that might enable us to do our jobs better," Ryan says. "Growth was always paramount. Wayne in particular really wanted to make things happen. They set some ground rules and then wanted you to tell them how you wanted to make the company succeed and grow. Rather than keeping the lid on, they took it off."

Aaron Spelling himself noticed the change. "Their interest was expanding and expanding and expanding," he says, noting that he was never made to feel like an employee. At one meeting Berrard attended, discussion went on for about an hour about a mini-series Spelling wanted to produce, "Texas" based on James Michener's novel. There were problems getting networks to ante up the fees. Finally, Berrard told Spelling that if this was a project he really wanted to do, then to go ahead and do it. Blockbuster would buy two copies for each of its stores and pay for it that way. The project ended up going a more traditional route, but with a switch, being released to home video first and then appearing on network television. But that Blockbuster was willing to make the commitment impressed Spelling.

Having interests in two Hollywood studios was only a start for Huizenga. Always looking for the bigger picture, the next step was to put Republic and Spelling together. Blockbuster continued to buy shares of both companies, gaining a controlling stake in Republic by March 1993 and two seats on Republic's board of directors. In early September, Huizenga and Berrard approached the other six Republic directors with a proposal to merge Republic and Spelling under Blockbuster's sponsorship. They negotiated a deal over the weekend and emerged with an arrangement under which Spelling would buy Republic's shares for $13 each. Spelling would finance the $100 million transaction by selling new shares of its stock to Blockbuster, which would end up with 70.5 percent of the new combined company.

As for Republic, Goldsmith felt it was a good deal and a fair price for stockholders. "The entertainment world was changing rapidly and the size and scale of companies was so immense that it presented a serious disadvantage to Republic," he says. (Not all shareholders agreed. A shareholders suit, later settled, was filed trying to block the deal claiming too low of a price. There was also a nearly year-long inquiry by the SEC into trading of Republic stock, but no actions were taken.)

It helped smooth the way that Goldsmith initially was to head up the new combined venture. But there were no employment agreements or contracts worked out for Goldsmith or other Republic executives in the combined company. When the merger was completed in April 1994, Blockbuster's own merger with Viacom was pending and Goldsmith says that made his situation uncertain. He left the company. Other top Republic executives had already resigned. What had begun as a casual conversation at a baseball owners' meeting with Huizenga wanting a small part of the picture had ended up, not surprisingly, with him controlling the whole show.

STREET DEALS AND STRATEGY

Some of the deals done by Huizenga and his team were as much for Wall Street as for strategy. Partnerships with IBM and CBS, announced with much fanfare, were particularly valuable for the credibility conveyed to Blockbuster. And the connection with a hot brand-name like Blockbuster was good for the stodgy image of its two partners. With IBM, there was an attempt to develop an in-store movie preview system being used at a store in Boca Raton, Florida. The idea was to give the "I don't know what I want to watch tonight" customers a tool to help them decide. "At least from the IBM perspective, this project was a real project, it really started bottom-up," says Antonio Romero, former general manager for IBM in south Florida and who later joined Blockbuster. It began with field reps and account engineers working with Blockbuster on an idea, and he didn't focus on it until later phases of the project. "This one was an exciting one because of the size of Blockbuster. This was an opportunity for IBM that represented tens of millions of dollars of revenue." Ultimately, the system wouldn't be adopted because of cost.

The CBS deal, announced in February 1993, was to develop a promotional ten-minute videotape magazine called "Hot Pix" to preview movies, videos and CBS programs. The alliance was good for CBS which would glean access to younger, video rental customers, many of whom have abandoned network television. For Blockbuster, the deal underscored the strength of its retail network and growing influence in the entertainment industry. But the partnership was never extended past a six-month tryout.

Meanwhile, Blockbuster's metamorphosis into an entertainment company moved beyond Hollywood. In addition to the investments with Republic and Spelling in early 1993, Blockbuster agreed to become a major franchisee of the Discovery Zone play centers for children. The story for the Street was of great cross-promotional opportunities and arguably there was some of that. But it was also an "old pals" deal.

In early 1992, Don Flynn brought the idea to Huizenga. Founded in 1989, Discovery Zone developed and franchised indoor playgrounds for children, emphasizing fitness and fun. Although there were similar concepts scattered around the country, here again was a chance to do what they'd done at Waste Management and were repeating with Blockbuster—conquer a fragmented market with a national rollout. Discovery Zone looked like a premier company with which to do that and besides, it would dovetail nicely with Blockbuster's broadening identity. Huizenga liked the idea but Baczko and Berrard didn't, mostly because of potential liability problems and the limited age appeal. The Flynns formed a partnership and invested in the company in July 1992, with Don Flynn becoming chairman and CEO. Waste Management Chairman Dean Buntrock bought in early, purchasing a stake in a private placement and committing the Blockbuster franchise owned with George Johnson to open 50 Discovery Zone centers under a separate company, but in the same markets as their Blockbuster stores. In April 1993, Flynn again talked with Huizenga about Blockbuster joining forces with Discovery Zone. He demonstrated that the legal liability was limited and that the business had promise. By then, Baczko was gone and Berrard, while still not enthusiastic, didn't object. Blockbuster bought 20 percent of Discovery Zone for $10.3 million, with an option for more shares and a commitment to opening 50 FunCenters within two years. Huizenga, along with Waste Management pals John Melk and Peer Pederson, joined as directors.

The credibility conferred by Huizenga and Blockbuster was parlayed into a sizzling share price. Blockbuster initially profited handsomely from Discovery Zone's public offering in June 1993 at $22 a share, which valued its holdings at $68.2 million, a whopping gain in just two months. So did the Flynns as well as Peer Pederson, John Melk and others who'd gotten in on the "old pal's" deal. In addition to basking in Blockbuster's success, Discovery Zone could also take advantage of Blockbuster's extensive research into site selection and market analysis, and hook up with its network of franchisees, particularly those abroad, to push the concept overseas. "What it really added was the franchise, the ability to build more units quicker," Flynn says. "It was always the intention that I would roll it out and then eventually (Blockbuster) would take control and there would be cross promotion and it would be part of Blockbuster's move into the entertainment end of the business."

FROM RENTAL TO RETAIL TO ENTERTAINMENT BUSINESS

As Blockbuster's profile rose, so did Wayne Huizenga's, both nationally and in the sprawling metropolis that is south Florida. By January 1991, Blockbuster had replaced bankrupt airline Pan Am in the Standard & Poors 500 stock index. The awarding in July 1991 of a National League baseball expansion franchise and the December 1992 award of a new hockey franchise lifted Huizenga's profile into the sports celebrity lexicon. And in keeping with its growth and evolution from an entrepreneurial start-up to a full-fledged corporate denizen, Blockbuster consolidated its headquarters in spring 1992, moving from its quaint Las Olas offices into a gleaming downtown Fort Lauderdale office tower, bought for a song and refurbished into a landmark of a hometown boy made good.

By Blockbuster's annual meeting in May 1993, Huizenga and his team had crafted a new persona for Blockbuster Entertainment Corp. and were ready for the great unveiling. With the music stores, movie studios, children's fun centers, and other moves, Blockbuster was no longer just in the video rental business. It seemed appropriate, though, that the company's new image was delivered to shareholders via video—a flashy show with video visits from Paul McCartney (whose concert tour was being promoted by Blockbuster including a televised live concert on Fox Network from the Blockbuster Amphitheatre in Charlotte, North Carolina), as well as Richard Branson, chairman of Virgin Cos., and executives from IBM, plus "tours" of the Republic and Spelling studios.

One deal introduced at that 1993 annual meeting was intended to boost Blockbuster's credibility, but it initially backfired. Back in 1990, Blockbuster had begun financing a small development company involved in "compression technology" which would allow music or video games to be recorded on blank compact discs on the spot. The idea was startling. Conceivably, consumers would never have to be told an item was out-of-stock because hard-to-find or mega-popular titles could be created while they waited. Huizenga was cool to the deal because it flew in the face of Blockbuster's strategy to concentrate on providing programming rather than getting caught up in any one technology. But it was a small deal initially, and Berrard funded it while looking for strategic partners. He found one in IBM, which financed it substantially with an agreement that the system would have to be made available to all retailers with Blockbuster getting a transaction fee while IBM would get the $30,000 to $70,000 for each of the machines.

But when news of the demonstration of the system at Blockbuster's annual meeting hit the music industry through the press, Berrard concedes now, it was totally mishandled. Berrard says he'd discussed the system with mid-level music company executives. Word never reached the top executives, and reaction in the music industry and among artists was swift and uniformly negative. Top concerns were over copyright protection, quality, and distribution control. This system was a potential threat to the very heart of their business.

Berrard was livid. But the mid-level managers he'd spoken with who hadn't carried the message to their bosses certainly weren't going to now. On a damage control mission, Huizenga and Berrard called top industry executives and explained Blockbuster's position. The rhetoric in the press cooled, but concerns over copyrights and other issues by the music industry remained. "I didn't do what a good executive should have done," Berrard concedes. "Wayne's comment to me was, 'Well, you know Steve, as upset as we otherwise might want to be, you could have headed this off, too.' He nicely told me that I could have used better judgment and could have taken that one additional step. He's right—I could have, and we didn't handle the media very well."

Once relations were restored and more access was granted by the music companies into their business processes and distribution systems, it became evident by early 1994 that the technology "price point" to make the system economically viable was still too high. All the components to build New Leaf existed, but most were in prototype or very early stage development and too expensive. The most difficult hurdle was in telecommunications technology. Clearly not geared to music, the system was then recast to augment the video game business in a test site in South Carolina. But again, the economics weren't there, though the plug on New Leaf wouldn't actually be pulled until many months later. Technology, which was supposed to threaten Blockbuster's core business of video rental, wasn't yet to the point to allow the company to launch new ventures.

NEW CONVERTS

For all of the aggressiveness Huizenga demonstrates in operating his businesses, he sticks to a conservative financial structure. It's part of his core philosophy that taking risks on the operating side dictates being conservative on the balance sheet and not mortgaging the future of the company by loading it with debt. It was an approach that suited new chief financial officer Greg Fairbanks as well.

Having not suffered through the sting of the earlier Bear Stearns report and the criticism by the short-sellers, one of Fairbanks' first suggestions was to change Blockbuster's tape amortization policy which he thought was too conservative. The idea was instantly rejected by Berrard and Huizenga, who'd been through that exercise. "I really did not think they were aggressive in their accounting at all," says Fairbanks. "If anything I believe and still believe to this day they were moderately conservative."

As a newcomer, he could see clearly the split in the market between skepticism and support of Blockbuster's skyrocketing success. "The whole problem with Blockbuster has always been it got so successful so quickly," he adds. "So people start looking for the smoke and mirrors, and they get very suspicious. At the same time, there was no major competitor to compare to Blockbuster to validate or legitimize Blockbuster. Everyone was looking for the skeletons in the closet. They quite frankly, just weren't there."

One of those who did a lot of scouting for skeletons early on and later became a believer was Larry Haverty, senior vice-president of State Street Research, which invests $7 billion of equities for various pension accounts. "I started out with (Huizenga) on the wrong side," he says. "I thought Blockbuster did aggressive accounting and Wayne and I would go at each other on several occasions." He remembers a particularly tense meeting at Merrill Lynch's New York offices in early 1990 where Huizenga was furious with him. "They went out of their way to point to their immaculate conversion and that they weren't doing anything wrong and I became convinced of that." As with Waste Management, Huizenga was trying to get as high a multiple as possible on Blockbuster's stock to make acquisitions. "He used legal accounting techniques to make earnings look as good as possible. When Blockbuster turned cash flow positive he changed the accounting." (Indeed, there was an accounting change once Blockbuster's incredible store buildout slowed, which amortized tapes on a slightly more conservative basis.)

It was when Haverty could see the cash flow generated by Blockbuster stores in 1991 and 1992, that he, like others, became a convert. State Street's largest holding, $100 million, was in Blockbuster stock and Haverty became, as he describes it, "the ultimate spokesman for them among the (institutional investor) community."

For all the attention paid to the multiple on Blockbuster's stock (the critics claiming it was too high, a bubble that would eventually burst) Merrill Lynch analyst Fran Bernstein says that Blockbuster "never got a multiple as high as a fast-growth retailer. It never traded close to its growth rate." She found Huizenga to be "extraordinarily forthcoming, accessible, and thoughtful and would tell you the positives and the negatives. He's a great presenter and tells a wonderful story."

Indeed it was in part that ability, and Huizenga and Berrard's effective repackaging and repositioning Blockbuster as an entertainment company, that boosted Blockbuster's stock to a year-long high of more than $21 a share by July 1, 1993. Press reports noted that the recent surge by investors wasn't because of renewed faith in the video-rental business, but because of approval of its move to become an all-around entertainment company. Blockbuster was benefiting from a higher public profile with partnerships with the likes of IBM "and a growing perception that H. Wayne Huizenga has a golden touch." While there were many believers, some analysts noted the smattering of investments and tempered their enthusiasm by wondering if Blockbuster was pursuing diversification or dilettantism by the launch in many strategic directions at once. That answer would never be quite clear as another set of circumstances would occur before the strategies could play out.

PARTNERSHIP PRESSURES

Making good on his promise of treating Berrard as a partner, Huizenga included him on private deals, like part ownership of the Marlins and on a few real estate investments. And he gave Berrard (and Rick Rochon at Huizenga Holdings) more and more of the lead in crafting deals. "We've been together all these years and if they can't step up and do it now, it isn't for me to do. That's part of bringing all these young people along. I like to do deals but so do they and they've got to learn," Huizenga says. Throughout the negotiations for Cityvision and other deals, Berrard would call and run points by him. "I'd just give him some ideas and then he'd follow through and get it done. So through all the years of starting out where I was at this level and gradually working myself down while Steve worked his way up, he just gained a lot of experience through that. Today, Steve's much better at the fine points of the deal than I am. If he and I were side by side on a deal, I'd defer to him every time."

Indeed, as he spearheaded Blockbuster's diversification efforts Berrard honed his deal-making skills under Huizenga's tutelage. He applied lessons learned from the first deals done with portable toilets, bottled water, pest control, and lawn care companies to music store chains, video store rivals and Hollywood studios. Despite the larger scope and dealing with publicly traded companies, most of the basic rules applied: Don't paint yourself in a corner. Never say anything that won't allow you to come back in the front door. Always leave room to back up. Don't say something is a deal-breaker. (Citing something as a deal-breaker and then backing up kills credibility and an edge in negotiating.) A deal is never dead if you don't let it die. Always let the other side set the initial price. Recognize what the other side really wants out of a deal. Know when to walk. Don't take no for an answer.

As Berrard grew more confident and prolific in his deal-making, it irked him at times that Huizenga was getting all the press and public credit. Articles would appear touting Huizenga's deal-making prowess, or about the nexus of investors among the Waste Management alumni, and not mention Berrard, who began to feel like the Invisible Man. Huizenga himself would take great pains to include Berrard in press interviews and give him credit in crafting deals, but the media attention still focused on the man at the top.

"The only thing that was always frustrating to me is I would pick up the paper in the morning and read how Wayne did this wonderful deal," Berrard says. "Wayne wasn't even there and never met the people. On the other hand, everyone has to find a place in life and what Wayne gave me in return was he let me go and do those things. He trusted me enough where he didn't hang on my shadow," Berrard says. "Sometimes it hurt. You'd read the paper and you'd think Wayne was out there all night doing this thing and I'm the one who was gone for three weeks and Wayne makes another great deal. Wayne didn't even want to do the damn thing."

As he was thrust increasingly into the role as frontman in dealmaking, Berrard would sometimes grow impatient and at times even irritated with his mentor. The perfectionism, the driving for the best deal, at times wore on him. "There's been a few times where I've been on the phone negotiating a deal, giving him where I'm at and had him tell me 'more, more, more.' And me finally getting fed up and saying, 'if you think you can do it any damn better, I suggest you get in the airplane and fly out here and do it yourself.' He's got me to that point before. But he's always known when to back off."

And as a surrogate deal-maker, Berrard was subject to the same criticism and analytical thinking that Huizenga directed at himself. "I don't ever remember Wayne telling me, 'good deal.' I've often heard him say to someone, 'well, yeah, it was an easy deal when you give them what they want.' I don't think in all the years I've been here I've heard, 'that was a great deal.' I've heard good job but I've never heard 'great deal.' He's always found something, 'well, we probably could have done this and we should have done that.' But that's Wayne. Hell, it almost got to the point where after I did one I would do the same thing. And before he could tell me, I'd say, 'I suppose if we could do it over again, here's what I probably would have done differently,' just to head off hearing that. Because it used to drive me bananas."

The pressure Huizenga placed on Berrard was grooming him for the next phase, as stage two of building Blockbuster was nearing completion. Huizenga again was sowing the seeds for that succession, being quoted in the press in early 1993 as saying he might take retain the role as chairman but relinquish the CEO spot. Though he did not name Berrard as his successor, it was widely expected that Berrard would take that place. Already underway were discussions about new strategies, perhaps splitting Blockbuster into various sectors like music and international, and taking those public. As with his personal life and his very persona, in building Blockbuster the motto was to "keep moving." He had to keep the company exciting, to keep the stock sizzling. His focus on Blockbuster's stock performance, while winning friends on Wall Street, drew veiled and sometimes not-so-veiled criticism within some quarters of Blockbuster. "You had a CEO whose whole focus was a financial strategy," says a former executive.

But to Huizenga, he was simply doing his job. To him, the mission of a CEO of a publicly traded company is simple: build value for shareholders. "We were building the company. Maybe some people didn't like the way we did it, but we built a big company in a short period of time and lots of people made lots of money in Blockbuster and that's what a CEO's job is, for his shareholders. It's to make money for the shareholders and that's what we did."

He didn't believe in staggered boards, golden parachutes, poison pills, or any of the other anti-takeover remedies adopted by U.S. corporations. "The best thing for shareholders is if someone wants to come in and make a run at the company, let them make a run. Run the price up, that's what my job was and I don't know why other people do it, I only know why I feel that way. To me, I don't need a job and so I'm not trying to protect my job. All these chairmen that want to put this in place and that in place, they all want to save their jobs. I don't care about my job. I was making $400,000 a year here, big deal. To me, it's the price of the stock and so the stock runs up and someone wants to make a run at the company, take off the manager's cap and put on the shareholder's cap and make the deal."

Indeed, as 1993 drew to a close, along would come a deal, the ultimate deal, the culmination of the making of a Blockbuster. But in doing it, some of his own rules of dealmaking would be broken and his reputation as a dealmeister would be battered. The stress would change the very nature of his relationship with Berrard, one which Huizenga valued most. Perhaps it was inevitable. Because in building Blockbuster, he had already broken the cardinal rule of the dealmaker: Don't fall in love.

9

Sports Inc.: Stadium Seats and a Baseball Team

The score was tied at half-time during Superbowl XXIII on January 22, 1989, as the San Francisco 49ers faced the Cincinnati Bengals at Joe Robbie Stadium. Now seemed as good a time as any for Wayne Huizenga to pay a visit down the hall to Suite 244, the skybox of Miami Dolphins owner Joe Robbie, whose 18-month-old, $110 million stadium was hosting the event. He'd met Robbie at a few charity events and had gotten to know him better during the commissioning of the USS Leyte Gulf in September 1987. It'd been an event that brought out much of south Florida's social set and Huizenga and his father, Harry, had been aboard as Robbie and some old Navy buddies had toured the guided missile launcher. The Super Bowl session was simply a chance to get re-acquainted with Robbie, but an idea had already been begun churning in Huizenga's mind.

For his part, Joe Robbie was at a vulnerable point in his ownership of the Dolphins. The South Dakota native and Minneapolis lawyer had plunked down $100,000 in 1965 as part of an investment group that included actor Danny Thomas which paid $7.5 million for a Miami franchise in the struggling American Football League and fielded a team a year later. Marketing the Miami Dolphins in its initial years was tough, with tickets nearly given away to help cultivate a fan base for the fledgling team. Among the first season ticket holders were Wayne Huizenga and his brother-in-law Whit Hudson. Gradually, Robbie bought out his partners and became sole owner. Three years after hiring coach Don Shula, the Miami Dolphins became the only team in NFL history to have a perfect record, culminating with a victory over the Redskins in Super Bowl VII. After the 1973 season, the Dolphins would again be Super Bowl champs, easily defeating the Minnesota Vikings in Super Bowl VIII. Over the next 22 years, the Dolphins would make two more trips to the Super Bowl as AFC champs, but only taste defeat at the hands of Washington in Super Bowl XVII and the 49ers in Super Bowl XIX.

The cantankerous Robbie tangled with the city of Miami in 1976 over the terms of a new lease at the aging Orange Bowl stadium. For six years, city officials bickered with Robbie, who insisted that a new stadium be built. By 1984, Robbie began pitching his idea for a privately funded stadium. Then, Miami Mayor Maurice Ferre dismissed it as a negotiating ploy. Nobody built a private stadium—the cost was simply prohibitive. "It got my Irish up," Robbie said later. "I suppose if they hadn't told me it was impossible, I wouldn't have done it." Construction started in July 1985 and by August 1987, the 73,000-seat stadium in northwest Dade County opened as Joe Robbie reveled in the glory. A giant football helmet in mid-field spewed balloons. A parachutist floated down with the game ball, which was handed to Robbie while fans in the packed orange-and-aqua stadium cheered as the Dolphins took on the Chicago Bears in the stadium's inaugural game.

But in less than two years, cracks appeared, not only in the stadium itself but in Robbie's dream, which he'd worked so hard to make a reality but which would later turn into a nightmare for his children. No banks had been willing to touch the risky project, so the stadium was financed with $90 million in Dade County industrial revenue bonds. Robbie pledged the income from the 10-year leases on the skyboxes and luxury seats to service the debt. The leases generated over $13 million a year, ample to cover the $10 million or so in interest costs. Central to the deal, the Dolphins were locked in to a 30-year lease at the stadium, which was also guaranteed a generous cut of the club's ticket revenues.

Meanwhile, zoning battles with local homeowners in the largely black, middle-class neighborhood had spawned a slew of lawsuits and limited the number of annual events to 18 until road improvements were made. Plans to provide more parking and to build a hotel-retail-office and a sports training complex on land next to the stadium were stymied by more lawsuits. The Dolphins suffered their worst record in 19 years during the 1988–1989 season. The poor showing, ire with the team's second highest ticket prices in the league and Miami's fickle fan base had left 23 percent of the stadium seats empty, and Robbie had been unable to lease 70 executive suites and 1,500 club seats. The lagging attendance cut into parking and concession revenues. Though Robbie was making the payments on the stadium, the facility grossed just $18.5 million in 1988, about 30 percent less than initial projections. Money was needed to rebuild the team, to finance roads, parking and maintenance for the stadium, and to fight the ongoing legal battles.

By summer 1989, Robbie was moving forward on plans to bring a baseball team to south Florida and the stadium, which had been designed to convert to baseball use. But baseball wouldn't come soon enough to meet his immediate challenges. Lenders became anxious and pressure mounted as the debt on the Miami Dolphins team itself ballooned, uncomfortably close to the NFL ceiling. "Joe Robbie should be applauded for his efforts but building the stadium was the biggest mistake he ever made," Huizenga says, now as owner of both the stadium and the team. "He pledged the team. If he didn't build the stadium, the family wouldn't have had to sell the team. There was too much debt on the stadium, the team was pledged, there was a lot of debt on the team and those kids had nothing to work with. Joe put the family in a terrible bind."

But the Robbies' problem became Huizenga's opportunity. Succession in any family owned business can be tricky, and sports teams are no exception. Joe Robbie and his wife Elizabeth had nine grown children and a handful of interlocking family companies. Getting an ownership stake in the Dolphins would enable Huizenga to be high on the list when and if the Robbies ever had to sell. "I think he saw opportunity to ultimately own the team and the stadium and he was able to invest some money (in the team) on reasonable terms and it was a reasonable investment if the family was going to have to sell," says R. Charles Shufeldt, president and CEO of SunTrust Capital Markets Inc., who advised the Robbie family during the negotiations with Huizenga. "It was a pretty good bet to anyone who had a keen interest in the Dolphins that when Joe Robbie passed away the team might have to be sold and Wayne is patient money by definition." As events would turn out, Wayne Huizenga would not have to be patient for very long.

His real fascination, however, was not with the team but with the stadium. How could such a facility possibly support itself on just 18 events a year? More concerts were a possibility. But through endless conversations with his friend and confidant Carl Barger, president of the Pittsburgh Pirates, the solution became clear—81 additional events generated by a Major League Baseball team. "What he saw with that stadium is a beautiful facility that he could buy dirt cheap," says Miami attorney Steve Roddenberry, who has represented Huizenga on a number of deals, including the stadium purchase. "We thought that you could generate a lot of revenue out of it (with concerts and other events) and I think that was a mistake. You can't generate that much revenue. Except for baseball. Baseball makes a lot of money."

By June 1989, before he'd even talked with Joe Robbie about his plans, Huizenga was already laying groundwork. "You know I've always had an interest in baseball," he told Jim Blosser during the attorney's first full-time day on the job June 1. "I think south Florida should have a major league baseball team and I'm curious why we don't. Why don't you look into that." So Blosser, a politically well-connected Fort Lauderdale lawyer, in addition to his role in representing Huizenga in government, political, and civic matters, became a key member of the team to bring baseball to south Florida. It was Blosser, through his wide network of contacts, who helped set up the initial meeting with Joe Robbie in the fall of 1989.

One late afternoon in early September 1989, Huizenga and his father, Harry, and Blosser met with Joe Robbie and Eddie Jones, president of the Miami Dolphins. The discussion was wide-ranging, with lots of vague promises and tantalizing possibilities on how Huizenga could help Robbie realize his vision. Suggestions ranged from taking a minority interest in the team at a high value and an interest in the stadium without managing control, to help in developing the adjoining properties and building a training facility. It sounded great to Joe Robbie. Lots of money with no strings attached—too good to be true. It was. As the old saying goes, the devil is in the details.

Brought in to help nail down the deal was Shufeldt from SunTrust through another contact of Robbie's. Once the parameters began to be pinned down, the promises came smack up against cold, hard reality. "Wayne was Wayne," Shufeldt says. "Wayne doesn't do anything that wasn't going to be good for Wayne. He was not giving money away. What we did was a heavily negotiated, reasonable deal for both sides."

Even years after the ultimate deal was announced, it's not quite clear when, how, or even whether Joe Robbie decided to part with a piece of his beloved Dolphins. At the press conference when the deal was ultimately announced, the *Sun-Sentinel* quoted Huizenga as saying "as close as the stadium and team are meshed, I felt to have a large percentage of the stadium beckoned for some percentage of the team. Initially, Joe didn't want to give away any of the team."

But, the finances of the stadium and the team were so intertwined, they were nearly inseparable. It was a package, and though Robbie may have preferred not to sell part of the Dolphins, he may have had little choice. "Joe was not adverse to selling a part of the team, he wanted to sell part of the team to raise some equity," says Eddie Jones, who was in on many of the initial negotiations with Robbie. Giving up 10 or 15 percent of the team to a minority interest with no rights, no liquidity, and no dividend in exchange for a cash infusion into the team didn't seem that onerous.

The real hangups were about price and control of the stadium. Huizenga was willing to pay for a minority piece in the team at a fair valuation but he wasn't willing to put nearly as high a pricetag on the stadium as Robbie, who had put his heart and soul into building it and knew he had a gold mine if he could just get more events into it. Moreover, Robbie insisted on retaining 51 percent. Huizenga refused to be a minority partner.

Just before Christmas, Robbie called Huizenga and during that discussion, Huizenga says, he told Robbie, "I'll do the deal, you can manage the thing, but it's got to be 50–50." Robbie agreed, according to Huizenga, then promised to meet after the Christmas holidays.

Ailing with a respiratory illness, Joe Robbie died January 7, 1990, at the age of 73. Before his death, Robbie had placed the Dolphins in a living trust naming three of his nine children as trustees, Tim, 36; Dan, 30; and Janet, 44. In addition, the three had managing control of the team with Tim as president. The three also controlled the stadium corporation. The decision by Joe Robbie to place the team in a trust may have been well-intentioned but it went horribly awry. Family members were pitted against each other and ultimately his goal of keeping the team within the family was thwarted.

Within a week of his father's death, Tim Robbie called Wayne Huizenga. He told the younger Robbie that his father had agreed to a 50-50 deal but not to take his word on it, to call Shufeldt. At the time of Robbie's death, says Shufeldt, there was no firm deal. "There was an agreement to keep talking," he says. Significant issues involving control of the stadium and the team still had to be resolved. Negotiations continued on a nearly daily basis with hard-fought points on both sides.

On a Sunday afternoon, February 18, the nine Robbie children gathered from various points in the country at their mother's home in Miami Shores. "That meeting was definitely a turning point," says Deborah Olson, one of the Robbie children, who as a board member of the family companies would be continually frustrated in her attempts to counteract decisions by her trustee-siblings who controlled the companies. The trustees brought up the negotiations with Huizenga with the clear message that they were going to explain the deal and that they intended to do it. Immediately, the other Robbies objected.

Only six weeks had passed since their father's death, there was confusion about the need for such haste and a strong sentiment that the deal be shopped to other parties. The family passed a resolution that they couldn't decide yet, there wasn't enough information. This was the only meeting of all Joe Robbie's children after his death—and it would be the last. As far as the three trustees were concerned, they were in charge and it was not a family decision.

On March 7—exactly two months after Joe Robbie's death—in front of television cameras and a crowd of reporters, Tim Robbie and a grinning Wayne Huizenga announced that the video store king had bought half of Joe Robbie Stadium and a 15 percent stake in the team. Terms weren't disclosed but would quickly become public. Huizenga paid $5 million for his interest in the stadium (plus debt assumption) and $12 million for his percentage of the team with an option for 10 percent more. He also agreed to finance stadium renovations and help develop the surrounding property, a plan which Joe Robbie had envisioned but had never been able to complete. It left majority ownership of the team and managing control of both the team and the stadium to the trustees, but with Huizenga to be consulted on capital expenditures.

This event ushered Huizenga into the world of professional sports, which to him was essentially a business. He eschewed the glamour of owning sports teams and looked to the bottom line. "To me, sports is a rental business and it's an entertainment business. And it does everything I've ever wanted to do in life, and that is rent things," Huizenga said years later. "You got a stadium. You sell skyboxes. You sell advertising. You got concessions. You get parking. But you have to have a reason to get the people there. So you get some players like a Dan Marino. That's your programming. And so that's how we look at sports."

But there was one difference: the glare of the public limelight. After the deal had been signed, Robbie had asked Huizenga his preference about a press conference. He was surprised, because to him it was a real estate deal, worth perhaps a newspaper interview or two, maybe a writeup in the local business press. "It changed my life big time. I didn't even think we had to announce it. To me, it wasn't a big deal. When you buy 15 percent of a company you don't announce it. My whole experience was making deals, so now we're buying 15 percent of a team and 50 percent of a building. You rent space to the Dolphins, it's no big deal. It's a piece of bricks and mortar with some dirt in the middle of it, right. It's like renting anything else, a warehouse or anything. So to buy half of Joe Robbie Stadium to me was like buying half of this office building. I guess I was pretty naive to think that."

Indeed, this was an introduction to the fishbowl of sports team ownership and though his friend Carl Barger would often warn him about the public spotlight—its positives and negatives—Huizenga would be amused, sometimes irritated, and at times even taken aback at the level of celebrity status conferred because of his sports team ownership, particularly in south Florida.

Meanwhile, the deal itself and the way it was done touched off a crisis within the Robbie family. Dissidence and distrust became the watchwords within the fractious family. "They panicked," is how Olson summed up her siblings reaction to the pending debt and the team's financial status. Her ire is not directed at Huizenga, but at her siblings. "You can't be taken advantage of unless you let it happen," she says. "I don't blame Wayne Huizenga. Wayne Huizenga looked out for Wayne Huizenga, and nobody looked out for me. I have respect for people who are upfront and Wayne Huizenga in my experience has always been upfront."

One clause in Huizenga's contract that wouldn't get much attention until later was a right to purchase the rest of the Dolphins team before any other buyer. "He always wanted to own the Dolphins," says Norman Braman, a Miami auto-dealership magnate and former owner of the Philadelphia Eagles, of Huizenga. "Football is his first sport, it's his favorite sport and his deal as concocted with Joe Robbie lent itself to that. I don't think he would have made that deal without the right of first refusal, which is a recipe for eventual ownership."

The clause was hard fought on both sides. The Robbies worried that having Huizenga in the shadows would chill the marketability of the team and depress its value. But Huizenga insisted that he wouldn't be a minority partner without some control over what happened to the rest of the team. "It was the most important thing we did in that negotiation," says Rick Rochon, who handled most of the dealings with the Robbies.

Timing is often cited by Huizenga as the reason for his success. In this deal, his timing was perfect. Just days after his initial Dolphins transaction was struck, a new television contract between the NFL and networks boosted each team's share by $128 million per team over the next four years, double what the teams got under the previous contract, and raising the value of NFL teams by perhaps as much as 15 percent, according to one account. Huizenga hadn't even signed the papers and already his stake was more valuable. And he would indeed be waiting in the wings with his right of first offer as the Robbie children battled over their legacy.

PERFECT PITCH: BASEBALL COMES TO SOUTH FLORIDA

By the spring of 1990, expansion excitement in America had reached fever pitch. After years of thumbing its collective nose at efforts to share more slices of its lucrative pie, Major League Baseball was finally bowing to mounting public pressure, angry congressional committees and the threat of losing the anomaly of its antitrust exemption—conferred on no other professional sport—and was deigning to grant two, but only two, National League expansion franchises.

The list of city hopefuls and owner wannabes was long. To baseball's grudging invitation, 18 groups from 10 different cities responded with a nonrefundable $100,000 deposit and a lengthy questionnaire. It seemed a sure bet that Florida would be tagged for one of the two expansion franchises. Every spring, the Sunshine State got a whiff of big-league baseball in the form of spring training, but efforts over the years to land a franchise in Florida had failed miserably.

Within Florida alone, three cities and at least five groups were vying for an expansion team by the time Huizenga entered the race. Some brought expensive dowrys, like the city of St. Petersburg, Florida, which had built a $110 million stadium in 1986 in hopes of luring a team and major league status. Instead, it had become a perfect foil for teams to wrangle more out of their hometowns in new stadiums or lease concessions by threatening to move to the empty Suncoast—sometimes dubbed the Sun Ghost—Dome. For more than a decade, the cities by the bay had flirted with baseball. The Chicago White Sox in 1988 were ready to quit aging Comiskey Park for St. Petersburg until the Illinois legislature, facing a midnight deadline, approved funding for a new stadium. Over the years, St. Petersburg car dealer Frank Morsani had bought an interest in the Minnesota Twins, and tried to buy both the Oakland A's and the Texas Rangers. But baseball wouldn't allow the teams to move and local buyers emerged who scotched his plans. Now Morsani and another ownership group in Tampa-St. Petersburg were among the expansion hopefuls. Meanwhile, Orlando hoped to make up for its demographic deficiencies and unimpressive television market with its principal backer, Rich DeVos, the $2.5 billionaire co-founder of the direct sales company Amway.

In addition, two groups in Miami were already vying for a franchise. Abel Holtz, a Cuban immigrant and prominent Miami banker as founder of Capital Bank, one of the largest minority-owned banks in the country, envisioned "baseball on the bay." In his all-white penthouse suite atop of his Brickell Avenue tower, he talked of a stadium to be built in downtown Miami fronting Biscayne Bay. The idea, backed by a few city councilmembers and powerful downtown interests, would appeal to Miami's baseball-crazy Cuban population as well as the city's wealth of visitors from Latin America and the Caribbean. An avid baseball fan, Holtz had talked with Joe Robbie about combining efforts to get an expansion team. Another group intrigued with the area's promise was headed by New York investment banker J. Morton Davis. Among these, Wayne Huizenga would emerge from a dark horse challenger to a major contender in just six months.

With the stadium and his initial stake in the Dolphins wrapped up, Huizenga didn't waste any time preparing his bid for a baseball franchise. On the afternoon of the press conference, his friend Carl Barger was already getting a tour of the stadium by Tim Robbie and being shown how seats could be reconfigured for baseball. Within three weeks of Huizenga's infusion, Robbie announced that more than $10 million would be spent on alterations to the stadium in an effort to catch up with other cities vying for an expansion team. South Florida Big League Baseball Inc. was incorporated with Wayne Huizenga as chairman. The office was in essence a campaign headquarters, a campaign to bring baseball to south Florida and vault Wayne Huizenga into the league of team owners.

Quickly, Huizenga assembled a cadre of consultants and advisors with the roles of key players mapped out. Jim Blosser would garner support from the government, civic, and political spectrum. Rick Rochon would crunch the numbers and plot the business strategy, with help from Steven Matt, an accountant with Arthur Anderson in Dallas, who specialized in sports team finances. Tal Smith, former general manager and now president of the Houston Astros was consulted for his expertise in the game. Don Smiley handled the press and marketing. Harry Huizenga took on the role of team mascot, sitting in on meetings where Wayne would be careful to ask his opinion, and passing out business cards that read "Harry Huizenga–shortstop."

Early in his quest, a year before he'd closed on the stadium, Huizenga had heard a presentation by Bob Hope, a public relations executive who'd been involved in bringing two expansion franchises, a hockey team to Ottawa, Canada and a basketball team to Charlotte, North Carolina. In that speech in March 1989, Hope played up Miami's chances for baseball by selling itself as a gateway to Latin America and the Caribbean, but warned that Miami was too far behind in the expansion process for groups, that it had to have an individual willing to step up to the plate. Huizenga asked Hope for a copy of his speech and if they could meet. During that session the next day, he asked Hope if he really believed what he'd said. Hope said yes. "Look me in the eye and tell me that because this could cost me a lot of money," Huizenga told him. Now Huizenga brought Hope on board to help spend that money and aid his effort to snare an expansion team.

Going into the September presentations, Huizenga and his group figured they were in last place. But Huizenga wasn't walking in as a virtual unknown. Blockbuster was the exclusive distributor of Major League Baseball videos. And he'd met Doug Danforth, chairman of the National League's four-member expansion committee, through Carl Barger, who as president of the Pittsburgh Pirates worked for Danforth. Barger had helped cobble together a partnership of seven corporations in 1986, including Danforth who was then chairman of Westinghouse, to buy the team and keep it from being moved. Danforth had become chairman and CEO of the team in 1987 and Barger had become president of the team he'd loved as a boy.

As Huizenga's group entered the windowless conference room and took their places around the U-shaped table, they knew they had to address the five points the committee could kill them on, ranging from the fact that Joe Robbie Stadium was not designated solely for baseball, to the substance of Wayne Huizenga. Stadium manager Glenn Mon took them on a "tour" of the stadium with overlays against other baseball parks. Smiley did the "gee-whizzers" about the area's appeal and marketability as a sports venue. Blosser stressed Huizenga's commitment to the community and support of the arts and civic organizations. Huizenga gave his best "presidential" address, highlighting where he'd come from, how he'd made his money, how sincere he was and that he alone would be behind the franchise to praise or to blame. He was willing to pay the full asking price of $95 million (some would say astronomical given the $7 million expansion fee in 1977). He'd sell stock rather than borrow to finance the fee and quipped that he'd write the check on the spot. "I've been lucky throughout my life by being in the right place at the right time, and I believe that this is the right place at the right time. I'll be a good person for you to do business with."

The presentation wowed the committee. In all the criteria—ownership, stadium, stadium location, capital structure, demographics, support—Huizenga's total score was higher than anyone else's. From number sixteen, he moved to number one and never left that spot. "Wayne was excellent, no question about it," says John McMullen, then owner of the Houston Astros and a committee member. "He didn't have to say 'I have to check with someone.' When the question was asked where the money was coming from, he said 'it's from me.' The demographics of Orlando were better, but he had a better presentation."

That reaction came as little surprise to some in Huizenga's camp. Steven Matt remembers he and Tal Smith coming home from their first meeting with Huizenga and his people to talk about baseball expansion and "there was no doubt in my mind or Tal's mind that this is a guy that baseball was going to want in their fraternity," he says. "We were telling him in our judgment that Florida was a given, that one of two expansion franchises would be going to the state of Florida," Matt says. "What swung it in south Florida's favor was Wayne."

In addition to his oft-cited ability to "write the check," Wayne Huizenga had another advantage. As a rich man, he understood intuitively how the wealthy thought, specifically, the 26 wealthy owners of baseball teams. He knew that the key was impressing the committee members and other owners. Nothing else mattered. Huizenga was the head strategist and would at times remind his team that a particular idea wouldn't do much to impress an owner. Posters in sports bars and fan rallies weren't the way to go. "We had a policy that we wanted to be as quiet as possible about this thing," remembers Don Smiley. "We didn't want parades and fanfare. We actually went the other way. We just did the opposite of what many cities did. It was very low key, conservative, just the way the other owners are, they're low key and conservative." If an idea didn't ring true with Huizenga, "he'd say, 'let's think about that again, now, because remember whose votes we're trying to get here,'" Smiley says. "I didn't have it. Jim didn't have it. Rick didn't have it. Wayne had it."

When the expansion committee visited Joe Robbie Stadium on December 18, initially there was talk within Huizenga's camp of a cocktail party for a thousand guests or a huge luncheon as other candidates had hosted to show community support. Huizenga quickly nixed that idea. Instead, he sponsored a luncheon for about 50 key community leaders, mayors, chamber of commerce presidents, and legislative reps on the club level at Joe Robbie Stadium. Meanwhile, committee members were ferried around on golf carts to explore the stadium and met in Suite 244, the orange-and-aqua executive skybox where Huizenga's discussions with Joe Robbie had begun 15 months earlier. Three presenters, including Blosser, went over details on demographics and the big question about south Florida's weather—indeed whether a stadium without a roof could withstand the hot and rainy season. Huizenga promised to put a roof on the stadium or build a new one if necessary.

The owners came out and sat at a table with Huizenga to continue their discussion and the guests from the community were introduced one by one. "They all smiled and waved, there was five minutes of 'grip and grinning' and the owners went back to their meeting," Blosser remembers. "Wayne was right on. He has a brilliant strategic mind. He cuts to the sense of a deal. What does it take to get this deal done. Instead of all the flag waving and all the flailing of arms and all the miscellanea, what does it take to get the deal done?"

It worked. That day, the committee announced that Huizenga's group would represent Miami as one of the six finalist cities, including Buffalo, Denver, Orlando, St. Petersburg, and Washington, DC. Huizenga had beaten out the other two Miami contenders because Holtz's proposed "stadium on the bay" was viewed as risky and too limiting a market. As a New Yorker, Morton was seen as not tied closely enough to the area.

"The two things that sold most of us was a visit to the stadium—before we saw the stadium, we were not sure a football stadium would work for baseball—and Wayne's personality and style," says Bill Giles, owner of the Philadelphia Phillies who replaced McMullen on the expansion committee. "He was self-assured but came across as not being a wild man. He gave an air of confidence but that he was not going to operate in any crazy manner like some owners we've had in the past who have been kind of mavericks, 'the hell with you and I'm going to do what I want and I'm not going to be a team player'. He's going to be a player."

The selection process continued with Buffalo and Orlando pared because of demographics. Washington's bid lacked a prominent investor. By March 1991, it was down to two Florida cities—Miami and St. Petersburg—and Denver. Now was an opportunity to have the community aid his effort. A massive, multi-lingual campaign to drum up support in south Florida from West Palm Beach to Key West, not to mention Caribbean countries like the Dominican Republic, Central American nations like Panama, and South American heavies like Brazil. On the last weekend of March, on a weekend that coincided with Passover and Easter Sunday, two exhibition games between the Baltimore Orioles and New York Yankees drew 125,000 baseball hungry fans. Huizenga sent a five-minute videotape of the jammed exhibition games to all 26 owners. The slide in Blockbuster's stock in the spring of 1991 in the wake of the Gulf War and short-seller campaigns caused a flap in the press in Tampa and St. Petersburg which reveled in the bad news. But it was of no concern among expansion committee members who understood that Huizenga's wealth was well-diversified.

As the vote drew near, expansion committee members became more leery about the commitment by the ownership group in St. Petersburg. "I went in with the predetermined mindset of St. Petersburg being the number one city and possibly Denver number two, and Miami number three," says Phillies owner Bill Giles. "I changed my vote because I felt more comfortable with one man controlling things than a group of people and the fact that (Huizenga) made a very good impression. He was not overbearing or egotistical and we certainly had confidence in his financial ability and his success in business."

On the morning of Friday, July 5, Fay Vincent called Huizenga at his vacation home in North Carolina, to find out where Huizenga could be reached just after the vote. Huizenga planned to leave about a half-hour before the 12:30 vote but the mountains would prevent him from taking a call on his car phone. With Marti driving and two carloads of family following, they reached the town of Hickory, North Carolina at 1:30 where Huizenga placed a call to Bill White, president of the National League, who told him the vote had been unanimous. "I told him, 'Not only do I want to be a team owner. I want to be a team player,'" Huizenga said later. Huizenga then called his team in Fort Lauderdale and Blosser, Smiley, and Rochon took the call. They popped open a waiting bottle of Dom Perignon (Blosser still has the empty bottle in his office) and drank a toast. "Then he came back and we all went back to work," Blosser laughs. "Next deal."

From long shot to dark horse to contender to winner in little more than a year. But even now Huizenga downplays his selection. "To me I don't think we won the franchise," Huizenga says. "I think Tampa-St. Pete had it all along. And all we were doing was, do a good job, hold our head up high, and make a good impression on people. Not step on any toes and the next time they would expand we'd be first in line. That's all we were trying to do. We were hoping all along that we would get it, but we never thought we would get it."

At a press bash that afternoon at Burt & Jack's in Port Everglades, Huizenga beamed before the crowd, wearing a wide red tie dotted with baseballs and a bright orange baseball hat emblazoned with "WAYNE'S TEAM" and in smaller letters beneath it, "Florida Marlins." (His father, Harry, Steve Berrard, Whit Hudson, and Wayne Jr. also had small stakes in the franchise.) On July 17, at the resort of Turnberry Isle in north Miami, a proper christening was held with 1,700 guests including Governor Lawton Chiles and Jeb Bush, who delivered a congratulatory telegram from his father, President George Bush. The team logo of a marlin jumping through a ring, and the official colors of teal and black were revealed.

A delegation from baseball led by Fay Vincent and National League president Bill White presented Huizenga with the official charter ushering him into the ranks of the exclusive club of baseball ownership, which Huizenga as a businessman, would soon find was a somewhat dubious distinction. Marti would later tease her husband that he would never spend so much money and have so little control as in professional sports, an observation he would soon come to share.

THE BUSINESS OF BASEBALL

It was to his long-time friend that Huizenga turned to build his new franchise into an actual team. Born in the central Pennsylvania town of Lewistown on August 18, 1930, Barger fell in love with baseball as a boy. He'd run downstairs in the early morning to get the newspaper to check the box scores and share the news with his dad, baseball being one of the greatest bonds between them. As a teenager, he'd hitchhike to Pittsburgh with his younger brother, William, to see his beloved Pirates play in Forbes Field. He worshipped New York Yankees star Joe DiMaggio, and considered it the honor of his life when his idol attended a roast held in Barger's honor in Fort Lauderdale in 1991. He pursued a career in law, joining the Pittsburgh firm of Eckert, Seamans, Cherin & Mellott upon graduation from Dickinson Law School in 1958. But baseball remained a cherished part of his life, and he often boasted that he'd known the batting averages of the Pirates and Phillies before he knew the alphabet, when baseball was a game and not a business. Yet it was business and law that provided the bridge into baseball, when as managing director of the law firm and a specialist in corporate finance, he helped put together the public-private coalition to purchase the Pirates and save the team from the threat of being moved. A year later, he became its president.

Warm, caring, and with an easy laugh, Barger was a driven man, a workaholic, and a heavy smoker (he'd tried many times but was never able to quit). He had an innately competitive spirit and a volatile, eruptive personality, which was egged on at times by Huizenga's deliberate calm. In Carl Barger, Huizenga had a friend to share his triumph of getting an expansion team and to count on in the birthing of a baseball club. It was "Carly," as Huizenga called him, who tried to fuse his love of baseball with the innate business bent of his friend.

Three days after the award of the franchise, Huizenga offered Barger the job and the prospect of a piece of ownership. There was some sideline jeering about Barger wearing two hats until August 2 when he reluctantly resigned as president of the Pirates. A hero in Pittsburgh, it wasn't an easy decision for Barger especially when the Pirates were in a pennant race, even given the excitement of presiding over the birth of a ball club. "Wayne saw that Carl left a lot of emotion in Pittsburgh and that was difficult for both of them," says Jim Leyland, manager of the Pirates, a close friend and confidant of Barger's. "Carl went through some tough times. It wasn't a snap decision."

With an office and a secretary, Barger set out to build his friend a ball club. The first major order of business was to hire a general manager. He'd been impressed by Dave Dombrowski, the young general manager of the Montreal Expos. He'd served on a few baseball committees with Dombrowski. Leyland also thought highly of Dombrowski, whom he'd worked with at the Chicago White Sox. They'd remained friends and whenever the Expos played the Pirates, Dombrowski would visit Leyland and occasionally with Barger as well. Dombrowski had heard through the baseball grapevine that there was interest in him for the Marlins job. A Chicago-area native, he checked with friends and heard favorable reports about Huizenga.

On September 18, Dombrowski and Barger met in Philadelphia and in short order, Barger offered him the job but said they also had to meet Huizenga. They left that afternoon in Huizenga's private plane to Fort Lauderdale. "There's no way that this guy can be doing the job—he just has got too much hair," was Huizenga's first comment. They visited for about a half-hour, and then finalized the deal. Over dinner at an Italian restaurant that night, the Marlin's newest catch talked with Huizenga,

Barger, and Smiley about the excitement of building a new club and their philosophy of baseball.

Initially, Dombrowski had little contact with Huizenga. He answered to Barger. "Carl was extremely enthusiastic and loved baseball, but it was made apparent that Wayne was not a baseball fan per se because he didn't know much about baseball and Carl was the baseball guy," Dombrowski says. "Carl used to joke that Wayne would prefer that there be three balls for a walk. Wayne made it clear that one of the reasons he bought the team was because of Carl, because Carl had talked to him about how fun it would be to own a baseball club."

Later, Dombrowski would discover an aspect of his new boss, which he would be shielded from at first. "Carl made it sound like, and this was a little misleading at the time, finances are no concern in this operation. Well, that was a misleading statement. It was basically as time went on, Wayne was going to give you what was very much necessary and very much wanted things to be first class but he's a businessman. So there's a distinction in the sense that he's in sports to run a first class operation, he will spend money to make money, he gives you the resources that you need, but you're accountable for the bottom line."

Indeed, throughout the expansion process, Huizenga had been careful to remind his team that the pursuit of baseball was not in fun, this was not a hobby. This was a business, a bottom-line, profit-oriented enterprise. At one news conference, he would describe a fly ball as a "transaction." Baseball was purely a business venture for Huizenga. "This could be a different kind of fun," he once said. "But I couldn't have fun if I wasn't making a profit."

"From the beginning, Wayne was approaching it as a business as well he should because he was talking about a very substantial investment," says Steven Matt, the sports finance expert from Arthur Andersen. "I always advise clients that people who buy professional sports teams are not motivated solely by economic consideration, there are many non-economic considerations—the prestige, the notoriety that goes along with ownership—and that's why the prices are what they are. But from the get-go, Wayne was approaching this as a business and that was evident from his extensive analysis and his extensive due diligence."

In calculating projections for his new enterprise, Huizenga had insisted that they be conservative to maintain credibility with the expansion committee and for his own comfort level. "In 20-20 hindsight, we were conservative in some respects and aggressive in others," Matt says. They assumed 30,000 tickets would be sold for each home game or 2.7 million fans total for the inaugural season. The Marlins would actually do better than forecast that first 1993 season, drawing nearly 38,000 per game for a total of

3.1 million "butts in the seats" at Joe Robbie Stadium. The Marlins and Colorado Rockies would be excluded from national television revenue for the 1993 season. Total revenue, plus the key in baseball, local media, was projected at $51 million. The team would actually do better, generating $58 million. And its first year out of the box, the Marlins would make money—$4.6 million or $1.9 million after interest costs.

The big expense was player salaries. Early on, Huizenga made efforts to dampen the expectations for his new ball club. "I think it would be a dangerous assumption for us to make—a dangerous road for us to go down—to try to get an expansion team in here . . . and set the world on fire the first or second year," he told the *Sun-Sentinel* just months after the franchise was awarded. The plan was to sign very few of the expensive free agents and instead hire young, inexpensive talent and develop from within.

The bottom-line orientation of Huizenga didn't bother Dombrowski, who'd been challenged by building a team at Montreal with modest resources. "We were always accountable for the bottom line, it was just that we had more bottom line to work with (at the Marlins)," he says. "What was impressive when we started the organization was that, with Wayne and with Carl, they allowed us to do the things we needed to do." The planned clubhouse and spring training facilities were first rate, and the emphasis was on hiring the best personnel, even if they cost more. For instance, Dombrowski recruited the scouting director from Montreal, Gary Hughes, considered top-notch but also one of the most highly paid. There were no restrictions put on Dombrowski when he left the Expos against hiring from the team, so he hired whom he knew and whom he considered the best. From the Expos, he also hired John Boles as director of player development, Whitey Lockman as a senior advisor and major league scout, Frank Wren as assistant general manager, Angel Vasquez as director of Latin American operations, and others. His raid on the Expos staff—a total of 14—drew a warning from baseball commissioner Fay Vincent.

Other preparations for the Marlins' grand entry were being handled by Jim Blosser, who worked to get the 18-event restriction on the stadium lifted. In presentations, he stressed the economic benefits conferred by having a major league baseball team. The restriction was rescinded, but attempts to settle the litigation were met with resistance by some community leaders, with whom the acrimony continued to be as great with Huizenga as with the Robbies.

Meanwhile, Barger was hiring the front and back-office personnel needed to run a baseball team in broadcasting, publicity, marketing, and finance. Just as crucial, he was instructing his friend on the vagaries of sports teams, particularly baseball, which would challenge Wayne Huizenga's precepts for running a "business." Though Huizenga could be made to see the logic in arguments, just because "that was the way it was done" was not a good enough reason. Early tussles involved company cars and credit cards. The Marlins scouts were given new Toyota Camrys, but only after Barger argued that they were needed to run a first-class operation and as lures to recruit scouting staff. Nor did Huizenga believe in company credit cards. Executives at Blockbuster and his other companies used personal credit cards and were reimbursed. But baseball staffers aren't highly paid and needed company credit cards. "Wayne doesn't understand why we need these things," Barger would mention to Dombrowski on occasion, but he always got them. "I can't remember anything that we really needed that we didn't get," Dombrowski says. "For someone like Wayne who'd never been in the game, it's hard to know if you have a scout in northern California, what his job is. Once he knew and once he understood, it was never an issue. It was more of a learning process for him."

As the Florida Marlins were getting ramped up and Wayne Huizenga was getting first-hand lessons on the inner workings of a ball club, he soon got plenty of exposure to the treachery within the ranks of his fellow owners and baseball itself. While often new team owners will hang back, not speak at meetings, and be low key for the first months, Huizenga quickly dispelled that notion. "It was very clear early on that Wayne, having invested $95 million to buy this franchise and knowing that he had to put a whole bunch more money in to get players and everything else, wasn't going to just sort of passively sit by and let decisions be made without putting in his two cents worth," says Stephen Greenberg, an attorney and deputy commissioner under Fay Vincent. "He was, without being abrasive in any way, assertive in terms of his views and what was right and what wasn't right and a whole bunch of issues that hadn't been thought through in terms of what players were selected or were eligible for selection for the expansion teams. It became really a push for fairness in terms of what kind of team they could assemble. It was very clear from the outset that short of spending money irresponsibly that Wayne was hell bent on putting a good team on the field."

Baseball stacks the deck against its new owners. All that $95 million had bought Huizenga was the right to a franchise and to spend another $20 million for start-up costs, to get the team to its first season. The expansion teams already were cut out of the national television revenue pie, and faced a host of expansion rules hobbling the ability of the Marlins and Rockies on the field. College draft picks with less than three years experience, and anyone with a no-trade contract were ineligible to be drafted by the expansion teams, which also got the last picks in the first round of the amateur draft. Barger complained to Greenberg, hoping that he could help lobby other owners or league presidents to change the rules. But baseball was baseball. "People want into baseball so badly they suspend judgment and then they get in and realize 'what have I done' and then they start complaining but it's too late," Vincent says. "Wayne was like that. He was so hot to get in, he didn't pay attention to 'I'm going to get screwed.' They [new owners] often don't know much about baseball and don't know how important that draft is."

While a lifelong baseball fan like Carl Barger knew a lot about baseball, now he was seeing it through slightly different eyes. That became clear to Greenberg, who had known Carl Barger at the Pirates and saw the change he underwent in his new post. "Carl became much more assertive when he became president of the Marlins," Greenberg says. "And I am convinced that it was a reflection of the difference between the Pirate's ownership and Wayne's ownership." The Pirates were owned by a group of companies, so they took a more corporate approach versus the entrepreneurial approach embodied by Huizenga and the Marlins. "Carl would be in our office or on the phone with me frequently, complaining about some of these procedures that were being set up either by the National League or by the television committee or whatever it was. And we ended up intervening in a number of cases at Carl's insistence. I'll never forget we had one meeting in our office—it may have been the first time I met Wayne in Fay's office, it was Carl and Wayne and Fay and me. And I was immediately taken, struck by the intensity that almost emanated from Wayne. I mean you look at his eyes and you want to look away because it's like they're lasers that are going to go right through you. That's when it struck me, because Carl did most of the talking. Wayne spoke a little bit but he let Carl do most of the talking, and that's really where it clicked. Carl really was becoming much more an instrument of Wayne at that point."

PROBLEMS, CRISES, AND CONFLICTS

The first crisis was touched off by a potential competitive threat across the state. St. Petersburg-Tampa Bay may have lost the expansion race, but they didn't count themselves out yet. Almost as soon as the ink was dry on the charter certificate for the Florida Marlins franchise, a courtship of convenience emerged between a new group lobbying to put baseball in the Dome and Jeff Smulyan, owner of the Seattle Mariners who wanted out of owning a money-losing baseball franchise in Seattle.

Through late summer and into fall, Smulyan and Seattle Mariner representatives talked with St. Petersburg city officials and community leaders about moving the team to the area. Baseball fans in Tampa and St. Petersburg dared to hope again, snapping up "Tampa Bay Mariners" t-shirts, and "May the Team Come True" posters.

But Smulyan faced complications, like an existing lease at the Seattle Kingdome and a media and political backlash in Seattle against moving the team. On December 6, 1991, he held a press conference announcing that the team was for sale with an asking price of $100 million. Acceding to an obligation at the Kingdome, Smulyan guaranteed local buyers an exclusive period of 120 days. If no one stepped up to the plate, he was going to move the team and though there were other suitors, the dome in St. Petersburg awaited.

In Fort Lauderdale, Wayne Huizenga and Carl Barger were livid that an established baseball team could be moved to the losing city in the expansion race, especially since they had won. Huizenga had explored the possibility of buying a team—after all, he'd preferred acquisitions to startups in nearly all his business ventures. If he had lost the expansion race, he would have gone after one. But word was that he had to go through the expansion process. "After he got the franchise he was very disappointed the way things were going," says Fay Vincent. "He said 'I'll give my money back, let me out of here.' He raised hell because he thought it was outrageous that he had to pay $95 million for a team and here was a team (moving) with all these stars when his team wasn't off the ground. He won the competition and they lost and here was Tampa Bay going to get something he was told he couldn't have with established stars and television value and he would be hurt. It was delicate because he couldn't be visibly against the team."

It was Barger who played the front man in the furor, complaining to the commissioner's office. But Huizenga took the hit among baseball fans in St. Petersburg and Tampa, who vilified him and plotted campaigns to boycott Blockbuster stores. Three state lawmakers from the St. Petersburg area threatened to cut Huizenga out of a state program that gave stadium owners $2 million a year for up to 30 years, arguing he was violating the spirit of the program by thwarting efforts to bring another baseball team to Florida.

The situation was defused when Nintendo of America, the Seattle-based U.S. division of the Japanese video game maker, in late January announced its intention to lead a local buyout group for the Mariners. Smulyan signed an agreement in early April and baseball officially accepted the $106 million bid on July 1, 1992.

But the threat to Huizenga's lock on Florida as a baseball market wasn't over yet. Just a month after the Mariners deal an ownership group in Tampa led by businessman Vince Naimoli announced that San Francisco Giants owner Bob Lurie had agreed to sell the team for $115 million. Lurie was weary of cold and windy Candlestick Park and sick of rejected ballot initiatives to build a new stadium. Naimoli, who had made his millions in the glass industry, had lent quiet support to the proposed Mariners move. Now he emerged in a more public role as the head of a group that would finally deliver baseball to Tampa Bay.

Huizenga was incensed. If the Mariners move would have been bad, moving the Giants was far worse—and he and Barger told Vincent so. He stood to lose up to $8 million a year if he had to share the Florida market, but the real impact would be far more damaging. "They were very upset," Vincent says. "The Giants moving to Tampa Bay would have been more a serious threat (than the Mariners.) It was a very strong National League team versus a weak American League team. Publicly he had to say he was very happy to support a team coming to Tampa but privately he was saying to me he thought it was outrageous." Huizenga argued the Marlins needed at least a year or two on the field to establish roots among fans. He and Barger "kept saying it was inherently outrageous, you don't treat partners and new colleagues this way, take their money and set them up and cut them off at the knees," says Vincent, who promised Huizenga he would block the move for at least a year.

But Vincent wouldn't be around to keep that promise. Having angered too many owners over too many issues, the barons of baseball conspired to teach their hired hand a lesson and issued a no-confidence vote. Rather than fight, a defiant but weary Vincent decided to resign in September 1992. When he called Huizenga with his decision, Huizenga had told him, "I think you're making a mistake. You're going to regret it. You don't ever want to back away from a fight."

As the weeks wore on and the ownership group in San Francisco strengthened and the Giants move began to look doomed, media reports kept surfacing about efforts by Huizenga or Barger or others on his behalf lobbying owners not to allow the deal to go through. Furious fans organized protests in front of Blockbuster video stores and hundreds more cut up their Blockbuster membership cards. State senators again threatened to cut Huizenga out of the state program for stadium grants while one even mentioned he was considering pushing for a new tax on videotape rentals. Again, Barger and others did the behind-the-scenes lobbying, allowing Huizenga to keep an increasingly tenuous public posture of support for his potential cross-state rival.

When the vote came on November 10, Huizenga voted for the move, even showing his ballot to National League President Bill White so his support would be publicly demonstrated. But the 9–4 tally cleared the way for a $100 million bid by Peter Magowan, president of the Safeway supermarket chain. The decision touched off a spate of lawsuits and countersuits.

There were outcrys from Florida senators Bob Graham and Connie Mack, who vowed to re-examine again baseball's antitrust exemption. And the dejected wannabe-Giants fans in Tampa and St. Petersburg held Wayne Huizenga personally responsible.

Though there were many reasons for owners to vote against moving the Giants—wanting to keep a National League team on the West Coast, a local ownership group, loss of a $95 million-plus fee from a city that had been in the running for an expansion team—the "Huizenga factor" can't be discounted. "I think his influence in killing the Giants move was pretty high," Vincent says.

To this day, Huizenga contends his role in both the Mariners and the Giants situation was way overblown by the press. "The way it's written up over in the papers in Tampa and St. Pete is that Huizenga stopped the deal or Huizenga controlled the deal. Now one new guy coming into the old boys network is not going to make or break a deal. The history of baseball is if you can salvage a team in its market, then it should stay and not move."

For his part, Naimoli doesn't put the onus on Huizenga for nixing the Giants move. "There were other people to blame and I wouldn't put Wayne in the top category," he says. "The area was looking for someone to lash out against and perhaps he was that person." He met with Huizenga afterwards who promised to support future efforts to get a team.

Indeed, on March 9, 1995, major-league baseball owners meeting at The Breakers in Palm Beach voted to award two more expansion franchises, one to Phoenix, and one to Tampa Bay, to begin play in 1998. Huizenga made the nomination for Tampa Bay. That, however, was after a presentation to baseball owners that succeeded in getting the expansion fee lifted from the proposed $115 million to a whopping $130 million. The rationale was that "they had such good stadium arrangements they could afford to pay more," Huizenga says. "They were playing in brand new facilities that were owned by the government and they were going to get all the sky box revenue and all the club seat revenue. And it was easy to see they could pay more." Even though baseball has its problems, franchise values are increasing, he claims, noting that markets like Colorado are doing very well. "These new markets will be just like Colorado. They're playing in brand new facilities that have sweetheart leases." On top of that, Huizenga argued that increasing channel capacity on television would make teams more valuable as programming. "He was so persuasive that the ownership committee raised the price $15 million based on a 15 minute presentation," Chicago White Sox owner Jerry Reinsdorf says. "In 15 minutes he changed everybody's mind."

There would be other skirmishes early on in Huizenga's baptism in baseball. One during the fall of 1992 involved George Steinbrenner. Since the Marlins were now playing in what had been minor league territory, Steinbrenner was demanding $10 million in damages for his single A Fort Lauderdale Yankees.

Huizenga told Steinbrenner that $10 million was outrageous, that he had paid $1.4 million for a Class A team and the most he'd pay was moving costs. Steinbrenner dropped his demand to $5 million. The matter was settled in July 1995 for $500,000. Of Huizenga, he says, "I find him calculating, cold, very smart, and a very good man. I don't mean cold and calculating in a negative sense. He's a cold, shrewd business man, very smart but he's a good man. He's a worthy opponent." For a newcomer, Huizenga was playing the hardball game that's played inside the world of baseball quite well.

Loss of a Friend

Though to the press, Huizenga always emphasized the business reasons for his decision to get into baseball, the real impetus was Carl Barger. "They had a wonderful relationship," says Marti Huizenga. "Carl was his closest friend." They were buddies, in a rare and special friendship born of comraderie and at times, mutual provocation.

"They were like big kids together," says Wayne Jr. "He did things with Wayne Sr. that I've never seen Wayne Sr. do. They'd sit around up in North Carolina and sometimes they'd sit for four, five, or six hours playing cards. You could just kind of feel a warmth, that they were comfortable together and I don't think he shares that with many people. They'd have a cocktail together out on the deck and sit and talk and they'd have their feet up, kind of day dreaming together a little bit. Carl was special. The whole baseball thing, part of it was because 'oh we've got the stadium and we need some more events here to make it really work out and it would be great to bring baseball to south Florida,'" says Wayne Jr. "But part of it was Carl and Carl's excitement about the game and Carl reminiscing about being a kid and the tradition of baseball. Carl made it more than a game. It was kind of a sexy, living, attractive thing. It was full of life and tradition."

The fusion of baseball and business between Barger and Huizenga wasn't always easy. From Barger, the Marlins would borrow some traditions, like striped uniforms and an old-fashioned scoreboard with hand-flipped numbers (with modern touches like advertising and two Sony Jumbotron scoreboards on opposite ends of Joe Robbie Stadium). But Huizenga, who hadn't grown up with the game, thought baseball needed to add some pizazz to appeal to a broader, younger base of fans. Indeed, fast-moving football and basketball were eclipsing "America's favorite past-time" and even baseball enthusiasts fretted over the game's greying fan base.

"Carl and I were the best of friends, but we were at each others throats all the time because all Carl wanted to talk about was tradition," Huizenga says. "And I have my own ideas of what the fans want and I'm not saying I'm right, but I just have my own ideas. Just because they did it this way in Pittsburgh didn't mean a damn thing to me. We'd go to dinner almost every night and goof around—it wasn't something that was going to end the friendship—but Carl would say 'that's tradition,' and I'd say, 'I don't care about tradition.'"

One source of friction was, as Huizenga describes it, "trying to create a better experience. There's no substitute in any sport for the game on the field or the game on the ice. That's the reason you go there, no doubt about it. But there is lots of other time, the experience of getting off the turnpike, getting into the parking lot, going to the stands, all these things are all part of (the experience). Getting your ticket taken, the atmosphere, the music you hear, the excitement before you even get into the building, is a big part. When you get to the game and you're a half-hour early, there's got to be some kind of excitement before the game, while you're waiting for the game to start. It doesn't take away from the big event. The big event is the game, but there has to be something to keep people occupied, whether it's music or whether it's some kind of promotion, whether it's getting a free gift, whether it's fireworks. Then there are lulls in the game and you've got to do things to liven it up a little bit. Carl didn't believe in that. Carl believed the game was the game. You don't do anything to take away from the game. So as we talked about doing all these things, Carl was 'no, no, no, don't worry, baseball's such a good game that people will come to the game to watch'. And I didn't believe that."

They also argued over budgets. In the week just after Thanksgiving in 1992, Huizenga and Barger went at it toe to toe. Huizenga wanted to stick to the conservative numbers they'd put together before the franchise was awarded. Barger was banging the table. "Damn it, Wayne, you can't do that. You can't run the club that way." The more emphatic Barger became, the calmer Huizenga was, making quiet comments that stoked Barger up even more. Barger won that battle and the player salary payroll went from the original $14 million to $19 million. "We had our budget of what we thought the team would do and then Carl had his budget as to what he thought the team would do and then we had the real budget. And neither one of us were right," Huizenga says. While revenue that inaugural season was more than anticipated, so was payroll, and a new television contract and the baseball strike would cost each team dearly in 1994. "So we never made our projections."

The tussles over tradition and battles over budgets aside, the excitement of starting something new buoyed both of them. From choosing the logo and team colors, to decisions like the Billy the Marlin team mascot to plans for a state-of-the-art spring training center near Melbourne, Florida, they were making sports history. Once the big work had been done, they were even planning for some shared fun. Anticipating that, there was a special "Barger box" built within the Marlins suite behind home plate, a small anteroom off to the side with a few seats, a phone, and a door where he and Huizenga and others could meet in private and Barger could smoke his cigarettes or light up a cigar without bothering anyone. And there were more challenges ahead, with Huizenga talking to Barger about helping with his anticipated award of a National Hockey League franchise, perhaps taking the role as chief intermediary between him and his growing legion of sports interests.

Friends worried about Barger as the fall of 1992 turned into winter. He was having a great time. The Marlins expansion draft had brought players like future all-star Jeff Conine and Bryan Harvey. He was excited about the prospect of signing name players like Orestes Destrade, who'd been playing in Japan, and catcher Benito Santiago. But he was depressed at times, separated from his fiance, his friends, and his hometown of Pittsburgh. And friends fretted he was working too hard. They urged him to slow down, to watch his blood pressure, to exercise, and most of all to quit smoking and take better care of himself—all promises made and broken before. A workaholic and a driven man, he'd found a challenge that drove him even harder. It was having a piece of ownership, it was starting something new, it was an obligation to south Florida baseball fans, and most of all, it was a vow to a dear and close friend. "We're going to make this a competitive ballclub in a hurry," he'd said when the Marlins franchise was awarded.

But on December 9 at the baseball owners meeting in Louisville, Kentucky, Carl Barger ran out of time. Excusing himself from a session, he walked out into a hotel hallway and collapsed shortly before 11 A.M. American League President Bobby Brown, a retired cardiologist, and Edward Rose, a partner in the Texas Rangers, administered CPR and mouth-to-mouth resuscitation until paramedics arrived. They rushed him to a nearby hospital where he died at 2:34 P.M., undergoing surgery to repair a ruptured abdominal aorta. In shock and disbelief, it was Marlins general manager Dave Dombrowski who called Huizenga, who then called Marti, Peer Pederson, and a small circle of friends in tears.

But Huizenga's world couldn't stop, not even for grief. The next day, the National Hockey League owners were meeting in Palm Beach to vote on granting an expansion franchise to Huizenga and south Florida, who'd applied for the franchise in November. "I've lost some friends, but none like this," he told reporter S.L. Price on what a *Miami Herald* headline called Huizenga's "worst good day."

"I didn't get much sleep last night. It wasn't so bad today. I woke up, I said, 'OK, I've got to come back to hockey.' But then I was walking out and the yardman had put the newspapers on a table so I read some articles and took them back to my wife. Then I went to the office. I tried to stop crying before I got there." The timing was all wrong. The last thing he wanted to do was wait in a hotel room for word of an expansion team, then hold a press conference announcing another push into sports when he should have been in mourning for the friend who'd helped usher him into that world. "I can't tell hockey, 'put it on hold.' When the opportunity presents itself, you jump on it—for south Florida. I knew I'd feel bad if I didn't take it."

The funeral service for Barger drew owners and players of the game he'd loved among the 400 mourners who gathered at St. Paul Cathedral in downtown Pittsburgh on December 12. George Steinbrenner and John McMullen and members of the Pirates and Marlins attended. Pirates' manager Jim Leyland gave the eulogy. "I called information this morning to get Carl's number and it was 1-800-Heaven and I got a message that said, 'I can't come to phone right now, but I have a meeting at 8, 10, 1, 3, and 5. At 6 o'clock there will be a press conference to meet my new Commissioner and join my new team. It's really great here. No arbitration, no salary disputes, no strikes. It's a great place to play and they have the most beautiful skyboxes I've ever seen. For all of you mourning my passing, please leave your message at the crack of the bat.'" At a memorial service in Fort Lauderdale a few days later, Huizenga assured mourners that Carl Barger would be there when the Florida Marlins took the field on opening day. "Carl will be watching from his new skybox." As the service drew to a close, organ music filled First Presbyterian Church with the unmistakable notes of "Take Me Out to the Ballgame."

On April 5, the Florida Marlins took the field against the Los Angeles Dodgers in their inaugural game at Joe Robbie Stadium. A fierce dawn thunderstorm dissipated and by game time, skies were clear. The day began for Huizenga with a toast of Dom Perignon at 8:30 A.M. and a presentation from "the original Marlins"—his father Harry, Steve Berrard, Rick Rochon, Don Smiley, and Jim Blosser—of an 18-inch cast bronze of a leaping blue marlin. (There was a dolphin, the fish, not the mammal, caught in its mouth. The symbolism too telling, they'd joked about having it removed and then decided to give the statue to Huizenga anyway.) Then he headed out to the stadium, where he signed hundreds of autographs and posed for dozens of photos, while 42,334 fans packed the stands and skyboxes, including 250 family members and friends brought to share this occasion. Amid the glare of television lights and cameras, Harry gave him a hug and a kiss and said quietly, "Congratulations son."

And Wayne Huizenga was right, Carl Barger was there. The flag at mid-field had flown at half-mast until Opening Day. The street fronting the stadium bears his name, as does the spring training center in Viera. That first game and throughout the inaugural season, the Marlins wore black armbands and a special patch. On Opening Day, Huizenga retired the No. 5 jersey. It had been DiMaggio's number, and it was DiMaggio who threw the first pitch in honor of the man who had idolized him as a boy. The broad grin and beaming smile on his face didn't banish the tears in Huizenga's eyes, and many times he was too choked up to even utter his constant refrain to family and friends, "Carl would have loved this." The Marlins won that first game, six to three.

In the Florida Marlins suite behind home plate, there is a collection of photos of the early hallmarks in Marlins history. An autographed photo of Joe DiMaggio wishing Barger well with his new team. Another of Huizenga and Barger with Fay Vincent and National League Commissioner Bill White when the charter was awarded. One of Huizenga at the initial press conference, with an orange baseball cap and his mother, Jean, standing at his side. The largest photograph is on the wall near the entry to what used to be the "Barger box," which with its door removed, is just an empty, rather odd room. It is a picture of two buddies in a joyful moment of triumph, taken with the backdrop of a baseball diamond at the stadium stretching endlessly behind them. There would be many wins for Wayne Huizenga in baseball, but never enough to erase this loss.

10

Sports Tycoon: Hockey, Football, and a Game Plan

In October 1992, Wayne Huizenga went shopping for an airplane and ended up buying a hockey franchise. While Huizenga was in California for business, his pilot, David Linnemeier had gotten word on a great deal on a 727, just the kind of plane they'd been looking for to use for the Marlins. It was owned by Bruce McNall, owner of the Los Angeles Kings and then chairman of the NHL's board of governors. While looking over the plane, Huizenga asked McNall when hockey was considering expanding because he'd like to see a team in South Florida. "I think it would go over well down there," Huizenga told him. McNall told him the league had considered South Florida for a team in 1990, but couldn't reach a deal and had awarded it to Tampa instead. But hockey was considering expanding again, and he encouraged Huizenga to speak with the interim league president, Gil Stein. Within weeks, Huizenga was in Stein's New York office talking about his interest in a hockey franchise.

Hockey envied the success enjoyed by basketball. The sport lacked national appeal in the U.S., its brawls on ice turned off many fans, and it was largely relegated to cable television. In recent years, it had cleaned up some and expanded its reach with new franchises in Tampa and San Jose where sunbelt residents were flocking to the game on ice. When Huizenga approached Stein, hockey was already talking to a potential owner who could lift the game's profile even higher. Walt Disney Co. Chairman Michael Eisner thought a team that played off of its movie "The Mighty Ducks" would be a great tie-in and a merchandising success. Now Huizenga's interest would provide hockey not only with a second expansion team, but also strong marketing possibilities.

A few weeks later in a conversation, Stein told Huizenga there was a chance at an expansion franchise being awarded within three weeks. "But you've got to tell me, do you want it or don't you." Huizenga hadn't planned on getting a hockey team so soon, his Florida Marlins hadn't even played their first game yet. But knowing that if he passed the chance up, it could be years before he or south Florida would have a chance at an expansion team, he said yes. There wasn't time to engage partners or shop the opportunity around. This was the one decision in sports, he admits, that wasn't driven by business but more by opportunity. "It isn't that I wanted a hockey team, but the opportunity was there to get it, let's go ahead and do that and we'll figure out what happens." If Disney is getting into the Mighty Ducks, this might well be a move for Blockbuster. Already, he could envision a sports component to Blockbuster's business as it stretched from video rental into an entertainment company. Blockbuster would guarantee a $20 million note in exchange for option to buy the team. In November 1992, Huizenga wrote an official request to the NHL for a franchise. Not more than a month later, on December 10, the franchise was awarded. If the phone calls that bombarded Blockbuster the next day were any indication, hockey in south Florida was going to be a hit.

Accustomed to moving fast, Huizenga's pace became to light-speed to get the conditions met for the franchise. Disney was committed to play the 1993 season and by March 1, Huizenga had to let the league know if he could make that same date. He was determined to meet that goal, even if he'd started behind the gate. "We're certainly not going to let Disney get a leg up on us," he said. "There's no way we're ever going to put ourselves at a disadvantage." He knew what was in store and what it would take. "There's going to be a lot of 20-hour days," he said.

By March, he had hired the Philadelphia Flyers' senior vice-president Bobby Clarke as general manager and Bill Torrey, former New York Islanders general manager, as president of the Florida Panthers. (The name was the favorite of a fan contest that drew 6,400 responses and, not so coincidentally, also a favorite of Huizenga's, who nominated the panther as the mascot and moniker for the high school teams at Pinecrest. It also tied in nicely to the "save the panther" campaigns to help preserve habitat for the endangered Florida panther.) A lease was signed with the Miami Arena, though unfavorable to the Panthers since the Miami Heat basketball team retained skybox, parking, and most advertising and concession revenue. Since Huizenga had indicated plans to build a competing arena for the team, the public-private authority controlling the arena drove a hard bargain. "We're not going to get $12.5 million like Disney is," Huizenga grumbled at the time. "I'm hoping I get a decent parking space."

Typical of his operating style, once he hired his managers, he deferred to them in building the team. "When we first got the franchise he basically has delegated to those of us who had been in the business," Torrey says. "He is very enthusiastic whenever we meet and has lots of questions like anyone would who had invested this amount of time and energy and money." But while Huizenga didn't know anything about hockey, he had strong ideas about marketing and design.

The first tussle with Torrey was over the color of the Panthers' uniforms. They'd tried iterations of Blockbuster colors (blue and yellow); and Marlins colors (black and teal); shades of green suggested by a designer friend of Marti's; softer, tropical colors with purples—and Torrey's choice, of red, navy, and gold—a total of 27 different configurations. The decision had to be made by July, and Torrey actually walked into NHL Commissioner Gary Bettman's office on deadline day with two different uniform patches, the one that Huizenga liked, which had more of a tropical twist, and the one he favored, more traditional hockey colors. Over the phone, Huizenga asked Torrey which one he liked. Torry repeated he wanted the red. It was more aggressive, reflecting the game's boldness and a color he thought players would want to wear on the ice. Huizenga told him to go ahead. "He was testing me to see how badly I wanted them," Torrey laughs. Indeed, Panthers' memorabilia sold second just behind that of the Mighty Ducks franchise by Disney. Huizenga attended the expansion draft in Quebec, querying Torrey on the players chosen and the rationale. "I've never heard of a lot of these guys, but I never heard of a lot of the baseball players we selected," Huizenga said. (Among the notables was goalie John Vanbiesbrouk, formerly of the New York Rangers, who had traded him to Vancouver and left him unprotected.)

The Panthers took to the ice for their inaugural game in Chicago, where Huizenga's childhood friend Dick Molenhouse and his wife joined the event. After the game they were set to leave when Huizenga bolted from the car and went to the locker room to congratulate the players on their 4–4 tie game with the Blackhawks. The Panthers snatched their first victory October 9 against the Tampa Bay Lightening in Huizenga enemy territory. Then it was to south Florida for the first home game October 12 for the unbeaten Panthers. They lost to the Pittsburgh Penguins, 2–0 but south Florida clearly considered it a victory. A crowd of 14,372 hockey fans gave Huizenga a standing ovation when he was introduced by NHL Commissioner Gary Bettman as Huizenga's hometown area became one of only nine cities in the nation to enjoy all four major sports. Yet this was only a start. Following his mode of bigger, better and putting things together, Huizenga was already onto the next part of his game plan.

BLOCKBUSTER PARK

All of his life, Wayne Huizenga has thought big. It's understandable then how a plan to build a 20,000-seat hockey arena for the Florida Panthers mushroomed into a proposal for a Blockbuster-owned 2,500-acre sports and entertainment theme park with its own quasi-governmental powers.

It started simply enough. Huizenga had promised the NHL a new hockey arena. South Florida cities in early 1993 began salivating at the chance to build him one. Competition between jurisdictions escalated, upping the ante with land or special financing breaks. But within weeks, what started to take shape were plans for a sports-entertainment complex with a hockey arena, baseball stadium, Little League stadium, movie studio, shopping arcade, and "virtual reality" center and movie studio. The dream was unveiled at Blockbuster's annual meeting on May 11, 1993, and quickly dubbed "Wayne's World" by the press. Even then, it was projected to be at most a 500-acre project but would grow to 2,600 acres.

Here was chance to parlay his sports teams into something bigger and enhance Blockbuster's image as an entertainment company. In the vision, Huizenga was borrowing pages from both Ted Turner and Walt Disney. He would, as Turner used his sports to provide programming for his TBS superstation, be able to use his teams as programming for a possible Blockbuster Channel. The Marlins and Panthers "would have been something to draw people into the Park and if the team didn't make any money but it drew people into the Park, that's the same thing as Turner getting his money over on the television station instead of the team," he says. The Blockbuster board had just weeks before the announcement flirted with buying the Marlins, but decided the company needed to do something more than just own a sports team. There had to be more "value added." Then, too, there would be questions generated by the chairman and major stockholder selling his sports teams to Blockbuster. Huizenga publicly vowed to sell the teams at no profit to himself, and reiterated that point in meetings with institutional fund managers.

From Disney, he borrowed the ideas for a theme park and studio—and another key point. As Blockbuster began buying up parcels of property southwest of Fort Lauderdale and getting Dade County and the state of Florida to cede 400 acres in northwest Dade for what had ballooned into a mega-complex, he realized to make this work, Blockbuster was going to free itself of the some constraints of three government jurisdictions, two counties, and the city of Miramar, Florida. A form of self-governance was needed. But getting it would be a battle. Not only would it have to be sold to local governments, but to a sensitive state legislature. "Not another Disney" was the common reaction among lawmakers, spoken or not.

In the early 1960s as Walt Disney was planning to turn 30,000 acres of cypress swamps, citrus groves and cattle ranches into what would become Walt Disney World, he hadn't wanted to have his ideas for innovative theme parks bogged down by local bureaucracies. Besides, he needed to finance the massive infrastructure of roads, sewers and water lines. Disney lobbied and won approval by the Florida legislature for a quasi-government, sometimes referred to as the state's 68th county. Among other points, it exempts Disney from local zoning restrictions, allows its own security and fire department and for the "government" to issue taxfree bonds to finance the infrastructure. Though the arrangement suited Disney well, it at times has created friction with the surrounding local governments, particularly Orange County. Legislators were wary of recreating the situation in south Florida.

Few of the political hands hired gave the Blockbuster Park process much of a chance to get through within a year the local government hurdles, let alone the myriad of legislative committees and the state legislature itself. But Huizenga knows the political process and what it takes. With Jim Blosser leading the charge with four other key executives Blockbuster quickly garnered approvals from the local governments and approached the state legislature in the spring of 1994. The lure was economic development and growth, as much a part of Florida as palm trees. The park was projected to draw as many as six million local residents and tourists a year, generate 16,000 jobs and $64 million in new taxes to state and local governments. It would have been a break in the endless suburbia of south Florida. But even in property already slated for development of 4,000 homes, the fight against Blockbuster Park became a fight to save the environment.

Hiring key lobbyists and a phalanx of experts who were on call to answer concerns of legislators, Blockbuster got its special jurisdiction on April 9, 1994, less than a year after the plan had been announced. It is testimony to Huizenga's political clout in Florida that the bill sailed through. Blockbuster had anted up heavily in support of civic organizations endorsed by politically powerful legislators. He'd cultivated ties with South Florida legislators over the years and those in the rest of the state knew him for his success with Blockbuster and baseball. "It's a salute to Wayne Huizenga that he had their trust," says Van Poole, former state Republican party chairman who was hired as a lobbyist. The district had broad zoning powers, could issue tax-exempt bonds and assess a one-cent sales tax on admissions and items sold, set hours for restaurants and attractions, down to when fireworks could start.

Already, Blockbuster had spent some $53 million assembling land, hiring consultants and lobbyists, and other costs on the park. Still ahead were complex environmental reviews and convincing public coffers to ante up hundreds of millions of dollars to help build it. Meanwhile, a backlash of opposition to the project was growing, protesting public funding and warning of environmental harm.

But what killed Blockbuster Park was not the environment, but economics. And it wasn't done in New York, but in Fort Lauderdale. After Blockbuster's merger of Viacom was completed, in a meeting on December 9, Steve Berrard, the new CEO of Blockbuster Entertainment, decided to kill what had been his mentor's favorite project. The rest of the Blockbuster Park team concurred. Viacom's newly acquired Paramount Parks sector, which reported to Berrard, didn't think it was the right site for expansion. The $2 billion price tag was far too much to swallow, and there weren't commitments by partners to share the costs. Viacom had to focus on paying down its debt from the Paramount acquisition and had already shed Madison Square Garden and the sports teams. Berrard's job was to realign Blockbuster within Viacom, not continue the strategy of an independent entertainment company and a vision Wayne Huizenga had for south Florida.

On the eleventh floor of Blockbuster Plaza, just outside Wayne Huizenga's office, is a five-foot by four-foot scale model of a sports and entertainment park—small, white cardboard renderings of a baseball stadium, a hockey arena, and a shopping and entertainment arcade connecting the two. A theme park sits north of the arena, the movie studio and sound stages are south of the ballpark. Minute, quarter-inch sailboats and powerboats make their way through connecting lakes, while a tiny fountain marks a water park. Broad swatches of green depict golf courses and areas for nature preserves and botanical garden. Huizenga points to where an amphitheater and hotels would have gone. "It would have been great for the company," Huizenga says, gazing at the model. "It would have changed Blockbuster's image." The model was delivered a week before the decision to axe the park. Even the special district had been dissolved May 3 by the state legislature. But five months after the project had been killed, Wayne Huizenga still hadn't yet been able to remove all that remained of his grand plan for Blockbuster Park, the key element of his long-term strategy for his sports empire.

Dolphins Deal

After Wayne Huizenga bought into the stadium and the Dolphins, his partnership with the Robbies remained uneasy at best. Fundamental disagreements arose over management of the stadium, from maintenance to concession stand prices. Patrons complained about dark and dirty rest-rooms, high prices for lousy food, expensive parking, and rude attendants. Huizenga made suggestions, which were ignored. At board meetings, he pointed out the revenue that could be generated by making the improve-ments, to no avail. "They thought I was negotiating with them all the time," Huizenga says. "I was putting up the money, but they didn't want to incur any more debt. They didn't want to owe me any more money. Well, it had to be done. The stadium was falling apart."

The first public rift arose in March 1992 at two exhibition games be-tween the New York Yankees and Minnesota Twins. The pitchers mound was poorly packed and the wrong height, the bullpen mounds disastrous, and the infield too hard. It was an embarrassment to Huizenga and word leaked to the press that he faulted the Robbies for the problems. "Wayne was ticked because the Robbies didn't hire the right consultant whereas Wayne would have hired the right guys," says Rick Rochon, who was often Huizenga's liaison with the Robbies.

That role was distinctly uncomfortable. "The Robbies basically didn't trust us and I don't want to say vice versa, but it was pretty damn close. We didn't really trust them and it wasn't as much trust, it was more philosophy of operation," Rochon says. "The Robbies make money by not spending money. Wayne makes money by spending money. Once your philosophies differ then you don't trust people. It was not a pleasant experience. Of all my time with Wayne, this whole Dolphins and stadium thing was probably the worst thing I've ever been involved in."

The distrust deepened as the fractiousness within the Robbie family continued. After Elizabeth Robbie died in November 1991, it became in-creasingly evident that the Dolphins would have to be sold to satisfy $47 million in estate taxes and stem the mounting legal battles. At first, the trustees sought to sell a minority interest in the team and keep control, but that clearly wasn't going to be enough.

With his right of first offer, the Robbie trustees had no choice but to deal with Huizenga eventually, but they wanted to avoid that as long as pos-sible. "When the Robbies decided they wanted to sell because the other side of the family forced the trustees to sell, it basically was, 'we want to sell but we don't want to sell to Wayne,'" Rochon says. "So I'm trying to negotiate to buy the damn thing and they don't want to sell to us."

In addition to the right to buy the team first, Huizenga held another valuable card which he skillfully played. In July 1992, he testified in a pro-bate hearing involving the Robbie estate that he might move the Marlins out of Joe Robbie Stadium after the team's five-year-lease. He was gen-uinely unhappy with the way the stadium was being managed, but moving the Marlins also served to try to jawbone down the price of the Dolphins.

The threat became a key piece of leverage as plans for Blockbuster Park took shape through 1993, just as the Robbies were trying to negotiate a sale of the football team. Without the Marlins to carry part of the debt burden, the Dolphins would be stuck again with one of the worst leases in professional football, about $3 million a year. That could affect the valuation of the Dolphins as much as $25 million, according to some estimates.

Through 1993, the Robbies entertained three potential suitors for the Dolphins. Financier Nelson Peltz and real estate investor Bruce Frey proposed a deal estimated at $150 million during the summer of 1993. Huizenga had dinner with Peltz to discuss the Dolphins finances and his interest in the stadium. Shortly thereafter, Peltz cut his bid to $120 million, which the Robbies rejected. Meanwhile, another suitor, New York investment banker J. Morton Davis, dangled a reported $148 million bid, but walked in October when they couldn't agree on terms. Commodities trader John Henry, along with Bruce Frey, kicked around a third offer for $142 million, but the Robbie trustees froze it out because of too many conditions. Then the Robbies provided telecommunications magnate George Lindemann a two-week exclusive negotiating period starting January 10.

A deal was struck on Friday, January 21, for $138 million. The three Robbie trustees and their attorney met that afternoon with Rochon and Huizenga. But the trustees said they were set to sign the deal with Lindemann on Monday. Seizing the moment, Huizenga offered to match the deal Lindemann made. Negotiations continued all weekend between Rochon, the Robbies, and their respective attorneys and on Sunday night, around 6 P.M. Huizenga arrived to sign the deal.

Essentially, including the 25% he already owned—the original 15% plus the 10% option—Huizenga paid $128 million for the team. Lindemann's annoyance at being beaten out of the deal was directed at the Robbies, not at Huizenga. Because the Robbies signed on Sunday night instead of waiting to sign his deal and then approaching Huizenga, they avoided paying as much as $500,000 in legal fees, he says. For his part, Huizenga notes that other prospective buyers called him during negotiations with the Robbies to gauge his intentions, but Lindemann never called until after the deal was done. "I'm surprised that he never called," Huizenga says. "I think he could have saved himself a lot of aggravation anyway (if he'd) just picked up the phone and called."

On Monday, January 24, at a press conference at Joe Robbie Stadium, Tim Robbie shook hands with a beaming Wayne Huizenga, introduced as the new owner of the Miami Dolphins. If the other National Football League team owners approved, he would also be the only man in America to own three major professional sports teams. He grinned for the TV crews and cameras would catch him celebrating with friends at the Florida Panthers game that night. It was a good deal, as would become clear a year later when mega-millionaire Malcolm Glazer bought the Tampa Bay Buccaneers, with one of the worst records in football, for $175 million—$47 million more than Huizenga had paid for a team with a spotty but generally strong record. (But one key reason for the difference in valuation again goes to the stadium—the Bucs could be moved and so set off a bit of a bidding war. The Dolphins, because of the stadium debt, are tied to playing in Joe Robbie Stadium.)

But reaching a deal with the Robbies was only a first step. Huizenga also had to clear his purchase with the NFL by getting approval of 21 of 28 team owners. The League had a long-standing rule against owners having controlling interest in other sports franchises and a few owners had been forced to divest themselves of various interests over the years. The rules prohibiting "cross-ownership" as well as corporate ownership had come under review recently, under some prodding by NFL Commissioner Paul Tagliabue, but no changes had been made. A day after the deal, Huizenga showed up for a Super Bowl party, hosted by Hugh McColl, chairman of NationsBank, in Atlanta attended by team owners Rankin Smith of the Atlanta Falcons, Jerry Jones of the Dallas Cowboys, and Jerry Richardson of the Carolina Panthers.

A little lobbying could help smooth his approval. But traditionalists like Bud Adams, owner of the Houston Oilers, and Ralph Wilson, owner of the Buffalo Bills, saw no reason to change the rules. The NFL owners haggled over the situation for two days at a meeting in March before reaching a temporary solution: Huizenga would put the team in a trust for more than two years, agreeing to sell the team in 1996 if the NFL still held firm on cross-ownership. That provision would be extended another year in 1995. While Huizenga's respectful demeanor and willingness to compromise helped break the impasse, he was prepared to play tough. "We had a contract and the NFL, in our opinion, didn't have any right to tell us we couldn't own a baseball team and a football team," Huizenga says. If the trust compromise had not been offered, "we would have sued the NFL."

While many of the owners agreed to the trust as a way to help out the Robbies and allow the sale to Huizenga to go through, Ralph Wilson of the Buffalo Bills abstained from casting a vote because he thinks the rule should stay. "I think it's difficult to own more than one sport and be really interested in more than one sport," he says. The dynamics of major league sports today takes a little time," he says. While Huizenga's marketing bent and business success impressed many of the NFL owners as potentially beneficial to the sport, there is a sharp distinction in approach from traditionalists like Wilson. "To me, sports is more of a personal matter and a real desire, a real interest in the particular sport," says Wilson, who's been an NFL owner for 35 years. "As a business decision it might be very good, but personally, I am interested in sports not to make money. The value of the franchises seem to be going up every year but there's not a lot of money to be made in sports on a profit and loss basis."

Now only one obstacle remained: the sale of the stadium. The sale of the Dolphins depended on the sale of the rest of the stadium to Huizenga. Though a price of $12 million was reached, Deborah Olson and some of the Robbie children objected to a clause that would allow Huizenga to change the name of the stadium. "My father built the stadium," she said, "I consider it a memorial."

But naming rights can be lucrative—United Airlines anted up $20 million for Chicago's United Center—and Huizenga's attorney Steve Roddenberry insists that they had information that other bidders had valued the naming rights at $1 million a year. The press took Huizenga to task, with *Miami Herald* sports columnist Greg Cote noting that it was Robbie's vision that had brought the Dolphins to Miami and his cherished dream to build the stadium. "To take away the man's name from this stadium or sully it by adding a commercial sponsor would be a shame. It would be corporate grave robbing."

For his part, Huizenga said he had no intention of changing the name. "I'm not going to call it Huizenga Stadium, absolutely not," he vowed. But

Reprinted with permission, *Tribune Media Services.*

the final agreement would not preclude him from securing a corporate sponsor. For Huizenga, the stadium name had nothing to do with memorials. It was strictly business.

SPORTS MONOPOLY?

By early 1994 with his sports menagerie full with the Marlins, Panthers, and Dolphins, Huizenga decided to go after the one professional sport in south Florida he didn't yet own—the Miami Heat of the National Basketball Association. An NBA team would provide another tenant for the arena planned for Blockbuster Park, and the Panthers and Heat could possibly split their seasons between downtown Miami and southwest Broward.

The franchise had been awarded in 1986 to Ted Arison, the shipping magnate and Carnival Cruise Lines founder, along with a handful of minority partners. Eager to snag a second professional sports franchise, the city of Miami built a 15,494-seat stadium in a blighted downtown area, hoping to spur new development, and gave the Heat a very favorable lease. But a reclusive billionaire, Arison disliked the notoriety of sports team ownership and over the years there had been periodic rumors of his interest in selling his family's stake.

In January 1994, Huizenga negotiated with the Arisons, mostly with Ted's son, Micky, to buy the Heat and offered $130 million. But managing partner Lewis Schaffel, who'd had a bitter falling-out with the Arisons, and part-owner Billy Cunningham, had to agree to the sale. They had no interest in having Huizenga as a partner and also wanted to cash out. Huizenga began negotiating separately with them.

Then Huizenga encountered his own set of complications. The just-completed deal to purchase the rest of the Dolphins was already running afoul of the National Football League's rules on owning other sports teams. While the Dolphins had been put in trust while the NFL sorted out the issue, a condition of the sale was that he wouldn't buy any more teams. Blockbuster was an obvious purchaser, but the pending merger with Viacom nixed that possibility. Deep-pocketed friends had taken a pass. Huizenga called his brother-in-law, Whit Hudson, in Colorado with a proposal that he take over the deal he'd been negotiating with Schaffel and Cunningham. Hudson, who owed his fortune to Huizenga, didn't hesitate.

Days later, on August 12, Hudson stood in front of television cameras as sports reporters grilled him about the deal. A slightly dazed Hudson admitted he hadn't spoken with Schaffel or Cunningham. The press demanded to know what Huizenga's role had been. "This is a complete surprise to me," he exclaimed at the press conference, but even Huizenga couldn't suppress a smile. Rick Rochon, Huizenga's point-man for sports, was the chief negotiator for Hudson, and already there were snickers in the press about "the old brother-in-law trick."

As rumors had surfaced over the summer, Huizenga had repeatedly denied an interest by either himself or Blockbuster in buying the Heat. Already, the word "monopoly" had surfaced in connection with south Florida sports. Now the press had a field day. Sportswriters and columnists weighed in on everything from fears of $10 hot-dogs and sky-high ticket prices to others discounting those concerns as Huizenga was too good at marketing but lamented all the area's professional sports teams being under control of one man—even if one owner had a different last name. There was open speculation on how much control and influence Huizenga had on the deal. Whit Hudson insists there was none. "Wayne didn't put one dime into it. I never talked to Wayne after we got involved except one time, Wayne asked me, 'are you sure you want to go through with this? You're really getting beat up bad.' I said, 'Yeah I know, but I'd really like to do something with it.' Because by this time I was pissed and I wanted to go forward with it."

But the deal never got done. The Arisons contended Hudson was reneging on various provisions. Hudson complained the Arisons wouldn't sign off on a definitive agreement and were using him as a front to set up a deal to buy out Schaffel and Cunningham. He sued the Arisons, Schaffel and Cunningham in January 1995, claiming they'd sabotaged his efforts to buy the team. Arison said that he was ready to close on the deal, but that Hudson was creating issues and couldn't get sale approval from the NBA. Arison threatened to countersue.

An ugly lawsuit naming Hudson, Wayne Huizenga, and Blockbuster would very embarrassing if filed just before the Super Bowl was set to play in Miami. Hudson denies the threatened suit prompted him to settle. "He'd already tried for four months to make me look bad and Wayne couldn't care less, Wayne had already told him to go to hell." But a suit between two such prominent members of south Florida's sports world wasn't in the best interests of the team or the community, says Albert Kania Sr., an attorney for Billy Cunningham, who played peacemaker. Just days before kickoff, Hudson and Arison settled with Hudson getting an unsold skybox and Heat tickets, a fraction of the $1 million in compensation Hudson had sought. The Arisons bought out Schaffel and Cunningham's interests and promised to keep the Heat in Miami.

But just two months later, it appeared that Huizenga may have yet had a final shot. In preparing for Blockbuster Park, Huizenga in July 1994 had bought half-ownership of Leisure Management International, which manages a dozen or so sports facilities around the nation, including the Miami

Arena. It was a small deal, by Huizenga standards, about $3 million, but through it he held a stake in the long-term operating contract for the arena. Huizenga was nervous about being viewed as trying to control too much of the south Florida sports market. But the LMI deal was done with initial encouragement by Miami city representatives, figuring that if Huizenga owned an interest in the arena, he'd have a vested interest in keeping the Panthers in downtown Miami, at least on a part-time basis.

As the Heat began negotiating for a new lease in 1995, LMI informed the team that terms would change substantially. Since the Heat was contemplating a short-term arrangement pending a rebuilt or new arena, perhaps the team would accept the same lease that caused the Panthers to lose $6 million a year? Micky Arison cried foul and the Miami establishment, including the mayor, sided with him while an editorial in *The Miami Herald* painted Huizenga as the spoiler. John Blaisdell, president of LMI says Huizenga's only directive has been "you negotiate the longest and best deal for the building." Blaisdell adds "the Heat has gotten spoiled. They got one of the best leases in the NBA ten years ago, they pay very little, and have a lot of rights." LMI cannot and will not renegotiate the Panthers lease based on any renegotiation of the Heat lease, he says. Any change in the Heat deal would affect the performance of the arena. The situation would have to be resolved, but while Huizenga didn't have the team, he had LMI, which controlled the action on at least part of the court.

SPORTS AS ENTERTAINMENT

To understand Wayne Huizenga's view of sports, a visit to Joe Robbie Stadium is a must. He's invested a great deal of time and money into the "fan experience." After buying out the remaining half of the stadium, he wasted no time in bringing it up to his standards. Instead of unfinished concrete, $2 million was spent on a blue-orange-black silica nonskid flooring, another $500,000 on paint. Additional parking, revamped restrooms with diaper changing tables and better lighting, more palm trees and new concession stands were added to the tune of $22 million spent on improvements in just the first eight months of sole ownership. Of that, about $1 million was spent on the club area with new carpeting and fixtures, and another $11 million on parking.

Restaurant areas such as the "Key Marlin" offers Caribbean fare like Jamaican-style jerk chicken, and another in a country-western theme serves up barbeque pork sandwiches, complete with local bands featured to provide pre-game entertainment. Another restaurant-bar with a nautical theme, the Port O'Call, offers beer and sausages from around the world.

The concession stands alone offer a greater variety of food, from health food—with vegetarian "Boca burgers"—to traditional ballpark hotdogs. But even hotdogs are researched by Huizenga. Fans tested and tasted various hotdog combinations and buns through football season until an all-beef hotdog with a special dijon-mustard bun was chosen in time for baseball to begin. Besides fan input, he also seeks input from his closest advisors, his family. Says Marti: "If he's working on a project or an idea or a problem, he'll call 15 different people, even our kids, and say, 'What do you think about having this kind of hot dog at the stadium?' or 'What's your feeling on the band?'" To keep the emphasis on family entertainment, alcohol sales after the seventh inning in baseball and after the third quarter in football, were eliminated. That change may cut into profits, but it also cuts down on rowdiness.

As stadium manager, Richard Anderson gets a first-hand experience for Huizenga's eye for detail and seeing the world from a fan perspective, down to popcorn containers. "When we're giving them this popcorn, we should get a better container," he told Anderson. Puzzled, Anderson asked him what he meant. "Well, you got a container and you've got this thing and the popcorn on the top and you walk away and somebody bumps you and now it's all over the floor. What good does that do us? Why don't we get a container that's deeper, give them the same amount but instead of having it piled over the top, now it's down here." Anderson laughs, remembering the exchange. "Here's a guy who's got billions of dollars worth of assets to worry about and he's worried about how you get your popcorn to your seat."

That attention to detail carries over to attention to convenience and unintended consequences. On one of his first trips to see the new spring training stadium being built in Brevard County north of Melbourne, Florida, Anderson waited anxiously for Huizenga to say something encouraging. He was proud of the effort that had been put into planning the $20 million center. "There's more than one elevator, isn't there?" Huizenga asked. "No, Wayne, there's one elevator." Huizenga was dumbfounded. All the patrons who had paid for club suites would have to wait for elevators jammed with press and game day personnel. No way. Before the building was finished, it was jacked up on one side for an additional elevator shaft to be installed. As for unintended consequences, in using the shoulders of the roads fronting Joe Robbie Stadium to handle additional traffic, Huizenga reminded Anderson to make sure he had a street sweeper come through so nails wouldn't puncture a patron's tire and spoil what otherwise would have been a pleasant game experience. "He challenges you and no matter how much effort you put into something," Anderson says, "it's never good enough. No matter how good it is. The challenge is to finally get something where he looks at that and goes, 'man, that was great.'" So far, that hasn't happened. "It makes me better. I strive for that."

That striving for perfection also plays into Huizenga's sense of humor at times. Before Carl Barger's death, Anderson hadn't spent much time directly with Huizenga. The first time he'd really recalls being alone with Huizenga was in the back of a limousine as a pallbearer at Barger's funeral. Anderson had been particularly close with Barger and was perceived as "Carl's guy" and was uncertain about what would happen to him without his patron. On Christmas Eve, Huizenga called and said he wanted to look at the spring training center. Anderson and Barger had been working closely on it and in recent meetings, Huizenga had made suggestions to change things that had already been done.

So on December 26, Anderson, Huizenga, and Harry flew by helicopter to the stadium, where Anderson had an experience that is the dread of any employee. Huizenga had scarcely said a word on the way up, and Anderson was already nervous. They got out of the helicopter and walked over to the stadium, and Anderson tried to open the door and it didn't open. There were windows installed where three days ago, there weren't windows and not a soul was around because it was a vacation day for the construction crew. "We couldn't even get in it, every door and window was locked and I'm petrified," Anderson recalls. "Wayne was great about it. He said, 'that's no problem, we can see through this window' and I started relaxing until a point where I thought, this is great, he's not going to kill me. Then he stopped me, grabbed my arm, and said, 'you know, I like this, but could we move this over about three feet.' And he pointed to this 20-foot-high wall that had a roof on it and he wanted me to move the building, the entire building, three feet. And I was so serious about it and I said, 'well, uh, uh, uh,' and he smiled at me. Then I realized he was pulling my chain. That's the first time I ever really had any insight into his sense of humor. And I loved it. It broke the ice and I realized that he was going to give me a shot to do what I could do."

His friendliness and approachability also provides Huizenga fodder for suggestions and new ideas from employees outside the top circles. A vendor hawking soft drinks saw Huizenga during a game, stopped him, and explained that he thought how the stadium could do a better job selling sodas, with the serving room needing to be revamped and more diet soft drinks offered in more concession stands. Anderson got a hand-written note from Huizenga and a phone call from Don Smiley within two days of that encounter. Better equipment and lighting were added to the serving room, and diet sodas were made more available. "Many people at Wayne's level would not have given this guy the time of day," Anderson says. "Not only did Wayne give him the time of day, but he was really genuinely interested in what he had to say and took the time to pass the information on. And now the guests that come into the stadium are going to have better service and experience. And that's the Wayne difference."

The "Wayne difference" also extends to staffing. Without having to duplicate the Robbie management organization, the full-time staff was trimmed by 20 positions. But the game-day staffing increased significantly, with 200 additional personnel for football games and 100 more for baseball games. Whereas the stadium had one attendant for every eight restrooms, it's now one attendant per restroom. Borrowing a page from Disney, "customer service representatives" are stationed outside the gates, watching for people who look confused and offering to help them find their seats. A customer service department was added to take suggestions and handle complaints, with three full-time staffers. And Huizenga thinks it's important that stadium attendants, as much as possible, staff the same seating sections every game, particularly in the season-ticket holder areas so "guests"—as they're referred to at the stadium—can establish a personal rapport with them. "Fans we consider shareholders," says Don Smiley, who was appointed Marlins president in February 1994. "That's the way I look at it, that's the way we here at the Marlins address our season ticket holders base, as shareholders. We address everyone as guests at the games and the reason you do that is because you are running a business and you want them to come back."

The goal is simple but difficult to achieve. "Wayne wants to go about building long-term loyalty that won't be nearly as impacted by our teams' performance," Anderson says. "You're not going to win every game and you're not going to have sunny weather every game, but if you have quality service, if your products are great and your presentation is great and you truly care, there's not enough seats to take care of that (demand.) We're all starved for that. I think the way a lot of people get in this business is because they're enamored with the team and they forget that it is a business. Wayne knows that it is a business and for him, business is quality customer service. And he understands that if he brings quality customer service, it'll be a successful business."

At Marlins and Panthers games—and now Dolphins games—there's always something extra. Pre-game bands playing in stadium restaurants, contests involving fans before the game and at breaks during the games, from bicycle racing on ice at a Panthers game to a race to stuff money into a sack at a Marlins game (too appropo given the on-going dispute between owners and players.) Gimmicks and giveaways—from caps to checkbook covers to cups to kids' batting helmets—are sponsored with local businesses. "We do a lot of things that are not done traditionally in other NHL rinks, but I am a firm believer that you don't present an attraction in South Florida in the same way as Winnepeg or Edmonton or somewhere where the game's been played for 150 years," says Bill Torrey, president of the Panthers. "The game is played the same once the puck is dropped, but obviously in a nontraditional market you have to market differently and Wayne's astute enough to see that."

Huizenga is constantly looking to add to the fan "experience." Within the league of baseball owners, one of his most outspoken stances was against the restrictions on scoreboard replay. Baseball has rules that prohibit showing controversial plays on the scoreboard to avoid stoking fan ire against umpires or provoking fights or riots. "He felt that the fans in the stands who are paying their $10 should be able to see the same thing as people on television as far as close calls," says Bill Giles, owner of Philadelphia Phillies. "We are going more and more in Wayne's direction." Giles is on the baseball committee on score boards with Huizenga and agrees with his stance. Baseball fans at the parks, Giles says, will see more controversial plays replayed, though not yet the same as someone watching at home. That "fan experience" and participation is something Huizenga also wants to carry over to football. He's suggested fitting the skyboxes with computerized call boards where fans can rerun a play or "play referee" in making a call. In an age of interactivity, the point is that fans no longer want a passive experience but want to participate in the game.

Within baseball, Huizenga's emphasis on the marketing and business of the game, and eschewing of tradition can rub purists the wrong way. Joe Robbie Stadium is a sea of advertising, from the directional signs to seating which act as billboards for cigarettes, scotch and beer throughout the facility, to the scoreboards with ads for Chevron, NationsBank, Ryder trucks, and Budweiser. Local sports writers lampoon the marketing emphasis—some say excess—especially over the loudspeakers where sponsors pay for mention from everything from pregame contests to the starting line-ups and calls to the bullpen.

He's also in favor of some fundamental changes in the game. Carl Barger used to joke that if it was up to Huizenga, there'd be three balls for a walk and two strikes for an out. While he may not go that far, Huizenga favored the new expanded playoff system and rule changes designed to speed-up play adopted during the 1995 season. He also supports interleague play, which would give fans a chance to see star players from both leagues, an idea that Giles has been pushing for five years. Even a traditionalist, baseball man like Giles, who's grown up with the game, sees merit in Huizenga's approach and some of his ideas. "I feel we have to appeal not to traditionalists and purists, we have to appeal to the fringe fan, the fan that follows the sport but doesn't come to ballpark 30 times a year," Giles says. "The way to do that is with promotion and marketing and making the event at the game so it's an outing so young people can say they had a good time and not be completely dependent on the outcome of the game. It's a fine line but I think you can keep both the traditionalists happy and create an atmosphere where the fringe fan enjoys the sport."

While Huizenga has been an agent for change in many of his business ventures—from garbage hauling to renting videos—that impact within sports is much more complex and difficult to effect. "I see him having strong opinions on certain issues," Giles says, "but he's found out now that it's a lot harder to make changes on baseball because you have 28 different opinions on things and harder to do in baseball than anything I know of." Indeed, as Huizenga was quickly discovering, sports is a very different sort of business.

FAN AND OWNER

Bringing two sports teams to south Florida vaulted Huizenga from a virtual unknown outside business and society circles in south Florida to a one-name phenomenon and local hero—"Wayne." Edwin Pope, columnist for *The Miami Herald,* gently parodied his last name as "High-zinger." The celebrity status never ceased to amaze Wayne Huizenga and Marti. Huizenga obligingly signs autographs for fans, sometimes for an hour or more. While he enjoys the attention, the notoriety has had its downside. Dinners at local restaurants became nearly impossible. "If we both had our druthers, we'd have a much more private, quiet life," she says. "Carl Barger really was the one that told Wayne, before the sports affiliation, that he had no idea what sports would do to his life. But nothing really prepared either of us, and particularly Wayne, in a million years, ever permitted him to think that he would be so popular, that people would just want to reach out and touch or talk or get his look or an autograph."

On most game nights when he is in town, Huizenga can be found in the stands at Joe Robbie Stadium taking in a Marlins game, or down at the Miami Arena watching the Panthers, or in his box on game day for the Dolphins. He attends out of town games as travel and time permits. His enthusiasm and ability to not take himself too seriously was evidenced by providing his own on-field entertainment, doing the hokey-pokey dance with the team's Billy the Marlin mascot in front of thousands of cheering fans.

But hero worship soon gave way to criticism about Huizenga's business bent about sports and not being a fan of baseball and hockey. What had been positive press took on a sour and at times sharply negative tone. Huizenga says he'd only been to three hockey games before owning the Panthers and since there wasn't a hometown baseball team in south

Florida before the Marlins, he didn't follow that sport much either. (Besides, he was busy building two billion-dollar businesses. And, it might be pointed out, he never owned a VCR or had rented a video before buying into Blockbuster, either.) "I would never try to pretend that I was a hockey fan. I certainly wasn't. And I wasn't a big baseball fan either. But I like baseball a lot more than I ever thought I would and I like hockey more than I thought I would. So I'm happy that I'm excited about the teams. Fact of the matter is that I didn't know much about them before they came here. Can't hide that fact and I've never tried to hide that. I've been right up front. Now a lot of people don't like that. A lot of radio talk shows say, 'well, he doesn't know much about the game.' What am I going to do? Try and pretend that I'm something that I'm not? I don't do that. This is the way it is. Take me the way I am."

Because of the fervor that sports teams evoke in their fans, some team owners prefer not to live in the communities in which they own teams. Norman Braman, a Miami Beach resident and former owner of the Philadelphia Eagles football team, was one such owner. "Sports is too emotional with too many people and it invades whatever privacy one has," he says. "The sports business is a very difficult business from an emotional standpoint and Wayne is finding that out. The honeymoon ends quickly and who the hell needs the aggravation wherever one goes. I don't want to turn on the television and hear and read about my franchise. I don't know how thick-skinned I would have been if I had lived in Philadelphia."

In the sports business, as Huizenga discovered, the goal in his personal game—making money—is considered by many fans to be a negative. Television contracts and escalating player salaries in all professional sports have fundamentally altered the economics of the games, and particularly in baseball, fan ire has been increasingly focused on the players. But owners who emphasize sports as a business evoke suspicion: if an owner is focused on earning a profit, many fans figure that means that ticket prices are too high or the team is skimping on paying for top players. Huizenga's repeated emphasis on treating sports as a business only fueled the criticism.

But his own competitiveness—and understanding of the dynamic within sports—acknowledges the difficult balance he wants to achieve. Again, it comes down to business. "If you're not competitive on the field you're not going to have anybody in the stands. So business dictates that you have to have a competitive team on the field in order to get people in the stands. So you really don't have a choice," Huizenga says. "It's not running a regular business. You have outside forces tugging at you all the time. That's different than running any other kind of business. Making money and having a loser on the field, that's not being a winner. But winning the championship and losing money that's not being a winner either. I think the smart person or the smart owner has to figure out how can I make money and still win the championship? You've got to."

For Huizenga, that means making the most out of the business end of the game on the marketing front, while keeping a rein on player salaries and—especially in the new teams in baseball and hockey—emphasizing development of young players rather than opening the checkbook to expensive free agents. As an owner, Huizenga gleefully shares triumphs of his teams and shows his disappointments, but he doesn't second guess his managers or his coaches, donning a uniform (Ted Turner) or berating them in public (George Steinbrenner.) During one Marlins game, when the team was losing, he asked general manager Dave Dombrowski about getting a new pitcher. He was reminded about the budget and about the trap of team owners who bet and break their budgets in pursuit of players. "Wayne is as competitive as anybody and when you're in my job, you know what the general marching orders are and you're careful not to act on people's impulses, not even Wayne's," says Dombrowski. "One time," says Huizenga ruefully about his lapse, "and I've not lived it down since."

There's a "sports side" and a "business side" to the teams, and Huizenga gives the "sports side" wide latitude on running their end of the operation. The marching orders are that each of the teams operates as a separate, independent business. He's kept informed but purposely stays out of decisions about players. "Dave's job is to go get the talent," he says. "I can't help him with that. But Smiley is responsible for the marketing side, for the season ticket side, the stadium side, the experience the fan has when he goes to the games. That's what I spend my time on. I can't help Dombrowski with a kid coming out of high school as to whether he's going to be a good first baseman or not. I can't judge that so why even get in the middle. Let Dombrowski do that."

He's kept his word. When the Marlins were weighing in December 1994 whether to re-sign shortstop Walt Weiss, who had joined the Marlins in the expansion draft and was a solid, dependable player, Dombrowski offered a three-year, $6 million contract. But Weiss and his agent held out for more, and the Marlins ended up making a deal for shortstop prospect Kurt Abbott instead. Just before the announcement was to be made, Weiss' agent called Huizenga to try and strike a deal. Huizenga called Dombrowski to ask what he should do. Dombrowski told him that the decision had been made to go with Abbott and advised him not to get involved. Huizenga told the agent to call Dombrowski. "If he does have personal feelings about players he has never said to me one way or another, trade a guy or not, he always says, 'do what you think is right,'" Dombrowski says.

The Marlins budget is run on a cash basis: If a ball player's contract calls for a signing bonus, that bonus is expensed against that first year, not spread over the length of the contract. That's a deterrent to paying huge signing bonuses, but it can be done, as the signing of outfielder Gary Sheffield illustrated. "He understands more than anybody what a good deal is," Dombrowski says. "If I was at my budget number, he has always made it clear to me that 'if the right person is available at the right price where we can make a good deal, you let me know. I don't want that bottom line number to stand in the way.' But that doesn't happen that often in baseball." Signing Sheffield was one example where the Marlins didn't have any extra money in the budget, but he told Huizenga that this was a chance to get one of best players in game, who was young and would be around for three years. Even though it meant big dollars, Huizenga gave the go ahead. "I would feel comfortable doing that again," Dombrowski says. "But what's tough with the Florida Marlins is that you're balancing the ability to get better now over the long run. There's not one player that's going to make us world champions. We're still building." Trading two young, promising players for one star, contends Dombrowski, could hurt in the long-run.

As with his other businesses, Huizenga supports his top managers, lets them do their jobs, but keeps abreast of the organizations and expects results. That management style is evident with the Miami Dolphins. When he became sole owner of the Dolphins, there was some apprehension, particularly given the animosity between the Robbies and Huizenga, on what would happen to the staff. As Dolphins president Eddie Jones remembers, Huizenga promised to keep the management in place and not make wholesale changes. On the business side, there are more regular financial review meetings, more input on goal-setting and emphasis on results. "On the business side, Wayne is always aware. He always sends us little notes and faxes and suggestions and he's always ready to come when we ask him to come sit in on a meeting, whether it has to do with a salary cap or marketing." He sends suggestions gleaned from reading about how other teams run their organizations. One idea came from a clip about the San Francisco 49ers, who won the 1995 Super Bowl, noting how the organization takes care of details for employees, observing births, birthdays, and anniversaries that make players and their families feel part of the team. The Dolphins had done some of that "personal touch" with their players, but now, for example, send out silver cups with inlaid dolphins to celebrate the births of players' children.

Huizenga's emphasis on performance racheted up the pressure on the Dolphins and on Don Shula. A growing favorite sideline sport of a faction of south Florida football fans was debating the future of Shula. Despite winning more games than any coach in NFL history (surpassing George Halas in 1993), many frustrated fans derided the Dolphins under Shula as an also-ran that couldn't quite muster the performance to make it to the

Super Bowl. With Shula's contract up for extension, speculation mounted that Jimmy Johnson, twice the winning coach of Super Bowl champs Dallas Cowboys, and hometown hero as coach of the NCAA champion University of Miami Hurricanes, might come out of his self-proclaimed retirement in the Florida Keys to replace Shula. It's been no secret throughout the NFL that the prospect of coaching the Dolphins has appealed to Johnson. Other NFL teams have been unsuccessful in luring the coveted coach away from his analyst duties at Fox.

But Huizenga backed Shula. "He's given us his complete support and he's there whenever he can be," Shula says. "That's very meaningful to our football team, knowing there is an owner that cares and that is emotionally involved as well as financially involved." Indeed, as is Huizenga's way with some of his top managers, he and Shula developed a personal relationship as well, often going out to dinner together. Whereas his relationship with Joe Robbie was much more owner-coach, "Wayne is much more interested in how you're doing and what's going on, much more personable."

That personal interest is extended in other ways as well. When stadium manager Richard Anderson in July 1993 recognized he had a problem with alcohol and decided he needed treatment, he was worried because it meant a month away in a treatment center in the middle of baseball season and he wasn't sure how Huizenga would react. He called Huizenga's secretary, made an appointment, and in one of the most difficult discussions he'd ever had with his boss, told him he had a problem and needed help. Huizenga told him to do what was necessary to take care of himself. Anderson entered a treatment center which looked a bit like a boot camp: sparsely furnished, two beds to a room, one pay phone in the common lobby area. One afternoon, one of his fellow patients told him he had a phone call. Anderson was puzzled, since his whereabouts where known to only a very small circle of people. "Richard, how are you doing? It's Wayne." Huizenga was calling from the airport in Holland, where he was traveling to attend a Huizenga family reunion. Anderson wondered how he'd gotten the number, but marveled more that he'd taken the time to call. Huizenga called a few more times, between meetings and once from a limousine in Los Angeles, asking if Anderson needed anything. "My own parents couldn't have meant more to me in terms of support," Anderson says.

At the end of the 28-day treatment, the clients with jobs are expected to call their supervisors for an "exit interview" to explain the program, the recovery process, and how the employer can help. Since Barger's death, it was Huizenga to whom Anderson reported, so he called and explained the request, adding that he didn't expect Huizenga to attend given his busy schedule, but that he had wanted to be able to say that he had at least asked. Not only did Huizenga come, but instead of the normal half-hour session, he spent more than an hour with Anderson and his counselor at an 8 A.M. meeting. As they walked to their respective cars, Huizenga turned to Anderson and told him there was a press conference in Miramar that afternoon where plans were going to be announced for Blockbuster Park and invited Anderson to participate. That Huizenga had made time for the counseling session on such a busy day impressed Anderson even more, since, as his later observations as a volunteer with working with the program bore out, fewer than ten percent of the executives in a role like Huizenga's who are invited to participate in such sessions with employees do so. "Here's a guy who knew very little about alcoholism and yet if he was like 99 percent of the CEOs in the world, he would have discarded me and I would have picked up the pieces and I would have been fine, but that says a lot about him," Anderson says. A year later almost to the day, Huizenga named him president of Joe Robbie Stadium. Anderson says Huizenga has never brought up the subject. "It taught me a lot about caring," he says. "He never said a word to anyone about it."

Labor and Losses

The nine months between August 1994 and April 1995 marked a period of Huizenga's tenure as a pro-sports team owner that he'd just as soon forget. Baseball's long-simmering labor dispute burst into open warfare as the players union rejected owners' demands for a salary cap. Among the owners, Huizenga stood as a "hard-liner"—one of the owners bucking for a halt to the ratcheting up of player salaries by imposing a limit on what teams could spend.

Overall, he believes, the players union has the deck stacked in its favor. "The unions have been smart, they have focused on every little sentence, every little word that they had to get changed," he says. "The owners are smarter than union when it comes to building highrise buildings and all that kind of stuff. But when it comes to the union contract, those union guys, that was their business and they just took us to the cleaners big time and we deserved it. We let them do it. But now, it's to a situation where you just can't go on."

The bitter strike that began August 12 wore on as talks between the two sides continued, then sputtered a month later. Owners insisted on a salary cap, which would limit players' aggregate pay to half of industry revenue. The players countered with a proposal for a "luxury tax" which would redistribute income from the richest teams from a levy against their total payrolls and revenues to the poorest teams. But owners objected because the players' plan didn't provide for a cap on salaries and held firm. On

September 14, the World Series was cancelled for the first time in 90 years, and would irreparably damage the national pastime.

But labor woes for Huizenga weren't confined to baseball. Unable to reach an agreement with players, the National Hockey League delayed the start of the season in October, then resorted to a lockout. Insisting on a salary cap, Huizenga took a tough line, willing to sacrifice the season if necessary to change the economics, and voted against the agreement that was finally hammered out January 11. Indeed, Panthers' president Bill Torrey, Huizenga's point man on the negotiations, was one of the most ardent supporters for a reopener clause within three years. "It's very simple—we're for a salary cap," Torrey says. "We think the only way we are going to overcome this problem is that there has to be some sort of capping on salaries so rich teams cannot outspend poorer teams and if it meant giving up a season, we were prepared to do it because it makes more sense business wise."

But Huizenga's season of dashed dreams wasn't over yet. After a strong start, the Miami Dolphins wavered with an inconsistent performance in the second half of the season. A win on Christmas Day against the Detroit Lions with a sold-out crowd and a national television audience on ESPN delivered a welcomed present to Huizenga. A playoff victory against Kansas City the following week fanned the hopes of a Super Bowl appearance. With the Big Game scheduled to play in Miami, an appearance and victory by the Miami Dolphins in the first year of Huizenga's sole ownership would have been especially sweet.

The January 8 playoff game against the San Diego Chargers started well and by half-time, the Dolphins led 21 to 6, after three touchdown passes by quarterback Dan Marino. But the Dolphins defense crumbled in the second half and a last desperate drive by Marino and a 58 yard field-goal attempt by Pete Stoyanovich failed to save the team from a shattering 22–21 loss. "I would have liked very much in our first year together of being able to get this team to the Super Bowl and win it," Shula says. "I think that would have been a great way to break Wayne into the National Football League. But unfortunately it didn't work out."

After the game, Huizenga went down to the locker room and expressed his condolences privately to many of the players. "He was very disappointed as we were, I was, and our football team was. It was a tough game to lose because we'd played so well in the first part of the game and then to see it come apart, missing a field goal by that much at the end of the ball game and all of a sudden, the season's over. Those are what you call crushing losses," Shula says.

In the wake of the defeat by San Diego, the clamour of the "dump Shula" crowd grew louder. Though Huizenga reiterated his support of Shula, the episode still makes the coach's jaw harden. "I don't think I need any defense," he bristles when the subject of Huizenga's endorsement is brought up. "He's always been supportive and he knew the magnitude of the loss and how deeply it hurt. He suffered with us."

The week of Super Bowl festivities in Miami only underscored the loss for an owner and a region that not only wanted to host the event, but to star in it. Huizenga made sure the stadium was spruced up for the attention, with more than $4 million spent on lush landscaping and palm trees. Though a private stadium, Huizenga donated it to the Host Committee for the Super Bowl, as are municipality-owned facilities around the country. Huizenga and the stadium earned nothing out of the event and he even had to pay for his own tickets and those of his family and friends—with the exception of a few free parking passes as the host. In the two boxes he personally hosted for Super Bowl, General Norman Schwarzkopf was among Huizenga's guests, who for this event were mostly family and close friends. When the San Francisco 49ers took on the San Diego Chargers on January 29 in a blowout game of 49 to 26, Huizenga himself couldn't help but wonder what all Miami Dolphins fans were thinking. "I kept wondering why we weren't in it," he says. To Shula, Jones, and the rest of the Dolphins, though, the focus was already on next year.

The start of spring-training approached without an end to the baseball strike in sight. In December, baseball's owners had declared an "impasse" with the union and imposed a salary cap, sparking a challenge by the union which complained to the National Labor Relations Board. Pressure by the NLRB prompted the owners to drop the cap by early February, but not even a deadline set by President Bill Clinton—of Babe Ruth's birthday February 6—could force the two sides to an agreement. The teams, with the exception of the Baltimore Orioles, began drafting "replacement" players for spring training and the baseball fans who were left braced themselves for baseball farce. But as the replacement Marlins and replacement Mets geared up for the season opener on April 2, the owners—facing an injunction—scratched replacement ball and accepted the players offer to return to work while contract negotiations continued. Replacement players for most teams were summarily dismissed, lucky to get a token check and a curt thank you. Huizenga opted to pay each of the 32 replacement Marlins players a $25,000 bonus, which technically wasn't due unless the season had actually started. "It was just a case of doing the right thing," Smiley said. "These players had their lives disrupted, leaving families, leaving jobs to endure scrutiny, name-calling and bashing. Wayne wanted to do something for them."

The regular Marlins faced the Dodgers for the opener of a shortened season on April 25. (The memento for fans was a promotional checkbook cover, an unwelcome reminder of what the game is really all about.) The Marlins lost, and the scarred baseball landscape looked much different from the bright beginning in 1993 when the Marlins triumphed over the Dodgers for their inaugural game. The Marlins had one of the worst starts in league history in 1995, and that poor showing, combined with strike-weary and resentful fans filled only a fraction of seats at the stadium. Empty seats plagued teams throughout baseball, adding to the $700 million estimated losses by the owners.

For Huizenga, the strike in baseball and lockout in hockey hurt dearly in the way he keeps score. Including interest costs, a projected $2.5 million profit for the Marlins in 1994 turned into a $10 million loss. With attendance off 10,000 fans per game, the Marlins were projected to rack up $12 million in losses in 1995. Though hockey would attract a strong showing, filling upwards of 90 percent of the seats at the Miami Arena, the small capacity, unfavorable lease, and lockout would combine to give the Panthers a $12 million loss in the 1994–95 season, on top of a $6 million loss in 1993–94.

In the third season of Huizenga's commitment to sports as business, the score was two strikes and a missed Super Bowl, and more than $38 million in losses for the Marlins and Panthers combined. With Barger's death, he'd lost both his best friend and key strategist. The merger of Blockbuster Entertainment with Viacom and the sale of Blockbuster Park had dealt a major blow to his plan. In the business of sports, Wayne Huizenga was short of his goal and in search of a new playbook.

11

Viacom:
The Deal from Hell

Bottles of Dom Perignon popped open and champagne flowed freely among the ten Blockbuster executives aboard the Gulfstream II jet as it rose through snow-choked New York City skies on its way back to balmy Fort Lauderdale. Emblazoned on its nose and tail were the symbols of some of the major pieces of H. Wayne Huizenga's empire—the fighting fish emblem of the Florida Marlins baseball team, and the snarling mascot of the Florida Panthers hockey team. Not far behind in the darkened skies raced the other plane in Huizenga's entourage, the eight-seat Hawker 700. Aboard both aircraft, exhausted Blockbuster executives, lawyers, and advisors, some of whom had worked non-stop for 72 hours straight, raised their glasses and toasted each other, then the man for whom they had toiled. Seated in one of the thickly padded soft-gray leather seats, Huizenga grinned and raised his glass in return.

And why not? A celebration seemed in order that night of January 7, 1994. They had just finished laying the groundwork for what was the biggest deal in Huizenga's storied career of deal-making. The "trash man"—the sneer one Hollywood executive had once conferred on Huizenga—relished his role in the takeover drama of the 1990s. In just seven years, he and his team had taken a $7 million chain of video stores and parlayed it into an $8.4 billion deal, or as much as $10 billion by Huizenga's estimation. Just hours earlier, he and Sumner Redstone, chairman of Viacom Inc., had inked an agreement that would merge Blockbuster Entertainment Corp. into Redstone's expanding empire and provide the ammunition needed to win the months-long battle for Paramount Communications Inc. against erstwhile friend Barry Diller, chairman of home shopping company, QVC Inc.

The combination made sense: Viacom could draw on Blockbuster's rich cash flow to pay down the debt it would take on to snag Paramount, valued not only because of its status as Hollywood's last remaining major independent studio but also for its Simon & Schuster publishing house, theme parks, and other divisions. And in one grand move, Huizenga would complete the transformation of the video rental giant into a full-scale entertainment company.

But there was a price. Even amid the celebratory toasts, Huizenga felt wistful. The tables had been turned. The Great Acquirer had become the acquired. He would no longer be chairman of an independent public company, becoming instead the vice-chairman of the combined companies. Since he had no desire to work for Redstone, or anyone, his role in shaping Blockbuster would largely be over. As financial advisors and lawyers had haggled over the last minutia of the deal and wording of a public statement, Huizenga had called his wife, Marti, and told her of the plans. "Wayne, are you sure?" she asked.

He hesitated. Blockbuster had brought him greater respectability, renown, and recognition in business circles than he'd ever garnered in his years as vice-chairman of Waste Management. Blockbuster had made him a force in Hollywood and had financed his new persona as a sports mogul. Through Blockbuster, "Wayne" as he introduced himself and was affectionately called by parking lot attendants to grateful south Florida sports fans, had become a folk hero in his hometown of Fort Lauderdale, and a national emblem of the modern entrepreneur. "It's the right thing to do," he answered.

As the sleek jet taxied to a stop in front of the Fort Lauderdale Jet Center at 10:20 P.M. to a waiting crowd of reporters, Huizenga repeated to himself that simple phrase. He and Steve Berrard had a lot of explaining to do, to the press, to shareholders, to Wall Street. In the firestorm of controversy and days of doubt that would soon follow, it was Berrard who would hold fast to those words. Little more than eight months later, a reluctant Huizenga would repeat them to Blockbuster directors as the deal hung in the balance. It was the right thing to do. As events would play out, it was the only thing to do.

*   *   *

In March 1987, as Wayne Huizenga was learning about video stores and his new investment in Blockbuster, Sumner Redstone was declaring victory in his battle over Viacom International Inc., a cable company which also boasted programs such as Music Television (MTV) and children's shows under the name Nickelodeon. At age 63, a point in life when many look forward to retirement, Redstone was launching his next career as chairman and architect of what would become one of the largest entertainment companies in the world. So began a chain of events in which the paths of two very different sorts of entrepreneurs, a Harvard-educated lawyer and a college-dropout, street-wise dealmaker, both of whom had become chiefs of billion-dollar companies, would cross.

Born in 1923, Redstone grew up in Dedham, Massachusetts. His father sold linoleum and eventually worked his way into owning nightclubs and opened one of the first drive-in theaters in the country. The younger Redstone entered Harvard University at age 17 and finished in just two and a half years. Fluent in Japanese, he joined an elite code-cracking team in the War Department's Military Intelligence Division during World War II. After the war, he earned a degree from Harvard Law School in 1947 and served as a clerk on the United States Court of Appeals before joining the Justice Department as a special assistant to the Attorney General during the Truman Administration. In 1951 at age 31, he became a partner in a Washington law firm and left three years later to join his father and younger brother, Edward, in the family's chain of 12 drive-ins. It was Redstone who quickly took the lead. Tough and autocratic, Redstone will negotiate ferociously over a $5 bet and in his theaters knows where every dollar is spent.

Redstone's experience as a lawyer proved handy. Like other small chains, National Amusements Inc., then known as Redstone Management, was fighting Hollywood to get access to first-run films. Redstone sued and won. Under his relentless drive, National Amusements expanded and became a pioneer in multiplex cinemas, the multiple-screen theaters that quickly metamorphosed into a mainstay of the movie-going public. Over the years, National Amusements became the preeminent privately-owned theater chain, with more than 900 theaters by 1995. On the walls of his office in Viacom's tower at 1515 Broadway in the heart of Times Square hang photos of Redstone with silver screen stars like Jimmy Stewart, Judy Garland, Gregory Peck, and others as momentos of the early years of that quest.

He also bears proof of another, much more personal and painful journey. The three gnarled, nail-less fingers on his right hand are the only visible scars of an oft-recounted, life-changing event that occurred in 1979 that tells of the man's singular tenacity. As fire swept through part of Boston's Copley Plaza Hotel, Redstone climbed out of the window of his third-story room. He clung to a window ledge as flames seared his body. After an agonizing ten minutes, he was rescued but the prognosis was grim. He endured 60 hours of excruciating skin graft operations. "I think I was always driven before, but out of that fire came most of the exciting things I have ever done," he said years later.

Using National Amusements' cash, Redstone had already begun investing in the industry he knew best and loved most—movie studios. He snapped up shares of Twentieth Century Fox in 1977 because he liked "Star Wars" so much. He cleared at least $20 million on his shares of Fox, in which he had a 5 percent stake, when Marvin Davis bid for the company in 1981. Handsome profits in the double-digit millions followed on his 10 percent stake in Columbia Pictures (bought out by Coca-Cola in 1982) and 8 percent of MGM/UA, sold when Kirk Kekorian bought out MGM's home entertainment division in 1985.

Initially, Redstone viewed Viacom International Inc. as simply another stock play, this time in the growing cable television and media programming business. Cable television was supplanting movie theaters as the entertainment engine of the future. Viacom was born in 1971 out of a forced government divestiture by CBS of its syndicated programming holdings. It expanded into cable systems and pay-television programming with Showtime and bought MTV Networks, which married two primary forms of entertainment, music and video, and became a cultural icon for the under-30 set across the globe and Nickelodeon, for the age ten and under group. Redstone started buying Viacom shares in 1985.

Worried that the company was a ripe takeover target. Viacom's management tried to take the company private with a $2.7 billion bid in September 1986. Suspicious of management's intentions, Redstone, who owned more than 10 percent of Viacom, consulted initially with Merrill Lynch and met, along with others, James Mason, an investment banker and mergers and acquisition specialist at Merrill with a background in the entertainment industry.

Following that briefing, Redstone was primed for battle. He formed Arsenal Holdings Inc. and learned all he could about Viacom's operations. On his side, Redstone also engaged Herbert Allen, the legendary key investment banker on many of the mega-entertainment deals of the decade. In early February 1987, Redstone, through Arsenal, countered the management proposal with an offer which, including debt, was valued at $3.1 billion. The fight escalated with management being forced to raise its bid five times, while Redstone parried and thrust three times, finally declaring victory on March 4, 1987 when Viacom's board of directors accepted his $3.4 billion offer. Then, Redstone relished the fight, telling Mason, "You know, James, this deal has given me ten years on my life." To which Mason would reply, "Sumner, I know where you got them from. You got them from me."

Canvassing his contacts in the entertainment industry, Redstone looked for an experienced chief executive to head up the company. Though he had won, the price was dear, with nearly $2.8 billion of debt and $500 million of his own equity at risk. Strong management was crucial. Repeatedly, the name of Frank Biondi Jr. came up. Born into a strict, Catholic family, Biondi grew up in New Jersey and over the years, retained a guy-next-door look with an easy smile and laugh lines etched into the skin surrounding his quick brown eyes. A strong, tough-minded executive, he prefers negotiation to confrontation. His thoughtful, calm manner would provide needed balance to Redstone's irascible temperament and overbearing overtones.

Then 43, Biondi had just months earlier been promoted to chairman and CEO of Coca-Cola Television. He'd been hired in January 1985, as executive vice president of Coca-Cola's Entertainment Business Sector by Fay Vincent, who then was running the division, which included Columbia Pictures and Columbia Television. After earning his M.B.A. from Harvard Business School in 1968, Biondi had spent nearly all of his career in various roles in the entertainment industry.

Though his recent promotion at Coca-Cola was a career milestone, the prospect of running Viacom intrigued Biondi. He met with Redstone over a three-hour breakfast on a Saturday morning in July 1987. Once he'd gotten assurances that Redstone would let him do the job without undue interference, he was on board. Indeed, Biondi's collegial management style and insistence on open communication was a welcomed boost to managers in Viacom's various divisions.

Meanwhile, Viacom's results and balance sheet continued to improve with pay-dirt deals such as the sale of syndication rights to The Cosby Show for a record $515 million in 1988. Redstone continued his combative use of courtrooms to preserve what he viewed as his rights. Against the counsel of others, including Biondi, he instigated the filing of a $2.4 billion suit against Time Warner, charging that the company had conspired to keep Viacom's Showtime and other cable programs off its cable systems. After three years of battle, Time Warner settled. Redstone acknowledges he has a reputation for litigiousness but contends it is unfairly conferred. "I hate litigation," he says. "Our point of view on litigation is very clear and simple. There will never be litigation in which we're the plaintiff unless we're right and unless it's critically important to the company."

Huizenga Targets Viacom—In 1991

In the late summer of 1991, a visitor arrived at Biondi's 28th floor office of Viacom's corporate headquarters. It was Wayne Huizenga, chairman of Blockbuster Entertainment Corp. Huizenga had just snared one of the two baseball expansion franchises. During conversations with baseball commissioner Fay Vincent about the cable industry and the impact of pay-per-view, he'd recommended that Huizenga call Biondi, who had worked for

Vincent at Coca-Cola Entertainment Co. Huizenga had followed up on the suggestion and queried Biondi about his perspective of the industry. Over a three-hour conversation, Biondi told him didn't think pay-per-view was much of a threat to video rental, at least not for the foreseeable future.

The visit to Viacom was part of Huizenga's continual fact-finding missions. As Blockbuster spread its reach further into the entertainment industry, Huizenga made the rounds, meeting with Time Warner Chairman Gerry Levin, Disney Chairman Michael Eisner, and others, building relationships, letting them know about Blockbuster's business and that it had plenty of cash to invest in strategic joint projects. He was sowing seeds for the right deal—maybe a merger sometime down the road—at the right price.

Nearly two years after his visit with Biondi, while considering further diversification into the entertainment industry, Viacom would cross Huizenga's radar once again. In a meeting in Blockbuster's offices in June 1993 with Merrill Lynch advisor James Mason to discuss the merger of Republic and Spelling (or "Duke and Donna" as they were referred to in code, "Duke" for John Wayne movies owned by Republic, "Donna" for a main character on Beverly Hills 90210) three companies were mentioned as potential partners in some form or another: Viacom, Paramount, and Polygram Inc., the music company subsidiary of Philips Electronics. As part of his industry forays, Huizenga met with Paramount Chairman Marty Davis for breakfast, and he and Berrard contacted executives at Philips about making a joint run at the Hollywood studio, perhaps even folding in Polygram as a three-way merger.

The timing was off. Philips was in the process of a strategic re-orientation and didn't want to take on that challenge. Without a partner with some cash to back the deal, it wasn't going to fly with Huizenga, who remained wary of Hollywood. Paramount was too expensive a target at that point. There was too much risk of ending up in a deal loaded with debt or too dilutive to shareholders. Moreover, the hit driven aspect of the movie-making business seemed at the same time, too chancy and too limiting. "I don't want to be negative on the studio industry, but to me, I like to build things—a hundred stores, a thousand stores," he says. With a movie studio, "the chances of having three hits next year when we had two last year, pretty skinny chance of that happening. You have two good movies next year, you lose two million and the next year you make five and at the end of ten years you're still making 20 movies a year like you always have. So where's the growth?"

With Redstone's National Amusements Co. owning 75 percent of Viacom's stock, the chances of Blockbuster acquiring that target were zilch. But that didn't preclude possibilities for joint projects. Through one of his charitable involvements, Huizenga had gotten to know Jack Schneider, who chaired a fund-raiser featuring great sports legends to raise money for the

Buoniconti Fund, founded by football legend Nick Buoniconti and his son, Mark, who is a paraplegic, to raise money for the Miami Project to Cure Paralysis.

It was through Schneider, initially, that the relationship with Viacom was fostered. Huizenga had mentioned to Schneider that a merger between Blockbuster and Viacom would be an intriguing combination. Schneider is a 20-year veteran and a managing director of Allen & Co. Inc., the match-maker-extraordinaire, advisor, and investment banking firm, to Hollywood and the entertainment industry. The firm was founded by Herbert A. Allen Jr. in 1964 as an offshoot of the legendary Wall Street partnership of his father, Herbert Sr. and uncle, Charles. Allen himself is regarded as a con-trarian who doesn't hobnob with the rest of the investment banking com-munity. Indeed, the firm's offices aren't in New York's financial district. Instead, Allen & Co. occupies a hushed floor in the ornate Coca-Cola building on Fifth Avenue in midtown Manhattan. It's a boutique shop with just eleven managing directors, 150 employees and exudes an air of exclu-sivity and secrecy that in itself adds to its allure. On the walls, like a fam-ily gallery, are photographs of deal-makers as well as employees, many of them taken at its ultra-exclusive conferences sponsored every summer at Sun Valley, Idaho. M&A, or mergers and acquisitions work, is only a small slice of the pie for the firm, which garners far more from trading and in-vestments, holding stakes in more than 100 companies, many of them small startups in biotechnology, energy and high-technology.

But it is Herb Allen Jr.'s role in the mega-mergers of the high-profile en-tertainment industry that has thrust him into the media spotlight. One of his first notables was the sale of Columbia Pictures to Coca-Cola in 1982, which netted the firm $40 million and a personal coup for Allen who, against the advice of his father and uncle, had bought a sizable stake nearly a decade earlier. Since then, the firm has been at the nexus of mega-deals between Matsushita's $7.4 billion acquisition of MCA, and the sale of Columbia Pictures to Sony for $4.8 billion among others.

Joining Huizenga, Steve Berrard, and Jack Schneider for breakfast on Tuesday June 29, 1993 in the Allen & Co. dining room were Frank Biondi and Tom Dooley, executive vice president at Viacom. The two-hour session was intended as a get-acquainted session by Schneider, who would be suc-cessful in making a match but lose out as the matchmaker where it counted—in getting the fees.

Two weeks later, Schneider would initiate another meeting at the an-nual Allen Conference at Sun Valley. The conference is renowned for bringing together a very select group of 150 titans of entertainment, in-dustry, and institutional investors for five days of power-fun activities like golf, tennis, skeet-shooting, and white-water rafting down the Salmon

River. It's a family affair, with Allen as the host, complete with babysitters for the children. Attendees include the power set overseeing huge corporate kingdoms: TCI chief executive John Malone, Time Warner chairman Gerry Levin, and Disney chairman Michael Eisner among others. An invitation confers an imprimatur of ultimate success in the numbers end of the entertainment industry.

Centered around the spectacular mountain resort of Sun Valley Lodge and outlying condos, it's a well-organized affair, with the fun carefully orchestrated so that the few dozen institutional investors, for instance, are paired with golf foursomes including CEOs. But there's plenty of time for conversations that become the preludes to major deals. Wedged in-between the fun and courtship are presentations by chosen participants. This year, Huizenga's third Sun Valley conference, he and Steve Berrard were scheduled to give a spiel on Blockbuster. Primed from the shareholders meeting, the investments in Republic and Spelling undertaken, they were ready, and there was no better audience to impress with Blockbuster's metamorphosis.

The duo from Fort Lauderdale wowed the crowd. The presentation was so good that the uninitiated became converts and the believers were smug at their foresightedness to be owners of Blockbuster shares. "If you make a good presentation there, things happen," says Larry Haverty, a senior vice-president of State Street Research, a $7 billion pension fund, who had started out a Blockbuster skeptic before his own conversion in 1992. "They made a great presentation. You're captive there for three or four days so everybody talks to each other and at the conference, there's always one or two things where everybody decides they're going to buy the stock and that year (Blockbuster) was one everyone was going to buy. It attracted an entirely different class of investors, long-term investors with a lot of staying power and the stock exploded out of the gate from that meeting." State Street stepped up its investment and others followed. ("Having Larry Haverty on your side was a big deal at the time because he could be so vocal," Berrard says.)

At the conference, Schneider collared Frank Biondi when he arrived the first day. "You know, Wayne and Steve would really like to meet Sumner," Schneider told him. Biondi had been intrigued by the possibilities of a business combination of some sort with Blockbuster and thought, too, that the conference would be an opportune setting to introduce Redstone to the concept. "I always loved the business and I always thought it was a better deal than Paramount and a better business than Paramount," Biondi says. "It's a stronger business and it has better growth dynamics—it's more predictable."

But Redstone, caught up with his multi-year courtship of Paramount Entertainment Corp. and its chairman Martin S. Davis, hadn't been able to conceive of talking to someone else until it looked like yet again, his hopes for snagging the beloved studio had been dashed. Talks with Paramount had broken off just before the Sun Valley conference. Now seemed as good a time as any, Biondi figured, to introduce a new prospect.

Over lunch on the back porch of Herb Allen's condo, Huizenga and Berrard made Blockbuster's case to Redstone and Biondi with Jack Schneider in attendance, looking for commonalties and opportunities and ways to keep a dialogue going. "Sumner really didn't know Wayne and didn't know anything about Steve and had somewhere between an open mind and grave doubts about the video business," Biondi recalls. "But we had a nice lunch."

One clue to the dynamics that would later play out was that just before the lunch, Huizenga said to Biondi, "Sumner's not real active, he's up in Boston."

"Are you kidding me?," Biondi replied. "He lives in New York basically. He's in the office everyday."

"Oh," Huizenga said. He'd known that Redstone owned control of the company, but hadn't recognized how involved he was in the business. Soon corrected, it was one of the few miscalculations in Huizenga's career. "I've always had the feeling that Wayne thought Sumner was somewhat of a recluse, not real active in the business and maybe his role was really to come in and become the defacto chairman, and he'd run the whole thing. The guy up in Boston would be clipping his coupons and worrying about other things. At this point, he'd never met Sumner. I always had the feeling that somehow, in Wayne's mind, he visualized this guy in a rocking chair with a blanket over his lap." (Indeed, Huizenga, in referring to Redstone often uses the word "old" to describe business practices and policies, even down to Redstone's insistence on maintaining voting control of Viacom.) "I sort of had this feeling that Wayne, when he first looked at it, says 'old man shareholder, young guy running the company. Ah, I can handle that,'" says Biondi. "And it turned out to be very different. It's not the first time that people have underestimated us and probably won't be the last time."

On Tuesday July 27, Biondi, along with Tom Dooley and Neil Braun from Viacom met again with Berrard and Huizenga to talk about joint business possibilities, everything from cross marketing campaigns between MTV and music stores to links between Blockbuster and Showtime. "Project Ruby" (for Redstone) looked better and better as a match. Weeks later, in August as Blockbuster's directors gathered in Paris to look over the Virgin-Blockbuster landmark megastore and met later at the Hotel Bristol, Huizenga brought up the possibility of a deal, perhaps eventually a merger, with Viacom. The board gave its approval to continue discussions.

But any budding relationship with Blockbuster had taken a backseat to Redstone's continuing romance with Paramount. The talks that had broken off in July were resumed. By Sunday, September 12, 1993 with a merger agreement in place, Redstone had snared his long-sought prize at last. Amid much media fanfare, Redstone announced that he and Davis would team up to restore the studio's tarnished allure and build on its stable of other companies, from theme parks to publishing. "Paramount was a passion," says Biondi of Redstone's focus on the company. "That was the Yankee bat boy buying the Yankees. He wouldn't have had the same passion about Warner Brothers. He wouldn't have had the same passion about MCA or Universal. It was Paramount, not a movie company—it was Paramount. To him, Paramount was the movie company when Sumner started in business. It was the king of the hill. There was a great emotional bond in getting Paramount."

But Redstone's celebration would be short-lived. Now that the long-rumored deal had been struck, it was a clarion call to the rest of the entertainment and media industry. Paramount was in play. Viacom's bid would soon bring out friend and now foe Barry Diller, chairman of QVC with a rival bid of his own. The chain of events unleashed by Viacom's announcement would end in the dethroning, by very different means, of three empire-builders: Davis, Diller, and Huizenga. When the smoke finally cleared little more than a year later, only Redstone would still hold a top spot.

THE MAKING OF A MERGER

When Huizenga's private line rang on Monday morning September 20 on his cherry wood desk in his downtown Fort Lauderdale office, he didn't need to guess who might be calling. It had to be someone from Sumner Redstone's camp, seeking contributions to a war chest in the battle for Paramount. Just hours earlier, home shopping company, QVC Inc., and its chairman Barry Diller had announced a rival $9.5 billion bid for Paramount.

Indeed, the caller was Robert Greenhill, chairman and CEO of Smith Barney Shearson Inc. who was advising Redstone on the Paramount merger. Just months earlier, Greenhill had left the number two job at Morgan Stanley & Co. to join Smith Barney. A tough 1980s-style dealmaker, he would feel in his element in the battle that lie ahead. Greenhill got right to the point. Viacom was looking for partners in the bid for Paramount. Was Huizenga interested?

The Viacom-Paramount engagement had unleashed a storm of speculation about a host of other potential suitors over the week. Stocks trading at high levels provided cheap currency and Paramount's array of properties and debt-free balance sheet were attractive lures. Nearly every major media company and Hollywood wannabe—including telephone companies eager to get a jump on the buildout of the much-trumpeted Information Superhighway—wanted a piece of the Paramount action. Within days, rumors on Wall Street and stories in the press had pegged players from media mogul Ted Turner to home shopping kingpin Barry Diller and Blockbuster Entertainment as possible players.

Indeed, news of the Viacom-Paramount deal had caught by surprise a contingent of Blockbuster executives—Berrard, general counsel Tom Hawkins, and Tom Byrne, vice president of development, along with advisor James Mason from Merrill Lynch, who were on the West Coast putting the final touches on the Republic-Spelling merger. Paramount had seemed such a promising possibility to complete Blockbuster's transformation. Berrard and Huizenga discussed a possible deal at length. It looked so good to Berrard that he wanted to do the deal with Blockbuster stock but Huizenga vetoed that idea. They'd need a partner.

With Wall Street investment bankers smelling takeover bait and huge advisory fees, there was no shortage of possibilities. During a quick trip to New York, Berrard made the rounds of investment houses, garnering Blockbuster mentions in press reports as considering a rival bid. But Huizenga quickly pulled the leash back. "There's no way in hell, Steve, that we're going to jump in the middle of this thing without someone with a lot of cash," Huizenga told him. On Friday, Huizenga had cautioned Berrard to leave the Paramount possibility alone. It was too big and he wasn't comfortable with it. Blockbuster's stock would never weather the public relations fiasco or the heated battle if it led a bid, even with a partner. The technology monster they'd fought so hard to beat down would surface again. If they lost, Blockbuster's stock would be devastated. And if they won, Huizenga wasn't sure it was much of a prize. "I wasn't willing to put a $10 billion number on movie studios," Huizenga says.

Teaming up as a partner with a lead player was another matter entirely. Berrard had just come into Huizenga's office to suggest that they call Viacom or Barry Diller when the call from Greenhill came. Frank Biondi got on the line and also pitched the possibility of working together. Just after the initial deal had been announced, Biondi had called Huizenga to explain that Viacom had been slow to act on the discussions about joint ventures with Blockbuster because of its on-going courtship with Paramount. Now, Huizenga figured, here was a way to cement that relationship. But it wasn't going to be cheap. Viacom executives and advisors made it clear to the dozen or so companies inquiring about wanting in on the deal that they had to pay to play—a minimum $600 million. There simply wasn't time or interest in negotiating a number of small deals.

But Huizenga wasn't ready to commit just yet. At the suggestion of Herb Allen, Huizenga called Barry Diller. As with Redstone, Paramount represented much more than just a studio for Diller. Paramount was a vehicle to expand beyond the home shopping channel he headed, adding its film and television libraries and providing a chance to create new cable services or even a fifth television network. And it was a chance to settle a score with Martin Davis, who had ousted Diller from his post as head of Paramount studio in 1984. The bitterness had lingered for years after Diller had become chairman of Fox Inc. and guided it into becoming a viable fourth television network. He'd left Fox in early 1992 and by year-end had plunked down $25 million as part of a buyout of QVC, a home-shopping channel. (One of the lures was Diller friend and designer Dianne von Furstenberg who had done a brisk business selling wares through the shopping channel and ended up becoming an investor.) Diller viewed QVC as an entrée into the amalgam of shopping, entertainment, and programming shaping up as part of the "new media." He had sizable partners in the venture with Tele-Communications affiliate Liberty Media Corp., controlled by John Malone, and cable giant Comcast Corp., the giant family-controlled cable company headed up by Brian Roberts.

Before Diller had made the offer for QVC in 1992, he'd paid a visit to Viacom's corporate offices to consult with Redstone. But with Paramount as the prize, any thoughts of disloyalty by mounting a rival bid were quickly dispelled. He'd already lined up allies in his QVC partners, Liberty Media and Comcast. There was no room for Blockbuster in the deal, Diller told Huizenga in a brief conversation. That rebuff would resound months later as a misstep on Diller's part and a contributing factor to the ultimate victory by Redstone.

With Diller out of the picture, Huizenga cast his lot with Viacom. The phone lines between Fort Lauderdale and New York sizzled over the next day or so as Huizenga and Berrard, together with their advisors from Merrill Lynch, James Mason and Chuck Lewis, caucused and conference-called with Sumner Redstone, Viacom's general counsel Philippe Dauman, and Greenhill and Michael Levitt, their advisors from Smith Barney. Then Huizenga's G-II was quickly fired up for a trip to New York so talks could begin in earnest.

Over the next week, Huizenga and Berrard negotiated a deal in which Blockbuster would buy $600 million in preferred stock paying a 5 percent dividend. The shares could be converted to Viacom nonvoting common stock at $70 a share, well-above the level that Viacom's stock was then trading. "What stood out in my mind was how fast Wayne and Steve were willing to move," says Biondi. "They clearly had made up their minds that they wanted into Paramount in some way, shape, or form."

Indeed, Dauman remembers that Huizenga at one point told him: "I only want to make the investment if I'm convinced. I want to be with the winner and I want to make sure that you are really going to go through and buy Paramount and do what it takes." But he also insisted on protecting Blockbuster shareholders. In case the deal with Paramount didn't go through, the amount invested would drop to $300 million. Dauman, who hammered out the details of the agreement with Berrard, remembers the entrepreneurial, no-nonsense, quick-decision attitude was refreshing compared with the more plodding, bureaucratic process posed by the various telephone companies who wanted in on the Paramount action. "In that initial meeting, Sumner felt very good about Wayne. He felt Wayne was the same kind of guy he was in that sense." Adds Redstone: "We both have the same background. We're both entrepreneurs. I started with a handful of drive-ins and Wayne basically did the same thing. He started with a handful of video stores and built this fantastic company."

On Wednesday September 29, Blockbuster directors gathered in New York and approved the investment. The advantages for Blockbuster were enticing: potential joint ventures involving everything from Paramount's film library and Viacom's cable operations to MTV and Nickelodeon, which dove-tailed nicely with music stores and Discovery Zone centers. The deal would further Blockbuster's penetration into Hollywood. Indeed, the press that appeared the next day not only heralded Huizenga as a player in the big-stakes battle for a prime Hollywood studio, but also noted Blockbuster's expanding reach as an entertainment empire. But the investment raised concerns among bond analysts on how Blockbuster intended to finance the investment and criticism that Blockbuster had put up too much cash for no tangible result.

But even then, and characteristically, Huizenga viewed the $600 million as only a first step. Besides the vague joint ventures and other publicly stated advantages of the deal, he initially saw other opportunities. One possibility was that if Viacom successfully snagged Paramount, perhaps he could persuade Redstone to part with its five theme parks in exchange for restructuring the Blockbuster deal. That would fit nicely with Huizenga's own plans to develop Blockbuster Park and grow that piece of the entertainment business. Or maybe they could swap some television and radio properties or other assets.

He figured Redstone might be willing to make such a deal because Viacom's appetite for such a large chunk of preferred stock would seem to be limited. But just five days later, Viacom announced that the telephone giant NYNEX had agreed to invest $1.2 billion in preferred stock. Even so, Huizenga figured he and Berrard had made a good deal. This was the price of a relationship, a means to an eventual bigger end, further protection against the misplaced but persistent perception that Blockbuster's core video business was doomed.

What happened just a week later drove that point home. On October 13, cable giant Tele-Communications Inc. and regional telephone company Bell Atlantic Corp. announced plans for a $30 billion merger, the largest in U.S. history. The marriage then signaled an ambitious push to speed construction of the "Information Superhighway"—the amorphous melding of delivery systems configured from telephones, television, and computers with favorite American past-times of entertainment, sports, and shopping. Over the past year, the "information highway" had already become part of the American lexicon, with nightly news programs heralding various experiments and alliances and even Vice President Al Gore making its construction a priority in the dawning of a new technological era.

Though no one was quite sure how to build this high-tech highway, who exactly would use it or how, nearly every major media, telecommunications and technology company wanted to be on it. Alliances between Time Warner and U.S. West, with plans for a new interactive system in Orlando, Florida, were being formed, while experiments like that of GTE Corp.'s interactive cable system in Cerritos, California, were already underway. Even Viacom was participating in a test in Castro Valley, California, with AT&T. In nearly all these tests, though it wasn't clear what consumers wanted or how much they'd be willing to pay, the ability to dial up movies on demand was heralded as the backbone of the systems.

None of this was news to Wayne Huizenga and Steve Berrard. They'd been deflecting the technology threat for years. They'd repeatedly insisted that the impact on video rental was a decade or more away, citing a recent Stanford Research Institute report which concluded that "reports of video-on-demand's imminent stranglehold on video retailing have been greatly exaggerated." Meanwhile, they'd hedged their bets by emphasizing Blockbuster's move into other modes of entertainment, including the recent alliance with Viacom. To Huizenga's satisfaction, the strategy was working, at least on a financial basis: Blockbuster's stock took nary a hit during the Bell Atlantic-TCI deal, an announcement that years earlier might have sent its stock on a downward slide. Still, the announcement made the drumbeat of the new technologies a bit louder, and would become a factor, albeit a minor one, in how events played out. The mega-marriage stunned the media world and business press and momentarily put the battle for Paramount in the background.

But not for long. In late September, Viacom had sued TCI, QVC, and its affiliates invoking antitrust claims and trying to stop QVC's bidding for Paramount. On October 21, Diller fired a volley himself, announcing plans to tender for 51 percent of Paramount's shares at $80 a share and suing Paramount and some of its directors for refusing to consider QVC's earlier bid. The suit named Viacom as "aiding and abetting" the breach of fiduciary responsibility. The battle wore on, with Viacom offers being met by counter-offers by QVC, with every move recounted prominently in the business and financial media. Not since the takeover battles of the 1980s had a fight ensued that was so vicious with the stakes so high.

During this, Huizenga had taken his place as a director on Viacom's board. The bonds between the companies were forming as Viacom and Blockbuster executives met to discuss joint ventures and projects, marketing alliances between MTV and the music stores, and ways to leverage the newly accomplished merger of Spelling and Republic. In daily conversations with members of the Viacom camp, either Greenhill, Biondi, or Redstone, Huizenga encouraged Viacom to continue its quest for Paramount. Yet it wasn't his battle. He'd gotten what he wanted and now had to wait for events to play out.

But as the conversations continued, it was becoming clear that Redstone was going to need more cash. For Redstone, Paramount had become the "deal from hell" as the battle took on aspects of waging a war, with constant meetings to plot strategies and fall back positions. Meanwhile, Blockbuster was preparing for a stock offering in November to help finance its $600 million investment in Viacom. This offering at $30 a share, near the all-time peak of Blockbuster's stock price, raised $424 million but would come back to haunt Huizenga as a benchmark comparison to the deal that would ultimately be struck with Viacom.

In early December, as the bidding for Paramount continued to ratchet up with the QVC offer now at $90 and Viacom's still valued at $85, the discouraged Viacom team—Biondi, Dauman, Greenhill, and Levitt—gathered in Sumner Redstone's office late one evening to discuss the next move. They felt the business combination offered by Viacom-Paramount was so much stronger, would result in a company so much better than Paramount and "The Shopping Channel" as Redstone referred to it. But it had turned into a contest of who could pay the most in hard cash and there was a real question of how much more Viacom could offer without crippling the company. Before they went any further, Redstone insisted, they had to consult their partners.

On the evening of December 9, the Viacom group gathered in Redstone's apartment in the Carlyle Hotel, overlooking Central Park. Also there were top NYNEX executives Bill Ferguson and Fred Salerno, along with Wayne Huizenga and Steve Berrard. Quickly, Redstone outlined the reason for the meeting.

"Look, I really view you as our partners," he told them. "You've been supportive and you've made big investments in our company and I thought before making the final decision it was only fair for you to tell me what you think we ought to do and what you're prepared to do."

The NYNEX executives demurred. The bidding was getting rich for their taste. Already NYNEX had come under fire by New York legislators and consumer groups who feared its telephone customers would be subsidizing its $1.2 billion participation in what was increasingly becoming cast in the press—with some justification—as a clash of egos for an overvalued prize. "We're with you to this point, but we don't have any more money to put into this," Ferguson said. "We just don't know enough. We're going to defer to you on whether you want to raise this bid or not."

It was Huizenga's turn to speak. "This is a once in a lifetime opportunity," he said, in one of his best coach-in-the-locker-room speeches. "Look, we've basically come this far, I think we ought to get it. If we decide to go up, we ought to make sure everyone in this room agrees we're going to get it. We can't go through this every time. We should be resolute about the fact that we want to get this, and we're going to do what it takes."

Conversation then centered on how to do it. Redstone was steadfast in his refusal to cede voting control. Biondi provided the road map. "There is one way we can do this without incurring further dilution and I'm telling you that, once you hear it, I'm not sure there's anybody who would do it." Viacom was offering a package of cash and stock to Paramount shareholders. The Viacom shares had been trading at $55 before the merger had beaten down the value of its stock. Biondi's suggestion was to have someone buy a portion of the stock, up to $2 billion, being offered to Paramount shareholders at that $55 price. Then the cash could be offered to Paramount stockholders.

"I'll do that but on one condition," Huizenga said. The room was stunned at both the breadth of the offer and the aggressiveness of his tone. "I want an unconditional merger agreement between the two companies on terms that have to be negotiated and we're going to do this really fast. I want to be clear about what I mean about unconditional. If we get Paramount, we merge. If we don't get Paramount, we merge."

Work began that night on hammering out the terms of a deal. Months earlier in discussing diversification, Merrill Lynch had code-named it "Project Orchestra" with Blockbuster as the brass, Paramount as percussion, and Viacom as wind. Now discussions would begin in earnest about the merits of a "duet" between Blockbuster and Viacom, versus a "trio," which included Paramount. Besides a merger, another possibility was that Blockbuster would get some assets—perhaps some of the Paramount library or theme parks—in exchange for its additional investment. But Berrard kept coming back to the value of a merger with Viacom. Though Huizenga had broached the idea publicly, now it was Berrard who became the driving force and who would ultimately carry it through. There was not another company in the entertainment industry that had the assets that Viacom had and was going to get through the Paramount deal. There was no way that Blockbuster would be able to obtain the likes of an MTV or Nickelodeon or Paramount studios, or theme parks, or publishing or premium cable networks like Showtime. And even if they could find similar assets, they would be prohibitively expensive. This was the deal they'd been waiting for.

In a second-floor private dining room at the Peninsula Hotel in midtown Manhattan on the evening of Saturday, December 18, the broad outlines of a deal were sketched out. (As fate would have it, the Peninsula is less than a block away from Allen & Co.'s offices, where Jack Schneider had made the formal introduction more than six months earlier and now, as Diller's advisors, would forfeit a hefty advisory fee.) In his suite, before the dinner, Huizenga had told Berrard, and his advisors Mason and Lewis, that he'd already made it absolutely clear to Redstone that this was a come-hell-or-high-water deal. No matter what happened with Paramount, Blockbuster and Viacom were betrothed and would merge. Viacom wasn't going to use Blockbuster just to win Paramount. Over a dinner of veal a short while later, Huizenga made that point again. Seated around a large oval table with Huizenga and Redstone in the center surrounded by their lieutenants and advisors, both groups listened and murmured assent. Aside from the signing of the initial deal three weeks later, this dinner would be about the only unifying event for many months.

"No Damn Deal"

Wayne Huizenga hates New York. He doesn't hate the city, or the people. But the crowds, congestion, filth, inefficiency, and inconvenience of it all offends his Dutch sensibility of order and cleanliness. Even arriving in his private jet and being whisked to Manhattan by private limo doesn't make up for the taxi driver tying up three lanes of traffic to stop and pick up a fare, or the delivery trucks blocking major intersections. It's a source of frustration for Huizenga, who relishes his five-minute commute from his waterfront Fort Lauderdale mansion down Las Olas Boulevard to Blockbuster's gleaming downtown office tower. And Huizenga never missed a chance to tell his advisors and soon-to-be-partners of his feelings. Redstone would get irritated with Huizenga. "New York is a wonderful place," he'd retort.

"Yeah, well let me tell you how much I don't like New York," Huizenga replied. "I don't even like to CALL New York."

Yet it was in New York, in the windowless conference center at the Shearman & Sterling law firm where Huizenga and other Blockbuster executives and advisors, along with those from Viacom, were trying to mesh together two complex companies led by strong-willed entrepreneurs and corporate chieftains into a unified body. In Sumner Redstone, Wayne Huizenga had met his match. Tough, shrewd, and a well-educated lawyer, Redstone wasn't a small-time garbage-company, lawn care, pest control, bottled water or video-store chain owner. Even Blockbuster's bigger deals with Philips, Cityvision, Republic, and Spelling hadn't measured up to the size and scope of this deal, the consummation of which would ultimately bend and even break some of Huizenga's own rules for deal-making.

In the days before Christmas, the teams worked to hammer out agreements. The $2 billion investment that Huizenga had initially proposed at that December meeting in Redstone's apartment was too rich, and was scaled way back to $1.25 billion. Control was never a bargaining chip, mainly because Redstone would never allow it to become one. Huizenga would get hammered on this point later by investors and the press. "I tried to get more of the A's because that's the stuff you can vote, but he just wouldn't budge," he'd tell other Blockbuster executives and his advisors.

Huizenga would never quite understand Redstone's attitude. He certainly controlled Blockbuster without having a majority of the stock. In his dealmaker approach, having two classes of stock inhibits someone from coming in and offering a better deal, the ultimate aim of his score-keeping approach to making money and building companies. "Sumner just thinks differently—he's got to have 51 percent," he says. "That's never really mattered to me, what's good for one is good for all." (Huizenga notes that Redstone's Class A voting shares rose higher—by 7 percent—than those of the Class B shareholders in the initial years of Viacom. "Sumner made out a lot better than his shareholders. At our place, everybody made out the same, management and shareholders made out the same." Indeed, in negotiating the deal with Viacom, Huizenga insisted that he receive no special treatment for his shares or an employment agreement. One caveat was that he and four other Blockbuster directors—Don Flynn, John Melk, Steve Berrard, and George Johnson—were covered by a provision which freed them from limitations on selling or pledging their Viacom shares.)

The deal snagged on a number of issues. The main obstacle centered around protecting Blockbuster shareholders, with Huizenga and Berrard wanting some premium for their shares and a mechanism to protect them if Viacom's share value dropped. There also had to be an out, a consolation prize, in case the deal for Paramount went through but the Blockbuster merger with Viacom was scotched for any reason as Blockbuster would have a sizable chunk of money, $1.85 billion, including the amount from September, invested in Viacom stock. But Redstone and Biondi insisted the merger couldn't be conditional, or that would make their offer for Paramount conditional. With his eye on plans to develop his Blockbuster Park concept, Huizenga wanted Paramount's theme parks to be conveyed as a "make whole" provision if the merger didn't go through and Viacom shares fell below $55 a share. But Redstone objected. He liked the theme park business. Finally, Biondi and Dauman convinced him to agree because Viacom retained the right to convey the parks and buy back a half interest within two years. But Huizenga figured Redstone would have no choice but to part with the parks instead of paying cash or shares because of the debt Viacom would take on with the Paramount deal.

The G-II got plenty of mileage shuttling between New York City and Fort Lauderdale. Talks broke down repeatedly. "He was a tough negotiator all along in every aspect of the deal," Redstone says. But Huizenga has a slightly different take. "I think the Viacom guys were tougher than we were. They may not perceive it like that but that's the way I see it." The first time Huizenga tried one of his favorite tactics and walked out of negotiations—polite and regretful that the deal couldn't get done—the other side was shocked. A half-dozen times, he left the negotiations, sometimes because of an impasse, other times as a ploy.

But as talks continued, that tactic got to be a joke among some insiders. At one point in the Shearman & Sterling Conference Center, both sides had caucused in their separate rooms to work out a response to a particular point in the deal. Huizenga came out in his long, black leather coat, shook hands with Philippe Dauman and said it was obvious they weren't going to be able to reach an agreement. "Good luck to you, it's been really great," Huizenga told him calmly. "I'm going to go back to Florida and it's too bad. It would have been a great thing, but it's all over."

They shook hands again. Huizenga left and Dauman went back into the other room where Greenhill and Levitt were waiting. They all started chuckling because they didn't believe it was really over, it was just theatrics. Indeed, Huizenga did return to Florida, but talks resumed a few days later. Another time when Huizenga walked, some participants swear, the G-II was simply fired up and circled around New York before landing again. Just hours later, Huizenga had called and said he was back in New York because of a dinner engagement and he'd had another thought on how the deal might work. One time, Huizenga and Berrard did simply switch to a different hotel.

As the holidays drew closer, the two sides were still far apart on the one issue that Berrard called a deal-breaker. Berrard and Huizenga were still angling for some kind of shareholder protection in case Viacom's stock, depressed because of the pending Paramount deal, didn't bounce back, or worse, fell further. Berrard wanted a "collar" which would kick in additional portions of Viacom shares at certain thresholds. But a normal collar, one that would take effect within weeks of the deal between Blockbuster and Viacom, wouldn't work because the "Paramount effect" might well still be weighing down Viacom's shares. Redstone in particular objected to a collar: it could become a self-fulfilling prophecy, resulting in more Viacom shares being issued and a still-depressed price because of the additional shares and greater dilution. And the resulting downward spiral in the value of Viacom's shares could hand victory in the Paramount battle to Diller. But Berrard wouldn't budge. "No collar, no damn deal," he snapped.

It was just two days before Christmas. Smith Barney Chairman Robert Greenhill let the talks break off, but Mike Levitt, who'd become friendly with Berrard, kept a dialogue going. Returning to Fort Lauderdale, Berrard asked Huizenga whether he should keep plans for a golf vacation in Arizona, the first vacation he'd had in about six years. "Go take your vacation," Huizenga told him. "There's no reason to stick around here. If it heats up, it heats up later. No big deal."

This time, Huizenga had written the deal off. The timing wasn't right. Redstone had until January 7 to raise Viacom's bid for Paramount so nothing was going to happen until that date grew closer. Nor was Huizenga sure the chemistry was there. He had no intention of working for anyone, but he wasn't even sure if he could work with Redstone.

It fell to the respective second-in-commands, Berrard and Biondi, along with the investment bankers, to keep the deal alive. Before talks had broken off, Berrard had mentioned that he might vacation in Arizona and Biondi had invited him to have dinner. Over the holidays, Berrard and Biondi and their wives met at the Biondi's vacation home in Scottsdale, Arizona. They talked cursorily about the deal, about what might have been. Biondi knew Berrard was still interested in a deal but was hanging tough on terms. It wasn't very substantive, but it was enough to keep the flame going. Berrard reported back to Huizenga as Biondi did with Redstone. On New Year's Eve, Huizenga spoke again with James Mason from Merrill Lynch who'd been advising them on the deal. Talk kept returning to the incredible collection of businesses each of the companies had, and how well they would fit together. To Huizenga, it sounded as though it might be time to get the plane engines going again.

Blockbuster shareholders had made an incredible amount of money in the past year. The market capitalization had risen $4 billion in the past year. "So if you could lock that in to something and protect their downside and give them the opportunity for some upside, that was the thing that we thought was the right thing to do," Huizenga says now. "Not necessarily the thing I wanted to do, but the right thing to do. I miss being CEO of Blockbuster. We were a company that had things on the roll, we had a lot of stuff going."

While the reality of video-on-demand was still years away, the perception would continue to dog Blockbuster's stock. Cash flows were good, the basic video business sound. "We weren't concerned about the ability to grow the company," he says. But "the ability for our shareholders to realize the appreciation that they'd realized in the past probably wasn't going to happen because of the perception out there." As Blockbuster's second largest shareholder (behind Philips Electronics N.V.) that meant that Huizenga wasn't going to get that additional appreciation for his 16 million shares or six percent of Blockbuster's shares either. The ride was going to level out. For a man who counts money as keeping score, here was a chance to lock in that score and go on to the next challenge.

By January 4, talks were back on. The solution: a collar cloaked in an appropriate acronym dubbed a VCR—a "variable common right"—which would grant additional shares if Viacom's shares traded at certain levels, but not until the first anniversary of the merger. The deal would give Viacom's stock a year to "breathe" and let the stock normalize and recover before more shares would be issued. Negotiations snagged over the valuation on the VCRs. "We were worried about our stock that had taken such a big rise and we didn't want our shareholders to go backwards," Huizenga says. "We weren't worrying so much about the upside potential as we were the downside protection." Repeatedly, the advisors from Merrill Lynch assured the Blockbuster executives that there was just a very "remote" chance that Viacom's shares would go below $36, the floor set by the transaction. But remote became reality.

Finally, after days of round-the-clock meetings to cover the myriad of issues, from the due diligence to stock valuations and other provisions, the deal was nearly ready to take to the respective boards. Just a day before Redstone and Biondi were to go to their directors with the deal, Huizenga dropped a bombshell. "I'm not going to stay," he told them. "I'm an entrepreneur. This is not what I'm about. I'm not about working for a big company. Hell, Sumner, put yourself in my shoes. You wouldn't work for me and I'm not going to work for you and I'm certainly not going to work for Frank."

Redstone and Biondi were stunned. They needed Huizenga to stay at least through a reasonable transition time. Though Berrard was increasingly in charge of Blockbuster, Huizenga's presence was needed at least for appearances to Wall Street. Redstone tried to talk Huizenga into staying. "But Wayne, you told me you might give me two years."

"Yeah, I did. But that was early and there's no need for that. Steve is going to stay."

Repeatedly, Redstone tried to have Huizenga change his mind. "I can't understand why you won't. You're convinced we've got the greatest thing going here. You're all excited about where we're going but you won't come to work for me. Why won't you be part of this great company?"

"Sumner, if I were doing this, would you come to work for me?"

"No," Redstone replied.

"Well," Huizenga answered.

Reflects Redstone: "Wayne's role was to be vice chairman of the board. I said to Wayne, you can play as big a role as possible. And I thought that role could be extremely significant. But he just did not want to be number two, basically." Finally, Huizenga agreed to stay at least six months after the merger but no longer than a year. Huizenga says he had never wanted to be a top executive at Viacom. "I enjoy building things," he says. As agreed, he would remain a director and be able to name two other directors. Divvying up exact roles would have to wait until the Paramount battle was finished, but one thing was clear—Martin Davis, who as Paramount chairman would have become CEO of the combined companies under the original friendly offer by Viacom—was out.

On January 7, Blockbuster board members gathered at the Ritz-Carlton to avoid the hoard of reporters camped out at the Peninsula. The meeting started after 4 P.M. Board members queried Mason and other advisors at length on the valuations, assumptions, and calculations of the deal. They examined thick, black-bound binders filed with documents detailing cash flows and projections and comparing the combined companies with other competitors in the entertainment field. Again and again, they heard that this was a Viacom-Blockbuster merger. With or without Paramount, this was a done deal, that Viacom's stock was artificially depressed because of the pending bid for Paramount and would bounce back, that there was only a very slim chance of it going below the floor set by the VCR. For each share of stock, Blockbuster shareholders would get a small fraction of a share of Viacom's voting stock, a much larger fraction of nonvoting (Class B) stock and a VCR. Huizenga and other Blockbuster directors committed to vote their 22 percent of the company's shares in favor of the merger.

Huizenga was already convinced this was a great deal, that Viacom's stock was worth much more than where it was trading. This was an $8.4 billion deal as it stood. If they got Paramount, great. But they'd also negotiated a clause where Blockbuster would have to approve any additional increase in Viacom's bid for Paramount, so if Barry Diller came in over the top, that was okay too. Maybe even better, since Viacom's shares would bounce back faster and the deal would shoot to $10 billion or more. The deal was valued at $31 a share, just below Blockbuster's all-time trading peak.

The board meeting ended after 1 A.M. Board members gathered at 8 A.M. the next morning and over a breakfast of muffins, began the sessions again in the second-floor conference room. Among the provisions was an agreement that Huizenga, Blockbuster directors, Philips and a few other shareholders such as Huizenga's parents, would vote their shares in favor of the merger. Just before 3 P.M. the Viacom contingent arrived—Redstone, Dauman, and Greenhill from Smith Barney—fresh from the company's own board meeting where the merger with Blockbuster had been approved. In an anteroom, Redstone and Huizenga and Berrard signed the deal at 3:30 P.M. Redstone went in to address Blockbuster board members about the great company that had just been created. Huizenga ducked to a telephone to call Marti, then via speaker phone addressed the Blockbuster employees assembled in Fort Lauderdale.

Then it was over to the Shearman & Sterling conference center for a call to Wall Street analysts and institutional investors. Already, there was a clue to the change at Blockbuster: Huizenga spoke only briefly during the conference call with Redstone and Biondi, leaving Berrard to handle the questions on business opportunities. He'd done his job, he'd signed the deal. But what is usually the end in such tales, in this case, turned out to be just the beginning.

SHAREHOLDER REVOLT

During the plane ride home, Blockbuster executives had joked whether they'd arrive before the first lawsuit was filed. They were confident this was a good deal, but it was controversial since it was a stock-for-stock transaction and Viacom's shares were volatile. Indeed, not one but four separate lawsuits would be filed within days. But neither Huizenga nor the others had an inkling of the firestorm that would hit. The press conference on Friday night at the Fort Lauderdale Jet Center was only a prelude. "We left Beavis and Butthead in New York," Huizenga joked, but with a glance to Berrard that signaled this phrase had been used before, perhaps to describe their negotiating partners at times. Before television cameras and a gaggle of reporters on "Wayne Watch," again and again, Huizenga defended the terms of the deal, the lack of voting stock, the valuation, his role as vice-chairman.

"By any stretch of imagination it is a mega company," he told reporters. "Our Blockbuster shareholders will end up with 62 percent of the Blockbuster-Viacom combined company and if we are successful in acquiring Paramount, we will own 52 percent of the three companies put together."

In just seven years, he reminded reporters, they'd sold the company "for what we consider will be a $10 billion transaction. I know that the press release says $8.4 billion and that's what we look at today because the Viacom shares are low and driven down by the Paramount transaction," he told

Reprinted with permission, *Tribune Media Services.*

them. "We delivered on our job and our job is to create shareholder value. I think this is a fantastic combination even though I will not be chairman of the company." As it neared midnight, the last of the television crews packed up and the reporters filed their stories. Huizenga thanked the Blockbuster executives who had stayed for the press conference, then signaled to his driver and bodyguard that it was time to go.

The next morning, weary but still triumphant, Huizenga and Berrard read through the Saturday *New York Times* story on the front page and shook their heads. The Viacom-Blockbuster merger "stunned" Wall Street but already the Viacom offer of $105 a share for Paramount was being pummeled as not much better than its previous bid, just a different configuration of cash and stock, and still below QVC's offer. In this and other press reports, the merit of the Blockbuster-Viacom merger would be whipsawed between the two widely divergent views on the fate of video rental—believers thought Blockbuster shareholders were getting too scant a premium and naysayers believed Viacom stumbled by getting into a business that would soon be obsolete.

"It's an open and shut case in my opinion," Huizenga said in an interview that Saturday morning January 8. "It might not be the way other people look at it but this is such a good deal for us as shareholders you can't not do it. We put our shareholders in position where we protect them on the downside and can go along for a significant ride on the upside. I'm willing to put my $500 million in there and so if I'm comfortable with it myself, I think I'm making the right decision for them. I'm giving up control because I think it's a wonderful deal and if I didn't think it was a wonderful deal for myself and other shareholders why would I give up control? We honestly believe their stock is being arbitrarily held down so we know we're going to get the upside. It's just a matter of is, it next week or six months but we know it's there." He noted repeatedly that the whole focus in the negotiations was to protect the downside. "The way Steve and I could get embarrassed is to not protect our shareholders." Those words would come back to haunt him just weeks later.

Signs came early of the trouble ahead. In an interview on the business television news show "Morning Business Report," Huizenga outlined the advantages of the deal but noted again that if Viacom didn't get Paramount, its stock would bounce back from $55 to $60 a share, a plus for Blockbuster shareholders. That was a reflection of Huizenga's deal-making approach to business, but that oft-repeated analysis would sow seeds of doubt early on about how much he really wanted the Paramount portion of the deal to go through.

Concerned that Blockbuster was getting sucked into an ego-driven battle for an already overvalued Paramount, analysts wanted to know what provision Blockbuster had to stop the escalating bidding. From the start of the takeover war, analysts had questioned how the skyrocketing price for Paramount could be justified by either Viacom or QVC. (In November an analyst with Oppenheimer had valued Paramount's assets at $7.1 billion or at most, $70 a share depending on its cash flow.) Huizenga assured analysts that Blockbuster had a veto provision on further increases in Viacom's bid. Meanwhile, Viacom's non-voting shares, which had traded at $41 before the deal was announced, dropped $2.75, reducing the value of Viacom's bid for Paramount. The market's negative reaction stunned executives and advisors on all sides of the deal.

That night, Huizenga and Berrard flew to Palm Springs to join Redstone and other Viacom executives at the Smith Barney media conference. Redstone and Huizenga took the podium together Tuesday, January 11 on the last night of the conference. They both outlined the benefits of the deal. But Redstone kept lauding the skills of "my team" which had worked the company down from high levels of debt and repositioned it to do a deal like Paramount. Huizenga said a few more words about the companies being a great fit. But Redstone's oratory skills just warming up, he launched into a tribute on his management team at Viacom which was the best out there. Annoyed and a bit embarrassed, Huizenga's fears of Blockbuster being treated as just the money bag for Redstone to get Paramount seemed to be underscored by the tone of this speech. Where was the credit for Blockbuster's team? For Huizenga, who can speak for hours without using the personal pronoun "I," Redstone's attitude and lack of recognition for the accomplishments of Blockbuster's management were irritating. "It was the proverbial slow-motion accident," says one advisor of the tense relationship that arose between Redstone and Huizenga. "It was the 'I' versus 'we' school." Still at the podium, Huizenga signaled to a waiter passing by. "Waiter, I'll have whatever he's drinking," Huizenga said. The remark got a good laugh from Redstone and the audience, but prompted an observer to say, "something tells me that Sumner has got a tiger by the tail."

Back in Fort Lauderdale, Huizenga faced a barrage of criticism being directed at Blockbuster by irate investors. Phone lines burned with angry callers, bewildered because the merger deal garnered so little premium near-term, no voting shares and placed Blockbuster as part of a debt-laden entertainment empire if the Paramount deal went through. "We underestimated what the market reaction would be to the whole thing," says Greg Fairbanks, who was chief financial officer of Blockbuster at the time and fielded most of the calls. "Our shareholders were saying, 'why in the hell, you guys are on the right track, your cash flow's good, you're not leveraged, why in the hell would you merge with a company and get involved with a company that's going to have $10 billion of debt after this thing is over with?' I think in a way we were our own worst enemy because in the 12 to 18 months prior to the merger, I think we had done such a good job of positioning the company away from that whole technology threat," Fairbanks says.

Analysts who followed Blockbuster were dismayed. Craig Bibb, an analyst with Paine Webber, was attending a consumer electronics show in Las Vegas when he heard the news. "My initial reaction was that I couldn't believe it," he says. "Analysts like me were recommending the stock through the buggy-whip days. The company had come from such a long way from two years prior when Wall Street was convinced that pay-per-view and video-on-demand were going to put the company out of business. I couldn't believe that they were going to sell out at a discount to current market value and a large discount to what the company was worth."

Portfolio managers like Haverty with huge Blockbuster holdings liked the Viacom-Blockbuster deal but "we didn't like the idea of Blockbuster getting into a bidding war for Paramount at a very high price," Haverty says. "Both parties (Redstone and Diller) were legally drunk and about to have one more drink. The bidding for Paramount was leaving reason behind. Whoever won, when the price started to hit $70 it was too much and we didn't like Wayne's cash flow to be used to further Sumner's ambition."

Analysis of the deal took a personal twist as well. On the Monday after the deal was struck, a headline in *The Wall Street Journal* read: "Blockbuster Merger Seen as Chairman's Bailout." With little premium being offered for Blockbuster's stock, the widespread expectation on Wall Street and in the media was that there had to be some other explanation for Huizenga's move, some hidden agenda, some piece of the puzzle that hadn't become clear. "There's a nasty way of looking at this and a magical way of looking at this," said Barry Bryant, an analyst with Ladenburg, Thalmann & Co., in *The New York Times*. "The nasty view is that Wayne sold out his shareholders for a chance to walk into the candy store. But the magical view is that Blockbuster stock is overvalued at $30 a share—especially in view of the threat from video-on-demand—and that Wayne is getting out of the horse and buggy before the automobile hits the road." Bryant took the more positive view, that Huizenga was being wise in selling out while Blockbuster was still a lucrative business. Even after the deal was done, a view prevailed in some circles that Huizenga was ready to move onto the next challenge and was looking for a big deal to take him out of Blockbuster that wouldn't be taxable. Steve Berrard would be in place to manage it and Huizenga would have a stake in Viacom just as he had kept a stake in Waste Management to use in building his next empire.

In crafting the deal, Huizenga had also underestimated the reaction of Blockbuster shareholders to the fact that they weren't getting voting shares in Viacom. Stockholders wanted some say in the future combined company and many on Wall Street questioned Huizenga's wisdom in the structure of the deal. "It is a reasonably good fit but selling the company without getting a premium for ceding control is surprising," Bibb said just days after the deal was done. "The market is disappointed that management of the company has shifted to Sumner Redstone and that Blockbuster shareholders don't get a premium for that."

As the war for Paramount waged on and Viacom's stock continued to sink, Huizenga's disappointment with the negative reaction to what he and Berrard had viewed as a brilliant deal turned to worry. At one point, he called Redstone. "Sumner, we're getting lots of feedback on the Street. People say your stock's going to go below 30." Redstone was livid. "It'll never happen," he snapped.

But as Viacom's shares continued to get hammered, Huizenga along with other Blockbuster executives, most notably George Johnson, began to actively hope the Paramount deal wouldn't go through. As Redstone prepared to raise the ante again in mid-January, Huizenga reminded him that Blockbuster held a veto right over any increases. But the clause hinged on a definition of "materiality." It was a distinction that had been lost on some Blockbuster directors. "I thought at one point that (the Paramount deal) wouldn't go through because I thought we had veto power over any subsequent raises and offers and we really didn't," says John Melk. "We really had a veto of significance. It was a nuance. Then it's a definition of what's significant. Do you want to kill the overall deal for that issue?" If asked that question directly a few weeks later, Huizenga may well have said "yes."

Instead, attorneys and advisors for both Blockbuster and Viacom examined the issue and deemed the hike that Redstone wanted as not "material." On January 18, Viacom raised its per-share price for Paramount to $107 a share and issued its "Diller-killer"—the same sort of delayed-reaction collar that Blockbuster shareholders had been granted but this time dubbed a "CVR" for "contingent value right." Says Redstone, "The final changes that were made in the deal were extremely modest. They were really fine tuning, they had extremely little in terms of dollar value." But the changes—particularly the collar—was enough to make Diller blink. He'd already concluded that Paramount was worth the $10 billion in cash and stock he was offering—not a cent more and certainly not the risk of having to make good on a $1 billion security owed at some future date if the stock didn't perform.

Still leery of Diller's threat, Viacom's board and its advisors huddled once more on February 1 to readjust the portions of cash and securities of its bid in time for the final deadline. Again, Huizenga threatened to veto the change, sure that the second bump combined with the first would trigger the "materiality" clause. But again, it came down to a matter of interpretation. The prevailing view was that they did not. What he had counted on as his club in bashing the dizzying bidding for Paramount turned out to be a useless stick. As a Viacom board member, all Huizenga could do was abstain from the vote, which he did. He still believes Viacom should have handled the situation differently by putting out more shares and less cash. "I just thought the price was getting to where it was too much," he says. "But Sumner because he's older and because he grew up in the movie business running movie theaters, his dream, his passion, was to have Paramount. I just thought the price had gotten too high, that's all."

As Viacom looked more likely to emerge as the winner for Paramount, Huizenga and Blockbuster shareholders looked like the losers. The "remote possibility" of Viacom's shares dropping below $36 had become a painful reality and then a mockery as Viacom's shares continued to fall. Tensions between the two companies turned to outright hostility as Huizenga and some top Blockbuster executives began to actively root for Diller to emerge as the victor.

Trying to pressure Viacom from going through with the Paramount deal or to sweeten the terms for Blockbuster, Huizenga in a meeting with Frank

Biondi in Fort Lauderdale on February 7 threatened to resign. Biondi turned to Berrard. "What about you, Steve?" he asked. Berrard was caught. During the negotiations with Viacom, Berrard had eschewed an employment contract because he didn't want criticism that he'd done the deal to get a plum for himself. But he'd promised Biondi that he'd stay on. Now he was faced with making good on the promise, or being disloyal to the man for whom he'd toiled for nearly 14 years and sacrifice a shot at being a top executive at one of the largest entertainment companies in the world. Arms crossed, he simply told Biondi, "Yeah, me too."

Biondi nodded and understood. "Steve was under an enormous amount of pressure," he says, reflecting on that tense meeting. "Steve wanted (the merger) to happen but had no idea whether the deal would happen and if he was contradicting Wayne, he would have been toast. So he said he was going to go with Wayne."

With the bidding deadline for Paramount drawing to a close, Redstone, Biondi, Dauman, and other members of the Viacom team gathered Valentines Day evening at the posh "21" Club in midtown Manhattan to relish their victory. Viacom had finally emerged victorious with its $10 billion bid, backed up by the guarantee for more shares within two years if the stock price didn't perform. Redstone had called Huizenga and said it looked as if they'd be victorious.

But Huizenga saw no reason to celebrate. The dour prediction he'd received about Viacom's share price proved true, and the stock dropped below $29 after the Paramount deal was announced. A series of events—the Paramount victory, a dismal first quarter by Paramount with dog movies like *Addam's Family Values* and *Intersection,* losses in a television joint venture—combined to impact the Viacom shares, which continued to sink. The thinly traded stock proved far more volatile than Blockbuster's advisors at Merrill Lynch had anticipated, and what might have been minor events had a Richter-scale-like effect on Viacom's shares.

Reaction on Wall Street among Blockbuster analysts and investors was swift and furious with the ire directed squarely at Huizenga. "This was the big deal of his career and now where does this leave him?," hissed one Wall Street analyst. "With or without Viacom, his reputation as a deal-meister is tarnished." The pressure by shareholders to get the deal with Viacom sweetened or break it off mounted measurably.

Initially, Huizenga put on a good front. A *Time* magazine story chronicling Redstone's victory featured a photograph of Huizenga and Redstone clasping hands with Huizenga flashing a "victory" sign. But tensions between the Viacom and Blockbuster camps were palpable by the time of a "get acquainted" meeting held in Vail on February 22. During one discussion, George Johnson was asked his opinion on the deal. "Well, you know,

I think this dog won't hunt," Johnson said in his Southern drawl. "It's all about stock prices and it's down. I've got my net worth tied up and this is not good. I don't want this to happen. And you can tell me all about promises and all I can tell you is the stock is nowhere right now and this ain't going to happen." Johnson recalls the meeting with a chuckle. "I wasn't the most popular guy at the picnic." He says now his concerns about the Paramount merger and resources for Blockbuster to grow its business were misplaced.

"It got to be a pretty lively conversation," Biondi recalls. "There was a very lively debate. It was a pretty good meeting, but it was pretty clear, at least to me, that the Blockbuster people were naturally on hold. You could sense they didn't quite know which way to go. There was a loyalty to Wayne and there was a loyalty to George." Again, it was Steve Berrard who at the end of the session, championed the deal. "This is exciting and we're going to work to make this happen," he said.

During the conference, Redstone and Biondi heard that Huizenga and Berrard were going to Denver to see John Malone at TCI to discuss a counter-deal. Redstone suspected that it was more a case of his nemesis trying to goad him than a serious consideration for Blockbuster but the fact that Huizenga was openly courting other suitors despite a signed merger agreement infuriated him. He already suspected Huizenga of trying to scotch the deal. And Redstone was right. "When the stock's at $26, all sorts of things run through your mind," Huizenga says. "What should we do now? Where should we go? Should we tube this deal? We had lots of ups and downs through that time. You start second-guessing yourself and so forth. You still don't have any problem mentally as to where the assets should go, but they're not getting there. Then you start wondering does the new management team have the ability to pull it off."

As Viacom's stock continued to sink in the wake of the Paramount deal, Huizenga was placed under enormous pressure. Instead of a triumph, the merger with Viacom had turned into his own deal from hell. From Wall Street to Las Olas Boulevard, analysts, investors, and media, even friends, either lambasted him for doing the deal or struggled to understand how he could have blundered so badly. In Fort Lauderdale, the hometown hero who had built Blockbuster into a multi-billion-dollar company and withstood withering attacks from doubters was now cast as the villain who had undersold his investors. Waiters, waitresses, parking lot attendants implored him not to go through with it. (At a formal dinner, one friend remembers a waitress served Huizenga his meal and whispered in his ear not to do the Viacom deal.) There was a daily barrage of phone calls from investors and analysts attacking his business acumen and urging him to have Blockbuster break up the deal and go it alone. Even the scuttling of the TCI-Bell Atlantic mega-merger in February and articles about the "potholes" on the Information Highway pushing back the threat to video rental played into the pressure on Huizenga to break up the engagement with Viacom as the view he and Berrard had long-espoused finally began to sink in at large in the mainstream press.

What had been the deal's strength—a merger with Viacom come hell or high water—became Huizenga's nightmare. Accustomed to being on the other side of the deal, Huizenga now found himself in the acutely uncomfortable position of having virtually no leverage. He'd committed a huge chunk of cash to Viacom. He'd left himself with no negotiating room and hadn't prepared for the worst that could happen. He wanted a better deal but absent that, he didn't want the deal anymore at all.

Ego played into the equation as well. In making the deal with Viacom, Huizenga had been torn between the right thing to do—merging the company and assuring value for shareholders and himself—and what he wanted to do, in remaining the CEO of a multi-billion-dollar, high-profile, publicly-traded company. He and his team had built Blockbuster farther— and faster—than they'd even believed possible and Huizenga wasn't quite as ready as he'd thought he had been to give up the ride. His dream for Blockbuster Park could be doomed under a debt-laden Viacom and with it his strategy for his sports teams. All the promised synergies with Viacom were subsumed in having lost where it counted most—keeping score.

He embarked on a campaign to pressure Redstone and Biondi to break the deal or up the ante. His shares were committed to the merger as were those of other directors. But he could try to get other Blockbuster shareholders to vote against the deal if it came down to a vote. Yet his actions over the next weeks, sometimes striking even other Blockbuster executives as bordering on irrational, would simply compound the complexity of the problem. With a signed merger agreement in place, he and Blockbuster executives were obligated to make a "good faith" effort to see the deal through. Instead, Huizenga in February had refused to join Redstone and Biondi in a road show to sell the new combined company to institutional investors, which had to be scaled back to meetings with a few key institutional investors.

HUIZENGA AND REDSTONE: AN UNHAPPY PARTNERSHIP

The tensions between Huizenga and Redstone were exacerbated over perceived slights. In early March at a media conference in Paris, it was Berrard who clued Biondi into that part of the problem. In scheduling a visit by Viacom executives to Paramount's studio, Huizenga hadn't been invited. And in deciding to recruit Jonathon Dolgen, president of Sony Pictures Entertainment, to oversee entertainment activities at the combined Viacom-Paramount, neither Redstone nor Biondi had thought to include Huizenga in the discussion or decision, instead calling him before the announcement was made. "His nose is out of joint," Berrard told Biondi of Huizenga's irritation over being treated more like an employee than a partner, a middling executive than the vice-chairman of the combined companies however that role was to be defined. Biondi was surprised, as he didn't think that Huizenga cared that much and moreover, had made it clear that he didn't intend to stay long in management. Biondi called Huizenga, who told him that he should have been invited and it was up to him to turn down the invitation. "It was a little tense," Biondi recalls. "We apologized and then I think we tried to bend over backwards to deal with the issue."

Caught between the two camps, James Mason from Merrill Lynch kept trying to salvage the deal and iron out differences. (Merrill Lynch took a lashing from investors and analysts for its role as Blockbuster's advisor and its valuations of both Blockbuster and Viacom, a sentiment that lingered months after the deal was finally done.) While the impasse was mostly over the price of Viacom's stock, a good part of it was how Viacom was treating Blockbuster and its executives, he'd tell Redstone and Biondi. At one point, Mason warned them, while Huizenga might be convinced the stock price might recover, he was concerned that the chemistry was wrong. "Seeds are being sown that can't be redone," Mason told them.

During the battle for Paramount and the immediate challenge of replacing management and cleaning house at the ailing studio, Redstone admits, "there may have been a period of some small neglect. There was never any intention to exclude Wayne from the process." After Huizenga complained, Redstone says he made it a point to include Huizenga in planning discussions and decisions. Says Huizenga, "There should have been more discussion. There should have been more of a meeting of the minds. There should have been more of a partnership. It wasn't a big deal. It's just something that, when you've made that many acquisitions and you've seen how people are affected when they're selling their companies, you're maybe a little more sensitive to some of that stuff." On a few occasions, Huizenga remarked to advisors and others that he resented being treated "as if we're the poor cousins from Florida," a glib remark but a clue to how deeply the issue cut.

As rumors on Wall Street and press reports surfaced about Huizenga's efforts to get the deal sweetened and hammered on Viacom's sagging shares, Redstone grew furious over Huizenga's comments that the deal couldn't go at Viacom's cratered stock price. Besides the articles in *The Wall Street Journal* and national press, Redstone would fax over to Mason copies of columns that had appeared in the local newspaper, the *Sun-Sentinel,* by business columnist Jack Neese, telling Mason it was obvious that Huizenga was trying to sink the deal. Though appearing merely to state the obvious, Huizenga's comments to reporters were calculated to goad Redstone into sweetening or scotching the deal, a tactic not lost on Redstone. "From the Viacom perspective we really were committed to doing everything we could to see the deal through," Redstone says. "I felt some of his statements that had gotten into the press was helping to sink the stock at the very same time that he was concerned about the price of the stock."

Says Huizenga, "I don't think we ever wavered in public. We were very candid with people but Sumner didn't like what we were saying. But it was factual. We said, 'I'll support the deal as long as the deal makes sense and if the deal doesn't make sense, we're not going forward.' Sumner didn't want me to say that. Sumner wanted me to say we're going to go forward under any conditions. Well, I'm not going to say that. So I could see where Sumner was coming from but he couldn't see where we were coming from. He just wanted an unconditional commitment that we were going to go forward at any price. Well, we couldn't do that."

Meanwhile, Huizenga continued his courtship with other potential suitors. Besides Malone, he met with Disney Chairman Michael Eisner and media baron Rupert Murdoch, letting Redstone know about the discussions, putting additional pressure on Viacom. Redstone didn't blink. "I haven't seen anyone come forward," he'd tell Huizenga. "I never saw any of it develop, I heard it primarily from Wayne," Redstone says. "I never took TCI seriously because I thought it might be a way to leverage us by TCI. John is very good at that kind of thing. Disney is a known bottom fisher—Eisner is fantastic, but he's not a guy who pays very much for anything so far, so I never took that seriously."

Talks did get far enough with Eisner and Murdoch to bring in investment bankers for due diligence. It was deemed that Viacom was indeed paying top dollar but big factors were that Blockbuster had already committed $1.8 billion to Viacom and was betrothed with a signed merger agreement in place. No one wanted to take a chance of incurring Redstone's wrath and reputation for litigiousness while having that chunk of money committed to a hostile partner. If Huizenga could break off the engagement, maybe there'd be further room for discussion.

In April, three Blockbuster board meetings were held in succession a week apart at the law offices of Skadden Arps where directors, as well as top executives and advisors from Merrill Lynch, met to look for ways to opt out of the agreement. Huizenga would call Redstone and bait him by telling him they were meeting to try to find ways to crater the deal. He continually made suggestions on how to end the merger, on what might be proper currency for going their separate ways, including ceding the theme parks to Blockbuster. "The parks were not an option," Dauman says. "We would never have done the parks. Sumner loved the parks."

But with the merger agreement not terminating until September, Redstone had time on his side. Alternately bewildered by Huizenga's actions and then enraged, he'd rant at advisors that Huizenga was trying to kill the deal. Huizenga's toughness exacerbated Redstone's tenacity. "Wayne, from our standpoint, what do we have to lose by waiting this out and hoping that our stock price will go higher?," he told Huizenga. He refused to issue more shares. "There's a dilemma Wayne," Redstone told him. "First, we're certainly not inclined to do it. We want to stay with our agreement. But even from your perspective, if we paid more the stock you have would go down proportionally, so it would be self-defeating."

The friction took on a highly personal note. In one session, Biondi and Tom Dooley were meeting with Huizenga. Biondi had left the room, but Dooley said, "give the deal a chance." Huizenga glared at him. "How many deals have you done?"

Taken aback at his tone of contempt, Dooley said, "I don't know. Enough."

"Well, I've done 800 so don't tell me about deals."

In another discussion with Biondi weeks later, Huizenga tried another version of an earlier threat. "You understand that if the merger actually happens, there's not going to be anyone down there? All the management is going to leave," he told Biondi.

"You know, Wayne, I've got two thoughts on that," Biondi said. "I'd really be sorry if you all did do that, including you. But the one thing you've taught me about your company is that you've got a much deeper management team than just you and Steve or George. But all that aside, if you all left, I guess it would be the second company I've bought this year that had no management, albeit for different reasons." (Adds Biondi in recounting this conversation: "He got really pissed. I mean smoke was coming out of his ears.")

"How can you say that?" Huizenga demanded.

"Look, I'm not here to threaten you," Biondi told him. "I'm just telling you that if you think that's going to dissuade us, you're barking up the wrong tree. That's not the way to deal with us and you will find us quite resolute in going forward."

Caught in the collision was Steve Berrard. Berrard was shielded from some of the heat of Wall Street and the press, which directed its ire at

Huizenga. Nor was it his reputation as a dealmaker that was on the line. Berrard, the biggest champion of the merger, quietly tried to keep the deal alive, the relationships with Viacom executives intact.

The pressure Huizenga felt was passed on to Berrard, who became the scapegoat for the way the deal had soured. Huizenga blamed himself and that blame carried over to Berrard. He wanted Berrard to be more supportive of his plan to kill the deal and help look for angles to get out of it. Berrard reminded Huizenga that he had been instructed to deliver a hell-or-high-water deal, and that's what he had done. He was simply trying to carry out Huizenga's vision, the mandate he'd received three years earlier to build Blockbuster into a diversified entertainment company.

Now he needed to save his boss from himself and Blockbuster in the process. Huizenga's actions were putting Blockbuster in a bind. They had a signed merger agreement and had to abide by provisions to act in good faith—or face a potential lawsuit, a point Berrard would make to Huizenga on occasion. He'd argue the fundamentals of the deal, the strategy, the synergies, all the reasons they'd wanted to make this marriage in the first place. He'd get Huizenga back on board with the merits of the merger, then another phone call from an irate investor or a comment from a neighbor or friend would touch off another round of trying to kill the deal.

The stress took a tremendous toll. Berrard's hair literally grew grayer. Other executives lost hair and weight. "They didn't really know where the chips were going to fall," Biondi says. "There was a lot of pressure at that point of time and I think Steve was like the pinnacle of all that pressure. The only thing I couldn't do was kid him during that period of time. He'd say, 'I can't talk to you about it now.'" Later, all that Berrard ever referenced to Biondi about that period was that 'I was under a lot of pressure. I was getting blamed.'

The executive floors atop One Blockbuster Plaza became almost unbearable with tension. The uncertainty weighed on the entire organization, causing anxiety even among rank-and-file employees. In addition to the normal uncertainty unleashed by any merger, many employees, as well as executives, had stock options and watched with alarm as the value of those options plummeted with Viacom's stock.

The letter Blockbuster sent in May to shareholders was a watered down version of the one Huizenga had wanted to send. He had wanted to say the board of directors couldn't recommend the deal but it was altered to simply read that "there could be no assurance" that the board could recommend it.

The Blockbuster annual meeting on May 24 was a lively affair. Sign-waving demonstrators outside the Broward Center for the Performing Arts protested plans for Blockbuster Park and the damage environmentalists feared would be done to the Everglades. Inside the auditorium, Blockbuster shareholders protested the merger with Viacom and the damage they feared would be done to their investment portfolios.

During the meeting, Huizenga repeatedly sidestepped the issue of the Viacom merger but made it clear it wasn't going to go at the current price. He outlined the reasons for the merger, that "the two of us would create a company with the ability to deliver a wide array of entertainment products to nearly every available medium around the world," Huizenga told shareholders. "And the addition of Paramount *at the right price* would create an entertainment company of even greater size and scope." He noted that because of the close of Viacom's stock price, the total value of the deal had fallen by more than $2 billion, from approximately $8.4 billion to approximately $6.3 billion. The Viacom stock Blockbuster shareholders would receive was worth only $23, substantially less than the $31 dollar price originally struck.

There had been no discussions with Viacom since the shareholder letter. "It's entirely possible that Viacom will wait as long as they can, in the hopes that their stock will rise further. Obviously, there's no guarantee that Viacom stock will be any higher in the coming months than it is today, let alone rise enough to restore over $2 billion of value to our shareholders." Blockbuster would continue to expand its reach in entertainment through its video rental, music, Discovery Zone outlets, its ownership of Spelling and plans for Blockbuster Park. "We have the utmost confidence in our management team, our franchise owners, our employees, our customers and you—our shareholders," Huizenga said, "to achieve our vision of the future with or without Viacom."

Meanwhile, Redstone was also getting pressure to break off the deal from other quarters. Viacom shareholders certainly opposed sweetening the terms, especially since some had questioned the wisdom from the start in buying into an obsolete technology. The benefit of Blockbuster's cash flow was over-rated and they feared issuing more shares for Blockbuster would further depress Viacom's stock price.

With the prospects for the Blockbuster deal appearing bleak, Redstone picked up the pace of asset sales, raising $317 million by selling a stake in Lifetime cable network and putting Madison Square Garden and the New York Knicks basketball team and New York Rangers hockey team, acquired via the Paramount acquisition, on the block. (The deal would close in August for $1 billion to ITT and Cablevision Systems.)

But by summer, Viacom's stock had started to edge up, in part because of an unsung hero in the Blockbuster-merger saga, a slow-witted, Alabama-born character named Forrest Gump. The movie, starring Tom Hanks and based on Winston Groom's novel by the same name, captured the hearts of Americans as they relived the tumult of the 1960s and 1970s through the eyes of a simple man with unabiding loyalty, love, and a collection of aphorisms ("life is like a box of chocolates") to guide him through challenges. "Gump" became a household name and a box-office smash for Redstone, the highest-grossing movie in the history of Paramount Pictures (surpassing *Raiders of the Lost Ark*) and unleashing a flood of Gump-related merchandise, from the usual hats and t-shirts to the "Bubba Gump Shrimp Co." cookbook based on the film's make-believe firm. The movie version of Tom Clancy's novel, *Clear and Present Danger,* also edged up Paramount's prospects and Viacom's stock, and therefore, the prospect of the Blockbuster merger.

The Sun Valley 1994 Allen & Co. power conference in July was a strange and strained affair. This one was immortalized, captured by Annie Liebovitz in a photo spread in the October 1994 edition of *Vanity Fair* on the "The New Establishment—Redefining Power in America." There, seated amid 16 of the most powerful corporate chieftains on the globe— Warren Buffett, chairman of Berkshire Hathaway; Gerald Levin, chairman of Time Warner; Bill Gates, chairman of Microsoft; Michael Eisner, chairman of Walt Disney Co.; Rupert Murdoch, chairman of the News Corp.— and a seat away from Sumner Redstone and next to Edgar Bronfman Jr., CEO of Seagram Co., is Wayne Huizenga. (But he is missing from the text of the story, which chronicles the rise of power of the barons of the media and information age.)

The night the conference started, Diller's proposed merger with CBS blew up, scotched by QVC partner and Comcast president Brian Roberts who had pulled the plug, which would lead to Diller's departure. As soon as he'd gotten the news at 5:45 that evening, Biondi walked over to Herb Allen who was greeting guests. "Have you heard?" Allen hadn't as yet. Biondi earlier had asked for a speaking spot at the conference and Allen hadn't been able to find one. Biondi felt he wasn't looking hard enough and Allen cited the awkwardness of the situation since they'd been on the other side of the Paramount battle. "If it's true, Barry doesn't have much to talk about," Biondi told Allen. "How about that speaking spot?" Allen laughed. "You're bad, you are really bad." Indeed, on Saturday morning, Redstone and Biondi, sans Huizenga and Berrard, made a presentation about the Viacom-Paramount merger. (During the conference, Redstone repeatedly referred to Diller as "my $2 billion ex-friend." To which Diller replied, "give it a rest. You won." They were each presented with a pair of boxing gloves.)

Relations between Redstone and Huizenga were distinctly cool during the conference during the public sessions. Privately, Huizenga was trying to break off the deal. "This thing is not going to make it, the stock's not coming back," Huizenga said in a meeting in Frank Biondi's room. "Why don't we just throw it in?" His argument was that there wasn't enough for Blockbuster shareholders in the deal, even with the VCRs. The discussion actually diverged into a debate and then a disagreement between Huizenga and Biondi on the mechanics of how capital markets work. "Look, there's no reason for us to cash it in," Biondi answered. "We like the deal and we think it's going to work and if we're wrong, it'll collapse on its own. That's why there's a break-up date."

In the end, Huizenga wasn't so sure he was right, checked and softened his public position after that conversation, Biondi says. "It was heated, it was lively," Biondi says of the discussion. "He was advocating a point of view and we were advocating a point of view and it wasn't like 'I'll never talk to you again and how could you do this to me.' Basically, it was issues of why should we do this?"

Redstone wanted more support for the deal, Huizenga wouldn't give it without getting it sweetened. He told Redstone, "Sumner, why should I, I'm already the schmuck of the year, how can you expect me to do more?"

"The issue of raising the price was never on the table from our perspective," Biondi says. "I don't think they picked up on that at all. I don't think anybody could read patterns very well. I think they always believed we were still negotiating and we may have believed they were still negotiating, simply because there were very good negotiators on both sides."

As the weeks clicked by toward the September 30 break-up date, Viacom's stock recovered further, aided by Paramount's movie successes, its sale of assets like Madison Square Garden and a well-timed, five percent stock purchase by investor Kirk Kerkorian. By early August, Viacom stock was hovering at $34 from its depth of $21.75 in April. Viacom executives insisted that the merger issue be put to a vote to Blockbuster shareholders, made their position known through the company's lawyers—and would have taken the matter to a Delaware court to force the issue. "We understood the difficulty of the situation but it was up to the shareholders to decide," says Philippe Dauman, Viacom's counsel. "We felt we had a merger agreement and it should at the very least be put to the shareholders of both companies." On Blockbuster's side, Merrill Lynch re-examined the transaction to judge whether it was still fair to shareholders.

No one was sure, not even Huizenga, how the decision was going to go as Blockbuster directors, executives and advisors gathered in a conference room at the offices of Skadden Arps at 9 A.M. on August 23. Merrill Lynch advisor James Mason and others went through the updated fairness opinion, the exchange ratios, the company fundamentals, the prospects for the share prices. Repeatedly, discussion focused on whether this was the best Blockbuster could do. Huizenga recounted his efforts to get Redstone to improve the terms, how much he had pushed during the one-on-one sessions with Redstone, the phone calls directed from advisors.

The advisors and executives filtered out of the room, leaving Blockbuster directors to decide its fate. As directors debated the company's course, Berrard reminded them of all the reasons they had made this deal in the first place, what the vision for Blockbuster had been and how the merger with Viacom fulfilled that vision. The decision had really already been made in January when the merger agreement had been signed. They had a fairness opinion from Merrill Lynch. There was a very real threat of a major lawsuit should directors vote against the merger and given Huizenga's actions, statements to analysts and the press, Blockbuster would have had a terrible case showing that it had acted in good faith. Blockbuster faced a potential legal liability in the billions of dollars and having $1.8 billion tied up with a partner with whom they were at war. The sniping by short-sellers and the technology threat they had faced down was nothing compared with this risk, which could ruin all they had worked for those intense seven years. Board members turned to Huizenga, wanting his cue. "I think we should go forward. I think it makes the most sense that we lock in what we've got," he told them. "It's the right thing to do."

But neither the reaction to the merger in January nor the ire by analysts and investors in February after Viacom had won Paramount, was a match to the fury unleashed by the decision by Huizenga and Blockbuster directors to go through with the deal. Blockbuster shareholders, who thought for sure that Huizenga would come back with a sweetened offer or wouldn't go through with the merger, felt betrayed. "When the guys at Blockbuster say they're going to do something, they usually do it and that was the sense of disappointment," says analyst Craig Bibb.

"We felt the stock was dramatically undervalued," remembers Larry Haverty, the portfolio manager for Blockbuster's largest institutional investor. "We were surprised that Wayne or the directors would agree to sell the company at that price. I was furious at Merrill Lynch for giving them a fairness opinion and felt the stock was worth much more and read the valuation and thought it was preposterous—they were coming up with a fairness opinion and specious logic to justify it. I was upset that the outside directors of Blockbuster caved and felt they could not vote against the fairness opinion of Merrill Lynch and how could they go to shareholders with this?" Haverty knows now that "sitting over their head was Sumner's sword of Damocles. Sumner felt he had a contract and if Wayne were to get into a legal battle and the court would uphold Sumner, Wayne could lose in one of those Texaco-Pennzoil cases and could lose everything he had built up."

On a conference call to analysts and investors on August 24, Berrard fielded questions and deflected the anger. Huizenga did not participate, a point not missed by the callers or by Berrard. He was tired of the abuse. Berrard had argued for this deal, let him handle the fire for a while.

Finally and firmly on board, it was Huizenga who suggested that the Viacom-Blockbuster management team undertake a road show to sell the deal. "I thought this was a really remarkable investment of time into what you knew was going to be uncomfortable abuse," Biondi says. "And he did it and he did it better than being a good soldier. He went in there and he really stood firm and he took the beating and he gave it back. A lot of people wouldn't do that. That's a sign of a big person and I guess underneath it all, I've always felt Wayne was a real big person."

The ten-day road show was grueling and exhausting, physically, mentally, and emotionally. "I don't know what was said to engender that kind of response and in about half of the situations there was sort of disguised and outright hostility directed principally at Wayne," Biondi says. Repeatedly, Huizenga stood his ground, telling them, "look, I believe in this merger and I think you're going to get value here. It hasn't been easy to do."

During one session, one fund manager from the Midwest "absolutely went ballistic on him," Biondi says. "I've never seen a guy do this. What was really funny was his argument 'I'm really unhappy, ten percent of my fund is in Blockbuster and it's down and I don't like it.' And he started

Reprinted with permission, *Tribune Media Services.*

saying something about Viacom and I said, 'hey, wait a minute. You can't like Viacom and be making that argument.' He said, 'I've got no ax to grind with Viacom, I think it's a fine company.' That was a major mistake because then the old prosecutor, Redstone, goes on this guy like a dog on a steak." Redstone argued that he couldn't like Viacom and not like the merger and why was he angry with Huizenga since he'd seen the wisdom in the deal.

During the roadshow, the entourage paid a visit to Haverty, who left Redstone and Biondi in the lobby when they came to sell the deal. He went over the situation again with Berrard and Huizenga—but Haverty still wasn't swayed. "There was never any doubt in our minds that the combined companies would be dynamite. We just wanted more going in. We voted against the merger and we felt that as Blockbuster shareholders we deserved a higher price for a change in control."

*   *   *

On September 29, 1994 just a day before the deadline for the break-up clause, Blockbuster held its last stockholders meeting in Fort Lauderdale. The Viacom shareholders had met and approved the deal. The shareholder lawsuits against Blockbuster had been settled just 15 days before for $1 million in legal fees. When the Blockbuster vote finally came through, 73 percent of the shareholders voting approved the merger, but because a blank vote counted as a vote against the merger, the final tally was 58 percent. (Marti Huizenga symbolically voted her shares against the merger.) After his tearful farewell and the well-wishers at the reception had left, Huizenga returned to his office atop One Blockbuster Plaza. Walking past the awards and framed newspaper articles chronicling Blockbuster's triumphs and his own achievements, it felt odd, an anticlimactic ending to an emotional day. He told his assistant, Valerie, that he was going home early. That night at dinner with John Melk and Don Flynn, he was subdued, not his usual self. Even when Melk asked him what he was going to do next, he wasn't sure. All of his intense focus and prodigious energy had been invested in Blockbuster and his sports teams, and even those he had envisioned eventually linking with Blockbuster. He honestly didn't know. It was too soon to answer just then.

12

After Blockbuster:
What's Next

The banner stretched between two palm trees read: "Wayne and Marti—
Thanks for the Memories." Beneath the words were the logos of Blockbuster Entertainment, the Florida Marlins, Florida Panthers, and Miami
Dolphins. In the late afternoon Florida sun on May 13, 1995, Wayne
Huizenga stood for more than an hour in a picnic area set up in front of the
stadium, posing for photos with Blockbuster employees, and their hus-
bands, wives, parents, cousins, and children. A photo opportunity with a
local celebrity. He signed pennants and programs, posed with the Billy the
Marlin mascot and greeted and bid farewell to dozens of Blockbuster employees. "He's signing anything," marveled one observer. "What about a
blank check from Blockbuster?" quipped another. "It's Viacom now," said
a third.

On stage, a six-piece band in tropical print shirts played Beach Boys
tunes and other rock-n-roll classics. The 1,000 or so employees and their
families milled around tables decorated in teal and white tablecloths,
munching on hot dogs, hamburgers, barbecue pork, and chicken, while
beverage stations served up soft drinks, wine, and Blue Ribbon water.
Notebooks were scattered around with a smattering of comments from employees, mostly jottings of thanks and appreciation for the free night of
baseball, some for their jobs, some for the attitude of the company. Marti
Huizenga took a plate of corn on the cob and BBQ chicken, sat at a table,
and struck up conversation while her husband continued signing autographs. Finally, they both took the stage.

"We've had a lot of fun over the years," Wayne Huizenga told the Blockbuster crowd, congratulating them on being the best employees in south
Florida. "We all realize things are changing and there are new faces but

305

we're still one big happy family. We love ya, the fun is not over. See ya later." Marti took the microphone, paused, then said, "I agree with Wayne on everything except one point, you're not just the greatest in south Florida, you're the best in the world. We've brought you here for another reason. You're going to help us win this game tonight. Have a good time and enjoy."

It must have been the good luck charm the Florida Marlins needed. The team had lost every one of their eight home games at Joe Robbie Stadium in 1995 and dwindling crowds made as pathetic a showing in the stands as the team did on the field. But on a beautiful Florida night with a sea-shell pink sunset fading into gray, the Marlins blimp coasting overhead, the Blockbuster video sign revolving on the Jumbotron scoreboard, and a full moon rising over the stadium, Huizenga sat in his box on the field fronting first base, still cheerfully signing hats and programs. The Marlins took the lead and beat the Colorado Rockies 8 to 2, earning a standing ovation. It was a good start for an ending.

*   *   *

On September 30, 1994, the morning after the emotional shareholder meeting at which he officially handed over the fate of Blockbuster to Viacom, Wayne Huizenga knew his world was different. "You don't want to be late on your first day," Marti teased him. "Sumner wouldn't like it." He sat through a series of press interviews, explaining again the rationale for the deal, his plans, still unformed, for the future. He took phone calls from well-wishers, head-hunters, and deal-dreamers and prepared for a series of good-byes.

The next landmark was the annual franchisee bash in October, and the first one that Huizenga didn't dress in costume for the theme party. "The last one was kind of bittersweet for Wayne and all of us," remembers Fred Montesi III, one of Blockbuster's earliest franchisees. The morning of Huizenga's farewell address, he had breakfast with him, Marti, and John Melk. "Wayne was nonstop joke telling for 35 minutes. You could tell that everytime he got a good response, it'd make him feel good enough to tell another. It was joke after joke after joke until Marti finally said it was enough." During his speech, similar to the one given shareholders, Montesi says, about two-thirds of the audience was teary-eyed. "It's kind of like giving up a baby," says Montesi. "I remember saying to Wayne, 'You need to look around the room and look at all these happy people. You've made them a lot of money, made them a wonderful business to be a part of. What a great ride we've all had.'"

As a thank you to some of the key team members who'd made that ride possible, Huizenga hosted a marlin fishing trip in Australia in late

November for 22 guests. Absent was Steve Berrard, who was caught up in Viacom budget meetings and already answering to his new bosses, Frank Biondi and Sumner Redstone. The trip was in grand Wayne Huizenga style, with "mother ships," (one 108-foot, the other 103-foot) seven sports fishing boats, and two dive boats, full crews and nonstop activity, from deep sea fishing to scuba diving to white water rafting. He fretted over details, calling his sister to make sure Whit Hudson wouldn't feel slighted being on the smaller boat, making sure that Don Flynn who didn't like the heat, was on a boat with air-conditioning, checked on everything down to food preferences and special diets. He matched captains with the experience of guests, checked that everyone who planned to go diving was certified, even had flowers sent to families since the trip was planned over the Thanksgiving holiday. At the end, an awards ceremony was held with bronze marlins and cash prizes given out for who was seasick the most, and who'd caught the ugliest fish, most fish, and biggest marlin. "That was the first vacation that he had since the beginning of Blockbuster in seven or eight years," says Wayne Huizenga Jr. "I haven't seen him have that much fun in a number of years. He really let himself go."

This trip, Huizenga was the host, and as the host, he let his guests have first chance at hooking a marlin. "The fish were kind of few and far between and he didn't want to be one of the ones (catching) unless everybody else had caught one already," Ray Huizenga says. "It's like there might be three people on the boat and it's kind of a team effort anyway, but there's only one person in the chair when you actually fight the marlin. So he was always letting somebody else take a turn." Besides, as exciting as Huizenga finds fighting a marlin, it's fishing for deals that really turns him on. It was time to start trolling again.

NEW LANDSCAPE

Change came quickly within One Blockbuster Plaza. Moving and construction crews rearranged offices in a new corporate pecking order. With Blockbuster no longer an independently traded company, the finance department was trimmed, and both that department and public relations were moved a few floors further below the executive suite, their services more insulated within the realm of a larger public company. Within months, work began to turn the sixth floor into the expanded but temporary home of Huizenga Holdings, pending a deal to lease three floors in a nearby office tower under construction.

But the changes were far more than cosmetic. The long and painful limbo before the decision to abide by the merger agreement between Blockbuster and Viacom made it easier for Steve Berrard to break out of

Huizenga's shadow. Following the merger, Huizenga attended only one Blockbuster executive management meeting. Initially, he and Berrard consulted often, but even those sessions became less frequent and shorter. Within weeks, Huizenga was spending a few hours and on some days, less than a half-hour on Blockbuster business.

The speed with which Berrard moved to make his own imprint on Blockbuster surprised even some insiders. In one of his first major actions, Berrard in December delivered the death blow to what had been his mentor's pet project, Blockbuster Park. By spring 1995, Berrard had unwound or revamped several other deals and directions Blockbuster had undertaken as a public company. In February, he finally pulled the plug on New Leaf Entertainment, the joint venture with IBM to create compact discs on demand, folding some operations into Blockbuster and disbanding the rest as neither music nor video games proved commercially viable for the system. Weeks later, the shaky partnership with Virgin Megastores was killed.

With Discovery Zone's performance continuing to deteriorate, in April Berrard moved to take management control of the company from the Flynns. The company lost $25 million in 1994 and those losses mounted in 1995. Flynn would remain chairman and a director, but his son, brother, and other board members resigned and the headquarters was moved to Fort Lauderdale. Flynn blamed the losses on a seasonal downturn and difficulties merging the newly acquired McDonald's play center company, Leaps & Bounds, but admits the company needed more operations expertise. "We didn't expect to lose money but we did. Doesn't happen to us very often."

The disengagement of Huizenga in Blockbuster's business was clear by the time of a Viacom board meeting held at Blockbuster headquarters in March. While he attended the board sessions, he skipped out for the Blockbuster presentations. "It was mostly a Steve show, literally, and that's the way Steve wants it," says Frank Biondi, chief executive officer of Viacom. "He wanted the challenge of running a major enterprise. He's sensitive to Wayne and doesn't want to make it difficult, but there are periods of time where they haven't talked much at all and then they talk a lot about other issues."

Huizenga kept the title of chairman of Blockbuster until June, but will remain vice-chairman of Viacom. His interest is in overseeing his $600 million plus stake in Viacom. Despite the months of discord during the uncertainty of the merger, Redstone says that Huizenga's participation is welcomed and he seeks his input. He discussed with Huizenga the negotiations regarding the sale of Madison Square Garden and the cable deal Viacom had struck with TCI. "The only limitation on Wayne's contribution would come from Wayne himself," he says. "Wayne can have about anything he wants—except my job. Putting that in a kidding way. Wayne is in as good a position to make a contribution to the strategy of this company as anybody I know. But I think he's on the path of gradually divorcing himself, going off on his own, and doing something else."

The atmosphere at Blockbuster was different, and defining that difference displayed conflicting loyalties. Long-time employees loyal to Huizenga described it as more corporate, less entrepreneurial, bigger and more bureaucratic. For others, it was seen as part of a natural evolution. "It's not Wayne's baby anymore," as one executive put it. "Steve is president and CEO now so by his very title, I no longer go to Wayne on a daily basis. I go to Steve and so does everybody else." Viacom's decentralized management mode kept most decisions in Fort Lauderdale, and for Blockbuster executives, vistas of new opportunities in sister companies beckoned.

The new era affected the relationship between Huizenga and Berrard as well. "It's different because I don't see him as much," Huizenga says. "Used to be he was in my office six times a day. Now he picks up the phone and he calls Frank." (To others, Huizenga would mutter privately on occasion during the early and most difficult stage of this transition that Berrard was "big-dealing" himself.)

"It's changed a lot," Berrard says of their relationship. "I don't see him every day and talk about what goes on here. But, I still tell him what's going on and we're still partners in a bunch of things so we'll still get involved in that. But I don't work as closely. I don't travel with him every day like I used to." Though eager to make his mark on Blockbuster as the top executive, the evolution is not without pain. Despite the personal toll exacted on his life, his alliance with Huizenga enabled him to achieve the position he now holds as a top executive in one of the largest entertainment companies in the world. "I've endured a lot, I've been through a lot, I've been a referee in a lot of situations," Berrard says. "I would do it again if I had to do it again. And I would do it for him. If I had two kidneys and I had to give one up, I'd give it to him. I just feel that way now. Where do we go from here? I'm working here and he's going off and doing something else, but that doesn't change the way I feel."

Looking back, which is not something that Wayne Huizenga does often, he's particularly pleased with one aspect of his tenure at Blockbuster. "I think it's results," he says. "You have to deliver and I think we've been good at delivering. We did what we said we were going to do. And it's hard to argue with that. Yes, we've had hiccups along the way and yeah, there's been ups and downs and there were a lot of things that happened that we didn't count on, but, when it was all said and done, we made our numbers. We did what we said we were going to do—and that speaks volumes."

As the new Viacom began to take root, the ire on Wall Street faded and Huizenga's tarnished reputation as a deal-maker began to recover.

Viacom's stock showed further gains—and the merger masked some underlying weaknesses within Blockbuster. Timing once again would work in Huizenga's favor. Competition within music retailing slashed margins razor thin, a warm winter compared to the record chill of the winter before sent same-store sales for video down to just three percent, and Discovery Zone would be a drag on investor perception of prospects for that business. "At the end of the day, Wayne did okay," says Larry Haverty of State Street Research, Blockbuster's biggest institutional shareholder. "The way it worked out, if you have to fault Wayne for doing what he did, it's only a fault in the short-term because right now, unquestionably a Blockbuster shareholder is better served by being in Viacom stock than in Blockbuster. If Blockbuster was independent, the stock would have gotten hit. He got an okay price but he got a piece of paper, ownership of Viacom, which is a dynamic company that is better able to hide any mishap in music, and video rental isn't the whole company if five or ten years later, the information highway becomes reality."

Perhaps Huizenga's greatest strength was knowing—with a bit of a persuasion by Steve Berrard—when to exit. "Wayne is an entrepreneur, he likes to build things," says Randall E. Haase, portfolio manger with Alliance Capital, who manages a $2.7 billion portfolio which started buying Blockbuster shares in 1992. "He is a dealmaker. He is not someone who falls in love with his businesses and that is a credit to him. The reason he is a success is that he doesn't own something forever. He gets involved in companies to create things. He creates asset streams, he created two multibillion companies. He's not someone who's going to run something for 50 years because he's not a manager. He is somebody who creates and builds companies that are going to grow at 30 to 50 percent for several years and then figure out what's best for the company." As an outsider, he sums up the Huizenga recipe for success: "He likes to take industries that are fragmented with no clear leader, take market share from moms and pops, in an industry that is growing and has economies of scale in having a large company and he likes service companies with repeat business." Applying that formula to a new venture was Huizenga's next challenge.

New Sports

"Retirement" wasn't even an option for Wayne Huizenga this time around. "I can't imagine Wayne not working," says Marti. "Wayne is driven from within." Wayne Jr. predicts more time will be spent with family, particularly with his two young children, Huizenga's first grandchildren, as well as with the other grown children, Pamela, Ray, and Scott. (But the pace wouldn't slacken much. After days of Super Bowl festivities, and after the big game itself, Huizenga and Berrard were on a 5 A.M. flight for a Viacom board meeting. And his assistant, Valerie Hinkell, would say that his schedule was as busy and hectic—perhaps more so—than with Block-buster as Huizenga scouted for new opportunities.) His father, says Wayne Jr., is still driven by the same force that's driven him since the purchase of that first garbage truck in 1962. "The deal. The excitement of making the deal. I think that's what drives him."

Indeed, that's why although, as Marti would remind him, he already had three businesses to run in the Dolphins, Marlins, and Panthers, the sports teams wouldn't be enough to keep his attention. He'd make more time for owners' meetings, but purposely keeps committee participation to a minimum. "I have a rule that I don't sit on an advisory board. When you sit on an advisory board your vote doesn't count. When you're on a committee in baseball or any other sport, your vote doesn't count. Your committee turns in its report but after that you have no authority, right? There's more important things to do than sit on an advisory board." Fur-ther, for all their glamour and public attention, the teams are modest-sized businesses by his standards. The three teams and the stadium are about a $250 million business.

The honeymoon already over with the sports press, Huizenga's focus on treating the teams as a business would garner him criticism but prompt no change in public posture. "It is what it is," he says. "And I'm not going to change. I'm not saying I'm doing it right, I'm just doing what I believe in. There are some owners out there, they lose a lot of money every year, just like we do in hockey and they don't care. They want to win. I want to win, too, but to me, you can do both. I think you've got to run it like a busi-ness." But with all the competing interests, the man who had made a suc-cess of nearly all his ventures was finding that the sports business was very different.

The first priority was figuring out how to stem his losses on the Pan-thers. The hockey team had been a financial disappointment for a man used to making millions. The opportunity for the franchise had come up before he had a place for the team to play. The Panthers had been losing roughly $6 million a year because of the unfavorable lease at the Miami Arena. Huizenga wanted a new arena to honor a commitment to the National Hockey League and to stem the team's losses.

But the ill-fated Blockbuster Park haunted his efforts to get public backing for a new facility. He'd spent much of his political capital on the project and his "do it fast" style of deal-making didn't sit well with a jaded public and suspicious press. He tried to get approval in the spring of

1995 for a restaurant and hotel tax to finance a $165 million arena before a site was selected and details were available on costs and benefits. Broward County officials wouldn't endorse the proposal in the face of local opposition.

Moreover, Huizenga's famed touch for timing was off. While public coffers had been tapped by various cities over the years to finance sports facilities, increasingly such ventures were requiring more private money. In July, Huizenga said he would move or sell the team unless a new arena was built which would allow him to keep skybox, concession, and parking revenues. He'd already rejected a proposal for an arena that would have required him to contribute as much as $65 million, contending the Panthers' losses would be too high by the time the facility was built to absorb that cost. "I'm going to do my damnedest to keep the team here in south Florida," he told reporters at a press conference. "But if it doesn't work, we're going to have to make some other decisions." While there was talk of working with NBA team owner Micky Arison to build a joint facility, options were limited and Huizenga was already talking informally with interested buyers for the team.

Then there were the lingering problems with baseball. The still-uneasy labor situation with the players' union leaves the Marlins an uncertain venture at best. "All of baseball's in a terrible situation right now," Huizenga says. Winning back fans will be quite a marketing challenge and an open-air stadium in Florida's heat poses an additional hurdle.

In addition, four teams now compete for sports fans' dollars in south Florida. "It's always been a tough area to draw—there's too many other things to do," he says, citing the mixed attendance record of the Dolphins despite their overall record as one of the winningest teams in the league. "If the team's not winning, forget it. Now we've compounded the problem because we brought baseball and hockey in. If you didn't have hockey, there would be more dollars to spend on the other sports. So by bringing the other sports here, we've split the market."

The bright spot in Huizenga's sports empire is the Miami Dolphins, which he's determined to get to the Super Bowl. The team in spring and summer 1995 spent $10.5 million to sign quality free agents like defensive lineman Steve Emtman, and Pro-Bowl tight-end Eric Green, among others. The strategy is to financially support the teams when they are ready to win a championship. "We want to win the Super Bowl badly," he says, as the Dolphins were heading into the season. "We have real good talent, first round draft picks and we're hopeful this is our year." When the Marlins are ready, he says he'll do the same. "We're ready to spend the money when Dave Dombrowski says we're ready to compete now and we'll fill the holes with whatever Dave recommends."

Meanwhile, he's scouting for ways to take advantage of synergies within his sports empire. Cross-marketing, like offering Dolphins season-ticket holders a reduced rate on Marlins tickets, was a given. There was discussion on offering fans a package of games for all three sports. To garner additional ideas for cross-promotions, the business-side sports executives—Don Smiley, Bill Torrey, and Eddie Jones—meet together occasionally with Rick Rochon to share suggestions.

As for the future, Huizenga will hold the teams as valuable assets while working for new ways to run them as operating businesses. "The only way it's going to work without Blockbuster Park is if you can bring in some other lines of businesses to tuck into what we've got," says Rick Rochon, who oversees the sports teams. "There's a business there. It just hasn't been defined yet. We're going to spend more time with them and try to make something happen." Meanwhile, Huizenga recognizes that he's not going to get the same rate of returns on the teams that he's been accustomed to getting in his other businesses. "What we hope to get is incremental value on the franchises and to cover a 10 percent return on equity while we're there," Rochon says. In Huizenga's favorite game—making money—the sports teams couldn't score high enough to merit his undivided attention.

New Choices

The steady stream of letters, calls, and personal entreaties to entice Wayne Huizenga into new business ventures turned into a flood once the merger between Blockbuster and Viacom was completed. In the month of October 1994 alone, some 140 proposals were received by Huizenga Holdings, everything from theme park suggestions to new inventions. A staff of four help evaluate them. But for the vast majority, they've missed their window as most of the ventures were too small and too limiting to intrigue Huizenga anymore. "It's pretty hard to get those deals going now," says Rick Rochon, president of Huizenga Holdings. "Ten years ago or eight years ago when we were doing smaller deals, that would work because these are mainly $5 million to $10 million deals. But you spend the same amount of time on the small ones as the big ones. He doesn't want to do that anymore. He wants to do deals where the company is already doing a couple hundred million in revenue."

But Huizenga would be very selective about what he'd invest his time and energy into. One new project was a 300 acre private golf course—for family and friends—being built near Stuart, Florida, designed by champion golfer Gary Player. Meanwhile, he still had other real estate holdings.

Real estate required money, but made money while freeing him for other ventures. "I like service businesses and to operate companies rather than own a piece of real estate but things change as you get older," he says. "A piece of real estate doesn't take as much time as running a business."

As a favor for a friend, on March 28, 1995, he bought one million shares of newly issued shares plus options on another million shares for a total $10 million investment for a 6 percent stake in OHM Corp., the hazardous waste treatment company which he'd continually tried to buy during his Waste Management years and instead had formed a lasting friendship with Jim Kirk, its chairman, president and CEO. Indeed, Kirk had instead turned the tables, as OHM was in the process of buying out the hazardous waste remediation business, Rust International, owned by Waste Management. News of Huizenga's purchase sent OHM shares up 38 percent within days, a result of the "Huizenga effect" as investors flocked to get in on what they thought might be his next deal. But this was just an investment, nothing more. (Even far from his sports teams territory, about 200 people in the small city of Findlay, Ohio, were waiting for him at 11:30 P.M. to see his G-II airplane and get his autograph. Huizenga cheerfully signed autographs and gave away shirts for an hour-and-a-half before heading back to Fort Lauderdale.)

The "old pals" network would also be plowing the ground for new deals. "I'm sure Wayne and I will do some things together," Flynn says. "We have done business for 25 years, there's no reason we won't. I plan to have a venture capital operation in Chicago and he plans to do the same in Florida and I'm sure we'll cross-fertilize." Flynn rattles off the criteria: "We all have a propensity toward service businesses, no products, no inventory and capable of a national rollout. On the other hand, you have to watch where the world is going. There are lots of opportunities in the entertainment, media, computer software and programming and where that whole world is going is a major, major business. There's going to be more privatization of government, companies that will run prisons more efficiently than today. School systems are going to get more private." Flynn personally likes the idea of private trade schools.

John Melk would also be scouting for ventures, while continuing to grow the personal care products company, H2O Plus, started with his daughter, Cindy. Huizenga and the "pals" are investors in that business, even though it doesn't fit their normal pattern of service companies.

Besides the service criteria, there are others that Huizenga was scouting for in his next deal. The company either had to be in south Florida or be able to have its headquarters relocated to south Florida. It had to have a "repeatability" component, like renting video tapes or garbage containers.

And size and potential returns were key. The aim is to make money, pure and simple. "Wayne likes companies with superior returns," says his long time friend and advisor Chuck Lewis at Merrill Lynch. "There are ideas that he has rejected simply because, while they produce good returns by anyone's standards, they can't produce these vastly superior returns that he expects." Even 25 percent annual returns aren't enough. "He understands and is attracted by the basic physics. He doesn't have to know all the details of a business," noting that Huizenga didn't know what an SKU (a stock-keeping unit, a method of keeping inventory in retail) was and said so during a meeting with analysts early in Blockbuster's history. But size is critical to making those returns.

While Huizenga no longer wants to do $5 million deals, he sees much more opportunity to make money in small deals than in mega-deals, and vastly more than he could taking over management of a big company. "I must have had 30 phone calls saying how about becoming CEO of this company. I'm not looking for a job. I don't want a job. So what we do, we'll do as an entrepreneur and we'll only do something that we think that we can double and double again and double again and that's how we make money. And the challenge here . . . I don't need any more money. I've got enough money, but the challenge is to make money. Why do you climb the mountain? Because it's there.

"Well, it's the same thing here. But if you can double every year and if your stock can double every year, let me tell you something, you've got a lot of people that are enthused and excited, you've got shareholders that are happy. You've got your neighbors and relatives that are happy. Everybody that is working in the company is charged and excited and they're all making a lot of money. They've got such an enthusiasm about them that they just can't wait to get up the next morning to go to work. No one has to ask them to come in on a Saturday or stay late. They want to be here. It's what we had at Blockbuster. People made more money here in two or three years than they could have made in a lifetime anywhere else. So that's what I get a sense of excitement about."

No matter what company he chose as his vehicle, his basic precepts of doing business remain the same. He believes in customer service. He confers credit to executives around him, but doesn't like others to take it for themselves. He gives authority, within boundaries, but demands accountability. He has an ego, but shuns pretension. He'll grow through acquisition rather than start-ups wherever possible to gain market penetration. He knows his value to the organization and expects to be compensated in stock and options—the method of keeping score—but still speaks of team effort. "I don't look at myself as ever doing anything. I'm always doing something with someone, whether it's Rick Rochon of Huizenga Holdings or whether it's Dean Buntrock at Waste Management. There was never a 'me.' There was never an 'I.' There was Don Flynn, John Melk, Dean Buntrock, Larry Beck. . . . Waste Management was never an 'I.' The only time it was an 'I' is when I bought my first truck and drove it myself. Other than that, it's always been 'we.'"

Anyone who works with him or for him will get a dose of the inner standard that drives him, the striving for perfection that goes beyond the excitement of the deal-doing. "He is never satisfied that he's done it exactly right," says Steve Berrard. "If the Marlins had a 162-game schedule and if they won 158, he'd probably have said, 'Well, we probably could have won two more.' But hey, that's part of him, that's part of the package. I also think in his personal life, that it never allows him to be anything more than just what he is and that's a down to earth person. That always self-critical analysis is really part of him and I think that's why if we were all walking down the street you couldn't pick Wayne out by identity. I think he prides himself on that and I think all of us are proud of that. I started here when his net worth was a helluva a lot less than it is today, but he's no different. He's the same guy he was 14 years ago so I think that's his whole psyche. I don't think it's just business, I just think he treats himself that way as well."

Oddly, that striving for perfection is evident in some of Huizenga's comments about Wall Street. Working "the Street" was considered by many within and outside of Blockbuster to be one of his greatest strengths. Yet, Huizenga professes still to not quite fathom Wall Street. "Every day is a learning experience and I don't think you ever quite figure out Wall Street. You might think you understand it but you don't." Indeed, Huizenga says contradictions and second-guessing were constant while building Blockbuster. One investor would complain they didn't use enough leverage, others would say not to use too much, some didn't want them to go international, others liked the concept. "That's part of the deal," he says. "If you believe in something you go do it. Same with sports. You make a trade for a player and some newspaper doesn't like the trade, boom, you get blasted. You got to do what you think is best. We also got assailed when we made some of the acquisitions we made. We also got assailed when the short sellers were out there. We also got assailed for bad accounting which wasn't bad. We got assailed for a lot of things. You make the decisions you got to make."

But on one major area, his interests and those of Wall Street converge. "To me building a company that makes a lot of money but doesn't give a return to its shareholders, that's not success. There are a lot of companies like that, they do great. The companies grow every year a little bit, but the stock really never does much. I'm not happy that way. I'd rather take this company to a certain point, fine, now we got a whole bunch of happy share-holders that followed us. We'll go off and find something else, go for the next one and go for the ride again." The vehicle Wayne Huizenga would find to take that next ride would be a familiar one—a garbage truck.

SAME SONG—NEW WORDS

After months of looking for the right company, it was a friend and a famil-iar business that would catch Wayne Huizenga's interest as the way to launch his third public company venture. He wanted to recreate the fast pace of the growth years at Waste Management and Blockbuster and had been looking for a shell, a company with a small base, that he could acquire and use its stock to move into three or four different high-margin service businesses ripe for consolidation. He'd checked in with an old friend from the garbage business days, Michael G. DeGroote, who'd built the third-largest solid waste disposal company in North America, Laidlaw, which was sold in 1990. He'd gotten back into the business in 1991 with a small outfit called Republic Waste Industries. The Atlanta-based company was one of hundreds of regional solid waste companies with that had continued to serve a profitable market niche despite competition by industry big guns Waste Management, Browning-Ferris, Laidlaw and others. But its haz-ardous waste business had dragged down its stock performance and hin-dered its acquisition strategy, since garbage company owners often didn't like the potential volatility of a stock riding on the regulatory vagaries of hazardous waste hauling and handling. DeGroote explained that he'd taken a few years to get the company back on track and was separating the haz-ardous waste business into a separate company. But DeGroote lived in Bermuda and was finding it difficult to oversee the company as closely as he'd like, given restrictions on how many days he could stay in the United States. Huizenga kept that bit of information in mind. The more he mulled it over, the better he liked the idea he was formulating.

Two months later, in late April, Huizenga called DeGroote and learned he'd be visiting in Naples, Florida, after going to the company's annual shareholders meeting in Atlanta on May 4. Huizenga invited him to pay a visit. Meanwhile, he'd approached brother-in-law Whit Hudson for the sec-ond stage of the deal he had in mind. Republic after the spin-off had nearly $49 million in revenues. If Hudson would sell Hudson Management with its six garbage-hauling companies and roughly $60 million in revenues to Re-public, right away they'd have a $110 million company. The deal looked great to Hudson, who stood to profit handsomely by taking Republic's paper—and even more so once Wayne Huizenga's name became associated with the company. On May 22, 1995, Republic announced that Huizenga and associates would invest $27 million in Republic in exchange for six million shares of stock plus warrants for an additional 12 million shares. Within days the stock was trading above $10 a share up from 3⅞. News of an additional $13.25 million infusion by Huizenga, plus an equal investment by John Melk and a $70 million private placement by Allen & Co., sent the stock skyward to a whopping $26 a share just before Huizenga closed the deal in August. The shares were trading at 98 times earnings—an incredible premium and a bet on Huizenga, who became chairman and chief executive.

"Unfortunately all the headlines were 'Huizenga's back to his roots, Huizenga's back in the trash business' and that wasn't the intent," he says. "The intent is to use the corporation as a vehicle to go on the acquisition trail to consolidate two or three or four or five different industries and we were looking for the right company." In Republic, he believes, they've found the right one. The company had made some problematic acquisitions in recycling and been caught by volatile scrap prices and bloated inventories, and had been plagued by the usual set of liability problems associated with the hazardous waste industry. DeGroote had sold some pieces of the company and spun off the hazardous waste operations. The new Republic seemed poised for promise and improved profits. Combined with Hudson's companies, the new venture would have $110 million in revenues, zero debt (once proceeds from sales are used to pay off all existing debt), $108 million cash in the bank, and after-tax margins of about 10 percent. "If looking for a jumping off point to make other acquisitions, here you have a company that's squeaky clean, no debt, cash in the bank, high multiple stock and a lot of shareholders equity," Huizenga says. "What we plan on doing with it is not just being in the waste business. We're gradually getting the word out that this is going to be a diversified service company."

One of the first orders of business would be selecting a name to reflect the new, expanded direction. "If I could pick the right name, I would call it Diversified Services but it's not a sexy name," he says. "It's not a good name, but that's exactly what we're doing. We only want to be in high margin stuff."

Essentially, Huizenga is dusting off the plan for Service USA, the company he was building before Blockbuster came along. But this time, he'll stay out of seasonal businesses like lawn care and for now, pest control. The aim is to grow quickly, to $500 million or so within a year or so, through acquisitions in the garbage industry and others. One industry that's intriguing is the security alarm business for homes and businesses. It's an industry with a few big players, and Huizenga believes, ripe for consolidation. As for other prospects, he's keeping mum for now, in part because they're still reviewing plans and "if we do enter them we want to sneak up on 'em, we don't want anybody to know what we're doing." Some candidates may be surprising because they're companies that might not be considered service companies at initial glance. The alarm business is a service business because of the monthly fees and because the equipment can be installed and rented as well as sold.

There may be some penalty by Wall Street, which generally likes "pure play" companies, but that's a dampening effect Huizenga is willing to accept. While conglomerates with divisions in manufacturing and health care or restaurants are so diverse as to be difficult to follow and value properly, he says, his idea is to go after industries with similar parameters. "I'm not saying these businesses are all going to be tied together or they're horizontal or vertical integration but they're all service businesses and you operate those differently. It's hard mentally if you're a manufacturer to decide how to serve the consumer in a restaurant, you just think different."

The idea is to springboard off the growth in several industries instead of just one. "Here's the way I would spin that story, okay, let's say we stay in the waste business—we go out and make a bunch of acquisitions and now we're a billion dollar company. We're no different than any other waste company. There's a lot of waste companies out there. So where's our growth story? Whereas, if we're in five different industries and they're all growing at 10 percent and we're growing within the industry, we can have a growth company that's a lot more exciting than having a pure play company that's growing at 10 percent a year. Some analysts will say 'I don't like that,' and we'll say fine, don't follow us. We've been around the Street long enough now that you can't try to please everyone. You have to do what you think is best."

The run-up in the stock price—the "Huizenga effect"—makes the challenge ahead much more immediate and difficult as expectations are already so high. He and DeGroote discussed that effect two days before the deal, with DeGroote warning that it would put a lot of pressure on him. "I said yeah I know, I've been there before, we know how that feels, but it's a joint effort around here." Huizenga and his family bought four million of the six million shares (plus warrants). The executives joining him and other employees also had the opportunity to buy shares and warrants—the shares at $3\frac{7}{8}$ and the warrants at an average of $5—and already had a sizable paper profit when the deal went through.

The warrants serve a two-fold purpose. Not only do they serve as future financial incentives, but they also provide a steady stream of capital into the company to use to pay down debt of targeted acquisition companies. While some shareholders won't like the dilutive effect of the warrants, the cash mitigates that concern.

In management, Huizenga will handle Wall Street, acquisitions and strategy. Hudson will take care of operations. "We learned something a long time ago, it's easy to go out and buy something but then someone has to run it and Whit's a good operator," Huizenga says. "Whit's trucks are spotless, he uses good new equipment that's well maintained."

The division of responsibilities is essentially the same structure they used in Southern Sanitation thirty years ago, but from a vastly different base. Though he had said it would be difficult to work for his brother-in-law again, working with Huizenga with clearly defined roles is a situation he can handle. "I'm going to be running the show," Hudson says. "Wayne and I between the two of us control the company and have the majority of the company. I'm still running my own show, just a little different than by myself." Although in charge of operations, Huizenga's deal-making machine will push him to new challenges. "My ways are more laid back and now I'm going to have to gear up like I did 20 years ago. I'll have to travel more, I've accepted that."

Also working with Huizenga on the new venture will be Wayne Jr., fulfilling the desire of both of them to work to build a company together. One of Huizenga's few regrets about Blockbuster is that Wayne Jr. did not work with him longer there. After working for some of his father's other companies, Wayne Jr. joined Blockbuster in 1987 at age 25 as an assistant store manager, then as a store manager, district manager, and administrative assistant to the chairman in 1989. He left a year later to start a frozen yogurt chain. Understanding of his son's sensitivity to being in his shadow, Huizenga was supportive but lukewarm on the business, believing the market too crowded with too many big players to be promising. He turned out to be right. For two years, Wayne Jr. toughed it out in a fiercely competitive market before selling for a loss of $2 million in February 1992.

Wayne Jr. admits he got caught up in Blockbuster's success. "I wanted to succeed not only for me but to make him proud," he says. "But in doing it, lost a fair amount of money. He was very, very reassuring about that. He said, 'don't worry, we'll work it out. You're young. You're going to go on. You're going to work in other businesses, we'll work it out. It's not a big issue.'" He returned to Huizenga Holdings to work in the bottled water company. Huizenga Sr. credits his son with helping to build that company and says the experience he gained in the yogurt company will serve him in good stead.

But there will be no special breaks at the new company. "I've always been able to get away with being friends with someone yet taking them to task if they need to be taken to task," Huizenga says. "I'm not afraid to do that. I'm probably harder on my kids and on my relatives because I don't want other people in the organization to feel there's favoritism out there and so I'm probably harder on Whit than I should be and on Wayne Jr. and that's natural." About the only friend not entirely happy about Huizenga's new line of business is Dean Buntrock, who wasn't surprised at Huizenga's choice.

While analysts following Republic put the growth target at $500 million in two to three years, Huizenga's eyes gleam at the prospects ahead. It'll get to that number "sooner, much sooner," he says. "If you take a company from $100 million to $500 million, that's $400 million of growth, you've grown five times and that's what we want and that's what makes life exciting for us."

Indeed, with his challenge ahead, there may not be much time for fishing for black marlin off the coast of Australia, so his goal of hooking a grander may still go unrealized for a while. But while he's not caught one as an angler, arguably, he's snagged two in corporate life. And like the angler always looking for next biggest fish, Huizenga is eternally fishing, too, always casting for the next big deal. There just might be another grander out there.

Author's Note

This project began with a call from Ruth Mills, an editor at John Wiley & Sons, Inc., saying she thought Wayne Huizenga would be a good candidate for a biography and asking if I would be interested in writing such a book. As I had covered Blockbuster and Wayne Huizenga for *BusinessWeek* since 1990, the prospect sounded appealing.

Although I had a fair base of knowledge about his years at Blockbuster and his entree into professional sports teams when I began this book, I had not written about his experience at Waste Management or much about other aspects of his life. What had struck me in reading various profiles that had appeared in local and national publications is that he is often portrayed as either a hero or a villain. What I sought to do was neither, but instead to write about who Wayne Huizenga really is, and what has led to what is unarguably great financial and business success.

The bulk of this project had to be reported and written over the course of six months, from December 15 through June 15, 1995. Although I already had plenty of material to draw upon, I knew it would be a more complete portrait if I had an opportunity to interview him again. He was at first reluctant, but then agreed to cooperate with the project while not requesting or requiring any editorial control or prior review to publication. True to his word, I have had the opportunity to interview Wayne Huizenga seven times for one to three hours each session during the course of reporting for this book.

I have also interviewed current and former Blockbuster executives and franchisees, current and former Waste Management executives as well as other business associates, industry sources, family members, and friends. Out of the dozens of phone calls and interview requests, only a handful refused to return calls or declined to be interviewed. A few others would speak only on background, not for attribution. I consulted numerous articles, legal, court, and regulatory documents, including some obtained via Freedom of Information requests from federal agencies.

323

What emerged was a man who didn't get to where he is by stealing wealth from others, but rather by creating it. Yes, critics may note that Waste Management and Blockbuster and what some would term their "hardball" business tactics may have contributed to force small, weaker operators out of business, but such is the economic Darwinism of the capitalistic system. Indeed, there are hundreds of owners of garbage companies and video chains who sold to Waste Management and Blockbuster in exchange for stock who are today far wealthier for doing so, as are shareholders who bought in, and in the lexicon of Wayne Huizenga, "went along for the ride."

For Wayne Huizenga, making money has now become, as he is often quoted as saying, akin to a game. The money is simply a way to keep score. By that benchmark, he's done well, indeed.

Acknowledgments

A project like this cannot be accomplished without the assistance of scores of others. For the time spent in interviews and on follow-up questions, I would like to thank Wayne Huizenga and the current and former Blockbuster, Huizenga Holdings, and Waste Management executives, as well as business associates, friends, family members, industry and Wall Street sources cited in the bibliography that accompanies this book. I would like to note particularly the time spent by Steve Berrard, Tom Gruber, Chuck Lewis, Rick Rochon, and Marti, Peter, and Wayne Huizenga, Jr. For her help with photos and arranging interviews, thanks to Valerie Hinkell, administrative assistant to Wayne Huizenga.

Thanks to Nancy Zell for her quick transcription work. Peter Valdes-Dapena proficiently probed the world of on-line research. Bob Andelman provided advice about book-writing and the world of sports, and his own book, *Stadium for Rent,* was a great help and a good read. For their valued suggestions and assistance in editing, my thanks to Antonio Fins and Robert Barker. I appreciate the support of this project by Stephen Shepard, editor-in-chief, and Keith Felcyn, chief-of-correspondents at *Business-Week.* Thanks to Ruth Mills, the editor at John Wiley & Sons who initiated this book, and to my agent, Dominick Abel, for his guidance. For my friends who provided hospitality, maps, and local lore during trips for this book—Jean and Mike Allen in Dallas, Jean Franczyk and Matt Brandabur in Chicago, Joanne Kenen in Washington, and Diane Goldie and Gary Bristol in New York—my sincere thanks and our home is open to you always.

To all my friends and family, most particularly my brothers and sisters and their spouses, who understood my absences and long silences and gave encouragement and support, many thanks. This project could not have been done without the help of my mother, Geraldine, who cheerfully and efficiently transcribed dozens of hours of interviews and whose faith in me kept me going. My deep gratitude for the love and guidance she and my father, Joseph, have always provided. Finally, for my son Kyle, who endured too many nights and weekends of "mommy working," and my husband, Shawn, who gave invaluable assistance in all aspects of this book as well as unfailing patience and love, my eternal gratitude and appreciation. I thank God every day for you and the love we share.

G. D.

Personal Interviews

Tom Adams, January 26, 1995
Clinton Allen, December 28, 1994
Ron Alsheimer, November 1, 1994
John Anderson, April 8, 1995
Kenneth Anderson, November 20, 1994
Richard Anderson, April 11, 12, 1995
Joe Baczko, February 3, 21, 1995
Bob and Judy Balfoort, January 30, 1995
Scott Beck, November 23, 29, 1994;
  March 8, 1995
James Beckley, April 18, 1995
Andrew L. Beja, January 9, 1995
T. Edward Benton, April 28, 1995
Steve Bergerson, May 4, 1995
Steve Berrard, January 7–8, 1994;
  February 15, 1994; December 22, 1994;
  February 15, 17, 1995; March 9, 1995;
  May 17, 1995
Craig Bibb, April 4, 1995
Frank Biondi, March 31, 1995
John Blaisdell, May 24, 1995
Fran Blechman Bernstein, March 13, 1995
James Blosser, March 16, 1995; April 6,
  1995
Albert (Budd) Bosman, February 7, 1995
Norman Braman, April 5, 1995
Betty Joanne (BJ) Buntrock, January 19,
  1995
Dean Buntrock, May 4, 1995
Joe Burke, November 9, 1994
Jeb Bush, February 27, 1995
Gale Butler, April 12, 1995
Tom Byrne, May 5, 1995
Harold Carter, March 8, 1995
Tom Carton, January 20, 1995
Hank Cartwright, January 26, 1995

Tim Casgar, April 20, 1995
Ron Castell, November 4, 1994; February 1,
  1995; April 20, 25, 1995
Rob Castleberry, February 10, 1995
James Chanos, April 10, 1995
Lowell (Mike) Clark, January 26, 1995;
  February 4, 1995
Bert Cohen, March 10, 1995
Michael Cole, May 3, 1995
David Cook, November 19, 1994
John Croghan, December 20, 1995
Ann Daly, February 13, 1995
Doug Danforth, May 30, 1995
Philippe Dauman, March 31, 1995
Nezida Sherman Davis, February 9, 1995
Phil deMena, November 30, 1994
Bill Denton, January 12, 1995
Taylor Devine, December 3, 1994
Dave Dombrowski, May 10, 1995
G. Jack Donson, Jr., January, 27, 1995
Herb Dorfman, February 7, 1995
Ian Duffell, February 9, 1995
Earl Eberlin, April 19, 1995
Jim Ellis, November 9, 1994
Roger Ellis, February 8, 1995
Greg Fairbanks, February 20, 1995
Carol Feinberg, February 21, 1995
Don Flynn, May 2, 1995
Jim Fowlkes, February 27, 1995
Barbara Gasser, January 27, 1995
Gerry Geddis, December 29, 1994
Harold Gershowitz, May 2, 1995
Bill Giles, April 10, 1995
Russell Goldsmith, March 2, 1995
Kevin Gowen, April 21, 1995
Stephen Greenberg, March 29, 1995

327

Jennifer Grisanti, February 8, 1995
Michael Gruber, October 11, 1994;
  March 8, 1995
Polly Gruber, January 13, 1995
Tom Gruber, October 27, 1994;
  November 2, 7, 22, 1994; December 22,
  27, 1994; January 6, 1995; February 10,
  14, 1995
Robert Guerin, January 6, 1995
Randall E. Haase, April 10, 1995
Samuel Harris, April 12, 1995
Larry Haverty, April 5, 1995
Tom Hawkins, April 13, 1995
Jerome Hoffman, January 26, 1995
Bob Hope, January 24, 1995
Bonnie (Huizenga) Hudson, January 19,
  1995
Whit Hudson, January 30, 1995; May 31,
  1995
G. Harry Huizenga, December 21, 1989;
  November 28, 1994; February 1, 1995
Marti Huizenga, December 21, 1989;
  January 17, 27, 1995; April 13, 19, 1995
Peter Huizenga, December 19, 1994;
  May 3, 1995
Ray Huizenga, April 19, 1995
Wayne Huizenga, January 7–8, 1994;
  November 14, 1994; February 14, 15, 18,
  24, 1995; March 6, 17, 1995; May 9, 1995;
  June 14, 1995
Wayne Huizenga, Jr., March 16, 1995;
  April 13, 1995
Gary Jacobson, January 27, 1995
George Johnson, December 21, 1994;
  February 10, 1995
Eddie Jones, April 19, 1995
Mariann and Garo Kalpakjian, January 25,
  1995
Albert Kania, Sr., May 30, 1995
Rick Karpel, January 11, 1995
Michael Katz, May 18, 1995
Doug Kinney, January 10, 1995;
  February 13, 1995; March 13, 1995
James Kirk, April 18, 1995
Dale Lampertz, December 1, 1994
John Leech, January 24, 1995
Charles Lewis, December 20, 29, 1994;
  January 9, 14, 1995; May 1, 1995
Jim Leyland, May 9, 1995
George Lindemann, April 24, 1995
David Linnemeier, March 9, 1995
Steve Littig, January 9, 1995

Norm McCarvill, March 9, 1995
Mike Machens, November 18, 1994
Bill McMillan, January 23, 1995
Jerry McMorris, May 9, 1995
John McMullen, April 7, 1995
Jonathon Mariner, April 19, 1995
Tom Marquez, November 18, 1994
Chick Martin, November 18, 1994
James Mason, March 25, 1995
Steven Matt, April 6, 1995
Bill Mechanic, January 9, 1995
Edward (Eddie) Meehan, March 16,
  1995
John Melk, December 16, 18, 20, 1994;
  April 26, 1995
Dick Molenhouse, May 4, 1995
Pixie Molenhouse, May 6, 1995
Frank Molstad, January 11, 1995
Fred Montesi III, December 28, 1994
Gary Moore, December 28, 1994
Bill and Jane Munsey, January 13, 1995
Vince Naimoli, April 18, 1995
Deborah Olson, April 5, 1995
Erol Onoran, March 23, 1995
Peer Pederson, December 15, 19, 1994
Van Poole, March 20, 1995
Wilbur Porter, January 31, 1995
Sumner Redstone, March 30, 1995
Jerry Reinsdorf, May 3, 1995
Tim Rice, January 11, 1995
Rick Rochon, April 19, 1994; November 2,
  1994; April 26, 1995
Steve Roddenberry, April 11, 1995
Antonio Romero, May 18, 1995
Barry Rosenblatt, November 14, 1994
William Rosse, January 27, 1995
John Ryan, February 13, 1995
Luigi Salvaneschi, October 31, 1994;
  January 10, 1995
John Schneider, March 29, 1995
Mark Schneider, February 27, 1995
Raymond Schneider, October 29, 1994
Marge Schott, April 12, 1995
Lee Seidler, November 4, 1994
Tom Sette, February 20, 1995
R. Charles Shufeldt, May 25, 1995
Ronald Shufflebothem, April 26, 1995;
  May 3, 1995
Don Shula, April 19, 1995
John Sie, February 9, 1995
Don Smiley, January 13, 24, 1995
Tal Smith, May 30, 1995

Aaron Spelling, February 17, 1995
Mike Starling, January 27, 1995
George Steinbrenner, May 10, 1995
Terry Stiles, May 8, 1995
Xavier Suarez, April 5, 1995
Jan Timmer, March 15, 1995
Dick Toplin, January 25, 1995

Bill Torrey, May 15, 1995
Fay Vincent, April 5, 1995
Gerry Weber, November 21, 1994
Fred Weinert, May 1, 1994
Ralph Wilson, May 8, 1995
Gary Wirt, January 9, 10, 1995
Andrew Zimbalist, April 10, 1995

Sources

CHAPTER 1 "ONE MAN'S TRASH": BUILDING A GARBAGE KINGDOM

BOOKS

George, Paul S., director, Broward's Flagship City: Ford Lauderdale 1945–1990/Broward County Comprehensive Survey Phase X, Historic Broward County Preservation Board, May 1990.

Jacobson, Timothy, "Waste Management—An American Corporate Success Story," Gateway Business Books, 1993, p. 51.

Volkers, Mark, "The Huizenga Family in America—1893–1990," July 1990, p. 8 (and others).

Weidling, Philip J., "Checkered Sunshine—The Story of Fort Lauderdale 1793–1955," Weidling & Burghard, August, University of Florida Press, Gainesville, 1966.

ARTICLES

Clary, Mike, "All Work, No Play Makes Wayne . . . ," *Florida Trend,* April 1990.

DeGeorge, Gail, "The Video King Who Won't Hit 'Pause,'" *BusinessWeek,* January 22, 1990.

Walsh, Matt, "Hat Trick Harry," *Florida Trend,* March 1993.

COURT AND OTHER DOCUMENTS

State of Florida vs. Harry W. Huizenga, Broward County, Florida, September 12, 1961.

Thomas L. Millwood vs. Harry W. Huizenga, Jr. (sic) and Herman Mulder d/b/a Pompano Carting Co. and Associated Independent, Inc., Broward County, Florida.

Associated Independents Inc. vs. All Service Refuse Co. Inc., et al. Broward County.

Jean Huizenga vs. G. Harry Huizenga, July 26, 1954.

Harry Huizenga vs. Jean Huizenga, July 28, 1954.

Joyce M. Huizenga vs. H. Wayne Huizenga, August 5, 1966.

CHAPTER 2 GARBAGE INTO GOLD: THE EARLY WASTE MANAGEMENT YEARS

BOOKS

Block, Alan A., & Scarpitti, Frank R., "Poisoning for Profit: Mafia and Toxic Waste," William Morrow and Co. Inc., New York, 1985.

Crooks, Harold, "Dirty Business: The Inside Story of the New Garbage Agglomerates," James Lorimer & Co., Toronto, 1983.

Crooks, Harold, "Giants of Garbage: The Rise of the Global Waste Industry and the Politics of Pollution Control," James Lorimer & Co., Toronto, 1993.

Jacobson, Timothy, "Waste Management: An American Corporate Success Story," Gateway Business Books, 1993.

ARTICLES

Franklin, Stephen, "Ex-Family Firm Got $158 Million in '74," *The Miami Herald,* March 16, 1975.

Hager, Bill, "Today's Waste Viewed as Tomorrow's Wealth," *Fort Lauderdale News,* July 15, 1970.

Schneider, Ben, "Garbage by Any Other Name Would Still Be as Profitable," *Fort Lauderdale News,* May 27, 1973.

Toner, Pat, "Amazing Garbage World Opens in Pompano Today," *Fort Lauderdale News,* September 29, 1971.

Toner, Pat, "Like Oscar, Wayne Just Thinks Trash $imply $well," *Fort Lauderdale News,* September 29, 1971.

COURT AND OTHER DOCUMENTS

Waste Management Prospectus, 1971; Annual Reports, 1970–1974; Proxy statement, 1972; 10K, 1974.

United States Securities & Exchange Commission, "In the matter of Trading of Securities of Major Video Corporation"—Deposition of H. Wayne Huizenga, December 5, 1988, Miami, FL.

Waste Management vs. Tony Reasons, et al., October 22, 1975.

CHAPTER 3   WASTE MANAGEMENT: REGULATORY WOES AND INDUSTRY TRIUMPHS

BOOKS

Block, Alan A., & Scarpitti, Frank R., "Poisoning for Profit: Mafia and Toxic Waste," William Morrow and Co. Inc., New York, 1985.

Crooks, Harold, "Dirty Business: The Inside Story of the New Garbage Agglomerates," James Lorimer & Co., Toronto, 1983.

Crooks, Harold, "Giants of Garbage: The Rise of the Global Waste Industry and the Politics of Pollution Control," James Lorimer & Co., Toronto, 1993.

Jacobson, Timothy, "Waste Management: An American Corporate Success Story," Gateway Business Books, 1993.

"Waste Management, Inc.: An Encyclopedia of Environmental Crimes & Other Misdeeds," Greenpeace USA, 1991.

ARTICLES

Akst, Daniel, "Waste Management Unit, 2 Other Firms Are Charged in California Antitrust Case," *The Wall Street Journal,* June 10, 1987.

"An Improving Environment for Waste Disposal Stocks," *BusinessWeek,* September 19, 1983.

Arnold, John, "Judge Enjoins Disposal Firm," *The Miami Herald,* April 1, 1976.

Atlas, Terry, "Chemical Toxic Waste Disposal: Firm Poised to Clean Up," *Chicago Tribune,* 1981.

Bailey, Jeff, "Garbage Firms' Antitrust Woes Pile Up," *The Wall Street Journal,* September 10, 1991.

Bailey, Jeff, "WMX Slates Big Write-Down, Job Cuts as Hazardous-Waste Industry Struggles," *The Wall Street Journal,* October 1, 1993.

Bailey, Jeff, "WMX's Stock Plunges 17% in Sell-Off Reflecting 3rd Period Loss, Other Woes," *The Wall Street Journal,* October 21, 1993.

Blumenthal, Ralph, "A Waste Hauler Under the Gun," *The New York Times,* November 25, 1984.

Blumenthal, Ralph, & Bonner, Raymond, "Giant Waste Company Accused of Illegal Acts," *The New York Times,* March 21, 1983.

Bonner, Raymond, & Blumenthal, Ralph, "Waste Hauler's Business Acts Faulted," *The New York Times,* March 24, 1983.

Bremner, Brian, "Recycling: The Newest Wrinkle in Waste Management's Bag," *BusinessWeek,* March 5, 1990.

Bukro, Casey, "Piled-Up Expectations Squeeze Waste Behemoth," *Chicago Tribune,* May 16, 1994.

Bukro, Casey, "Waste Management Suit Denies Organized Crime Link," *Chicago Tribune,* October 15, 1992.

Delp, Doug, "Hollywood Hires Defense Team," *The Miami Herald,* October 28, 1975.

Dreyfack, Kenneth, & Hoppe, Richard, "Waste Management's Image Is Still Less than Pristine," *BusinessWeek,* September 9, 1985.

Duffy, Brian, "State Finds 'Technical Violations' at Hazardous-Waste Storage Facility," *The Miami Herald,* April 27, 1983.

"Government Wins Trash Collection Merger Challenge in Dallas, Loses in Houston," The Bureau of National Affairs, Inc., *Antitrust and Trade Regulation Report,* May 5, 1983.

Liss, Robert, "Garbage Pact Is Voided," *The Miami Herald,* September 19, 1975.

Liss, Robert, "Legal Fight on Garbage Suit Seen," *The Miami Herald,* October 26, 1975.

Litinsky, Ruby, "Police Report Spurs Garbage Pact Delay, *Fort Lauderdale News,* July 17, 1975.

Parker, Steve, "Hollywood Investigates Bid by Waste Management Inc.," *Fort Lauderdale News,* July 13, 1975.

Pasztor, Andy, & Richards, Bill, "Unit of Waste Management Accused by U.S.," *The Wall Street Journal,* September 25, 1987.

Peterson, Cass, "Firm Finds Profit, Controversy in the Hazardous Waste Business," *The Washington Post,* March 31, 1983.

"Reaping Profits by Sticking to Garbage Collections," *BusinessWeek,* March 13, 1978.

Richards, Bill, "U.S. Targets Waste Haulers in Big Inquiry," *The Wall Street Journal,* June 4, 1987.

Richards, Bill, "Waste Management, Browning Ferris Are the Subjects of Grand Jury Inquiry," *The Wall Street Journal,* May 6, 1987.

Richards, Bill, "Waste Management, Browning Ferris Faces Charges of Nationwide Price Fixing," *The Wall Street Journal,* February 17, 1988.

Richards, Bill, "Waste Management Faces More Inquiries," *The Wall Street Journal,* September 28, 1987.

Schenker, Jennifer L., "Federal Grand Jury Probing Garbage Collection Companies," *The Sun-Sentinel,* November 14, 1982.

Schmidt, William E., "Denver Lawyer's Role in EPA Decisions is Focus of Inquiries by Congress," *The New York Times,* February 25, 1983.

Schulte, Fred, & McClure, Robert, "The Titans of Trash: Big Profits, Big Problems," *Sun-Sentinel,* December 6–December 10, 1987.

Schwartzman, Bob, "Intricate Dealings Cloud Investigation of Garbage Firms," *Fort Lauderdale News,* June 21, 1979.

"Seeking a Toehold in Nuclear-Waste Disposal," *Chemical Week,* July 7, 1982.

Shabecoff, Philip, "Propriety of EPA Aides' Talks Questioned," *The New York Times,* February 16, 1983.

Strasser, Fred, & Hickey, Mary, "Lawyers Trip over Zeros in 'Mega-Divorce,'" *The Miami Herald,* February 6, 1983.

"Waste Management: Change with the Market or Die," *Fortune,* January 13, 1992.

"Waste Management: How It Found a Growth Dynamo in Chemical Disposal," *BusinessWeek,* September 13, 1982.

Weiner, Steve, "Garbage In, Profits Out," *Forbes,* December 12, 1988.

Whiteshield, Jim, "Hollywood Approves Lawsuit's Settlement," *Fort Lauderdale News,* March 4, 1976.

COURT AND OTHER DOCUMENTS

Waste Management Annual Reports, 1975–1984, 1988, 1994 (plus 10K, proxy statements, and other documents for various years in that period).

State of Florida vs. Albert Carlson, Broward County Circuit Court, January 29, 1976.

United States Securities and Exchange Commission—In the matter of Waste Management—Deposition of H. Wayne Huizenga, July 3, 1975.

United States Securities and Exchange Commission vs. Waste Management Inc., Harry Wayne Huizenga, Earl Edward Eberlin, March 26, 1976.

Waste Management Inc.—Final Report—San Diego District Attorney, March 1992.

A Critical Analysis of the San Diego County District Attorney's Final Report on Waste Management, O'Melveny & Myers, (Warren Christopher, William W. Vaughn, et al.) May 28, 1992.

CHAPTER 4   WAYNE'S COMPANIES AFTER WASTE MANAGEMENT: TOILETS, LAWNS, BUGS, AND WATER

ARTICLES

Altaner, David, "Boston Firm Buys Control of Pier 66," *Sun-Sentinel,* August 28, 1987.

Altaner, David, "Houston Quits S. Florida Savings," *Sun-Sentinel,* May 6, 1986.

Andreoli, Tom, "Waste's Legacy: Recycling Wealth; Following the Trail of Firm's Founding Cadre," *Crain's Chicago Business,* January 18, 1993.

"Corporate Sleaze," *Crain's Chicago Business,* February 8, 1988.

Edwards, John G., "U.S. Takes Over S. Florida Savings," *Sun-Sentinel,* March 26, 1987.

Gershowitz, Harold, "Wrong Assumptions," *Crain's Chicago Business,* May 4, 1987.

Goodman, Cindy Krischer, "Wayne's Gang," *Daily Business Review,* January 28, 1994.

Kelley, Lane, "Ailing Thrifts Woes Tied to Too Many Commercial Loans, Not Enough Home Mortgages," *Sun-Sentinel,* February 14, 1988.

Kimmins, Dick, "Chemlawn Drops Suit, Insider Trading Issue Not Resolved," *Business First-Columbus,* March 30, 1987.

Malandro, Margie, "Pier 66 Union Files Complaint, Calls for Boycott Dispute," *Sun-Sentinel,* January 7, 1986.

Melcher, Richard A. with DeGeorge, Gail, "Here's to 'Old Pals,'" *BusinessWeek,* February 28, 1994.

O'Connor, Matt, "Suitor Withdraws ChemLawn Bid," *Chicago Tribune,* March 26, 1987.

O'Connor, Matt, "Waste Firm Bid Surprises Chemlawn," *Chicago Tribune,* February 27, 1987.

O'Connor, Matt, "Waste Firm Moves into Pest Control," *Chicago Tribune,* October 13, 1987.

O'Connor, Matt, "Waste Management Purchases TruGreen," *Chicago Tribune,* September 17, 1987.

Pounds, Marcia, "Current and Former Waste Management Officials Help Rahn," *Sun-Sentinel,* April 21, 1986.

Pounds, Marcia, "Developers Check in at Major Hotels," *Sun-Sentinel,* April 21, 1986.

Richards, Bill, & Bailey, Jeff, "Waste Management Case Reflects Murkiness of Insider Trading Laws," *The Wall Street Journal,* February 9, 1988.

Sympson, Ron, "Houston Purchases Dade S&L to Form Financial Conglomerate," *Sun-Sentinel,* October 28, 1983.

"Waste Management Execs Must Give Up Profits," *Crain's Chicago Business,* April 6, 1987.

COURT AND OTHER DOCUMENTS

United States Securities and Exchange Commission, "In the Matter of Chemlawn Corp.," Testimony of H. Wayne Huizenga, March 24, 1989.

CHAPTER 5   VIDEO VENTURE: TAKING CHARGE OF BLOCKBUSTER

BOOKS

Lardner, James, "Fast Forward: Hollywood, the Japanese, and the VCR Wars," W. W. Norton & Co., New York, NY, 1987.

ARTICLES

Adams, Tom, "Bustin' Out: While the Skeptics Still Snicker, Blockbuster Video's Retailing Gamble Shows Early Signs of Paying Off," *Video Store,* February 1987.

Altaner, David, "Fort Lauderdale Investors Close Deal on Video Stock," *Sun-Sentinel,* February 1987.

Up & Down Wall Street, *Barron's,* September 1, 1986.

DOCUMENTS

United States Securities and Exchange Commission, "In the Matter of Chemlawn Corp.," Testimony of H. Wayne Huizenga, March 24, 1989.

Blockbuster Entertainment Corp. annual reports, 10Ks and proxy statements, 1985, 1986, 1987.

CHAPTER 6   FAST FORWARD: BUILDING THE BLOCKBUSTER MANAGEMENT TEAM

ARTICLES

Alpert, William M., "What's Wrong with This Picture? Too Many Companies Are Making the View Scene," *Barron's,* September 21, 1987.

DeGeorge, Gail, "The Video King Who Won't Hit 'Pause,'" *BusinessWeek,* January 22, 1990.

Kelley, Lane, "Making Money at Fast Forward," *Sun-Sentinel,* June 19, 1988.

Reveron, Derek, "Video-Rental Chain Bets $5 Million," *The Miami Herald,* June 11, 1988.

DOCUMENTS

United States Securities & Exchange Commission, "In the Matter of Blockbuster Entertainment Corp.," Testimony of H. Wayne Huizenga, September 21, 1990.

Blockbuster Entertainment Corp., Company Documents, 10K and proxy statements, 1987, 1988.

CHAPTER 7   DEAL DU JOUR: BLOCKBUSTER SWALLOWS UP THE COMPETITION

ARTICLES

Ames, Joe, "Blockbuster of a Deal: Cox Will Invest in Video Stores," *The Miami Herald,* September 20, 1989.

Ames, Joe, "Blockbuster Triples Its Earnings," *The Miami Herald,* April 12, 1989.

Curley, Catherine D., "Busting the Video Block," *Rental Dealer News,* August 1988.

Engardio, Pete, & Fins, Antonio N., "Will This Video-Chain Stay on Fast-Forward?," *BusinessWeek,* June 12, 1989.

Finefrock, Don, "Dallas Trial Shines on Blockbuster Early Years," *The Miami Herald,* September 25, 1994.

Goldberg, Jeffrey, "Video Wars: Blockbuster Gets Set to Take on Erol's for Control of the Local Market," *The Washington Post,* January 9, 1989.

Kaminsky, James, "Franchisors Race for Dominance," *Video Store,* July 1988.

Kelley, Lane, "Making Money at Fast Forward," *Sun-Sentinel,* June 19, 1988.

Lowenstein, Roger, "Analyst's Bashing Rocks Block Blockbuster Entertainment," *The Wall Street Journal,* May 10, 1989.

Miller, Michael W., "Blockbuster Contradicts Official, Saying It Won't Sell Rental Data," *The Wall Street Journal,* January 2, 1991.

Miller, Michael W., "Marketing: Coming Soon to Your Local Video Store: Big Brother," *The Wall Street Journal,* December 26, 1990.

Norris, Floyd, "Behind the Plunge at a Video Chain," *The New York Times,* May 10, 1989.

Poppe, David, "Class Action Follows Blockbuster Criticism," *Daily Business Review,* May 12, 1989.

Postlewaite, Susan, "Texas' $123 Million Version of Blockbuster's Birth," *The Miami Review,* Friday, September 16, 1994.

Pulliam, Susan, "How Blockbuster Polishes Its Profits," *Corporate Finance,* July 1989.

Savitz, Eric J., "An End to Fast Forward?—Growth Faces Obstacles at Blockbuster Entertainment," *Barron's,* December 11, 1989.

Stilson, Janet, "At Home Where They Range," *Multichannel News,* September 1994.

Waldman, Peter, "Huizenga Says Blockbuster Won't Bomb," *The Wall Street Journal,* May 19, 1989.

DOCUMENTS

Blockbuster Entertainment Corp. company documents, 10K's, proxy statements, press releases 1988–1990.

Charles D. Howell vs. Blockbuster Entertainment Corp., Scott A. Beck, et al., amended complaint, June 27, 1994, and proceedings.

United States Securities & Exchange Commission, "In the Matter of 'Trading of Securities of Major Video Corp.'" Testimony of H. Wayne Huizenga, December 5, 1988.

Bobby Cox et al. vs. Blockbuster Entertainment Corp., Major Video Super Stores, Major Video Corp., complaint filed July 19, 1988, and proceedings.

CHAPTER 8   DON'T HIT PAUSE: BLOCKBUSTER IN TURBULENCE

ARTICLES

Carlson, Gus, "Blockbuster, CBS Create Promotion," *The Miami Herald,* February 25, 1993.

Carlson, Gus, "Blockbuster to Build Family-Fun Park," *The Miami Herald,* December 5, 1992.

Carlson, Gus, "Blockbuster's Purchase Shakes Music Retailers," *The Miami Herald,* October 25, 1992.

Carlson, Gus, "The Next Disney?" *The Miami Herald,* March 14, 1993.

Carlson, Gus, "With No Competition, Huizenga Stands Tall," *The Miami Herald,* March 18, 1991.

Cooper, Helene, "Blockbuster Entertainment, UK Firm Plan a Chain of Megastores in the U.S.," *The Wall Street Journal,* November 17, 1992.

DeGeorge, Gail, "Blockbuster's Grainy Picture," *BusinessWeek,* May 20, 1991.

DeGeorge, Gail, "They Don't Call It Blockbuster for Nothing," *BusinessWeek,* October 19, 1992.

DeGeorge, Gail, "Wayne's World: Busting Beyond Video," *BusinessWeek,* November 1, 1993.

Dorfman, Dan, "Money Manager Trashes Blockbuster," *USA Today,* May 10, 1991.

Fabrikant, Geraldine, "Blockbuster President Quits As the Company Revamps," *The New York Times,* January 5, 1993.

Faiola, Anthony, "A Grand Opening: Blockbuster, Virgin Plan 12 Stores," *The Miami Herald,* March 16, 1993.

Faiola, Anthony, "Blockbuster to Buy 2 Largest Franchisees," *The Miami Herald,* July 17, 1993.

Faiola, Anthony, "Blockbuster Make-Over: Restructuring Includes Exit of President," *The Miami Herald,* January 5, 1993.

Faiola, Anthony, "Blockbuster Watches Revenues Soar," *The Miami Herald,* October 21, 1993.

Faiola, Anthony, "Merging LA Studios Would Let Blockbuster Control New Outfit," *The Miami Herald,* September 14, 1993.

Faiola, Anthony, "Profits from Video Soar," *The Miami Herald,* February 3, 1993.

Goodman, Cindy Krischer, "Blockbuster's Global Strategy," *Daily Business Review,* March 15, 1993.

Goodman, Cindy Krischer, "Blockbuster Ups Its Stake in Republic," *Daily Business Review,* March 31, 1993.

Goodman, Cindy Krischer, "How Huizenga Went Hollywood," *Daily Business Review,* September 17, 1993.

Goodman, Cindy Krischer, "IBM, Blockbuster Pushing Ahead," *Daily Business Review,* August 17, 1993.

Govoni, Stephen J., "Shorts, Lies & Videotape: Blockbuster Battles the Shorts," *CFO Magazine,* December 1991.

Grossman, Laurie M., & Stern, Gabriella, "Blockbuster to Buy Controlling Stake in Spelling in Swap," *The Wall Street Journal,* March 9, 1993.

Hooper, Laurence, "CD Ventures Planned by IBM, Blockbuster," *The Wall Street Journal,* May 11, 1993.

Kelley, Lane, "Blockbuster to Operate Tour Boat," *Sun-Sentinel,* January 15, 1991.

Le Batard, Dan, & Carlson, Gus, "Look Ahead: Chief of Blockbuster Envisions New Role," *The Miami Herald,* February 24, 1993.

Lohr, Steve, "Record Store of Near Future: Computers Replace the Racks," *The New York Times,* May 12, 1993.

Lopez, Ed, "A Return to the Spotlight—Blockbuster Stock Hits 52-Week High," *The Miami Herald,* March 27, 1992.

Lopez, Ed, "Blockbuster on Defensive," *The Miami Herald,* May 21, 1991.

Lopez, Ed, "Blockbuster Gets Ready to Invade Europe," *The Miami Herald,* December 10, 1991.

Lopez, Ed, "Cox Puts 82 Blockbuster Stores on the Market," *The Miami Herald,* May 7, 1991.

Lopez, Ed, "Videos Attracting Buyers: Sales Increasing Faster Than Rentals," *The Miami Herald,* February 12, 1992.

McCarthy, Michael J., "After Frantic Growth, Blockbuster Faces Host of Video-Rental Rivals," *The Wall Street Journal,* March 22, 1991.

McCarthy, Michael J., "Blockbuster Moves to Enter Record Business," *The Wall Street Journal,* October 20, 1992.

McNair, Jim, "Blockbuster Picks President from Toy Chain," *The Miami Herald,* January 17, 1991.

Meisler, Andy, "From Spelling, a New Programming Adventure," *The New York Times,* July 11, 1994.

Niebuhr, R. Gustav, "Cox to Pull Out of Video Rentals with Sale of Its 82 Blockbuster Stores," *Atlanta Constitution,* May 6, 1991.

Poppe, David, "Blockbuster, Cruise Line Deal Sinks," *Daily Business Review,* May 24, 1991.

Poppe, David, "Blockbuster Growth on Horizontal Hold?" *Daily Business Review,* May 21, 1991.

Sandomir, Richard, "Wayne Huizenga's Growth Complex," *The Business World/The New York Times Magazine,* June 9, 1991.

Shapiro, Eben, "Blockbuster Buying Music Stores to Expand," *The New York Times,* October 20, 1992.

Strouse, Charles, "W. Dade Amphitheatre to Seat 20,000," *The Miami Herald,* September 30, 1992.

Walsh, Matt, "Hat Trick Harry," *Florida Trend,* March 1993.

DOCUMENTS

Blockbuster Entertainment Corp. company documents, 10K, proxy statements, press releases, annual reports, 1990–1993.

Discovery Zone, 1993 Annual Report, press releases and other documents.
Spelling Entertainment Group Inc., 1993 Annual Report and other documents.
Republic Pictures, 1991, 1992 Annual Reports and other documents.

CHAPTER 9 SPORTS, INC.: STADIUM SEATS AND A BASEBALL TEAM

BOOKS

Andelman, Bob, "Stadium for Rent—Tampa Bay's Quest for Major League Baseball," McFarland & Co., 1993.

Sands, Jack, & Gammons, Peter, "Coming Apart at the Seams—How Baseball Owners, Players and Television Executives Have Led Our National Pastime to the Brink of Disaster," Macmillan Publishing Co., 1993.

Whitford, David, "Playing Hardball—The High Stakes Battle for Baseball's New Franchises," Doubleday, 1993.

Zimbalist, Andrew, "Baseball and Billions—A Probing Look Inside the Big Business of Our National Pastime," HarperCollins, 1994.

ARTICLES

Allen, Kenneth S., "Politics Is Key Player in Baseball Expansion," *St. Petersburg Times,* April 16, 1990.

Barns, Craig, & Kelley, Lane, "Dolphins Pick up Video Investor, Get $30 Million Dolphins Deal," *Sun-Sentinel,* March 8, 1990.

Christensen, Dan, "Is Huizenga Sabotaging Giants' Florida Move?" *Daily Business Review,* December 22, 1992.

Cote, Greg, "Blockbuster Deal for the Dolphins," *The Miami Herald,* March 8, 1990.

Cote, Greg, & Price, S. L., "A Dome for JRS? Huizenga Is Willing," *The Miami Herald,* June 19, 1991.

Davidson, Tom, "Heavy Hitter: When Wayne Huizenga Steps up to the Bat, Look for a Home Run," *Sun-Sentinel,* December 23, 1990.

DeGeorge, Gail, "The Dolphins, Never Played This Rough," *BusinessWeek,* October 28, 1991.

Edes, Gordon, "Barger's Death Leaves Void Marlins' President Won't See His Dream," *Sun-Sentinel,* December 10, 1992.

Helyar, John, "Baseball's Expansion Is a High-Stakes Game of Money and Politics," *The Wall Street Journal,* December 21, 1990.

Henderson, Joe, "Danforth Defends Miami," *Tampa Tribune,* May 29, 1991.

Hyde, Dave, "Huizenga Has Teams; His Smile Is Missing," *The Miami Herald,* December 11, 1992.

Nickens, Tim, "Tampa Bay: We Wuz Robbed," *The Miami Herald,* November 11, 1992.

Niedzielka, Amy, "Barger Service Tears, Smiles," *The Miami Herald,* December 16, 1992.

Phillips, Mike, "No Teasing: Tampa Has a Team," *The Miami Herald,* May 10, 1995.

Postlewaite, Susan, "Robbie's Finances: Playing for Cash," *Daily Business Review,* March 15, 1989.

Postlewaite, Susan, "The Selling of the Dolphins," *Daily Business Review,* May 14, 1990.

Price, S. L., "It Was Huizenga's Worst Good Day," *The Miami Herald,* December 11, 1992.

Price, S. L., "Marlins President Dies at Baseball Meetings," *The Miami Herald,* December 10, 1992.

Price, S. L., "Never-Stop Barger Ran Out of Time," *The Miami Herald,* December 10, 1992.

Price, S. L., "Play Ball? Miami a Baseball Finalist," *The Miami Herald,* December 19, 1990.

Price, S. L., "Problems Continue on JRS Mound," *The Miami Herald,* March 22, 1992.

Robertson, Linda, "Miami Throws Out First NL Pitches Today," *The Miami Herald,* September 18, 1990.

Satterfield, David, "Feud Could Throw Robbies for a Loss," *The Miami Herald,* September 15, 1991.

Satterfield, David, "Huizenga Is Just Bubbly During the Big Day," *The Miami Herald,* April 6, 1993.

Satterfield, David, "Robbie Widow Lashes Out at 3 Children," *The Miami Herald,* October 2, 1991.

Taylor, John, "Halfway Up a Cliff," *Florida Trend,* August 1987.

Walsh, Matt, "Hat Trick Harry," *Florida Trend,* March 1993.

CHAPTER 10   SPORTS TYCOON: HOCKEY, FOOTBALL, AND A GAME PLAN

ARTICLES

Barnes, Craig, "Robbies Won't Sell Dolphins, Trustees Say," *Sun-Sentinel,* January 19, 1992.

Bricker, Charles, "Huizenga Hits Atlanta, Joins Owners," *Sun-Sentinel,* January 26, 1994.

Cole, Jason, "Huizenga Says Choice Up to Shula," *Sun-Sentinel,* June 29, 1994.

Conrad, Eric, "A Few Bad Bounces," *Sun-Sentinel,* April 29, 1995.

Conrad, Eric, "Arisons Take Over Heat," *Sun-Sentinel,* January 28, 1995.

Conrad, Eric, "Huizenga Bid Still in Limbo," *Sun-Sentinel,* February 18, 1994.

Conrad, Eric, "Huizenga Denies Bid for Heat," *Sun-Sentinel,* July 23, 1994.

Conrad, Eric, "Huizenga Strikes Fast to Complete Dolphins Deal," *Sun-Sentinel,* January 25, 1994.

Conrad, Eric, "No Strings Attached: New Heat Owner Harris Hudson Aims to Prove He Is Not Just a Puppet of H. Wayne Huizenga's," *Sun-Sentinel,* August 25, 1994.

Corbett, Sue, "Huizenga's Team Describes Vast Dade/Broward Complex," *The Miami Herald,* October 5, 1993.

Cote, Greg, "Do the Right Thing and Do Nothing to JRS' Name," *The Miami Herald,* May 22, 1994.

Cote, Greg, "Dolphins 2nd-Most Valuable," *The Miami Herald,* April 19, 1995.

Cote, Greg, "The Fans Strike Back," *The Miami Herald,* May 21, 1995.

DeGeorge, Gail, "At Least It Won't Be Huizenga Stadium," *BusinessWeek,* June 13, 1994.

Ferman, Gary, "All in the Family: Whit Hudson's $60 Million Stake in the Miami Heat," *Florida Trend,* November 1994.

Fialkov, Harvey, "Hat Trick for Huizenga," *Sun-Sentinel,* December 11, 1992.

Finefrock, Don, "Never Land: Huizenga Theme Park Is Dead," *Sun-Sentinel,* December 10, 1994.

Goodman, Cindy Krischer, "Blockbuster Gets Option for Stake in Sports Teams," *Daily Business Review,* September 22, 1993.

Hammer, Joshua, & Starr, Mark with Andelman, Bob, "Is It Show Time for Hockey?" *Newsweek,* December 28, 1992.

Helyar, John, "After the SuperBowl of NFL Feuds, Wayne Huizenga Wins," *The Wall Street Journal,* January 28, 1994.

Helyar, John, "Hockey's Delay May Check Rise in Its Popularity," *The Wall Street Journal,* October 3, 1994.

Hyde, Dave, "All McWayne Diet Bland, Unhealthy," *Sun-Sentinel,* August 14, 1994.

King, James, "Right to Name Sports Facility Can Turn to Gold," *The Plain Dealer,* February 25, 1994.

LaPointe, Joe, "NHL is Going to Disneyland, and Miami, Too," *The New York Times,* December 11, 1992.

Le Batard, Dan, "Blame Shula: He's Making the Decisions," *The Miami Herald,* January 9, 1995.

Le Batard, Dan, "Huizenga's Handouts Show Class,' *The Miami Herald,* April 4, 1995.

Markowitz, Arnold, "Hockey Joins Mix in a Crowded Field," *The Miami Herald,* March 21, 1993.

Marvez, Alex, "Hudson Plans Second Offer," *The Miami Herald,* November 2, 1994.

Merzer, Martin, "Batter Up! Yup," *The Miami Herald,* April 3, 1995.

Merzer, Martin, "JRS Opener Canceled, Subs Let Go," *The Miami Herald,* April 2, 1995.

Neal, David J., "A Veto, a New Plan, a Tuesday," *The Miami Herald,* January 8, 1995.

Neal, David J., "Breakneck to Icebreakers in Just 7 Months," *The Miami Herald,* March 2, 1993.

Neal, David J., "Panthers Stop Lightening, Get First Win 2–0," *The Miami Herald,* October 10, 1993.

Nease, Jack, "Heat Deal Would Fan Flames of Antitrust," *Sun-Sentinel,* July 26, 1994.

Philips, Mike, "Marlins Winless at JRS," *The Miami Herald,* May 10, 1995.

Phillips, Mike, & Merzer, Martin, "Play Ball? Strike Ends, Owners at Bat," *The Miami Herald,* April 1, 1995.

Rafinski, Karen, "Critics Express Strong Distaste for a Food Tax," *The Miami Herald,* April 17, 1995.

Reed, Ted, "Heat Owner Says Team Not For Sale," *The Miami Herald,* January 6, 1994.

Salguero, Armando, "Shula Tries to Stay Stern Amid the Storm," *The Miami Herald,* December 25, 1994.

Satterfield, David, "A Big League Challenge: 4 Pro Sports Now Facing Fans' Dollars in S. Florida," *The Miami Herald,* October 18, 1993.

Satterfield, David, "Bid to Buy Dolphins Fizzles; Robbies Seeking Other Offers," *The Miami Herald,* November 11, 1993.

Satterfield, David, "Robbie Sibling: Deal a Steal—For Huizenga," *The Miami Herald,* January 26, 1994.

Satterfield, David, "Robbies Take Battle into Court," *The Miami Herald,* January 10, 1992.

Satterfield, David, "Settling Robbies Estates Holds Key to Taxes," *The Miami Herald,* March 29, 1992.

Satterfield, David, "Suit Reveals Depth of Dolphins' Debt under Joe Robbie," *The Miami Herald,* July 8, 1992.

Satterfield, David, "Teams Are Secretive but Here's a Glimpse at Finances," *The Miami Herald,* October 18, 1993.

Satterfield, David, "Will Huizenga Be a Name-Dropper?" *The Miami Herald,* May 19, 1994.

Spencer, Clark, "NHL Acts Quickly, Quietly to Land Huizenga, Eisner," December 13, 1992.

Spencer, Clark, "Panthers All Smiles," *Sun-Sentinel,* October 7, 1993.

Spencer, Clark, "Step No. 1: Find a Place to Play," *The Miami Herald,* December 12, 1992.

"Warm Welcome—Cold Result, *The Miami Herald,* October 13, 1993.

Wyche, Steve, "Spring Training of a Different Sort," *The Miami Herald,* February 17, 1995.

CHAPTER 11   VIACOM: THE DEAL FROM HELL

ARTICLES

Antilla, Susan, "Analysts Skeptical on Viacom's New Bid for Paramount," *The New York Times,* January 8, 1994.

Auletta, Ken, "Redstone's Secret Weapon," *The New Yorker,* January 16, 1995, p. 46.

Bulkeley, William M., & Wilke, John R., "Can the Exalted Vision Become Reality?" *The Wall Street Journal,* October 14, 1993.

Cox, James, "Matchmaker Shuns the Spotlight," *USA Today,* August 24, 1994.

DeGeorge, Gail, & Landler, Mark, "Call It Blockbummer," *BusinessWeek,* May 9, 1994.

Fabrikant, Geraldine, "Bell Atlantic Said to Make Huge Bid for Cable Giants," *The New York Times,* October 13, 1993.

Fabrikant, Geraldine, "Hard Choices Are Seen in Any New Viacom Bid," *The New York Times,* December 27, 1993.

Fabrikant, Geraldine, "New Bid Starts Takeover Fight for Paramount," *The New York Times,* September 21, 1993.

Fabrikant, Geraldine, "Viacom Announces Merger and Raises Bid for Paramount," *The New York Times,* January 8, 1994.

Fabrikant, Geraldine, "Viacom Gets Help from Blockbuster," *The New York Times,* September 30, 1993.

Fabrikant, Geraldine, "Who'll Survive in Media Deal? Paramount Chief's Job Is Uncertain," *The New York Times,* January 10, 1994.

Faiola, Anthony, "Merger Brings Information Age Home," *The Miami Herald,* October 14, 1993.

Fanning, Deidre, "Sucking up to Herbert," *Esquire,* June 1991.

Finefrock, Don, "Blockbuster-Viacom: A Tough Sell," *The Miami Herald,* September 12, 1994.

Finefrock, Don, "Viacom Stock Value Gives Huizenga Leverage," *The Miami Herald,* March 5, 1994.

Goodman, Cindy Krischer, "Blockbuster Looking to Acquire Paramount's Theme Park Chain," *Daily Business Review,* January 20, 1994.

Greenwald, John, "The Deal that Forced Diller to Fold," *Time,* February 28, 1994.

Grover, Ronald with Landler, Mark, "Down and Out in Beverly Hills? Get Real," *Business-Week,* February 28, 1994.

Grover, Ronald with Landler, Mark, "Gump Happens—and Viacom Is Thanking Its Lucky Stars," *BusinessWeek,* August 8, 1994.

Landler, Mark, "The Paramount Bout: Both Sides Could Take It On the Chin," *BusinessWeek,* December 13, 1993.

Landler, Mark, "Will MTV Have to Share the Stage?" *BusinessWeek,* February 21, 1994.

Landler, Mark, & DeGeorge, Gail, "A Marriage Made by Gump," *BusinessWeek,* September 5, 1994.

Landler, Mark, & Grover, Ronald, "Why Barry Needs Larry," *BusinessWeek,* July 18, 1994.

Landler, Mark, & Grover, Ronald with Rebello, Kathy, "Maybe They Should Just Call It Sumner Inc.," *BusinessWeek,* July 18, 1994.

Landler, Mark with DeGeorge, Gail, "Paramount: Not so Fast, Barry," *BusinessWeek,* January 10, 1994.

Landler, Mark with DeGeorge, Gail, "Sumner at the Summit," *BusinessWeek,* February 28, 1994.

Landler, Mark with Grover, Ronald, "Paramount: Talk about the Plot Thickening," *Business-Week,* October 18, 1993.

Landler, Mark with Grover, Ronald, "The Ending of Paramount's Script May Not Be Written Yet," *BusinessWeek,* September 27, 1993.

Landler, Mark with Grover, Ronald & DeGeorge, Gail, "Scaling Mount Paramount," *Business-Week,* October 4, 1993.

Landler, Mark with Grover, Ronald & DeGeorge, Gail, "Sumner Redstone Gets a Little Help from His Friends," *BusinessWeek,* October 11, 1993.

Landler, Mark with Grover, Ronald & Weber, Joe, "Comcast Plays Spoiler," *BusinessWeek,* July 25, 1994.

Landler, Mark with Smith, Geoffrey, "The MTV Tycoon," *BusinessWeek,* September 21, 1992.

Landler, Mark, Grover, Ronald, & Weber, Joseph with DeGeorge, Gail, "Collapse on the Info Highway," *BusinessWeek,* March 7, 1994.

Landro, Laura, & Naik, Gautam, "Viacom Partners Seek to Toughen Terms on Cash," *The Wall Street Journal,* December 29, 1993.

Landro, Laura, & Roberts, Johnnie L., "QVC's $9.5 Billion Bid for Paramount Brings Industry Titans to Fray," *The Wall Street Journal,* September 21, 1993.

Lenzner, Robert, & Matzer, Marla, "Late Bloomer," *Forbes,* October 17, 1994.

Levy, Clifford J., "Blockbuster Hopes Deal Can Expand Its Realm," *The New York Times,* September 30, 1993.

O'Shaughnessy, Elise, "The New Establishment," *Vanity Fair,* October 1994.

Postlewaite, Susan, "Viacom Gives Huizenga Long Leash to Sell Stock," *Daily Business Review,* October 17, 1994.

Roberts, Johnnie L., "Viacom, Blockbuster Try to Negotiate a More Limited Joint Venture Accord," *The Wall Street Journal,* May 5, 1994.

Roberts, Johnnie L., & Landro, Laura, "Viacom Is Said to Be Exploring the Sale of Madison Square Garden, Two Teams," *The Wall Street Journal,* April 11, 1994.

Sharpe, Anita, "Blockbuster Notes Recent Lack of Talks Regarding Viacom's Acquisition Plan," *The Wall Street Journal,* May 25, 1994.

Smith, Randall, "Viacom Stock Sinks on Blockbuster News, Cutting Value of Paramount Offer," *The Wall Street Journal,* January 11, 1993.

Smith, Randall, & Roberts, Johnnie L., "Viacom Faces Anger from Shareholders of Blockbuster as Price of Deal Sinks," *The Wall Street Journal,* February 18, 1994.

Smith, Randall, & Sharp, Anita, "Blockbuster Is Said to Seek a Higher Offer," *The Wall Street Journal,* March 4, 1994.

Steinmetz, Greg, & Sharpe, Anita, "Blockbuster Holders Register Objections to Viacom Merger's Terms; Stocks Slide," *The Wall Street Journal,* August 24, 1994.

"The Very Private World of Allen & Co.," *BusinessWeek,* November 5, 1984.

Tully, Shawn, "The Man Who Scored in Coca-Columbia," *Fortune,* February 22, 1982.

DOCUMENTS

Blockbuster Entertainment Corp. press releases, proxy statements, and other company documents.

Viacom Inc. and Blockbuster Entertainment Corporation Joint Proxy Statement, August 31, 1994.

Viacom proxy statement July 7, 1994.

CHAPTER 12 AFTER BLOCKBUSTER: WHAT'S NEXT

ARTICLES

Filkins, Dexter, & Hartman, Todd, "Huizenga Keeps Race Deal on Track," *The Miami Herald,* May 19, 1995.

Finefrock, Don, "Yo, Wayne: Let's Make a Deal!," *The Miami Herald,* October 17, 1994.

Goodman, Cindy Krischer, "Huizenga Is Back in the Trash Business," *The Miami Herald,* May 23, 1995.

Pope, Edwin, "Paying the Cost to Be the Boss," *The Miami Herald,* June 11, 1995.

DOCUMENTS

Republic Waste Industries, Inc., 1994 Annual Report and other documents.

Photo Credits for Insert

Index

345